On Eagle's Wings
The Secret Crossing

By:

John A. Bolden

ISBN: 978-0-9976855-0-3

DEDICATION

DISCLAIMER

THE STORY YOU ARE ABOUT TO READ IS TRUE. THE EVENTS THAT YOU WILL READ ABOUT ARE OF THE AUTHOR'S EXPERIENCE, MYSELF, JOHN A. BOLDEN. I HAVE WRITTEN THIS STORY TO THE BEST OF MY ABILITY THROUGH MY MEMORY OF THE EVENTS THAT I HAVE WENT THROUGH DURING MY TIME AS A BERLIN BRIGADE SOLDIER IN THE UNITED STATES ARMY INFANTRY. SOME OF THE NAME'S IN THIS STORY HAVE BEEN CHANGED TO PROTECT THEIR IDENTITY. I CAN NOT SPEAK NOR WRITE ABOUT THE EXPERIENCES THAT OTHERS MAY HAVE GONE THROUGH DURING THE TIME FRAME OF THIS STORY. I HOPE THAT THIS STORY IS WELL RECEIVED AND WILL SERVE A GREAT PURPOSE AMONG OUR FUTURE GENERATIONS.

THIS BOOK IS DEDICATED TO MY MOTHER,

MARY "BRIDGET" MILLIM BOLDEN,

FOR ALL WHO KNEW HER, KNOW THAT SHE IS A LOVING CARING SOUL FOR ALL HUMANITY. SHE TAUGHT ME THIS WONDERFUL VALUED ATTRIBUTE OF LIFE SO

–

THAT IT MAY BE CARRIED FORTH UNTO OTHERS.

ALSO, I WISH TO DEDICATE THIS BOOK, TO MY SISTER,

LEA ANN BOLDEN

WITH HER CARING, LOVING NATURE, SHE HELPED ME TO LIVE AND TO BRING FORTH THIS STORY, SO THAT IT WILL HELP MANY OTHERS AS OUR FUTURE GENERATIONS UNFOLD.

Table Of Contents

ACKNOWLEDGEMENTS

As this story was written, there is another tale of how it came to be finished and ready for publication. There are many people that had a part in helping me survive and to live in order to accomplish this task. I wish to give them the credit that they deserve for having the faith, trust, and confidence in me, as we continue upon our journeys together to serve the greater good of all. May they be recognized as gifted, loving, caring souls that serve a purpose much greater than themselves!

The story begins with my move from Wisconsin to Arizona. After having purchased a home and securing employment in Arizona it was time for the move to a comfortable warm place. My two best friends,

JIM CONANT and JEFF PARKER

they gave of their time to help with my move. Jim bought a couple of my weapons then later gave more of his time and energy in selling a few items from my home in Wisconsin and sending me the money, when I discovered that the job that I had secured before my move was no longer available. Jeff did of the same thing and had borrowed me $300 then another $500 to help with my expenses in order to find a job here in Arizona. Jim later paid my water bill for me so that I was able to keep the water on in my home. Hundreds of applications I placed out there for employment with no contact back. These two men helped me to survive, And For That I Am Forever Grateful! My friends,

Tim and Theresa "Lady T" Reeher,

helped me with my move from Wisconsin. With their cards and letters of encouragement that I received in the mail, it gave me strength and courage to move forward And For That I Am Forever Grateful!

As the months passed and the bills mounted up, I was directed to the,

Mesa Veteran's Center
Mesa, Arizona

where I met with my brothers and sisters from the military. It is here that they gave me many resources to help get me back on my feet. With these resources in hand, I searched many of them and asked them for help. During the week days I would travel to these resources, then at night and on the weekends I continued on with my writing. I went to

Veteran's Employment Services
Mesa, Arizona

where they helped me to place in more job applications then they directed me to sign up for food stamps, which was in the same building, which I did.
The state of Arizona,

Arizona Department Of Economic Security
Family Assistance Administration

awarded me food stamps to be able to get some food. For All Of That I Am Forever Grateful! From there I was directed to go to,

Mesa Community Action Network
A New Leaf
Mesa, Arizona
Yvette Reed
Client Services Supervisor

Where as, she helped me to fill out the paperwork to apply for utilities assistance. It is here that they awarded me $485 to pay for my water, gas, and electric services to keep them going in my home. For That I Am Forever Grateful! I was worried about losing my home in Mesa as I expressed this to her, she handed me a piece of paper that had, Save My Home AZ, on it. She directed me to go to the website and sign up for it, which is exactly what I did. A few weeks later I received a call from,

Mario Nevaraz, Jr.
Housing Counselor
for
Chicanos Por La Causa, Inc.
from
SAVEMYHOMEAZ

with the paperwork set in motion, a few months later they qualified me in to the program then paid my back mortgages and are continuing to support me, to save my home in Mesa, until I am able to get back on my feet. For This I Am Forever Grateful! As the days moved forward my utility bills were becoming due once again, as the summers here are hot, so are the utility bills. I am, once again, directed to call upon my brothers and sisters of the military forces and seek help. I called the,

American Legion Post #26
Mesa, Arizona

to see if they would help me. With paperwork finished they awarded me $300 to pay my utility bills. It wasn't enough to cover all of them but it sure was a helping hand. For This I Am Forever Grateful! During all this time, I was selling some of the valuables that I had to cover other expenses. I was at a time, where some of my weapons and ammunition had to come into play, in order to survive. As I did not want to sell them, it had to be done. I contacted,

Ed
at
Bear Mountain
Mesa, Arizona

to see if he would be interested in buying them. He informed me that he really did not need to buy any guns or ammunition, then supplied me with some resources to sell them on, which I tried for a week. I called him back up and explained my situation. He agreed to purchase my guns and ammunition to help me. For This I Am Forever Grateful! My sister,

Lea Ann Bolden

during all this time, with as little income that she receives, was sending me as much as she was able to and continues to do so, to help me get by. For This, I Am Forever Grateful! I am finally called in for an interview, after hundreds of applications and not being called, there was only one. It was part time at $10.59 per hour. I was asked "Are you still interested?" My answer was straight and to the point, "YES!!!" I knew it would not be enough to cover my bills but it was something, I had to take it so that I was able to get my son some money through child support. It had been way too long without a job and this job offered with it many opportunities for advancement. Three weeks to go to get my first check. Will I be able to afford the gas to get back and forth to work? Sold a few more things that I had, to keep me going. I go to Starbucks, which is where I go, in order to get on the internet, and do some work with the book. I built a website to place some excerpts from the book on there and created a Go Fund Me account to see if there was anyone out there that was able to help me through this rough time. Asking for any type of contributions and offered a copy of the book with any donation, to help me advance with it, in order to get it published. There was only one person,

Dennis Zeiter

that came to my rescue and gave me a donation of $30. This is a man, a friend of mine, that I had not seen since 1983. That $30 helped me to get many things that I needed. For This, I Am Forever Grateful! While at Starbucks, I talked to a lady that I had met there a few times before, this lady,

Kathy Phelps

has only known me for a few months. She listened to my story then offered me $40 to put in my gas tank to get back and forth to work, in order for me to get my first paycheck. With my first check, I paid her back the money she loaned me to keep going. It was about a month a go that the alternator in my truck went out and I had to get another one. $250 is the price for such a part and she borrowed me the money to get it as it would be able to get me back and forth to work. For This I Am Forever Grateful! It was about a week later when the recovery company showed up and repoed the truck, as I was behind in payments, for five months. What was I to do? Four days left to work before my two weeks assigned paid vacation for the job that I just started a few months ago. Frantic, I called to try and save my job. My four days are picked up by my co-workers. I get a call from,

Henry Hurd

We started the same day at our new job. We were classmates for a few weeks when we first started. He has only known me for 100 days and has a vehicle for me to use and to purchase from him if I wanted to. He told me that I could pay him whenever I could and that he wanted me to stay working where we were at. The day I went to pick up the vehicle, two people offered him more than double of what he had paid for the vehicle and declined their offers saying,

"No, I can't do it. This is my brother from another mother. A situation has come up and I want him to keep his job where we work together." For This I Am Forever Grateful!

Now you know the story of how this book came to be. It has become clear to me, through this new journey that I embarked upon, and throughout my whole life, that the evidence is there. God is with us always, in all ways, at all times. At this time in my life, I may be a poor man but I will always be Wealthy in Spirit and Faith! And For This, I Shall Be Forever Grateful!!!

ON EAGLE'S WINGS:

THE SECRET CROSSING

BY: JOHN A. BOLDEN

1
ONE DAY IN EAST BERLIN

The sun was shining brightly on Sunday, March 24, 1985 as two American soldiers headed off into East Germany, near Ludwigslust, on a surveillance mission to monitor Soviet activity. In the afternoon they followed a convoy of Soviet tanks returning from target practice. Doing their typical mission of counting the force and observing the exterior of Soviet equipment, it seemed to them normal duty activity. They break away from their surveillance, after all was complete, and drove to a near by tank shed, looking around and being cautious as to their approach, knowing this area was frequently guarded, they discover there was no one around and they begin to think they are alone. The two soldiers on this surveillance mission were Army Major Arthur D. Nicholson and his driver SSG Jessie Schatz. As they approached the tank shed they took pictures of sign posts and positioned their vehicle in such a way that SSG Schatz could pull security while Major Nicholson could look for any type of armored vehicles to include in his report.

Despite the team's best efforts of observation, a soviet sentry had remained undetected, concealed in the woods across the way. The sentry had been walking near his post when the surveillance team had driven up to the tank shed. The soviet soldier had positioned himself about 50 meters to the rear of the surveillance team. SSG Schatz notices the sentry just a moment before the sentry open fires upon them. The Soviets claim the sentry issued two verbal challenges, warnings in two different languages, one in Russian and one in German, fired a warning shot into the air, and then fired a shot to disable. SSG Schatz, being a native German, heard no such challenge in any language and the first shot that rang out was a miss, not a warning shot. As Major Nicholson turns and starts running back to the surveillance vehicle he is hit by the next round fired by the sentry, he is struck center mass into the upper abdomen. His whole body becomes numb with the burning sensation of the projectile entering his body. Placing his hand over the entrance wound, he groans, falling to the ground as he calls for SSG Schatz and then loses consciousness. SSG Schatz jumped from the vehicle to administer first aid to Major Nicholson but is halted by the Soviet sentry who was pointing an AK-47 directly at his head. The Soviet sentry motions him back to the surveillance vehicle where SSG Schatz could do nothing but comply with the demand. He then secured the equipment and locked the vehicle. Shock was imminent and as it set in he realized there is nothing he can do for his fallen brother.

As the next three hours went by Soviet officers and soldiers came to secure the area and collect data about the incident and prepare their defensive statements to give to the United States as an excuse for shooting and killing an American Soldier. During that time, no one, not even the medical personnel that was on hand that day rendered any type of medical aid to Major Nicholson, as he laid there all that time, his blood ran out of his body, ensuring the intent of the AK-47 projectile fired by the Soviet Sentry, was proved to be fatal. As an unidentified person in a blue jogging uniform knelt down by Major Nicholson, checked his pulse and found there was none, declared him deceased.

2
TRACK VEHICLE COMMAND

As the sun shined brightly on the warm spring day of March 24, 1985 at the motor pool of HHC 1/8 Cavalry Regiment, 4.2 Mortar platoon, Ft Hood Texas. The platoon was doing regular maintenance on their vehicles and gun tubes making sure all was in order. Usually not working on the weekends, there were only a few of the soldiers down at the motor pool. Squad leaders were being reassigned to different duty stations so all equipment had to be accounted for and reassigned to other squad leaders. PFC John A. Bolden was the assigned driver for one of the mortar's tracked vehicles and his squad leader was one that was being reassigned to another duty station. He was looking for being promoted to assistant gunner as there was a fresh E-1 waiting to be assigned a track. As all the equipment was laid out and accounted for his previous Sergeant released all the material including the track back over to the platoon. As was proper duty protocol, the Specialist 4th Class Promotable, gunner, was to take the reigns as the new squad leader, he quickly declined the position, stating he was not ready to be in charge. The offer was made to the assistant gunner who was a Specialist 4th class, he to, declined the position, stating the same reason. Now, SSG Rhone was in a dilemma, there were no more Sergeants, Specialist 4th Class promotable nor Specialist 4th class to offer the position to. He had to assign someone to finish the day's duties. SSG Rhone turns to PFC Bolden and asked him if he wanted the job and PFC Bolden accepted the position. Bolden was in a strange situation. Trying to figure out a solution to his problem, he asked,

"How is this going to work, Sgt Rhone? I've got two men that out rank me and one man the same rank as I am. How do I give an order to someone that outranks me when they can easily refuse it?"

As Staff Sergeant Rhone handed the inventory sheet to Bolden to sign for the tracked mortar vehicle and all of it's equipment, his response was simple and direct,

"I'll make sure they are E-1s by next week, I'll Guarantee It!"

As PFC Bolden signed the inventory sheet, SSG Rhone turns to the Specialists and barks out his order,

"From now on PFC Bolden is in charge of you, you will obey his every order as if it was an order coming from myself, You should be ashamed of yourself for refusing such a command and having a private in charge of you, You will be wrote up, placed on report, and I will try my best to take your rank. PFC Bolden, they are your men."

Bolden quickly responded back,

"Yes Sergeant!"

Bolden then proceeded to give out his orders to his newly assigned squad,

"Alright men let's get this equipment loaded up and lock it down so we can enjoy the rest of the day."

Bolden's new squad worked diligently in securing the track vehicle and it's equipment. His men had no problem following his orders. Strange as the situation was, Bolden's new squad seemed happy and confident with their new leader.

Monday morning formation, 0600 Hours, SFC Farabee is addressing his platoon, as he looks at the beginning of the third row he looks at PFC Bolden standing at the head of the third squad formation.

"Bolden, what the fuck are you doing in the squad leader's position? You better get your ass in proper formation right fucking now! Where is your squad leader?"

Bolden shouted back,

"I am the squad leader and tank commander for third squad Sergeant"

Sergeant First Class Farabee yelled,

"Holy fucking shit! Why is this Private First Class in charge of Spec. Fours, Staff Sergeant Rhone?"

Staff Sergeant Rhone began his explanation,

"Because those two Spec 4's refused to accept the duty, stating they were not ready to be in command yet. PFC Bolden volunteered for the position and signed for the track and it's equipment."

Sergeant First Class Farabee barked out his orders,

"You get that promoteable in my office right after formation, Sergeant Rhone, is that fucking clear?!"

Staff Sergeant Rhone, complying with the order given, said,

"Yes Sergeant!"

By that afternoon, PFC Bolden was no longer the squad leader "nor" the tank commander of third squad; he did get his Assistant Gunner Spot in third squad as he had hoped to receive.

3
ORDERS FOR NEW DUTY ASSIGNMENT

As new troops were pouring in from Germany and being added to HHC 1/8 Cavalry Regiment 4.2 Mortar

Platoon, the troops that had entered into the unit almost two years ago after their basic and Advance Individual Training, were being informed that their orders will be coming soon to be assigned to a new duty station, most likely overseas. The orders started coming in September of 1985, there were three soldiers that stood out among the rest. PFC Gary "Swag" Swaggerty, Fire Direction Center, PFC Joe "Joey" Perez, Ammo Bearer and PFC John A. Bolden, Assistant Gunner. Sgt Pinkney starts calling out the names and their next duty station,

"Swaggerty, you are headed to Anchorage Alaska, Perez, lucky you, going to Korea, Bolden, you are on your way to West Berlin Germany to join "The Berlin Brigade." Get your boots shined up and order a case of brasso, that's a spit shine unit, son!"

Bolden pipes up!

"Sergeant there must be some kind of mistake. I am a FORSCOM soldier, my whole four years of duty is to be here in the states, and not to be shipped anywhere overseas."

Not really asking but making a witty statement, Sergeant Pinkney said,

"Ahhh, you did not read your contract did you private?! After two years the army can send you anywhere they have to have you and you are going to Berlin whether you like it or not. All you have to do is keep your uniform pressed and your boots shined. The thing about Berlin is, if we should ever go to war with the Soviets, you are already considered a "Prisoner Of War", with the Wall in place. Bolden, you have earned this duty station with what you did a few months back. There are only a few hand picked soldiers that get the privilege to serve there so, accept it and feel honored, to be able to go serve in the Berlin Brigade."

Bolden, feeling a bit disappointed, replied,

"Yes Sergeant."

After formation the three discussed their next duty stations, wishing that the three of them could stay together through out their military service. Always looking out for each other and always working well together even though they were never in the same squads within the mortar platoon. Perhaps this is what made their platoon so special each of them knowing their duty and excelling at their job, never hesitating to accept a challenge when ever it presented itself. These men together were exceptional and they knew it. Swaggerty, being a man that was about average height with a few extra pounds on him, would have made a good First Sergeant, he was so quick at calculating fire missions that he would have been a mortal danger to any enemy we came up against, started out the conversation,

"Bolden, what are you bitching about? Sounds to me like you got the best new duty station out of all three of us."

Joey Perez, being a short Puerto Rican, this man could whip a 4.2 cannon into shape within a blink of an eye, having it ready to fire accurately hitting it's mark five miles down range. If you were standing within an 80 meter radius of the blast, you would wonder who was the soldier that did it and would want to give that bastard a medal just for doing that good of a job, began nodding his head in agreement with Swaggerty, then said,

"I will have to agree with Swag on that one Bolden. Look at me, I'm headed to Korea where they still shoot at us and get away with it. Bolden when you get to Germany you are going to find one of those German girls, marry her and bring her back to the states, you know you are, so quit your whining."

Swaggerty bounced back in to the conversation,

"Yeah, I can see that happening to Bolden. Perez is married, I just got married. So, what is your deal? Find a nice German woman and marry her."

Bolden coming back at them with a quick response,

"No, I don't think so guys. I like being a soldier and being care free. Women like soldiers but most of them don't care for their lifestyle, especially if we should get deployed to a war zone. I'm happy the way I am right now. So Swag, don't forget to pack an extra pair of long winter underwear where your going. Perez you better load and carry an extra magazine of ammo with you on patrols over there buddy."

Swaggerty, being his usual smart aleck personality, said,

"You best take your own advice Bolden. It is not the warmest in Germany and they just shot an officer over in Berlin. You watch out for yourself and maybe sometime in the future we will see each other again."

Two months later the three of them boarded different planes to start different lives and to serve their country in different countries.

4
REST AND RELAXATION

Returning home to Tomah Wisconsin for forty five days leave, PFC Bolden is greeted by his parents and his sister after not having seen them for almost a year he is feeling good within their company and after a few days starts to feel comfortable with his family. After a while he begins to figure out what to do with his time and decides to go deer hunting at the nearby Fort McCoy, gets his deer the first few hours of the first day. Now what to do? All he knows is training as a soldier and misses his active status while on leave. Going to Fort McCoy to the gym to keep in shape makes him feel more at home than actually at home and decides to visit the army recruiter the next day and volunteer his services to help recruit new troops. He puts on his class A uniform, sporting his blue infantry chord over his right shoulder, the cross rifles in place on his lower collar, the army service ribbon, the army achievement medal he was awarded for helping his platoon reach first place for an army training mission while at HHC 1/8 cavalry regiment

Ft. Hood TX. Making sure everything was in the proper places and all metal shined to a glossy finish. He was proud of his uniform and the awards he had received. He gained from the army a higher self esteem, training him, that if he sets his mind to it, he can accomplish anything and everything. A sense of definition to his life that he never had before, a purpose worth caring for and now he was ready to relay this to other souls seeking to gain self respect. Traveling to Sparta, Wisconsin he arrives at his destination, the army recruiting station, and introduces himself to SFC Barnes, he was not PFC Bolden's recruiter from before as he was newly assigned to this post. Bolden relays to him what his purpose is for coming to his office and volunteers his services. SFC Barnes eagerly accepts PFC Bolden's proposal and immediately puts him to work. Through the next thirty days, Bolden is running errands, making calls to old class mates, and visiting high schools with SFC Barnes, and explaining to the young men and women what the army had given to him and how proud he is to serve his country. Within this time he lapses on his physical training and knows, in his thoughts, that he must keep up with the physical demand, that is required from an infantry soldier, but time is fleeting and so are the goals of obtaining new recruits. The monthly goal must be met and is strictly adhered to. His voluntary services to SFC Barnes and the United States Army served well, as he helped gain two new soldiers, one male and one female, for our country, with that, the goals of recruitment were met for that month of December in 1985. PFC Bolden did not expect anything in return.

Christmas was special that year for the Bolden family for they did not know when the next time they would see their soldier. They made it a special occasion knowing that his departure was soon in coming. Gathering around a fabulous turkey dinner, that PFC Bolden's mother had prepared, they give praise for the time they have together, asking for his safe return. It will be almost two years before they get to see him again.

5
THE FLIGHT TO BERLIN

New Year's Day, Bolden starts packing his duffle bag, preparing for his flight, that would leave in just a few hours. His orders state that he must report to duty in West Berlin January 3rd, 1986. He is to report in civilian clothing due to the rise of terrorist activities. The ride to Lacrosse airport was very quiet until PFC Bolden broke the silence by speaking of his forty five days home with his family, how good of a shot it was to get his deer the first few minutes of his hunt and how it would provide food for them for some time. He explained how much fun he had helping the recruiter and how his experiences in the army made him feel like he had a purpose in life and how he looked forward to making it his career by serving twenty years or more. He felt as if he was able to provide security for his community and by being in the army it created within him a sense, a feeling that he was able to give something back to those that helped him accomplish so much with his education and awareness of what a democratic society stands for. People standing together with different voices, different opinions and still be able to come to an agreement on certain things. With a little give and a little take we come to a conclusion that is beneficial for everyone. It is as if the human spirit places a blanket around us to give us warmth, provide us security, and to protect us from our own vices. Unbeknownst to him, PFC Bolden was giving his family a calm peaceful feeling, allowing them to know that with every bit of his training and of his pride being a soldier he would take every bit of caution available to him to return home safely to them. They arrive at the Lacrosse airport in time for his departure. His mother and sister, with tears streaming down their face, hugged and kissed him, his father standing proud, eagerly shook his hand and said,

"We will see you when you come home son!"

With that, PFC Bolden, withholding his tears and hiding his nervousness grabbed his carry on luggage, did an about face and walked to his plane without looking back.

The flight plan was simple. Lacrosse,Wisconsin to Minneapolis, Minnesota. Minneapolis, Minnesota to Zurich Switzerland. Zurich Switzerland to Templehof Airport ,West Berlin, Germany. Departing the plane in Zurich was quite a surprise to PFC Bolden as he started to notice the police carrying automatic weapons. His thoughts were direct as he said to himself,

"These people are not playing around. The United States is nothing like this!"

These exact actions only validated his reasoning for staying in the States as his duty station. There is nothing in the world like staying in your comfort zone and to stay with what you know that makes life much easier. However, in order to expand one's comfortableness in life one must step out of their comfort zone to broaden their horizons. Bolden, with a slight, silent chuckle, said to himself,

"YEAH RIGHT! Try telling yourself that, if you should be running, from shots fired, out of those automatic weapons they are carrying."

Having had a few hours to spare before his next flight to Berlin he decided to take a stroll around, inside of the airport, and see what the difference, life was there as compared to back home. Staying within the confines of the airport, determined not to miss his next flight, he visits a few shops and admired some of the art they had on display and also some of the architecture that was on the outside. Things there were not that much different from home except that he noticed smaller details in their building's designs and how intricate some spots were and imagined how the creators of such magnificence came up with their brilliance. PFC Bolden was never much for building things or using his imagination to create. His training was in how to destroy things, blow them up if you will, and with a good team of men, your will, was seen to it, mission accomplished! Keeping to his self while there, for the simple reason he did not know the language they spoke, so there was no point in trying to converse with any one, and besides that, he was intimidated by the fact of being in another country and not knowing what the customs were like. After looking around a bit he found his boarding gate and sat down in the lobby waiting for it to load up. He had already decided that when it was time to board the plane that he would hang back for a bit and observe the others as to what they did and then follow suit. He was wearing blue jeans with a red flannel shirt and his fake black leather jacket, you know the type, the kind that made a crinkling sound when it got cold as if it were made out of glass and ready to shatter at any moment you moved in any direction. It looked good on him and that is all that mattered to him. He had his carry on bag which would droop over his shoulder that had the essentials in it. Change of shirt, pants and toiletry articles. That is one thing the infantry teaches you. Travel light and when you reach your destination then scrounge what you can to survive, in other words,

"STICK AND MOVE!!!"

The time came to board the plane and he started to watch what the people were doing. They handed over their ticket and moved to the plane. Simple enough! He is sure he can do this. PFC Bolden hopped up off of his chair, grabbed his carry on and headed for the gate with his ticket in hand. When he arrived at the head of the line and went to hand over his ticket, two armed guards emerged from the set of curtains that were located to the left of the entrance to the plane. They started yelling something at him and of course if someone is yelling at you in the military then you better be at the double time march. PFC Bolden picked up his pace toward the plane's corridor, the next thing he knew those two guards had a hold of him, one on each side grasping his arms and leading him behind the curtain, yelling at him, in the language that they spoke, the whole time. Not knowing the language they were speaking, let alone what they were saying to him, he could tell by the tone of their voice this wasn't going to be good and wondering what it was that he may have done for them to be shouting at him. It didn't take long to figure out that they wanted him to unload his carry on bag on to the table as well as the contents in his pockets for an inspection. That is exactly what he did. When he threw his wallet down on the table the billfold came open and his green military I.D. card was in full view. He notices the two guards talking to each other and as he looked into their eyes he sensed fear among them. One of the guards that seemed to be in charge put his hand up as to say,

"Stop".

He then motioned to Bolden with one finger as to say

"Wait One Moment"

then the guard left the enclosed curtain area. The other guard looked at him with a glance and had somewhat of a smile and then looked away quickly. After about a minute or so the guard that had left returned with a taller guy that had the uniform on of an officer and he was sporting a pistol on his left side, holstered. He picked up Bolden's wallet looked at his Military I.D. and asked.

"Is this you?"

PFC Bolden confirms to him that he is the soldier in the picture. The officer apologized to him and asked him to pack up what he had on the table and to board the plane quickly. PFC Bolden nods his head and did exactly that. His hands were shaking and all he could think about was getting to Berlin and getting situated with his new platoon. There were no other service men around to talk to on the whole trip and if there had been, then it would have made things, much easier. From what he had heard, before going to Germany, was that each soldier went to Frankfort, West Germany before being assigned to their new units, but for some reason Bolden was to report directly to Berlin. As he boarded the plane, his nerves were calming down and his hands had stopped shaking, then the anger kicked in. Bolden's thoughts start ranting.

"Those arrogant no good bastards."
"Just who do they think they are?
"Once they discovered I was a soldier in the United States military they sure did change their attitude real quick. God, get me to my unit, quickly, please!"

That's the thing about many people when an initial conflict begins, nerves start to act up and they begin to shake, the vision begins too blur, the throat begins to swell and they can hardly breathe, the moment all of those things dissipate the opposing party had better watch out and be careful because what they will have coming at them is nerves of steel, a clear vision, and heavy breathing coming straight for them with a purposeful goal in mind and there is nothing that is going to stop it, except for satisfaction.

You are trained that with your green Military Identification Card that you show it to no one else except for other U.S. military officials or if you are stationed stateside to members of law enforcement agencies if so called upon. This is to protect yourself and to protect your identification card from being duplicated and used to gain access to U.S. Military installations. It is a wise thing to do and to keep in mind. The only reason they were able to see PFC Bolden's identification was because his wallet flew open upon hitting the inspection table, which was most likely a good thing for all involved.

As soon as his plane landed in Berlin, PFC Bolden immediately locates his liaison and started the registration process. His security blanket was back and felt much more comfortable. Later he learns he is to be assigned to CSC 6/502nd Infantry Battalion. He was once again in a 4.2 mortar mechanized platoon doing the same thing he had done in Ft. Hood, TX. Easy Enough!!!!

6
ROOM ASSIGNMENT

Upon entering McNair Barracks located on Goerzelle, PFC Bolden is taken to CSC 6/502nd Infantry Battalion and assigned his quarters. Top floor, down the end of the corridor, on the left, next to a set of double glass doors that led to a set of stairs, when descended, led to the battalion commanders head quarters. PFC Bolden was then introduced to his room mate Specialist 4th Class Michael Broadway. He stood about 5 foot 10 inches, wore black framed military issued glasses and had a medium frame for a body. An average soldier from what PFC Bolden can figure out at first glance. As he shakes Broadway's hand and introduces himself, Bolden is cut short as Broadway starts to lay the ground rules for them being room mates,

"This is my room, now that you are here, the right side, from these wall lockers, that are in the middle of the room, is my Area Of Operation."
"The left side is your AO."
"You stay out of my area and I will stay out of your area." "That is my computer by the window, DO NOT TOUCH IT!!!!"
"Oh and by the way, we have a small group of us that go over to the East if we find out that you're cool, we might take you with us."

Bolden's reply was simple and direct, giving back the same energy Broadway used in setting down the ground rules of "Areas of Operation's"

"I don't know anything about computers and really am not interested in them."
"I'm good with the AO situation."
"As far as going to the East, I don't know what you are talking about and really don't care."
"I am here for training, soldier and that is what I will do."
"It is nice to meet you!"

Bolden's thoughts on the other hand were quite different.

"What an arrogant, pompous ass, if they are all like this then this is going to be one wild ride."

Little did PFC Bolden know that Specialist Broadway would be a true soldier when the time would arrive.

7
McNAIR BARRACKS

McNair barracks is a compound that consisted of many buildings connected together. This is the home for many infantry soldiers with the U shaped parking lots, for the different battalions, where company formations are held. It has within the confines everything a soldier could have. A small PX store, church, barber shop, restaurant, bank, bowling ally, that consisted of four lanes, which was located by the Star Light Club, where many soldiers went to have a relaxing evening with a few cocktails and enjoy the camaraderie of friends. What stands to attract attention is a tower with four clocks at the top of it which faced in all four directions. There was no excuse for a soldier if he should ever show up late for formation if he was anywhere near that clock tower. The hands of time will always be ticking as it watches the future unfold with every stroke of the second hand. Time waits for no one, nor should it, as it is the keeper of history, the value of the present, and the creator of the future. The clock tower located on 4th of July Platz at McNair barracks will always stand in the memory of an infantry soldier as it is a pillar of strength that upholds his honor, dedication, and courage for the time he spent defending the city as a member of The Berlin Brigade.

Training is always a part of a soldier's regimen and part of his training is how to interact with the local people of the country they are assigned to defend. All new soldiers assigned to West Germany were required to take a class that teaches them how to speak the German language, understand the difference between the United States dollar and the West German Mark and how to calculate the current exchange rate, know how to move around the city with the transportation systems the German's had provided such as S-Bahns and U-Bahns and many other topics that would help gain the confidence of the soldier as well as the German people so that both know the soldiers are there to defend and not dictate. This school was called The Iron Soldier's School Of Standards. The special thing about this school in West Berlin was that it taught you some of the history that surrounds Berlin and how the Berlin Wall came to be. This school of standards, whether knowingly or unknowingly, gave the Berlin Brigade soldier his reason for being there.

8
A SMALL HISTORY OF BERLIN

At the end of World War II, Nazi Germany had been defeated, with their leader Adolf Hitler and some of his higher ranking officers diminished after taking their own lives and the others taken prisoner, Berlin was a conquered and devastated city, which had to be rebuilt. A meeting was held at Cecilienhof Castle, located in the Potsdam district of Berlin to determine the fate of the city. This castle was chosen because of the safe haven it provided the leaders of the four conquering nations, The United States, Great Britain, France, and The Soviet Union. The city had been air strafed and bombed numerous times with many undetonated shells left in the ruins. The castle was completely intact, missed by the air raids with the nearest shell exploding almost two kilometers away. President Truman, Prime Minister Churchill, and General Secretary Stalin would be safe there to devise a plan and save the city from ruin. Berlin was divided into four sectors. France had the north west part of Berlin, Great Britain controlled the middle west sector of Berlin, The United States controlled the south west sector of Berlin, and The Soviet Union controlled the Eastern Sector of Berlin. Each power was assigned to rebuild their part of the city the best they could. From the beginning of the negotiations the Soviet Union had continuously argued of how Berlin was to be divided and controlled. The Allied Powers were persistent with their part of the city to be governed by a democratic society and capitalism was the game where freedom of choice was to reign with the people. The Soviet Union consisted of communism, where anything and everything was owned and controlled by the government. The people were told who they were to be and what they were to become. Berlin was a city surrounded by Communism, for Germany had been divided into two states, West Germany and East Germany. The Allied Forces watched over West Germany while the Soviet Union controlled East Germany. Berlin was located in the East German state controlled by the Soviet Union, thereby creating the western part of Berlin, Occupied territory by the Allied Forces. The Soviet Union was determined to push The Allied Forces out of Berlin, claiming that Berlin was in their occupied part of East Germany and that the Allied Forces had no right to be there. That is one thing you should not tell a people that are raised to believe in their inalienable rights and who have been taught to protect those rights at all cost. This was put to the test by the Soviet Union.

9
THE BERLIN AIRLIFT

The Soviets, trying to push the Allied Forces out of Berlin, countered this move by requiring that all Western convoys bound for West Berlin traveling through Soviet Germany be searched. The Tri-zone government, recognizing the threat, refused the right of the Soviets to search their cargo. The Soviets then cut all surface traffic to West Berlin on June 24, 1948. American ambassador to Britain, John Winnant, stated the accepted Western view when he said that he believed "That the right to be in Berlin carried with it the right of access." The Soviets, however, did not agree. Shipments by rail and the autobahn came to a halt. A desperate West Berlin, faced with starvation and in need of vital supplies, looked to the West for help. The order to begin supplying West Berlin by air was approved later by U.S. General Lucius Clay on June 24. President Truman, wishing to avoid war or a humiliating retreat, supported the air campaign, against many advisers wishes.

In the early hours of June 24, 1948 by order of Joseph Stalin, Russia halted all traffic into and out of the Russian sector of Berlin at Marienborn, which was the Russian checkpoint located nearly one hundred miles from the city of Berlin. Stalin also cut off all electricity to the city of West Berlin claiming "Technical Difficulties". General Clay who was the Military Governor of Germany at the time contacted General Curtis LeMay who was the Commander of the United States Air Forces in Europe and asked him if they could start flying food supplies into Berlin. General LeMay agreed and the airlift started on 24 June, 1948. At the beginning of the airlift General LeMay had hoped to concentrate the men of the 60th and the 61st Troop Carrier Group at Rhine Main AFB which had one 6,000 yard runway. Rhine Main had been used as a fighter station after the war by the Air Force and was composed entirely of "Marston" steel matting.

At the beginning of the airlift there were three supplying airfields: Rhein Main and Wiesbaden in the American zone, and Weinstorf in the British zone. However, by the end of the Airlift there would be nine airfields. All six would be located in the British zone to cut down the length of time of flying supplies into Berlin. The only route into Berlin was by means of three, twenty mile wide corridors across the Soviet zone of Berlin. Once the allied forces were over the city, western aircraft shared airspace with seven Soviet airfields.

At the start of the airlift the main aircraft used was the C-47 and they first were to carry 80-tons of milk, flour and medicine into the suffering city of West Berlin. The American name for the Berlin Airlift was first called " The LeMay Coal and Feed Delivery Service". The British called it "Operation Plainfare". The primary goal of Russia was to force the United States, Britain and France out of West Berlin.

On July 2nd, 1948 Britain's Lt. General Brian K. Robertson demanded after conferring with the U.S. and French leaders that the Russians lift the entire blockade. On July 14th Russia informed the western powers that they no longer had any right to be in Berlin and that the blockade was invoked to protect "The economy of the soviet zone". The Russians claimed that by setting up a west German government, issuing separate currency and through other alleged violations of "Big Four" agreements on Germany and Berlin, the west had rendered "Null and Void its' Right" to participate in the occupation of Berlin. Moscow asserted that West Berlin is in the center of the Soviet zone and is part of that zone".

The Western reaction to the allegations made by the Soviet Union was responded to during the Anglo-American, French meeting in London that began on July 15th. The Russians were told that "No Threats, pressure or other actions could squeeze the United States out of West Berlin". Ex Major General William J. (Wild Bill) Donovan, Wartime OSS Director, declared on July 17, 1948 The place to make a stand against Russia is right here in Berlin. This is not a Cold War. It is Hot as Hell...Their motives are just what the Soviets have said - to stop the ERP - and what they have not said - to drive us out of Europe. If the soviets want war they can start it 500 miles to the west just as well as here."

On July 17-19th 1948, Sixty B-29 Bombers landed at Scampton, Waddington and Marram England. Six RAF Vampire jet fighters reached Montreal from England on July 16th. Sixteen F-80 Shooting Stars reached Greenland on July 17th, bound for Germany just in case the Russians thought of cutting the air link to Berlin. During that time, General Clay was asked if the U.S. War Department had given him permission to start the airlift. General Clay responded by saying "I did not ask permission". So the Berlin Airlift was actually started without President Harry S. Truman's permission.

Also in July of 1948 General William H. Tunner arrived in Weisbaden to set up an Airlift Task Force which was independent of the Headquarters USAF. By October of 1948 the Combined Airlift Task Force had been born. Up until this time there had been a set target for the amount of goods airlifted into Berlin, but provisions under the CALTF was written a sentence which allowed the airlifters to deliver the maximum tonnage possible in the safest way possible.

Soon after the C-47's had started transporting goods into West Berlin the Air Force realized that the C-47 was not large enough to haul the weight required to reach their goal of 4,500 tons a day. So General Clay ordered 72 C-54's which was approximately eight squadrons because the C-54 could carry much more cargo thus making it possible to reach their target goal. Along with the 72 C-54's 2,500 crew members were also brought along. By September of 1948 the Airlift was transporting 5,583 tons of supplies into Berlin. By the 26th of August the total tonnage delivered to Berlin by U.S. planes had reached the 100,000 mark.

In October of 1948 General Clay asked the National Security Council to grant him more DC-4 aircraft to increase the tonnage of supplies. The members of the council chose to ignore his request but then President Harry Truman asked Clay to "Step into his office." He also asked Secretary of the Army Kenneth C. Royall into his office and stated to General Clay "I'm afraid your very unhappy, General, but don't be. You're going to get your airplanes".

In November of 1948 the Russian Military authorities threatened to force down western aircraft if they flew outside the 20 mile wide corridors regardless of weather conditions. On December 6th a C-54 taking off from Fassburg Germany crashed within walking distance of the airfield and 3 airmen were killed. Undaunted by several deaths by this time on the 20th of December 1948 "Operation Santa Clause" began to fly gifts to the children of West Berlin which totaled close to 10,000 children receiving gifts.

By December 31st of 1948 the 100,000th airlift mission was flown since it's beginning on the 26th of June. By years end nearly 750,000 tons of supplies had been airlifted into Berlin.

The week of March 12th, 1949 was a record breaker. In just 7 days 45,683 tons of supplies were flown into Berlin. Surviving a normally harsh German winter, the airlift carried over two million tons of supplies in 270,000 flights within 328 days. The blockade of Berlin was finally lifted by the Soviets on May 12, 1949. Berlin became a symbol of the United States resolve to stand up to the Soviet threat without being forced into a direct conflict. The Airlift continued however, hoping to build a 200,000 ton supply reserve in Berlin. Then in July of 1949 The U.S. and Great Britain announced their plans to phase out the Berlin Airlift by October 31, 1949. During that time the United States lost many aircraft, some shot down, some from the weather conditions, and some from mechanical failure along with the equipment lost were the brave airmen and servicemen that manned these aircraft. Their honor, courage, and dedication to the freedom that we hold so dearly is memorialized with the Berlin Airlift Monument located in Berlin – Tempelhof. The monument displays the names of 39 British and 31 American airmen who lost their lives during the operation.

10
A Small History of the Berlin Wall

In 1949, Western and Eastern Germany formed separate governments. In the 1950's the West East Gap continued to widen. In West Berlin and West Germany building boomed. In the East, food and housing were scarce and people began voting with their feet, fleeing to the west after East Berlin businesses had been seized by the government. More than 3 million people left East Germany for a better life in the West. By 1961 the communist government knew it had to stop the exodus. At 2:00 A.M. on August 13th, 1961 a low barbed wire barrier was strung between East and West Berlin, it effectively divided the city in half. On August 15th cement slabs and cinder blocks began replacing the barbed wire. Within days, workers cemented concrete blocks into a low wall through the city. In 28 years the Wall claimed at least 239 victims, shot by guards, drowned in the waters of the Spree, or one of the lakes, or killed jumping out of their houses. An estimated 10,000 tried to escape to the West about 5,000 made it. 19 year old, Hans Conrad Schumann was the first border guard to defect on August 15th, 1961 two days after East Germany sealed off the borders with the wall, after him about 2,000 soldiers fled to the West. With so many people fleeing from East Germany to West Germany and especially when a country's soldiers are not willing to fight and defend that country's way of life, one must ask the question

"Why?"

What is it that these people are willing to place their life at risk to change what they feel is "NOT" how they wish to live?

The Iron Soldier's School Of Standards, answered a few of those questions. As PFC Bolden sat in his chair and listened attentively to the instructor of the class many things came to his mind of how he appreciated the country that he was born in and how the United States Constitution came in to play with his life and how fortunate he was to have the Bill Of Rights protect him as a citizen of the United States. He learned that people living in the DDR were assigned to positions of work that fit their social class description and how they performed on certain tests; if they were members of the communist party then they had more privileges. The government chose who were to attend the universities and who would work at other labors. East Germans could be detained at any time, questioned/interrogated, and imprisoned for any length of time without probable cause. If the picture on your passport/visa did not match the hair style you sported when that picture was taken, then you could be questioned for that simple reason. It was said that it could take an East German thirteen years to get a car and to get your own apartment could take up to ten years and only if you won it through a lottery type system. Private farmers had been forced to join large scale collective agricultural enterprises in the 1950s. Some practices that were used, to help the farmers, with their decision, were to cut off all electricity to their villages or to close down a local shop where they could get supplies. People who lived in East Germany that had family in West Germany were not allowed to see them or have any other contact with them in fear, that if they did, they would be considered

"Enemies Of The State" and be under constant surveillance by the State Security, otherwise known as "Stasi". With your ideas and motivation and you were able to create a successful business from it, you were then required to produce a final balance sheet and then hand the business over to state ownership without any compensation, this was called "Being transferred over to the People's Ownership". At any time Stasi agents could enter your home and property, place you under arrest, take any or all of what you have acquired and worked for your whole life. There were a few who stood up against this type of government by leaving East Germany and going to the west to have a better life but it was a 50/50 chance to make it successfully across the border. East Germany was serious about escape attempts, serious enough to shoot and kill their own people or send them to prison should they be captured alive. Successful escape or not, it did not stop there, as their family and friends were subjected to interrogation and sometimes imprisonment for knowing the escapees as the government considered them to be enemies of the state. For those that did escape successfully from East Germany to West Germany they were granted instant West German citizenship and accepted as one of their own people to live freely in a democratic society shielded by the allied forces.

The class instructor's voice began to fade as PFC Bolden's thoughts were becoming louder in his mind.

"No, no this can not be, a person can not live like this, being in constant fear that everything you worked for can be taken away from you just by saying what is on your mind."

"Where is one's motivation for success in their life and for their family?"

"How can you bring out the best in someone if you suppress what they wish to do?"

"Are the East Germans that passive of a people that they will allow that type of government to control their lives in such a manner?"

"The courage it took for those who escaped is amazing it is equal to that of being a soldier and actually fighting to defend that which is your inalienable right to be who you are and what you wish to be for you and your family."

"What strength one must have to make that decision, to trust what you do not know to be true and to push forward upon faith, trust, and hope that everything will be fine."

"Alone in a world knowing that every move you make, every decision you make, is an independent choice of your own, for your life's fate depends upon this."

"What an adventurous spirit these people must have to make such a bold move to create a life of their own and to not be dictated to as to what their life should be."

"I would be proud and honored to stand next to someone like that for they are the spirit that is within me."

"They are me and they are what I believe in, the right to be my self!"

The instructor's voice became louder as PFC Bolden snapped back into reality and started to listen to what the instructor had to say. He reminded the class that on the last day they had to wear their class A uniforms, no name tags, as they would be taken on a tour to East Berlin and to change American dollars into East Marks if they planned on buying anything there. As PFC Bolden left the classroom his thoughts were heavily on those that made their escape from East to West and became quickly saddened by those that did not make it successfully.

11
A TOUR OF WEST AND EAST BERLIN

On PFC Bolden's last day at the Iron Soldier's School Of Standards everyone that had attended his class boarded a tour bus for the Berlin tour. Once everyone was seated the bus proceeded on its way with the class instructor giving his narration. Once again the instructor's voice is muffled as PFC Bolden's thoughts took control as he was observing the architecture of the buildings and of course observing "The Berlin Wall" and the guard towers, whenever they came close to either one.

"The Wall was tall enough that if you ever tried to scale it on either side would take too long to do, by the time you reached the top, they would have spotted you on both sides and if you reached the top the round smooth construction had no grip to hold onto and flip yourself over."

"How many East German soldiers to a guard tower?"

There are two men to a guard tower, as was later explained, they did this for a couple reasons. If one guard decided to escape the other guard would shoot him and if one guard brought anything up about an escape the other guard would report him. On the other hand if the one East German guard shot anyone trying to escape over the wall he would have a witness to say he was doing his duty as a soldier. In PFC Bolden's opinion, if you had to have one soldier watch another soldier so that he does not desert his guard post then it is wasted energy on something that should be given within a soldier's belief system, and that is, if a soldier believes in his government and his way of life, then he is willing to fight and defend it at all cost.

The tour bus parked on the street next to a government building which was later described as The Reichstag Building, it was built to house the German parliament. It was an impressive piece of architecture and what stood to grab one's attention was the scripture embedded at the top of the entrance, "Dem Deutschen Volke", (To the German People"). Touring the building some parts of it had been closed off to general public access as it was close to the Berlin Wall. Walking along a second floor corridor the tour guide placed everyone's attention to the floor below them. As you looked down you could see a round room with many chairs surrounded in a circle. It was explained that no one was to enter that room until Germany was reunited. The West Germans dreamed of the day when this would happen and their hopes ran high that they will be together with their countryman once again to build a great nation, a free society where likes and dislikes come together to make decisions that are forged from the words and actions of each individual, voted by majority to be their voice, to come to an agreement that what they have decided will best serve the people of their country. What an honor this would be for a soldier who was a part of this if it should ever happen. To be part of bringing together a country with the same ideals and belief system as his own country, the pride and glory one must feel from this should it ever come true would be worth fighting to defend it. The purpose of one's life is measured by the accomplishments no matter how small or great those accomplishments maybe it is all part of a series of events that leads to the end result that best serves the majority. If we fly with the wind and allow it to take us, it will lead us to where we are needed the most and if we hoist our sails and navigate using the wind it will take us to our deepest desires, either way the wind will take us to what will become and that is the will of the majority combined together in spirit.

After the Reichstag building tour, everyone boarded the bus to continue on to East Berlin. The tour guide instructed everyone not to take pictures of the government buildings which could quickly be identified by having the Soviet symbol of the hammer crossed with a sickle and a star in the upper canton and also the symbol of the D.D.R. (Deutsche Democratic Republic) which was a hammer and a compass in the middle of a ring of rye. The instructions were clear, giving an indication that if you were to take pictures of the government buildings, that you could be considered a spy, which would constitute a reason to any communist soldier to shoot or capture anyone caught in this type of situation. As the tour bus passed through Checkpoint Charlie his attention fell upon the buildings. They were old buildings that were denied care from reconstruction and evidence of World War II was still visible as bullets holes from 50 caliber machine guns and 20mm (mike

mike) cannons had not been patched up. The reason the communist government had given for this non-restoration was to remind their people what war was all about and what it would be like if war should ever happen again. One had to wonder if that was the sole purpose of leaving those bullet holes there like that for that particular reason or was it a ploy to divert the people's attention away from their leader's neglect or lack of funds to reconstruct the buildings to create a better life. One could only speculate. Crossing the border through Check Point Charlie you immediately sensed the difference of life energy. In West Berlin it was vibrant and full of activity, like a bright sun shining day that held warmth for the love of life's adventures. It was magnificent with its architecture, beautifully designed and crafted with utmost care. The pride of West Berlin was visible with every step you took, from the cobblestoned streets and sidewalks to the Kaiser Wilhelm Memorial Church that stood on the Kurfurstendamm along with The Europa Center. They stood as symbols for West Berlin's vitality and durability. The Kaiser Wilhelm Memorial Church had been badly damaged in a bombing raid in 1943. With its delicate design and intricate structure it was rebuilt to stand in a fashionable way and served as a reminder of what war could do to such beauty. With its steeple still missing it stood tall with pride and shined with the brilliance of its creators. The Europa Center was equally impressive, the complex with a total floor space of 80,000 square meters, divided into distinct units: a two-story foundation with a basement and two inner courtyards, a cinema, a hotel, an apartment block, and the box-shaped high-rise with a height of 86m, 21 stories and 13,000 square meters of office space. The main notable features of the Europa Center being on top of the high-rise, and visible across Berlin, is a large metal star-in-a-circle symbol, the logo of car manufacturer Mercedes-Benz, a symbol of West Germany's quality of productivity. It weighs 15,000 kg, has an outer diameter of 10 meters, completes approximately two revolutions a minute, and glows at night with the help of 68 fluorescent tubes. It can be tilted back for maintenance work, and in stormy weather it automatically turns into the wind. The "Clock of Flowing Time" (*Uhr der fließenden Zeit*) in the western courtyard portrays the passing of hours and minutes in twelve-hour cycles. Globules of colored water flow up and down a tower through a system of communicating tubes in such a way as to display the current time. The system is emptied every day at 1am and 1pm and the cycle begins again. There is a world fountain at the entrance to the Europa Center. A pool in the second courtyard contains the Lotus Fountain, by the Parisian artists Bernard and Francois Baschet, a "water play" with optical and acoustical elements. It was originally commissioned for the staircase of Berlin's New National Gallery and was installed there in 1975. It was deemed expendable in 1981 and was transferred to the Europa-Center in 1982 for free as an extended loan. The reconstruction and remodeling of the two buildings silently spoke the words of the Western Powers that democracy and capitalism were there to stay. It stated the strength of faith that the Allied Powers have for the free society of the West German people. In East Berlin the opposite was apparent. It sensed of a gray dismal day shrouded by clouds. Fear was apparent as if walking on your tip toes not knowing that if your next step would be right or wrong and what the consequences would be if it was the wrong step. Could an American soldier talk to an East German asking for a simple common courtesy of where the nearest bathroom was without that person being placed under suspicion by their government? Going from West Berlin to East Berlin in 1986 was like going back in time to the late 1940's or early 1950's. One thing that looked close to being modern were the communist government buildings but were built of a simple architectural design that resembled a box structure. The tour bus headed toward a place called Alexander Platz and as it got closer to the center of the market square PFC Bolden sensed an odd odor emitting from the air. The smell pierced his nostrils like a lightening bolt from the sky. It was an old musty, but not moldy type of smell. It was, as if the soil was fermenting to become fertile for the nourishment of new seed to grow, the smell of compost brewing to begin a new life. It was explained on the tour that Alexander Platz was called the Ochsenmarkt or ox market, but in 1805, after a visit by Russian Czar Alexander I it was renamed to Alexanderplatz. Most of the buildings on the square were destroyed by allied bombing during the Second World War. After the war it became the center of East-Berlin and the square was used as a showcase of socialist architecture. This resulted in some plain bulky buildings and a huge television tower. The TV tower, known as the Fernsehturm or the Tele-spargel (toothpick) is one of the largest structures in Europe. The total length to the top of the spire is 365m or 1197 ft. It was built in 1969 by a team of architects with the help of Swedish experts. It contains a concrete shaft, a steel-clad metal sphere and a TV antenna. The sphere contains a revolving restaurant

(Telecafé) at 207m and a viewing platform at a height of 203m. The explanation continued stating that this building was nicknamed “The Pope’s Revenge”, because the money that was allocated to this project was supposed to be constructed into a church. When the sun shines on the Fernsehturm's tiled stainless steel dome, the reflection usually appears in the form of a cross. This effect was neither predicted nor desired by the planners. As a jibe against the atheist foundations of the Communist government, and the ongoing suppression of church institutions in East Germany, Berliners immediately named the luminous cross *Rache des Papstes*, or "Pope's Revenge". Virtually ever since, the authorities have been working to correct what they view as the tower's one major flaw: treating the glass sphere at the top with paints and chemicals of every kind. Yet even today when the sun strikes that sphere, that sphere that towers over all Berlin, the light makes the sign of the cross. There in Berlin, like the city itself, symbols of love, symbols of worship, cannot be suppressed. The World Time Clock is one of the Alexanderplatz’s most well-known features. It was constructed in 1969 as part of the square's redevelopment and has become a popular meeting point.

Weighing 16 tons and 10 meters tall, it features a revolving cylinder with the world's time zones bearing the names of major cities in each zone. The mechanism constructed in a way which enables the current time in each zone to be read.

The clock is topped by a simplified model of the solar system, which revolves once a minute. The Neptune Fountain in Berlin was built in 1891 and was designed by

Reinhold Begas. The Greek god Poseidon (Neptune) is in the center. The four women around him represent the four main rivers of Germany: Elbe, Rhine, Vistula, and Oder.

The fountain was removed from its original location at the Schlossplatz in 1951, when the former Berliner Stadtschloss (Berlin City Palace) there was demolished. Eventually, after being restored, the fountain was moved in 1969 to its present location between the St Mary's Church and the Rotes Rathaus. The diameter is 18 m (59 ft), the height is 10 m (33 ft). The changing of the guard was a sight to see at the Neue Wache as the East German Government had made it a monument to victims of the Nazi period. The East German Guards would march in a goose step fashion to the monument to relieve the current guards on post then the relieved guards would goose step back to their building to begin other duties or take the rest of the day off. Many tourists found this change of guard interesting to the point of the guard's discipline through his drill and ceremony. All of these things stood out to PFC Bolden but there was no color to them, no real life essence that illuminated outward. There definitely was a thought behind these structures and the way they were built but the passion behind their artistry was hidden, suppressed in such a way that even a child could pick up the message that was being delivered subliminally. The message being as this, "We, the government of our people, have taken care of everything, you, the people do not have to worry about anything. We know what you have to have to live peacefully. You do not have to think about anything for we have your best interest in the decisions we have made for you. It would be best if you did not question the decisions we have made for you because it serves the best interest of our people. It was at this point in PFC Bolden's life that he saw how powerful symbolism was to a country. Buildings and structures carry with them the life and idealism that a country holds for their people. They could be used for liberation or suppression of ideas. Give happiness or sadness to those that view them. A nation's history of lifestyle can last throughout the ages communicating to the future their belief and customs from what they build as this has been proven through archaeology.

The tour guide allowed everyone to go through the market place to look around and purchase items if they so desired. The monetary exchange rate was 11 East German Marks to 1 American Dollar which to an American soldier created him to be wealthy even the lowest ranking ones. PFC Bolden exchanged forty dollars and turned it into 440 east marks. He did not know what he was going to buy. One thing was for sure he had to have something that was vibrant, something that stood out and showed a happy purpose. It was then he saw what he was looking for, a musical instrument that resembled a harpsichord with it's black lustrous background and beautiful painted flowers on it. He did not know how to play the instrument he only knew that it would make a great present for his mother. The price was 35 east marks equivalent to around $3.50. There was a harmonica with the bright chrome finish that glittered in the sunlight and the case it came with was light blue the color of an American infantryman's blue chord. An East German flag and a Soviet flag with their bright colors, to PFC Bolden purchasing these flags were like capturing the enemy's fortress, taken in the heat of battle. These were all that were of interest to him. Having over 300 east marks left he did not know what to do with them. He decided he did not want to come back to this side of Berlin and he handed what he had left to a passing stranger. The stranger declined the money and pointed his finger at a camera that was situated on a corner pole. PFC Bolden started looking around and saw many cameras on the street poles and corners of buildings. He could not believe what he was seeing, he then knew the whole Alexanderplatz area was being monitored at all times. It was then that PFC Bolden knew, that no matter how good his intention were, if that stranger took the money it may be considered as a bribe and that stranger could be taken in for questioning. He then placed the money back into his pocket and wished the stranger to have a good day. Returning back to his quarters at the McNair Compound after his tour of Berlin had ended his thoughts were on the surveillance cameras and their placements on Alexanderplatz and also took into his thoughts about what he had learned for the day. As he sat quietly on his bunk, not saying a word to his room mate, he wished he was back in the United States and to be in the company of his friends as he felt that he did not fit in with the company of his current platoon and living on a small island of democracy, surrounded by a country that supposedly placed a high value upon their working class people but gave to them so little trust, that they had to monitor their smallest activities. It made no sense at all to PFC Bolden. As the sun settled into the west he closed his eyes and fell asleep in hopes that all would get better and more clarity would be given to him for his purpose there.

12
BACK TO INFANTRYMAN'S TRAINING

The next day at 6 A.M. PFC Bolden was standing in formation ready for physical training, the one thing he worried about on his days of leave at home and being in the school. It was to be a three mile march with the company full gear and ruck sack weighing eighty pounds. Being the end of January it was a bitter cold day so he decided to wear a sweater on the company march. Marching along the cobble stoned streets and singing cadence was a good feeling for him because he was back into training as a real soldier. The first two miles were easy then after that the formation started to do a yo-yo effect in which the end of the formation had to run to catch up to the beginning of the formation. The mortar platoon was one that was almost to the end of the formation. As the sweat started to pour off of PFC Bolden he could sense his uniform was getting wet and heavier. The last mile of the company march was the worst as he thought about falling out, if he fell out of this march it was cause for remedial physical training and that was one thing he did not want to do. He pressed on and as they entered the McNair Barracks Compound he breathed a sigh of relief but noticed he was starting to get dizzy, his breathing was shallow, and his skin was cold, clammy, and he was starting to turn pale. With a nauseous feeling in his stomach he knew he was dehydrating even after drinking all the water he had in his canteen. As the company came back into formation in the parking lot he could not wait to be dismissed and return to his room to recuperate. Instead he heard the orders for cool down exercises and knew he wasn't going to make it. Immediately he whispered to his squad leader what was going on and his sergeant knew what was happening just by looking at him. He dismissed him quickly but sent him down to the mortar platoon's area of operation instead of back to his room. Bolden snapped a back step then a left face and at a quick time march went around the formation and quickly down the stairs toward the mortar's AO. He saw the bathroom to his right and headed inside taking off his equipment and leaving a trail to the nearest toilet knowing that once he got there he was going to vomit but all he could do was go through the motions because he did not eat anything the day before as he was not hungry from the tour. Dry heaves had taken there toll on him and he passed out with his head lying on top of the porcelain. The next thing he knew his squad leader was shaking him asking if he should go get a medic. Bolden came to, looking at the clock, he had been passed out for ten minutes. He explained to his squad leader that he was fine and had to have a few minutes to regain his posture. The sergeant barked back at him saying he better gain his composure back quickly and be in formation at 0800 hours because he had heard Bolden was getting promoted to Specialist 4th Class at that time. The squad leader also instructed Bolden that he was going to cover him this time but if it ever happened again he was going to recommend him for remedial PT. Bolden assured him it would not happen again and nothing else was said about it. Bolden picked up his gear and headed for his room. Turning the key in the lock and opening the door, his room mate Broadway was on him, asking if he was okay and if there was anything he could do for him. Bolden without saying a word shook his head no and proceeded to get ready to take a quick shower in the community bathroom, return to his room to get dressed in his best BDU's and then head down to formation. Broadway started to console Bolden saying that it was okay and that he had seen many soldiers coming from the States, with so many days off from before, falling out of physical training for lack thereof. Bolden reminded him that he did not fall out of the march and that he made it completely then told him to leave him be as he was in hurry to get to formation and that he was being promoted. Company formation had gathered promptly at 8:00 A.M. as PFC Bolden was called to the center front of the formation. The Captain had read the order of promotion to Specialist 4th Class, it is read as follows:

"To All Who Shall See These Presents, Greeting: Know Ye, that reposing special trust and confidence in the fidelity and abilities of John A. Bolden, I do promote him to Specialist 4 in the United States Army, you are charged to discharge carefully and diligently the duties of the grade to which promoted and to uphold the traditions and standards of the Army. Effective with this promotion you are charged to execute diligently your special skills with a high degree of technical proficiency and to maintain standards of performance, moral courage and dedication to the Army which will serve as outstanding examples to your fellow soldiers. You are charged to observe and follow the orders and directions given by your superiors acting according to the law, articles and rules governing the discipline of the Army. Your unfailing trust in superiors and loyalty to your peers will significantly contribute to the readiness and honor of the United States Army."

The Captain proudly placed the rank of Specialist 4th Class upon Bolden's uniform collar. Bolden snapped a quick salute to the Captain and returned to his platoon. After formation many of his platoon members shook his hand and congratulated him on a job well done. The next day was a two mile run with the company's physical training and it went like a breeze for him completing the cool down exercises. He was getting back into shape to be a fighting infantry soldier and his confidence had returned. Company formation 0800 hours, Specialist Bolden is called to the center front of the formation. To his surprise he double times it to the front not knowing what to expect. The Captain with a letter and a plaque in his hands stood in front of Spec. 4 Bolden, he read from the letter of appreciation the recruiter's office had sent.

"This letter is in expression of our appreciation of PFC John A. Bolden's efforts in support of our activities in December 1985. This fine young soldier unselfishly donated his time to assist us in achieving our mission for this month. By his attitude and soldierly bearing, he has shown himself to be a credit to himself, his unit, and the United States Army. We respectfully request that this letter be entered in PFC Bolden's permanent record and that the accompanying plaque, a token of our appreciation, be presented to him in an appropriate ceremony."

The Captain presented Bolden the letter of appreciation plus the plaque, shook his hand and asked if he had really helped recruited anyone into the army which Bolden replied with his accomplishments about the two fine people he helped to recruit. The Captain replied with

"Outstanding Work" Bolden!

Saluting the Captain, Bolden returns to his platoon to start the work day. The following day at 0800 hours company formation Spec. 4 Bolden is called once again to the front and center of the formation. The Captain standing in front of him held a folded green folder that had the Army symbol imprinted in the middle with a gold color that read,

"DEPARTMENT OF THE ARMY UNITED STATES OF AMERICA",

he was also holding a blue box that Bolden knew was a medal of some sort but did not know what it was for. The Captain opened the green folder and started to read,

"Department Of The Army, This is to certify that the secretary of the Army has awarded The Army Commendation Medal to Specialist 4 John A. Bolden, United States Army for outstanding meritorious service while assigned as driver, assistant gunner, gunner, and squad leader with the Mortar Platoon, Headquarters and Headquarters Company, 1st Battalion 8th Cavalry, 1st Cavalry Division, Fort Hood, Texas, during the period 15 February 1984 to 15 December 1985. Specialist Bolden's constant thirst and drive to be the best at whatever he does enabled him to advance to squad leader over his peers in a very short period of time. Specialist Bolden aided the platoon's placement as #1 in the Brigade during the Division Mortars Shoot Off. He played a key role in mission accomplishment at the National Training Center,

Fort Irwin, California. Specialist Bolden's outstanding performance of duty reflects distinct credit upon himself, The First Team, and The United States Army. Given under my hand in the city of Washington this 9th day of December 1985, signed Kent E. Harrison Colonel Armor Commanding and John D. Marsh Jr. Secretary Of The Army."

Hearing the words that the Captain had read, Bolden was thrilled and proud that his old unit had remembered him but he did not expect the ARCOM, it was one of the highest medals you could receive during peace time. Standing tall with his head held high as the Captain opened the box and pinned the medal on his uniform. He reminded Bolden of how hard that medal was to get and told him he was proud to have him as a soldier in his company serving with the Berlin Brigade. He handed Bolden the green folder and the blue box then once again Bolden salutes the captain and returns to his platoon. After formation the men in his platoon shook his hand and many were asking him if he was a super soldier expecting more awards. He was starting to receive respect among the soldiers of his platoon but still did not feel like part of them. The mortar platoon was dismissed from formation and was ordered to report to the motor pool which was located across the street of Goerzalle from the McNair Barracks Compound to do regular maintenance on their vehicles and gun tubes. They were to report within one hour. Bolden went up to his room to place his new medal and the folder in his wall locker when he saw another green folder that he had received when he was in Texas. He had been awarded the Army Achievement Medal while training in Ft. Irwin, California. It read as follows:

"DEPARTMENT OF THE ARMY: This is to certify that the Secretary of the Army has awarded THE ARMY ACHEIVEMENT MEDAL to Private First Class John A. Bolden, United States Army for Meritorious Achievement during the period 15 July 1985 through 9 August 1985, as a member of the 1st Battalion 8th Cavalry Task Force, 1st Cavalry Division, during Operation "Mojave" conducted at the National Training Center, Ft. Irwin, California. His devotion to duty, tactical and technological knowledge of Soviet Tactics, and hard work were instrumental in the outstanding results achieved by the 1-8 task force. His superior performance of duty reflects distinct credit upon himself, The First Team, and The United States Army."

As he read those words he came to the realization that he had now seen the enemy face to face in East Berlin wearing those Soviet uniforms he had seen in mock battles at Ft. Irwin, California. It was the real deal now and his training was starting to take shape in the form of dedication to his purpose of being a soldier. The next day as the company formation began to assemble the anticipation grew as many thought Specialist Bolden would be called front and center again but his name was not mentioned and he was relieved that his name was not called again. Walking up to his room to get ready to go to the motor pool again he passed by the CQ (Charge of Quarters) desk as the CQ runner called to Bolden and handed him a letter. When Bolden returned to his room he opened the letter and it read:

"Dear Private First Class Bolden, Congratulations on your assignment to Berlin. On behalf of all the Non-commissioned officers of the Berlin American community, I want to welcome you to this assignment in one of the world's most interesting cities. As you probably know, Berlin is 110 miles inside East Germany. We are actually closer to Poland then to West Germany. Because we are surrounded by communist territory, the western sector of the city, protected by U.S., French, and British soldiers, stands as an example of our commitment to the goal of freedom. As a result, we have a significant mission here which includes preparing for the defense of West Berlin, as well as protecting our rights of access into the city. To accomplish this mission, we expect every soldier to be professionally competent, personally disciplined, and physically fit. The training and operational requirements are challenging and demanding, but the results are professionally and personally rewarding. Again, congratulations on your assignment to the Army's finest organization. I personally look forward to having you as a member of our professional team. Sincerely, Gary D. Donelson Command Sergeant Major. U.S. Army."

This letter stated it all in a clear vision of what was expected of you as a United States soldier being stationed in West Berlin. There was no retreat, there was no surrender! If war was to break out between the Allied Forces and the Soviet Union it was going to be a fight to the finish and it would be the will of the Allied fighting soldier that would determine victory or defeat. The spirit of these types of soldiers only knew of one thing and that was victory through his training and determination.

13

A VISIT TO A SPECIAL FRIEND

Still feeling not at ease with his new platoon Specialist Bolden received a letter from his best friend Jim Conant who was serving on board a ship, as a sailor, in the United States Navy. Reading the letter he found out Jim's brother John was stationed in Carlstadt West Germany, located in the northern part of West Germany a few miles south of Bremerhaven, where Jim and John's mother Marie had boarded a ship heading to the States during World War 2 to escape Nazi Germany. John was stationed with an infantry unit there and had only a few months left before he transferred back to the States. This was Bolden's chance to feel a little more at ease with his current situation and to get together with someone he actually knew would make him feel like he was at home. Asking around on how to get a pass to go see his friend's brother he found out he had to take the duty train there and back. Getting a three day pass would be a questionable feat for he had only been with his unit a couple weeks after the School Of Standards training was complete. He had to go, the anxious feeling he felt inside of him to be with someone he knew took full control of his decision to put in for the pass. The next day his platoon Sergeant called him into his office, handed him his three day pass, and explained that all of his superior officers had granted this to him because of the outstanding efforts he had shown in the past with the awards he had recently received. Specialist Bolden was to leave that Friday night after close of business formation and to return the following Tuesday for 0600 hours, company formation. He was informed that there was not much time he could spend in Carlstadt with his friend's brother because of the schedule the duty train had to follow. The Duty Train could only travel at night through the Soviet sector of East Germany, all windows had to be closed and the curtains drawn at all times. The duty train had only two stops in East Germany and that was upon entering and leaving these Soviet controlled parts. It stopped to present paperwork to the Soviets showing travel documents of each individual that was present on the train and cargo that the train was hauling. With the time of travel involved this meant that Specialist Bolden would arrive in Carlstadt on Saturday afternoon, have Saturday night and Sunday Day with his friend's brother then would have to board the Duty Train Sunday night to arrive back in West Berlin Monday morning in order to be at company formation Tuesday morning. They would have to make their time together the best way they knew how. He was reminded not to drink the water on the train for it was not potable water and not for human consumption. He had called John from the CQ desk and informed him of when he was to arrive in Carlstadt and was quickly assured that John would meet him at the train station Saturday afternoon.

14
THE DUTY TRAIN

The Duty Train was special. It was to provide safe transportation in and out of West Berlin and West Germany for American soldiers and there families. On September 10, 1945, the four Victorious Powers enacted regulations for rail traffic in the occupation areas. Western Allies were allowed two railway connections, through the Soviet Occupation Zone, to the beleaguered

City of West Berlin. The tracks ran from Helmstedt via Marienborn, Magdeburg, and Postdam to West Berlin. The other route was via Potsdam, Stendal, Magdeburg, and Oebisfelde to Hannover. In 1945, American Forces used the West Berlin railway station Wannsee, later on the station -Lichterfelde-West- also called RTO, near Drake Strasse. It was about a half mile away from the primary U.S. installations, including Headquarters, McNair, Andrews, Roosevelt, and Turner Barracks. On December 1, 1947, the Americans activated RTO. The British and French Armies used different stations for their railway traffic. The railway route led from Lichterfelde/RTO via Steinstuecken (after 1961, next to the Berlin Wall). Public rail traffic already had to stop at Griebnitzsee Station, the first East (communist controlled) Bahnhof (railway station) after Bahnhof Wannsee. In November 1945, the very first U.S. Duty Train traveled from Frankfurt am Main (U.S. Zone of West Germany) via Helmstedt (British Zone) to Berlin-Wannsee. From November 25, 1945 this Duty Train made three trips per week in each direction. From December 13, round trips were made daily. By 1946, all railroad tracks, damaged during World War II, had been repaired. This provided the Western Allies to make use of the rails to transport troops and supplies. On May 2, 1947 a second train was activated, providing daily connection between West Berlin and Frankfurt. Allied railway traffic operated with no major problems through 1947 when disagreements among the Victorious Powers escalated into the Berlin Blockade (1948-1949). On 24 June 1948 at 0600 Soviet forces suddenly severed all traffic between West Berlin and West Germany.

Following a successful -Luftbruecke- (Air Lift) by Allied Air Forces, on May 4, 1949 the "New York" or "Jessup-Malik" contract allowed Allied rail traffic to roll again. The "old" practiced system from March 1, 1948 was active again. An agreement gave permission for sixteen daily trains between Berlin-Magdeburg and Helmstedt to supply Allied troops. During the mid 1980s, U.S. Duty Train couples ran three times a week from Frankfurt am Main and Bremerhaven via Helmstedt/Marienborn-Potsdam to Berlin RTO. Altogether there were twenty eight U.S. Duty Trains per week. British ran fourteen and the French ran six. All Duty Trains changed from West locomotives because the Soviets allowed only Deutschen Reichbahn locomotives were allowed to pull Allied Duty Trains across communist territory. Locomotives were changed at Potsdam and Marienborn and was considered typical Red Army harassment; a waste of time and money. At the borders of West Berlin and the West German Bundesrepublik, U.S. Train Commanders were required to dismount and present "flag orders" prepared in three languages (English, French, Russian) to Soviet military authorities. Soviets were not allowed to enter Duty Trains or to check its Allied passengers but insisted on inspecting travel documents. Similarly, Soviets authorities looked over supply lists but were not authorized to inspect supplies on board. Military Police of the U.S. Army's 570th M.P. Company (Railway Guard) and later 287th M.P. Company had responsibility to for Duty Train security. There was a special order that all Duty Trains had to be inspected and locked from outside to prevent escapes from the "Workers' and Farmers' Paradise" of communist East Germany. The RTO was the beginning and end of all military Duty Train rides from and to West Berlin. Hundreds of thousands of soldiers and their dependent family members used that connection to leave and enter the "Freedom Island" of West Berlin. The Duty Train was considered a fine alternative to travel on, than by the Autobahn or flight by aircraft. For this rite of passage for safe travel one had to give special consideration of what it took to provide this. The allied soldiers with their “Show of Force”, their willingness and dedication to fight and defend, had protected this easement to provide safe passage for all Western travelers.

Specialist Bolden’s travel orders read that he would depart West Berlin, stop in Helmstedt West Germany, then continue on to Carlstadt. The return travel orders read just the opposite. Upon boarding the Duty Train that Friday night his attention was on the Sergeant in charge as he was barking out his orders from the rules and regulations of the Duty Train. The orders were that once they entered into the Soviet sector of East Germany all personnel will be in their bunk areas only coming out of their bunk areas to use the lavatory and then to return to their bunk areas after such use of the lavatory. All windows will be in their upright positions, locked and the curtains drawn, no one is allowed to lift these curtains at any time. Drinking of alcoholic beverages was not allowed on the train and if you appeared to have been drinking too much of an alcohol beverage you could be denied access to the duty train. The last standing order was,

“DO NOT DRINK THE WATER ON THE TRAIN!!!!”

Simple enough thought Specialist Bolden and then he was assigned his bunk area. After a hard day of work he laid down on the bunk and went to sleep excited about arriving at his destination. Saturday afternoon rolled up and there was John waiting his arrival in Carlstadt as soon as Bolden walked off the train they shook hands and expressed how happy it was to see each other. John showed him around his Army base and then later introduced him to his room mate and fellow platoon members. They were a good group of men and you could tell they were a tight bunch, all of them being 11B infantrymen. The first thing to do was to open a Budweiser to begin the celebration. They were amazed as John told them Bolden came from Berlin and the questions about the Berlin Brigade were nonstop. All of them assured Bolden that even though John was going back to the States soon that if anything should happen they would be to Berlin within a couple days to regroup and to fight on against the Soviets. Once they halted the Soviet forces at the Fulda Gap, which was the only real possible full scale frontal attack of a major Soviet tank assault, it would be only a matter of time for them to get to Berlin. Now there was the fighting spirit Bolden admired, he felt at home with his new 11B buddies and his comfort zone was back. The celebration continued into the night as the empty Budweiser cans started to accumulate and be formed into a huge pyramid only to be knocked down with a drunken stumble. Upon awakening late that Sunday morning they discover it was too late to get breakfast as the mess hall was closed. It did not matter to them as they were not all that hungry and decided to take a walk around the town of Carlstadt. John showed him some of the old cottages that were still up and a wind grind mill that was frozen in the ice. John wanted to know about home as he knew Bolden had recently come from there. He assured him that his mother was doing good and that she eagerly awaited his return home soon. They pass by a small pub and decide to go in for a drink. This is where John started to teach him about how to drink socially among the Germans. John ordered a shot, small bottle, of Jaegermeister. It was in a small but slender green bottle and John explained to him that once Bolden was finished drinking it all at once he was to lay it down on it's side so as not to let the spirit of the elk out of the bottle, if he set it up right then he would have to buy the whole pub a round of drinks. Simple enough thought Bolden as the two prost each other and drank from the small containers. With the bitter biting taste of Jaegermeister, Bolden, finishing his drink, shook his head and went to place the bottle upright on the bar. The pub grew silent and all eyes were on Bolden. With the silence and eyes upon him he remembered what John had previously told him and laid the empty bottle of Jaegermeister on its side and breathed a sigh of relief. John was laughing at him and patted him on the back saying it was a good thing he listened to him. They each ordered a golden weissen beer and John proceeded to teach him about the Sonderspiel machine that was hanging on the wall, the same as a slot machine in the states. The three dials would spin around and hopefully you could get three suns to line up which gave you a chance to win more West German Deutsche Marks by hitting a button and landing on the upward scale of what was available to win. They talked of home again drinking more and more beer. Bolden reminded John he couldn't get to drunk in order to board the Duty Train back to Berlin. As the time approached they stumbled to the train station, on time for the Duty Train. The NCOIC of the train took one look at Bolden and almost declined him access to board as the reasoning being he was too drunk. John explained to him that Bolden had to get back to Berlin before Tuesday formation otherwise he would be considered A.W.O.L. (Absent With out Leave). Bolden assured the Sergeant that he would be okay and that he would go to his assigned bunk immediately. With that he was granted access on board the Duty Train went to his assigned bunk and as promised went to sleep. Monday late morning, early afternoon, Bolden was awakened by a sharp loud rap on the door of his bunk area as the Sergeant yelled they were approaching West Berlin and it was time to get up and get ready. The Sergeant asked him if he threw up in there and if he did Bolden was cleaning it up. Bolden responded that he was fine and would be ready in a few minutes. He knew he would be okay because he and John had not eaten anything the day before. Bolden got up from his bunk and walked to the lavatory, he was hung over and his mouth was dry from all the drinking him and John had done. He had to have something to quench his thirst but remembered the warnings about not drinking the water on the Duty Train. There was the sink in front of him and when he looked up he saw a full flask of water in a holder with plastic cups covering the top of it. In his mind he was rationalizing why they would put a full flask of water next to the sink on the wall. They did say not to drink the water on the train, maybe from the sink, but heck they put that water in the flask to drink, so it must be drinkable. Without another thought of it Bolden picks up the flask and downs every bit of it. Feeling somewhat refreshed and analyzing the water he had just drank as being sweet and quite tasty. Yes, he thought, it had to be safe to drink. Non-potable water doesn't taste that good or does it? As the Duty Train was coming to a stop in West Berlin, the sweat from Bolden's brow increased with intensity, his face was turning red, his stomach was churning, burning, a strong sharp pain came from inside his stomach. He knew instantly what was going to happen next as he headed for the lavatory once again with that salty taste of saliva accumulating in his mouth. With his swift movements the lavatory door burst open then shut, as he knelt down toward the toilet bowl he started vomiting phlegm, it was non-stop for a couple minutes and the pains in his stomach were increasing. After the phlegm was all spewed out there was nothing left to throw up and the dry heaves kicked in. The NCOIC of the train was ordering everyone off of the train and as Bolden walked out of the lavatory the sergeant asked him if he was okay. Bolden nodded, thanked the sergeant for his help and allowing him permission on the train, then disembarked the train. As he was walking through the train station the pains in his stomach hit again and he headed straight to the W.C. (Wash Closet/ bathroom). He noticed the ceiling was quite high and that the doors to the stalls of the toiletten were kind of antique in nature. The toilets did not have any water in them like the States. This did not really matter to him at the time as it all came in a flash as he bent down over it to vomit again. Still nothing came out as the dry heaves were taking hold and he could feel his stomach muscles begin to pull and ache. This type of movement would not allow him to be silent in his actions as he knelt there for a moment with a little moan of agony. As an infantryman you do not show pain or fear, you hide these emotions the best way you know how in order to achieve your objective. He heard the footsteps of another person entering the W.C. and tried to be quiet but another wave of pain came and bent him over the toilet. This lasted for about a minute and then he heard the man's voice.

"Are you all right in there buddy?"

"Should I get you some help?"

"No, I will be okay, just drank the water on the train is all", was Bolden's response.

"Hmmm, You dumb ass, next time listen to what they tell you!"

This was the response of the kind stranger that was offering help just a few seconds ago.

"Must be an officer." Bolden thought.

That's right, next time listen to what they have to say. DO NOT DRINK THE WATER ON THE DUTY TRAIN!!!

15
THE GRUNEWALD AND DOUGHBOY CITY

Mid-February of 1986 was cold, below zero weather, and snow piling high within the city. It did not stop the training of an infantry soldier, as a matter of fact, that is the type of training weather an infantryman was expected to be his best at. One of their mottos is, "If it ain't raining, we ain't training", the same could be said of the snow and cold. The Grunewald forest was 12.5 square miles and mostly used as a training area for Berlin Brigade soldiers. Their training also consisted of urban warfare in a place called Doughboy City. In the 1950s, U.S. Berlin Command created a special training area called PARKS RANGE. It was located at the end of Osdorfer Strasse in Lichterfelde. Two sides of it were next to the DDR (Communist East Germany) borderline. On the western side, about 30 yards away from the so-called DDR "Death Strip", began one of the biggest U.S. training sites in West Berlin. On the opposite side of the fence was the village of Teltow. Parks Range was shaped like a large triangle; about 1.5 km long and about 1 km wide. The smallest part, just about 300 yards long, has been on the street side. But here were the two main gates, the first one for wheeled, the second gate for tracked vehicles. Far in the rear of the Range also has been the back gate. The muddy area had previously belonged to the German Reichsbahn. In the rear were still parts of some old railway tracks. Now there were lots of young birch trees, which gave U.S. assault troops good cover.

For many years, the U.S. Army practiced urban warfare at Parks Range. Typically, the goal was to capture a little village on the opposite end of the compound. Over time, this mock village took on three different versions: At first, it was called "Moba City". Except of a few buildings made of bricks, it was a simple wooden construction. The colored front looked very realistic but its back was wide open, like a Hollywood movie set. On the ground, fox holes and fighting emplacements had been dug. There, one could find cartridge cases from M1

Garand rifles and Browning .30 caliber machine guns. Here the Berlin Brigade constantly practiced Combat in Cities. During work days Berliners would often see U.S. infantrymen marching from McNair Barracks to Parks Range, often escorted by tanks and long military convoys.

Urban warfare was a stressful and important specialty of America's Berlin troops. The reason was right behind the DDR fence. The Cold War was a very dangerous time for all West Berliners and the protecting powers. The U.S. Army constantly prepared to fight in an urban environment. Occasionally, U.S. troops from other assignments visited and tested this modern training site.

At the end of the 1970s, a big change took place at Parks Range. Several real concrete houses (1 to 4 floors) replaced the simple old wooden scenery. The new village was called "Doughboy City". It was surrounded with trees and bushes. The large front sides were wide open and you still could see the DDR border line. Tankers from the famous Co. F, 40th Armor found good training conditions. There was no need to maintain the landscape as in the Grunewald where realistic training was almost impossible because of concerns over maneuver damage.

In the mid-1980s, the Army created a 2nd village. A realistic U-Bahn station, with an original U-Bahn wagon on railway tracks, was built between two combat cities. Now the Army could practice with different units on the same compound. Everything looked very real. There was a church, a city hall and all kind of concrete houses with a different number of floors. At the end, the Army also had replaced the sandy trails and walkways inside and outside of Doughboy with real concrete streets. The streets even had names. There were bus stops and many abandoned vehicles which all gave a very realistic touch.

16
WARM DRY FEET

The Grunewald Forest was a special place with a history to it. Training for a Berlin Brigade soldier there was also tedious. Not only did they have to perform their military tactics with sharp precision but also they had to watch out so that they did not create any damage to the forest itself. Kind of a difficult feat for someone who is trained to blow things up, mow things down and advance as quickly as possible, but it was good moral ethics and respect to the West German people to let them know that we were there to protect, build, and secure their freedom of democracy. It was 6/502nd Infantry Battalion's turn to train in the Grunewald and their turn just so happened to be one of the coldest times in February. Three days of snow and subzero temperatures in the outdoors. Bolden had been assigned as a driver of one of the mortar tracks. It was nothing new to him as he was a driver in Ft. Hood, TX. The battalion moved out of the motor pool headed for the Wansee then into the Grunewald where each company divided up and set up into their positions. A few yards into the Grunewald CSC 6/502nd infantry platoons split up and set up into their own positions. As the mortar platoon entered their positions the tracks were strategically set into their fighting positions into the wooded area, then set up camouflaged positions. In front of them was an open spaced area where the grass had been now there was a blanket of snow undisturbed. It was left undisturbed as to keep our position secret and hidden from any air surveillance. It was a perfect set up. The cool afternoon was quieting down as a jeep pulled up and dropped off Specialist Tim Copsovic. He stood about 5'8", about 180 lbs. and held a top muscular frame. He had an arrogance about him Bolden didn't care for, just by looking at him. After a few words with the platoon sergeant Copsovic started heading towards Bolden's squad. Once he got there he reported to the squad leader and stated that our gunner had to go back to the rear and take care of some personal business and that Copsovic had been assigned to our squad as the new gunner. Bolden learned later on, that Copsovic had been with the mortar platoon for a long time but somehow managed to become the battalion Colonel's personal jeep driver. He had been arriving late to pick up the Colonel, as it was a 24/7 on call duty position. With the cause of his lateness, the Colonel relieved him of his position as a driver. After that he went out and got drunk then found the Colonel's jeep, in which, he then commenced to damaging the vehicle. The Colonel, looking to keep this incident quiet, did not give Copsovic an Article 15 or a court martial, instead he ordered Copsovic to take a Genesis program. Genesis was equivalent to that of Alcoholics Anonymous in the civilian world. He had to attend the meetings regularly and was not supposed to drink alcoholic beverages. Now he was reassigned to the mortar platoon to train on a regular basis. There were no fancy balls or halls to attend anymore for him. It was the smell of mechanic grease, mogas fuel, oil, dirt, and gun powder emanating from your uniform on a weekly basis. As he was being introduced to his new squad, Bolden could sense there was something just not right with this guy but held his opinions to himself as he tried to make the best of the new change. As the day went on, the mock battle proceeded and each mortar crew performed their duties with outstanding precision with each fire mission. Shot, over!!! Shot, Out!!! Was the communication relay between the Mortar FDC, (Fire Direction Center), to the Forward Observer (Scout) that was ordering the fire missions. The temperature began to drop dramatically and with the snow fall lightening up they knew it was going to be a cold night. Most had already put on their Mickey Mouse boots, which were appropriately named because of their size and shape. These boots were designed to go over your combat boots. Some had a tube in them so that you could blow them up to make them fit. They were designed to withstand temperatures of 80 below as well as the sleeping bags that we were issued. Bolden was assigned early guard duty around the perimeter which made him happy because this meant he could get a full night's sleep, that is, if he could get any sleep with the temperature being 40 degrees below zero. He placed his Mickey Mouse boots on over his combat boots. Under his combat boots he had on two pairs of socks, OD green in color, standard issue. The guard shift was two hours in length, at the beginning it was only going to be one hour because of the subzero temperatures but everyone was asked what they would prefer. To pull two hours at one time meant more sleep, to pull one hour meant to be woke up from a nice warm sleeping bag in the middle of the night and adjust to the outside. It was unanimous with the two hour shift. Bolden walked his guard post wearing his army pile cap which was fantastic for keeping the ears warm, his sweater, BDU jacket liner,

BDU jacket, LBE belt (Low Bearing Equipment), strapped around his shoulder was his M-16A1 automatic rifle, long winter underwear, two pairs of socks, combat boots with his mickey mouse boots over them. The only thing cold on him was his hands, wearing his standard issue set of gloves with the liners in them. Walking the guard post he started to shiver from the outside temperatures, staying alert to any movements within and outside the perimeter he started to cite in his mind the first three general orders of a soldier. 1st General Order: I will guard everything within the limits of my post and quit my post only when properly relieved. 2nd General Order: I will obey my special orders and perform all my duties in a military manner. 3rd General Order: I will report violations of my special orders, emergencies, and anything not covered in my instructions, to the commander of the relief. Over and over again he recited them hoping that the time would arrive when he was properly relieved from his guard post. The time came when he woke up his relief who had been sleeping away from the track. The heaters in most of the tracked vehicles did not work and the parts had been on back order for more than a year. There were only two tracked vehicles where the heaters were working. That was the FDC track and 1st squad. It didn't matter anyhow because the whole battalion was under noise discipline throughout the maneuvers. Some decided to place their sleeping bags on the cold steel of the tracks while others opted for the snow covered ground. Bolden decided to set his bedding up on the ground which in his mind was warmer than the steel. As he started getting into his sleeping bag he was reminded by his relief to take off his Mickey Mouse boots so that his feet would not sweat while he was sleeping in them. Being that his feet were warm he decided to leave them on as he snugged into his sleeping bag zipping it all the way up to his nose. His body started to warm up quickly then his body stopped shivering. As the warmth enveloped his body he fell into a deep sleep. Awakened by the rising sun and the commotion of the other soldier's movements around him he was reluctant to get out of his sleeping bag. It was warm and pleasing and he knew the temperature outside had not risen much. He forced himself up and out of the warm sleeping bag and headed for the chow area to get the first morning cup of coffee and breakfast. It was the usual field breakfast of watered eggs, soft bacon, dry bread, a possible dry cereal, if you wanted it, juice, grits or hash browns. It was a hot meal and to a soldier in the field a most welcoming gift. It had been prepared by the field mess hall and brought to them in OD Green canteens which were rectangular in shape and contained three separate containers. They had their MRE packs (Meals Ready to Eat) which was used for lunch or dinner whenever a hot meal was not able to present itself. The temperature had risen somewhat and a heavy snowfall began once again. Within a couple hours after awakening Bolden began to feel the cold starting to set in throughout his whole body especially his feet. With all that had been going on he had not changed his socks to keep his feet warm and he knew it. The only thing he could do was to keep moving to stay warm and even then that wasn't working. His feet and toes were becoming numb and he knew frostbite was near. He then heard the order for everyone to report to the FDC track. They were to take off their boots and socks to have their feet inspected for frostbite. This was his chance to change his wet socks for dry ones. He quickly opened his duffel bag and extracted two pairs of OD green socks and reported to the FDC track. As his feet were being inspected he was told that he was very close to having them frostbitten and to change his socks and to next time not wear his Mickey Mouse boots while sleeping in his sleeping bag. There were a few others who were not so lucky and had to be sent back to the rear to get treated for frostbite. The most important thing for an infantry soldier is WARM, DRY FEET!!! These are his greatest assets that keep him mobile on the battlefield. Lesson taught, lesson learned!!!

17
THE KU'DORF

CSC 6/502nd was back to the McNair barracks by Friday night and ready for the weekend to rest and relax with training complete. Specialist Broadway had received his status as a promotable to sergeant and had been assigned a room of his own which left Bolden to a two man room all to himself. They were both happy and thrilled with the situation at hand. Bolden still not comfortable being with his new platoon and not really trying to make any friends found himself up at the CQ desk talking to the runner and asking questions about the local night spots downtown. The CQ runner started talking about one of the American hot spots called the Ku'dorf. He said it had so many clubs inside that you wouldn't know which ones to go into first and so many people partying there all the time. Specialist Ivey a member of the mortar platoon came through the two bay doors headed towards his room down the hall. The CQ runner stopped him and asked him what he was doing for the night. Ivey, who stood about 5'10" tall with a slender build, a little balding on the top of his head, sporting military issue glasses with the black frames, otherwise known as birth control glasses because of their 1950's look, and looked to be about 25 years of age, said,

"I'm doing nothing but relaxing in my room for the night."

"Good, then take Bolden downtown and show him the Kudorf, you know he's new and has been here awhile and still doesn't know anybody." spouted back, the CQ runner.

"Have his roommate Broadway take him downtown, that's what a roommate is supposed to do besides that I don't have any money to be going downtown.", was Ivey's reply.

"Shut up you rich prick and take him downtown, Broadway's heading over to the East you know it and I know it, all that money you're saving up isn't going to do you much good anyhow, so live a little and take Bolden downtown and show him the ropes, while you are at it tell him the rules about The Level and the Kudorf, By the way Broadway is not his roommate anymore, he's a promotable now, and he's got his own room, you snobbish bastard!!!

"You got any money Bolden?", asked Ivey.

"Yes, I do was Bolden's response.

"Well then be ready in about thirty minutes and we will head down town."

Excited Bolden went to his room, changed his clothes and groomed up for the evening then met Ivey at the CQ desk, from there they went down the stairs and walked to the bus stop. They waited for the bus where Ivey informed him,

We do not have to pay for public transportation. They know we are military by our hair cut and attitude so they rarely ask us for our I.D.s and if they do ask you, just show it to them quickly, other than that you know the rules about presenting identification."

He started showing Bolden how to get downtown and how to get back by using the color codes of the bus routes in case they got separated. When they arrived downtown, departing the bus, they walked about a block where there were many people standing outside of the club, "Kudorf". Standing in line to get in, Ivey started to explain about the differences between the two clubs. The one called "The Level" was upstairs and that was reserved for the British soldiers, "The Kudorf" was downstairs and that was reserved for the American soldiers. The British soldiers were not allowed to go into the Kudorf and the American soldiers were not allowed to go into the Level. The simple reason being that American and British soldiers could not get along with each other and each time that they did get together there was a fight between them.

Bolden's thoughts started asking questions about,

"Why that would be?"

He thought it would be cool to party with the Brits, heck they are supposed to be our allies,

"Aren't they?"

The cover charge to get in to the Ku'dorf was five West German Marks which was equivalent to be around $2.50 from there they walked down a couple flights of stairs that winded down into an entrance way, turn left and there was club after club after club with people all over the place partying and having a good time. Each little club had their own array of music. Walking down the hall looking left and right these small little pubs were full of people as you were coming to what look like the end of the hall, you took another left, to the right was a small bathroom with about 3 urinals in it and an elderly man that tended to the small W.C.. You were supposed to tip him as you left the bathroom after doing your business as he kept the area clean for your use. He spoke very little English but was a very enthusiastic and jovial type of person.

Bolden asked Ivey, "Why is there someone in the men's bathroom, seems kind of weird to me?"

Ivey replied, "That's how some people make their living over here. It's like being a janitor in the States only here they are always on duty in one place. That is what the tip plate is for as you exit the bathroom."

Once this was explained to Bolden he made it a point that every time he used the W.C. upon his exit he would place a couple of West Mark coins onto the tip plate. He admired the working man for he was a working man himself. He was not born into richness or pleasantries. Bolden had left home when he was fifteen years of age, he held three part time jobs and still went to school. He knew he had to finish school to get his diploma. After graduation he dropped one part time job and made the other two jobs, he had, full time. He remembered the closeness of his friends and their families that helped him accomplish his education. They were working class people to. To Bolden, the elderly gentleman that attended to the W.C. was not just a janitor, he was a working man that had the duty of making sure that everyone, who entered that bathroom, stayed in good health by keeping it clean. His job was more important than a doctor because he was at the front line of the battle for disease control. His success rate is unrecognized to many people but his job is fundamentally important. Ivey took Bolden further along the path then took a right that led into a type of square round open area, a dance floor somewhat with small pubs on each side of it, this area was mostly the rock n roll type area with much Lynyrd Skynyrd being played on the turntables. Continuing on, the open space led into a small corridor path that led into another wide open space, this was the disco and it was always packed with partying type of people. The dance floor was full as Saturday Night Fever type of music was playing and a new type of music called "Technik" with its laser light show being introduced onto the scene. Visions of John Travolta dancing on the floor came to Bolden's thoughts as the music played on. After all, that is where he learned how to dance was watching Saturday Night Fever and the way Travolta moved. If you wanted to get the women you had to know how to dance and dance well.

Ivey asked Bolden, "Do you want to get a beer here or someplace that is more quiet?" Bolden knew Ivey wasn't comfortable being at the disco and neither was Bolden.

“No, not here, let's go someplace quiet.” was Bolden's response.

They went back to where the S-curve was in the middle of the Kudorf, found a table, and ordered a couple of golden weissen beers. The texture was smooth and soothing to the palette as they both sipped their beers slowly.

Ivey, asking, but making more of a statement rather than a question,

“I notice you don't drink beer very fast. You aren't much of a drinker, are you?”

Bolden agreed with him and stated,

“No, not at this time, I like to keep my senses about me, this way, I will remember what you are teaching me.”

They made small talk mostly with their time there, admiring some of the beautiful women that would walk by and give them a glance back or two. After a couple more beers Ivey decided it was time to go.

“Are you hungry?” asked Ivey

Bolden nodded and followed Ivey through the corridors, up the stairs, and then out into the open market area where they came across a small Imbiss food stand with a line in front of it. This is where Bolden got the knowledge of the best food in the world, “The Doner kebab”. It is a Turkish dish made of lamb meat cooked on a vertical spit and sliced to order, add some vegetables, special sauce, between a hunk of bread and it makes the world a place worth living in. The sensation of it all together is an eye opening experience, after eating one you wish to have another. Ivey ordered two of them, one for him and one for Bolden. They started to walk to the bus stop, after the third bite into Bolden's Doner kebab he stopped and said to Ivey,

"Man, these are great! I've got to go back and get a couple more to put in the refrigerator in my room at the barracks."

In doing this he would have breakfast waiting for him when he got up and didn't have to worry about waking up to go to the mess hall.

"Hurry it up! The bus is coming soon and I am going to be on it, with or without you."Ivey shouted.

As Bolden stood in the small line he noticed a couple of British soldiers in front of him. He could tell they were British by their accent, even though they were speaking in English, Bolden couldn't understand what they were saying so he kept to himself and listened to them talk. One of them looked up and saw Bolden watching them, the man asked him,

"Yau a yahnk?",

"What?", was Bolden's reply.

"YAU A YAHNK?", the British soldier asking again, only this time much louder.

" Man, I apologize, but I'm not sure what you are saying", said Bolden.

Again the British soldier asked him the same thing, this time with a bit more urgency in his voice. Just then Ivey shouted out,

"YES, HE IS A YANK, IS THERE A PROBLEM?!!!

"Glaud ta met yau dar mate!!!"

as he stuck out his right hand in greetings toward Bolden. Bolden extended his right arm and shook the British soldier's hand.

"Ahhh, nice to meet you to, I think", said Bolden with a smile on his face.

The handshake is important to a warrior and some say it comes from the knight's code of chivalry. To offer your right hand in friendship, for a handshake, you are saying to that warrior that your fighting arm is free of any weapons and that you wish to do no harm unto that warrior. You are giving to that person your trust and alliance to them allowing them to know that you feel no harm from them. It also denotes your thoughts being expressed spiritually. The left side of the body is the receiving port of energy which allows you to sense the thoughts of others. The right side of your body is the exiting port of your energy which allows you to express your thoughts without speech. There is much energy placed into your thoughts as it exits out the right side of your hand. Which is why, drill instructors are taught to point with all their fingers on the right hand instead of the one index finger. It calms down the soldier you are giving instruction to in order for them to listen to what you are relaying to them instead of them thinking you are trying to insult them. When the two right hands embrace each other in a handshake each warrior is relaying their thought of intention to each other thereby relaying peace and friendship toward one another.

Bolden received his order of two Doner kebabs just in time as the bus pulled up to the stop and was letting passengers off and then on.

Ivey calling out to him said,

"You better get your ass moving we're pulling out, now!!!"

Bolden looked at the British soldier and said with a smile,

"See ya later mate."

Bolden jumped on the bus and waved at them as they waved back and felt much more at ease with himself. He looked at Ivey and said,

"No wonder why the Americans and the Brits don't get along, they can't understand what the heck each of them are saying and we speak the same language."

"There are a couple of things you have to remember about the British", Ivey said. "One, they are well disciplined and two they will fight at the drop of a hat if they sense something is wrong. They respect those that stand up for themselves so don't ever back down from them in any type of confrontation, that is why I shouted back at them when they asked if you were a yank. I could tell they were getting a little agitated." "One other thing about the Brits, they are sticklers for rules, so watch what you do around them."

"Ok, point taken there Ivey, I appreciate the good time tonight and your words of advice. Bolden stating back in the way of gratitude.

They both arrived at McNair Barracks and each went to their own rooms. With the Doner kebabs in the frig and

Bolden in his sleep wear laid down on his bunk and ended the night filled with the nights events into a peaceful sleep.

18
A FINE LINE

The beginning of March brought with it the promise of warming temperatures. The sun was appearing frequently throughout the days. The winds had calmed down into a slight breeze and with the temperatures rising a bit the snow was melting slowly as the days progressed on, leaving in its path a few slushy spots of puddles. Bolden was starting to get familiar with a few of the guys in his mortar platoon and he had acquired a new roommate. He was a Spec. 4 already and was married. His wife was in transit to West Berlin so the arrangement was only temporary on the rooming situation. Bolden was good with that because this guy was much different than the rest of the platoon members. He was talkative, liked to joke around a bit, and he loved to party. Jack was about 5’ 8” tall, not stocky but had a muscular build to him with fiery red hair that matched his personality. He was always motivated, kept his AO clean and as a team, Jack and Bolden, kept their room in immaculate shape. Jack was mostly gone from the room after duty hours visiting an army pal in another company that he had met on his travels to West Berlin. Bolden did not know much about him but he liked him. He was a mighty fine soldier and knew his job well as a mortar man. Three weeks in West Berlin and with his wife due to come within a couple days Jack walked into the room with his head down and his face looking a little pale. It was only about an hour after they had been relieved of duty from the regular company formation end of day routine.

"What's up Jack, that pretty little thing at the small PX turn you down or what?", Bolden asked, jokingly.

"No", Jack said with his head slightly looking upward, they caught me shoplifting in the store so now I have to see the Colonel.

"Holy shit!", Bolden remarked. "What did you have to have that was so important Jack?" "Man, if you had to have some money I could have lent you some till payday."

"I have money", said Jack. "Just wanted a candy bar is all, I've done it plenty of times since I've been here, this time they saw me do it and took action."

"Awe, Jack that sucks, well you most likely will get an Article 15 and busted down in rank not to mention extra duty and pay, think they might send you back to the states?"

"I don't know, not sure, that's what I'm wondering about to, my wife is supposed to be here in a couple days, she's not going to like it too much if we have to head back."

"I know you have a clean record otherwise Jack, you wouldn't have been assigned to the Berlin Brigade if you did. Hope he goes easy on you."

The Colonel did not go easy on Jack though, when all was said and done, Jack received about the max punishment you could get for a field grade Article 15. He had found Jack guilty and his punishment was a full reduction from Specialist 4th class to Private E-1, 45 days extra duty, half a month's pay for two months, and 60 days restriction. There was probably more attached to it that Jack didn't tell us but that was his affair. The majority of the platoon had felt it was a harsh punishment for just a candy bar but the Colonel made an example of him and it served the purpose. He was able to stay with the company and with the Berlin Brigade which many of us were happy to hear. He was a fine soldier with great merit toward working as a team. In a war type situation his ability to scrounge whatever he could at a time of survival, without getting caught, which he said he had done so many other times before, would have been rewarded with a medal but we were at peace in a place where we were surrounded by the enemy at all times and discipline had to be adhered to always!!! What creates you to be a hero in one circumstance can also create you to be an outlaw in the same circumstance under different conditions. It is a fine line to be judged in times like those for this will place you at a crossroads in your life to exam it, define it, and then take action upon it. The only thought you have left at that moment is hope. Faith in what you have done all the way to the conclusion of that matter, that it will ultimately define its purpose later in life and help you lead the way by example. Jack's sacrifice of his reputation, by doing what he did, would serve Bolden in the near future for the difficult decisions he will have to make.

19
A SCOUT'S INVITATION

Tracy Guill was a scout with CSC 6/502nd, he stood 6 ft. in height, maybe a little more, about 190 lbs. he had short black hair with an eccentric personality other than that of your typical enlisted soldier. In other words, he did not fit in with his other platoon members and he knew it. This did not bother him at all, in fact, in some ways, he gave off that air that he took pride in being different from others. He wasn't arrogant about this, he mostly kept to himself but tried to make friends as he went along the way. He dressed and talked differently than the average infantry soldier. He spoke fluent German and was highly intelligent, sometimes trying to hide his high IQ but somehow wasn't able to camouflage it too well, possibly his pride taking over when he was constantly correcting those who would question anything about him. His room was at the other end of the hall where the scouts and snipers were located, whereas the mortar platoon had a hall of their own. Guill approached Bolden at the CQ desk and struck up a conversation. He knew Bolden was still new and did not have very many friends there yet. It was not hard to figure this fact out about Bolden because he spent most of his time at the CQ desk talking to the runner. There was not much else to do he did not have a television set in his room. Bolden would write letters home and to his friends. That didn't take up much time. He would call home every so often to talk to his mother or sister but he had to keep a limit on the phone calls home because he had to call collect and a call collect to the United States was not cheap. He had decided to send an allotment home to his mother of $400.00 a month from his pay to help with the collect calls and other bills. He did not have to have much money there for he had room and board. His meals were paid for, medical, and dental. He had decided it was better for his family to use it rather than it be used up for drinking alcohol or other foolish things. The Army had provided a place where you could make calls home for free but the time was limited on how much you could talk and it all depended upon the ionosphere if it was favorable to make a call that day or not. There were many soldiers that stood in line to make their calls home and Bolden having stood in line for chow, in line to draw your weapon, in line to get a hair cut, in line to get into a club, was not interested in standing in anymore lines than were necessary to.

Guill asking Bolden, Will you like to go to East Berlin with me this coming Saturday?"

Bolden, being hesitant, replied, "I wasn't to impressed with East Berlin when I went on that tour from the school. I really don't have any inclinations of going over there again."

Excitedly Guill started to explain his inclinations in order to change Bolden's mind on going to the East with him.

"The night life is totally different over there and I can show you some really neat places, more than what you saw on that East Berlin Tour. Over there the woman treat us like we are wealthy at the discos and they flock around you like a magnet. We will dine at one of the fanciest restaurants they have there and to us it will be cheap. Take $40.00 and convert it to East Marks that will be more than enough to cover anything you do over there. I've been over there plenty of times and know many places, besides that I speak German."

"It is nice to have some company with you while you are there, so what do you say?" asked Guill.

Bolden was getting motivated by what Guill had been saying and eagerly accepted his invitation. He was ready to go out and enjoy himself and to have the comfort of having someone to converse with.

Bolden asked Guill, "What is the procedure for paperwork to go over to the East."

Guill excited in knowing that Bolden was accepting his invitation said, "It's easy, I'll take care of it."

It was simple, all you had to do was fill out the form for an East Pass, it went through the chain of command all the way to the Colonel with everyone's permission. Once that was accomplished you took your East Pass to the Checkpoint, show it to the M.P.s as you were going across and you were in East Berlin. Simple! The CQ runner already had anticipated what was going to happen next as he got up from his chair and walked into the Captain's office returning with two East Passes to be filled out and handed them to the two soldiers. With the East Passes filled out and turned in all they had to do now was wait for the chain of command to approve them, which was almost a given thing depending on if you had duty, or done something that would have given them a reason not to sign it. Guill and Bolden had agreed to meet around 1600 hours that Saturday in front of the CQ desk and then take off from there.

20
BACK TO EAST BERLIN

Saturday, March 8th,1986, 1600 hours, standing in front of the CQ desk, Bolden was wearing his Class A uniform. Cleaned and pressed he was showing off his ARCOM, AAM, and his ASR medals, the Berlin Brigade

Patch on his left arm, STRIKE symbols pinned in their proper position, shoes spit shined to a mirror gloss finish, and the most important of all to any infantry soldier, the light blue infantry cord that was over his right shoulder. Looking sharp, feeling good and standing proud he spots a figure way down to the end of the hall walking toward him. It was a shadow it seemed at first and Bolden thought it must be Guill coming to meet him but as the figure came closer the uniform this soldier was wearing resembled that of a Soviet Officer. The black military long winter coat, unbuttoned, the lower portion swaying back and forth with each step that he took. On the top of his head for cover were not the usual style Class A garrison hat and definitely not the cover that an enlisted man would wear. It was an olive drab, cold weather, fur flyers hat, fur ear flaps on each side clasped together with their buttons on top of the hat. The United States Army bronze symbol attached in the middle front of the fur flap shining brightly as the light hit it. The hat resembled the Soviet soldiers Ushanka winter hat worn by Soviet officers. As the silhouette came closer it became clear that standing in front of Specialist 4th Class Bolden was Specialist 4th Class Tracy Guill being his different self.

Bolden chuckling out loud asked, “Are you really serious?”

Guill looking surprised and serious came back with, “Yes, why are you asking?”

“You look like an officer not just an American officer, a Soviet officer at that.” “Is that hat you are wearing regulation for an enlisted member such as yourself?” Bolden asked.

"Yes it is!" Guill answering back in earnest. "Look it up in the regulations for yourself if you don't believe me". Said Guill.

"Well I hope you don't drink too much alcohol over there. I'd hate to have to get shot at while carrying your ass across the border with them thinking I'm trying to capture one of their officers for interrogation on our side." Bolden said half-jokingly.

"I like dressing up like this, who knows I might even get one of those bastards to salute me over there." Guill stated with a smile on his face.

As they both started laughing Bolden looks at Guill and said, "You look squared away, let's get going so we can catch the bus on time."

They approached Checkpoint Charlie and presented their East passes to the M.P.s in charge.

The NCOIC snapped at Guill the moment he saw him, "You are a spec 4. What are you doing wearing that officers hat in your Class A uniform soldier?"

Guill responded back, "It is regulation sergeant: you can look it up if you like."

Guill stood his ground as the NCOIC knew that Guill was correct. The Sergeant examined their East passes then waved them through reminding the both of them to be back before midnight. As the two of them started walking toward the East they entered into a small corridor boxed in with plywood and plastic. There was barely enough room for two people walking in either direction to get through shoulder to shoulder. The slush of the melting snow mixed in with dirt was not difficult to pass through however they walked carefully trying to keep their uniforms and highly shined shoes in sharp appearance.

Bolden looking over to Guill asked, “What happens if we are not back by midnight?”

Guill answered quickly, “They will send a search party out for us. Once they find us we will be reprimanded to the Colonel, receive an Article 15, and our passes to the East revoked. This is something you do not want to happen. So make sure you are back in plenty of time to check in.”

Checkpoint Charlie was well known to many East and West Berliners, as well as to the Allied Forces. This was the name it was given by the Western Allies. It was a symbol through the Cold War representing the separation of East and West Berlin. For some East Germans it was a “Gateway to Freedom.” Soviet and American tanks briefly had a face off at that particular point during the Berlin Crisis in 1961. Tourists from abroad, diplomats, and the military personnel of the Western Powers were only allowed to enter East Berlin through that crossing point. It was tightly guarded on both sides. The passing point on the street for cars was narrow as the long, thick cement blocks formed an S-curve shape to prevent vehicles from high acceleration for an escape to smash through into the West. East German Border guards patrolled the area with loaded AK-47 Kalashnikov automatic rifles with orders of “Shoot to Kill” on any and all escape attempts. As they were walking by the East German guard shack Bolden noticed how the border guards were checking visas and passports of the people that were leaving East Berlin. He saw how one would check the documents and another guard would walk around to the back of the vehicle examining the exterior and then the interior as much as possible. The border guard would continue on around to the passenger side and then would stop just before the end of the passenger's side front tire. Bolden could tell immediately these men were well trained and knew exactly what they were doing. Guill started to remind Bolden that if they saw a Soviet officer that they were to salute him as they were still considered to be our allies. The East German Border guards and soldiers, though there was not much difference in their defined roles for military status, were our enemies and we were to seriously consider them as such. The Soviet military could question us slightly but the East Germans could not. They had declared the Western Powers as there enemy and we kindly returned the favor. Passing the East German guard shack they passed by two East German border agents that were standing together waiting for the next vehicle to be inspected as it came up the line. There was a slight bit of tension as their paths crossed. Bolden wrote this off as being a newbie entering into East Berlin on foot and it soon went away as they continued on their path. Looking at the old buildings walking down the sidewalk he felt that strange sensation he felt when he was there on the tour from the Iron School of Soldiers.

Guill breaking the tension asked Bolden, "Are you hungry?"

Bolden nodding his head in affirmation to Guill's question and asking back, "Do you have a place in mind?"

Guill said, “Of course I do, it is one of the fanciest places they have here and they have great food. You might have to order two plates though because the portions that they serve are kind of conservative: it has something to do with etiquette, I think.”

“I am not well rehearsed in etiquette and I’m not much for fancy, Guill. Hope it isn’t too expensive, was Bolden’s reply.

“You are in East Berlin now, YOU’RE RICH!!! You’ll see.” Guill stated, optimistically.

Continuing on their journey they reached a T intersection and then took a right to head toward the main square of Alexanderplatz it seemed like it took forever to get to the downtown square with the sun starting to set in the west and the night coming in to take its place they finally arrived at the fancy hotel named The Palast. To Bolden it didn’t seem extravagant at all to him it resembled an old hotel in downtown Chicago during the 1920’s or 1930’s era a comparison he made from watching old gangster movies when he was a child growing up in Illinois. They walked through the double doors straight ahead was an old fashioned elevator with a gate in front of it, to the right was the check in station to the hotel, to the left was the restaurant. It did not seem very big in size. Tables were lined against the big bay windows that overlooked the city street so you could watch the people passing by. Open tables and chairs were placed brilliantly in the middle of the floor to accommodate as many customers as possible for the dining area. They chose a middle table that was against one of the big bay windows for their dining pleasure. It was taking some time for them to be waited on as the waitresses had huddled together discussing which one of them were to serve the American soldiers and take their order. Possibly discussing who spoke better English, who had the bravery to be seen serving them, who would take the tips they would most likely leave for the service providing that they felt that American soldiers to them were wealthy, their kindness, or maybe it was all of that. All of them were nicely dressed and carried themselves with a posture of uncertainty within them. The one that served them was it seemed like the older of them she looked to be in her late 30's to mid 40's with short curly brown hair and green eyes with a medium frame about her. Her complexion was one that did not stand out, though pretty in her own way, there was something subtle about her, something that was holding her back from her true qualities. There was the slight smile as she came to the table that a waitress would provide but she did not make eye contact. Bolden had been a cook in a few restaurants back home before joining the army and had watched the waitresses that he worked with at the time. How they carried themselves and joked with the customers to help them feel at ease while dining in the establishment was the determining factor of how much a tip they would receive for their services. When Guill started speaking German to her, her eyes lit up somewhat relieving the anxiety she must have felt about the communication process. He had ordered us two Pilsner beers which came in a fancy shaped glass. Pilsner beer wasn't a favorite of Bolden's as it had a strong bitter taste that came with it but as long as it was cold and carbonated he was happy to deal with it. As he looked at the menu he saw it was all in German and asked Guill to order for the both of them and informed Guill he would like to have some kind of steak for dinner as his diet had consisted mostly of cheeseburger and French fries from the mess hall or the burger bar in the McNair compound and an occasional Doner kebab from the Imbiss by the barracks.

When Guill finished the order he explianed to Bolden, “I have ordered us two plates for each of us. I will pay the tab.”

Bolden refusing his offer stating, “No you won't, I will get this. I appreciate you very much for bringing me over here to the East side and teaching me what the other members of my platoon would not do. I insist, you allow me to pay for dinner!”

Guill with a satisfied look on his face accepted Bolden’s offer. As they waited for their food to arrive Bolden expressed his thoughts about how East Berlin appeared to him how everything looked so dull there. The people with the clothes that they wore, their silence, their reluctance to talk, the buildings of how they hid the thoughts of the architect that designed them. He told him how he wondered about where the life force was, the brilliance, the shine of energy that was in the West. The amount of cameras mounted on almost every city block and how he could not fathom the idea of that being in the United States.

Guill started to inform him, “Be cautious of what you say and do in both East and West Berlin, the reason being, there are more spies in East and West Berlin than all over the world.”

With that said Bolden quieted his tone and took his advice and changed the subject as the dinner plates started arriving to the table. Guill was correct in ordering two plates as the portions were small in comparison to an American meal. The salads were small, the steak was thin and it's shape resembled that of a pork chop, a small side of mashed potatoes, and a few green beans, with a hard roll (Brochen), and a side dish with a small scoop of butter. This butter was different than anything Bolden had ever had before. Its texture was grainy and had green bits of herbs in it, and unlike the Eastern side of Berlin, it had a Golden yellow shine to it. This had personality to it. He picked up his butter knife which had a thick handle to it and the spreading portion was wider than he was used to. After splitting the brochen in half he applied the butter with the sharp personality to it with his over-sized butter knife. After placing the knife back onto the thick square napkin he then bit into the hard roll. As soon as the butter started to melt onto his tongue his eyes widened with satisfaction as the herbs danced along his palette. The sharpness of it with its vibrant character and color was outstanding and no other butter would compare to this. He had to know what it was called and asked Guill.

"HEY, WHAT KIND OF BUTTER IS THIS?"

Guill told him, "It's called Krauterbutter."

"What's in it?" Bolden asked.

"I don't know but it sure does taste good." Guill said.

He called the waitress over and asked her what was in the butter that made it taste so good. She told him that the ingredients were fresh parsley, tarragon, dried dill, minced chives, chervil, minced onion, lemon juice, and salt.

Guill asking Bolden, “Why are you so excited about the butter? They have this butter on the West side to, ya know?”

Bolden responding back, “This is the first time I have ever been in a restaurant since I've been in Germany. They have some really good food here!”

To Bolden it seemed as if a whole new world had opened up for him and it just so happened to be in a place that he wasn’t very fond of to begin with. He watched as Guill placed his thick square napkin onto his lap and started to use the different forks that were available. One for the salad, one for the dinner, to Bolden there was no use for the extra utensils that were at his disposal. He proceeded to cut his steak up into bite size pieces all at once and saw Guill cut his steak one piece at a time and then eat it. With all the plates they had acquired from ordering two meals each, that were sitting on the table, they had acquired some attention from the other guests within the restaurant. As Bolden was cutting his steaks up into small pieces he could sense the stares of some of the other guests, looking up cautiously he saw many of them looking his way and stopped cutting.

He asked Guill, “Why are these people staring at us?”

With an earnest look he replied, “They aren’t staring at us, they are staring at you.”

Bolden with a surprised look on his face asked, “Why is that?”

"Because proper etiquette dictates that you cut your meat one piece at a time, small pieces so that your cheeks don't puff out while you are eating it. This gives you an air of sophistication." Responded Guill.

Bolden with his new found knowledge and sense of aristocracy settled into a relax state and commenced to enjoying his wonderful meal. With their meals and after dinner coffees finished it was time to go. The waitress placed the tab on the table with a small dish as Bolden picked it up and looked at the numbers it had come to about 100 East Marks equivalent to around $10.00 U.S. dollars. The price of four complete meals, two pilsner beers, and two coffees in East Berlin cost the same as purchasing four Doner kebabs in West Berlin. After paying the tab they walked into the hallway as Bolden was going to the right to exit the hotel Guill had stopped and asked,

"Are you possibly interested in having some female company?"

Guill said he had heard rumors that on the top level of the hotel were available high class call girls that to us would be very affordable. He had always wanted to check this rumor out to see if it was true and Bolden could tell his spirit of adventure was high. Listening to what Guill was saying Bolden's eyes were fixed on the elevator. He could feel from the pit of his stomach a small knot starting to develop as a warm sensation of eerie goose bump shivers started to rise up his spine then to the top of his head. He knew right away it was his instincts telling him that was not a good idea. High class call girls, fancy food, a top rate hotel was an open door invitation to a spy network and he was not trained to handle a game like that. This was a game he could not afford to play nor was it one that he could afford to lose. He shook his head from side to side and followed his instincts and refused Guill's high spirited sense of adventure.

Bolden responding respectfully, "No, I'm not much for the company of prostitutes, though I do not condone the profession, I think my money can be spent better on other things besides sexual favors." What is the local night life like in the area where we can have a drink together and talk a little more?"

Guill answered, "There are a couple of good discos around here. Follow me, I will show you."

They proceeded down Alexanderplatz into the big square where the local markets were located. Bolden had a Kodak disc camera he had purchased when he was stationed in Ft. Hood Texas that served him greatly. It was compact and portable that fit perfectly in his pocket for easy storage. The film was easy to load with a complete disc of 15 exposures per disc. Snapping photos of anything he found of interest to him. He saw that the Pope's Revenge Tower was coming closer as well as the World Time Clock that kept time throughout the world, still looked kind of weird to him but art is art and that's all there is to that. They came up to what looked like a government business type building and walked in. It was dimly lit as a soft yellow glow from the light bulbs came through. They walked up a flight of stairs turned to the right on a level platform then started up another flight of stairs that led them to the top of the second floor. Looking straight forward he saw the men's bathroom door was opened wide. The wall was painted a dull yellow. One thing that caught his attention was a payphone that hung on the wall to the right.

"Why would they have a pay phone in the bathroom?" He wondered.

They took a right and walked by the women's bathroom. It was the same. The door left open, same dull yellow color and a payphone on the right wall which a line had formed to use it. The second story hallway was painted a dull gray. Everywhere he looked nothing shined of brilliance. It was dull, dull, dull! They walked through a set of steel doors that were held open by steel bolts that set into the floor. The music they were playing was American songs which surprised Bolden. The whole disco was barely lit up except for the dance floor which had a subdued light show going on around the dancing area. To the left was a few tables that were barely being occupied as his eyes followed from there to the right in a slow circular motion was the dance floor then a small couple tables. On the back far wall was the bar area to order drinks from. It stretched the whole length of the back wall then coming up on the right side were more tables with a bit more lighting to them. This seemed to be the area where many people liked to party at as all of the tables that were there had been filled. It was filled with laughter and drinking. Smoke filled the air with the scent of clove cigarettes being smoked. To their immediate right was a long set of tables that were placed together end to end with chairs on both sides. The table had big thick champagne bottles at least ten of them that Bolden could count. Coca cola cans empty and full were sitting on the table. Packs of Kool cigarettes were laid out in the open. Though the lighting at that table was dim he saw the Class A uniforms of American soldiers and sitting in the middle of the table was his old roommate Spec. 4 Michael Broadway drinking a glass of champagne and smoking a Kool cigarette which was his brand. Along with him was Spec. 4 Kevin Festerman and one other soldier he had not seen before. Bolden was eyeing the table and counted five women sitting at the table with the soldiers. All of them drinking champagne and smoking Kool cigarettes. The women started staring at Guill and Bolden then Broadway turning his head to see what they were staring at looked at Bolden and said,

"Johnny, what the hell are you doing with a scout? You're a mortar man!"

Bolden snapping back proudly said,

"Guill was nice enough to invite me over here with him and show me a few things I did not get to see on the tour where as you bastards would not bring me over here with you. So I accepted his offer and he has been a pretty good host I may add."

"What does a guy have to do to get a drink around here anyways?" Bolden asked.

Broadway offered a seat at their table sitting opposite from him that Bolden accepted and then looked at Guill to see if he was going to sit with them which he did but took a chair about three seats away, that was kind of odd Bolden thought. It looked as if Guill's personality had changed. He had gone from being very talkative and assertive to shy and silent quickly. Broadway motioned over a waitress and asked her to bring two more champagne glasses over. She was very prompt with her service and as soon as the glasses were on the table Broadway poured two glasses of champagne from the oversized dark green bottles that they were stored in. He placed the full glasses in front of both the newly arrived guests, lifted his glass and said

"Prost!"

Bolden picked up his glass and sipped a little from the glass. The moment it hit his tongue it immediately started to dance on his taste buds. First it was sweet then it kicked up into second gear and switched over to being bitter that made Bolden's eyes widen, then into third gear turning bittersweet all within a matter of seconds before swallowing the East German made beverage.

"WOW!", Bolden thought, "That's enough to make you think twice about drinking that kind of alcoholic concoction."

Broadway could tell by the way Bolden looked after sipping on the champagne that it wasn't really his cup of tea so to speak and offered this thought as a consolation prize.

"Yeah it's a little rough at first but at 30 East Marks a bottle which is equal to $3.00 in our currency you will get used to it. Gives you one heck of a good buzz and the women here like it!"

"Well then if that's the case let's get us three more bottles and have a good time", Bolden said while motioning to the waitress and saying

"Drei Bitte (Three Please)"

to bring the next order of champagne to the table. Guill ordered a different type of mixed drink instead of the champagne, as far as Bolden could tell, Guill did not like the taste of the champagne, for he had not drank any from his glass. Broadway proceeded with the introductions with the ladies sitting at the table. He first introduced Bolden to his girlfriend Jacqueline. She was a skinny kind of woman with short black to dark brown hair. Bolden had noticed before approaching the table that she was very active conversing with everyone at the table. When Bolden sat in the chair across from Broadway, she was still and very observant of him. Ignoring the stares from her, Bolden shook her hand and bowed his head toward her, as in a polite manner of chivalry, acknowledging her presence. He was very uncomfortable around her as her hand shake was vague in nature. The next one Broadway introduced was Mandy. She was a very cheerful young lady, though her English was not that good, she could be understood, as she joked around and made many people laugh around her. She was a little chunky, had curly brown hair, with a chubby face. The laugh lines she had around her mouth, created the appearance around her, that she loved to have fun and make people laugh that was around her. She was about five feet five inches in height but her personality made her more noticeable than anything. Bolden liked her immediately and could sense no danger from her whatsoever. One thing Bolden noticed right away, was that she was wearing a United States Army Major oak leaf bronze cluster insignia on her sweater that an American soldier had apparently given her. Though it seemed harmless for her to wear it on her sweater Bolden knew it wasn't the right thing to do. If she had been taken into custody for interrogation the Stasi could have confiscated it and used it for infiltration into any U.S. Military establishment. An officer that was a Major carried enough clout within the U.S. Army ranks that not many people would question. She was sitting next to Kevin Festerman who was a member of the 4.2 mortar platoon and Bolden knew him already. He did not know him well but had worked with him a couple of times on the mortar guns. An excellent soldier from what Bolden could figure out and had no problems with him at all. He was about five feet six inches tall had an average frame for a soldier with short brown thin hair. He and Mandy made a natural looking couple being together and it looked like they enjoyed each others company. Sitting next to him was a soldier that Bolden had not been acquainted with. He was a sergeant and Broadway introduced him as Ray Williams. They shook hands as they were introduced and Broadway explained that Ray was a mortarman assigned to the mortar platoon but had been transferred to supply as they were shorthanded at the time and Ray had past experience in that field from his last duty assignment in the States, which explained why Bolden had not met him during training with the platoon. Ray had somewhat of a chunky face with thin hair. He was drinking coca cola and did not smoke, which was kind of odd for a soldier, as Bolden allowed his thoughts to be expressed verbally out loud to Williams. He explained that he did not care for the taste of alcohol or cigarettes and besides that he was the driver of the van. He wished to make sure everyone got back safely. Bolden just shrugged his shoulders and said,

"To each his own, man. I can respect that. Then Guill and I will go back through the checkpoint with you guys."

Immediately, the response was quick from all the soldiers at the table, at the same time,

"No you can't, you have to go back over the same way you came in. If you walked over you have to walk back."

It was definitely a clear message, no doubt about it. Mike continued on with his introductions to Babette and Ushi, two blonde young women with average body frames. They could not speak English very well so they were kind of quiet sitting next to each other. Nice enough as they were, they did not stick out in a crowd. They seemed kind of timid to Bolden as he bowed his head slightly to them acknowledging their presence. Then there was Tanje, a skinny young female with black hair. She seemed to be uncomfortable sitting at the table with everyone and after the introduction she got up and left the table. Bolden wasn't quite sure how to take her personality but did not really care for her attitude. As Bolden sat back down in his chair and lifted his glass of champagne to take a drink he felt a presence come up from behind him. It was a strong essence of energy that seemed to be pressing against his. As he saw movement from his left side he looked up and standing there beside him, looking into his eyes, was a woman that stood way out from the crowd. She had blonde hair that waved slightly down to her shoulders and clear blue eyes. A glow about her that shined so brightly it seemed to light up the room. She was different, way different from any of the other women that were in the club. The clothes she was wearing were made in the west and she had an air of sophistication about her that made her distinct from all the rest. She stood tall and straight with her chest out that gleamed with pride and strength. Staring into his eyes that seemed like an eternity, Bolden could sense she was checking him up and down. His blood was pulsating through his veins with excitement. The music drowned out in the background as did all the other voices that were speaking at the time. He couldn't take his eyes off of her and he watched carefully for her mannerisms. His mind was made up that he was going to get to know her and she was going to know him. As he was about to speak to her she made the first move and asked him,

"So, where do you come from?"

It was clear to him she spoke English well and it was a relief to him because he spoke very little German. Being witty and looking for what kind of reaction she would have Bolden piped back quickly with,

"I came from the West, how about you, where do you come from?"

Instantly he saw the left side of her lip slightly open as if holding back a smile and a tad bit of laughter. Oh yeah, she liked him and he knew it. As Bolden began to stand up to introduce himself, immediately Broadway intervened with his continued introductions,

"Jackie, this is John, John this is Jackie."

As the two of them shook hands Bolden felt the firm but delicate grip of her female handshake. By the feel of her grip he could sense she was a woman with a strong sense of character that was true to her word and ideals. He had to know more about her and the best way to do that was to have a conversation over a few drinks. He offered her some champagne which she accepted and he motioned to the waitress to bring another glass. He pulled a chair out from the table and asked her to have a seat next to him. As she sat down he noticed the slight smile she had earlier disappeared and a serious look came upon her face as her and Jacqueline, Mike's girlfriend, looked at each other. He could sense the tension between those two women and he knew there had to be a history between the two of them. Bolden had to break the tension that was apparent in the air between them as he intruded with his words while pouring a glass of champagne for Jackie,

"To seriously answer your question of where I come from, have you ever heard of the State of Wisconsin?"

"Yes I have", was her direct and immediate response.

"I know all of the States in the United States of America", she proudly stated.

This was odd to Bolden because there were a few people that lived in the United States, that he knew, that did not know all of the States and they did not really care to know. For a woman in an Eastern Block Communist State to know of America seemed quite different for him. He asked her how she was able to speak English so well. Her response was,

"From school and talking with American G.I.s."

She told him that in school they had to speak a different language of their choice, which she also told him that they emphasis to them to learn to speak Russian, but she chose English because she liked it and did not care to speak Russian. Right away he could sense she was a rebel against overbearing authority. As the night continued on they engaged in small talk getting to know each other, Jackie would interpret to the other women at the table that were asking questions about Bolden, small things about how he liked the champagne and so on but his attention was mostly on Jackie for they had something in common. He did not know what it was but he definitely liked her. To him, she was a breath of fresh air in a place that was stagnant and stale bringing in a life of excitement and beauty. He hoped he would be able to see her again in the future. The time went by quickly and before he knew it Guill was tapping him on the shoulder saying it was time to head back to the West, remembering they had to be back before midnight. Bolden had forgotten Guill was even there for he had been so quiet through everything. As the both of them stood up Bolden expressed his appreciation to everyone that was at the table for the wonderful time he had at the club. He then turned to Jackie, shook her hand again and said,

"It was very nice to meet you and I hope to see you again soon."

"Ja, me too", was her reply.

Leaving the table and walking toward the exit, Broadway yelled across the room,

"I'LL MEET YOU BACK AT YOUR ROOM."

Bolden nodded and waved good bye. Walking back to Check Point Charlie Bolden engaged Guill with many questions about the women at the table and especially Jackie. He did not express much in his answers simply saying he did not know them that well and cautioned Bolden to be careful of what he said around the women for the reason being they could be spies. Bolden acknowledged the possibilities that a couple of them could be spies but he knew the woman he had just met, Jackie definitely was not a spy. Bolden asked Guill, "What is going on between Jackie and Mike's girlfriend Jacqueline? I sense there is something going on there." Guill's response was simple,

"Don't know, you will have to ask Mike about that."

"Of course I will." Bolden said with a smile on his face.

Guill and Bolden returned safely back to McNair Barracks after having stopped at an Imbiss stand to get a couple Doner kebobs. Thanking Guill for taking him over to the East and having a wonderful time, both of them returned to their rooms. Thirty minutes later while munching on one of the Doners there was a knock on his door and as he opened it, Broadway is standing in the opening. Immediately he exclaims.

"From now on you go over to the East with us instead of a scout, we have to hang together, man!!!"

"What, so am I cool enough to take over there with you now?" Bolden replied with a smug smile on his face.

"Yeah, yeah, eventually we would have taken you with us sooner or later. You made quite the impression on the girls you know, especially Jackie. They were asking many questions about you, a lot of questions!"

"So what's the deal with your girlfriend and Jackie? I know something's up." John asking inquisitivly.

Mike shed some light on the subject by saying he had asked Jackie to be his girlfriend before asking Jacqueline so there was a bit of difference between the women.

"Say no more, I know the situation well then."

He knew Mike did not wish to speak about it. Changing the subject Mike asked John if he wished to go over to the East with them the next weekend which John eagerly accepted. He wished to see Jackie again and get to know her.

21
MEETING TWO

The next Saturday came and Bolden met up with Mike and Ray in the parking lot of 6/502nd Infantry Regiment. They hopped into Ray's VW van quickly and headed towards Checkpoint Charlie. Bolden was starting to become more comfortable around Mike as Mike's attitude toward him had changed for the better. John started to make small talk with Ray in order to get to know him a little better. Asking Ray why he wasn't with the mortar platoon. Ray replied quickly saying that he really did not miss training with the mortar platoon.

"While you guys are out freezing your balls off in the winter during field training I'm back in the rear wear its warm handing out gear to the soldiers and keeping inventory, I've been in a while now and I still can put a gun up quicker than you guys can so I will stick with what I have right now." Ray, stating this with full confidence in his voice.

Bolden was satisfied with the way Ray had answered his question and left it at that. They pulled onto Alexanderplatz and then into the market square where the discos were located. John asking excitedly,

"So do you think Jackie will be here tonight?"

Mike answering back with a small bit of hesitation said,

"Who knows, she shows up when she wants to and leaves when she wants to, she doesn't really hang out with any of the other girls."

John stating back,

"Yeah, I kind of figured that by the way she was last weekend. She is way different from the other girls, kind of like a wild stallion."

Mike and Ray both started laughing and nodded their heads in agreement. They jumped out of the van and headed for the Disco on the second floor. Mike was in the lead as he was anxious to see his woman. As they entered the door to the disco the women were already there with the tables and chairs pushed together. Mike ordered five bottles of champagne right away and a round of glasses for everyone. John spoke up and said,

"Order five more, I'll get it and an extra glass in case Jackie shows up."

Mike threw a few packs of Kool cigarettes on the table for the women to share and then asked John,

"Did you bring any extra packs of your cigarettes? If you did, then put them on the table."

John was a bit hesitant about placing his Marlboros on the table as cigarettes and alcohol to an American soldier was rationed. They were only allowed four cartons of cigarettes a month and he smoked a carton a week. John threw his extra pack of Marlboros on the table and the women crinkled their nose at them saying they liked the taste of Michael's cigarettes, seeing that his cigarettes were menthols. It did not bother John at all he was quite happy with it and picked up his extra pack of smokes and put them back into his pocket.

"Just leave them on the table!" Mike said with a firm tone of voice, we might have to have them later.

"You smoke as much as I do Mike. What about your rations, man?" John asked with a concerned look on his face.

"How much liquor do you drink?" Mike asked.

John answered "Not very much at all. Why?"

"Then find someone that does drink alcohol but doesn't smoke then trade your liquor ration for their cigarette ration." Mike suggested.

"That sounds like a pretty good idea. The only problem with that is I don't know anyone like that. I've been here a few months now and I still don't know too many people. I still don't know why they ration cigarettes for us over here anyways, sounds stupid to me." Responded John.

Mike looking at John with a confused look on his face said, "You're fucking kidding me right, you aren't serious are you?"

"Yes I'm serious, why what's up?" John asked.

With a bit of a Hmmpf and with a tone of voice that seemed disgusted with Bolden's lack of intelligence upon the current topic of conversation Mike explained why they rationed the cigarettes,

"It's because you can get at least $50.00 a carton for American Marlboro and Kool cigarettes here on the black market. At $2.00 a carton at the PX store for us that's a really good profit, dumb ass!!!"

Immediately Bolden stood up from his chair, his chest was puffed out, and anger filled his eyes. The blood flowing through his veins, pulsating rapidly with each beat of his heart. He was ready to fight for he was feeling embarrassed and insulted.

"Who the fuck, are you calling a dumb ass? Just because I don't know something doesn't justify you calling me a dumb ass. Is that clear enough for you Mike?"

Instantly Ray stepped into the situation.

"John calm down that is just the way Mike phrases things. He did not mean anything by it. You should know him by now. Both of you shake hands and remember where you are at. We have to be on our best behavior over here and you both know that."

Ray made sense and calmed the two men down, both of them realizing the ladies were present. There were no apologies given as Mike and John shook hands then raised their filled champagne glasses and "Prost" each other then took a drink. Everyone at the table followed suit, except for Ray who was drinking his Coca cola. The alcohol soon set in and there was laughter at the table as everyone started to enjoy each others company. Mandy had been eyeing John up from the moment they entered the club. He would look her way casually from time to time as he was busy in conversations with others present at the table. John enjoyed Mandy's humorous spirit with the way she made others laugh. As he was talking to Mike he noticed from the corner of his vision Mandy standing up from the table, grabbing a champagne bottle, then her glass, walked over to him and pulled the chair out next to him and sat down. She grabbed John's almost empty glass filled it up and then filled hers up. John watching her lift her glass up and said to him

"Prost".

John followed suit clicked her glass and repeated the well-known phrase back to her. He sensed her attraction to him but wishing to set things straight asked her

"Aren't you Kevin's Girl?"

"Art der", she responded.

Looking at Mike and asking what she said he responded back with,

"She said kind of."

Mandy looking at John said

"Kevin is not here right now, you are!"

Then they both heard a familiar voice say,

"And So Am I!"

As they looked up it was Jackie. Her lips were pursed and her eye sight was concentrated straight onto Mandy. The look Jackie had was not one of anger but of determination. Her will was strong and forceful as the energy she placed forth carried a message of concern for she was claiming her territory and the boundaries had just been placed. It was then John knew from that moment on that they were a couple but yet an unofficial couple. He knew that Jackie had claimed him as her own and by looking at the way she was handling herself without words, while she was present, there would be no other woman that dare come near him. For some odd reason John was comfortable with that. He felt much pride being around Jackie. The way she carried herself, the way she talked, and the way she held a conversation amazed John.

He felt Mandy get up from the chair she had sat down in, only moments earlier, and looked at her. Mandy had a disappointed look in her eyes but still had a smile on her face and then started to laugh as she said,

"Ok, kuss kuss, later!"

John smiling back at her gave her a wink and said,

"Later!"

He then offered Jackie the chair and grabbed her empty glass that he ordered for her earlier and filled it up with champagne.

"I was hoping you were going to show up." He said to Jackie.

"Ja I was hoping you would be here also"

, responding back as she accepted the glass from him and took a small sip.

"Tell me more about Wisconsin where you are from." She said with an interested tone.

"Not much to tell you. It is mostly farm country and looks a lot like Germany from what I have seen of it so far." John stated shrugging his shoulders.

"Have you traveled much?" She asked inquisitively.

"A little bit. I lived in California for a few months and South Carolina for a few months also. I have seen both oceans and I have to say that I like the Pacific Ocean better. It is so blue and is much cleaner. I love Las Vegas, Nevada. There is so much to do there and so much to see. The city when the lights come on at night is exciting to see!" John said with an upbeat tone.

As he was looking at Jackie he could tell she was getting excited in what John was telling her.

"Were you born in Wisconsin?" She asked.

"No, I was born in Aurora, Illinois, near Chicago. My parents moved us up to Wisconsin when I was about ten for a quieter setting. My father likes to hunt and fish. There is much open land in Wisconsin which is perfect for that. How about you were you born here in East Berlin?" John asked.

"Ja, been here all my life. I wish to see all those places you talked about, especially California!" Jackie said excitedly.

"Have you traveled much?" John asked.

"Jaaa much, where am I to go?" Jackie expressing this with a sarcastic tone of voice.

She continued on,

"I have been everywhere first it was school, school, school, then it was work, work, work."

John picking up on her sarcasm and disdain quickly offered an apology.

"Forgive me, when I am around you I forget where I am. You are different Jackie and I think you know that."

Jackie responded back, "Ja I am. I don't like it here. I wish to see America. It seems so bright and full of life. I think it would be fun there. Here, because of the way I dress and talk with American G.I.s the Stasi is always questioning me.

Why do I dress in western clothing?

What did you talk about with the soldiers?

Don't you like being here in our wonderful country?

Yack, yack, yack on and on they go and I tell them nothing. I hate them very much!

She proceeded on, telling John about an experience she had with the Stasi after receiving a book from an American G.I. They had taken her down into the bunkers below the city where a prison was located. It housed the so called "Enemies of the State." People who tried to escape to the West and got caught, people who had tried to help the escapees and got caught with them, and other so called political prisoners. They had led her into one of the rooms for questioning where they told her they had seen her receive something from an American soldier which looked like a book and they wanted to know what it was that soldier had given her. She said she would not answer their questions and then they left her sitting in the room by herself for a couple hours. Then as the door opened stood a man who was tall with a serious look on his face wearing as she put it, "A fake leather jacket." He pulled out the chair that was across from her and sat down. He asked her what the book was she had received from the American soldier. As she sat their quietly, not answering his question. He leaned over to her and said,

"We have you on camera receiving this and it would be in your best interest to tell us what it is."

She refused to answer his question stating she did not receive anything. Standing up he looked down upon her and said in a calm but forceful manner,

"You can change your clothes and stay here for a few days until you decide to tell us what it is. We have a room ready for you. It is your decision. What will you like to do?"

Looking up at him she told him,

"It is an English dictionary, I speak English and want to know what the words mean, Ja!"

With a slight smile on his face he said, "Gute, that is all we wanted to know."

He proceeded on asking her if she would spy for them as they had seen her talking with other American soldiers and they knew she was friendly with them. She asked,

"What do I get for this if I do this for you? Do I get a car, a bigger apartment, money?"

With a surprise look on his face he stated back,

"No, you get none of this. You will do this for your country to keep us safe from the Americans!"

Jackie responding back saying, "No, I will not do this! I have nothing to fear from the Americans! Now let me go home!"

With a disgusted look on his face he tells Jackie,

"You are free to leave but know that we are watching you!"

Jackie got up and left the room hurriedly. As Jackie was telling her story John had listened to her intently and was astonished at what she was expressing. He was having a hard time with this and could not believe that he was hearing this from someone who had actually gone through what the Iron School of Soldiers had expressed to him about the interrogation tactics from the Stasi of East Germany, "The DDR." John trying to change the subject to lighten the mood asked Jackie,

“Do you have any brothers or sisters?”

Jackie answered back,

“No, I have an Uncle who lives in the West. My Uncle, his wife, and their daughter escaped to the West in 1961 when they started to build the Wall.”

Jackie continued on about her Uncle in the west.

“When I was a little girl he sent me a Christmas present from the West. It was a little toy with little round candies in it made in America. It was so pretty and the candy had different colors. They were very shiny and beautiful. The smell was so fresh. I can still smell them. Ever since then I had always dreamed of going to see America. This is how I see the United States, very colorful, bright, shiny and beautiful. John nodding his head said,

“Yes, I know what you are saying, that is the way I see West Berlin. There is so much life over there. Everywhere you go there is always somebody doing something and it is very beautiful there. Some day you will see it, I am sure you will.”

“Ja, someday I will!” Jackie stated back.

She said this with so much confidence and earnest from her heart that it was difficult for John to look away from her eyes. The music started to get louder as if it was calling them to the dance floor. John stood up and without asking grabbed Jackie’s hand and led her to the dance floor. Jackie with a surprised look on her face went along with him and as soon as they hit the dance floor their bodies were in motion, swaying with the beat of the music. It was an American disco song. The dance floor was filled with youthful energy as the beat of the music carried into their spirit of joy. Time flew by quickly again and before they knew it, it was time for the three soldiers to go back to the west. Ray being the highest ranking among the three of them took charge and reminded Mike and John it was time to go. Arriving at the VW van John thought they would be saying good bye to the girls but they were getting into the van. Ray, taking his spot at the wheel started up the van ready to go. Mike, sitting on the passenger side as his woman, Jacqueline sat on his lap. John piled in from the passenger side back seat then slid over to the driver's side while Jackie came in and sat on his lap. John was very comfortable with this as Jackie had placed her left arm around the back of his neck and with her right hand opened she placed it upon his chin and lifted his head up, leaned down and gave him a slight kiss upon his lips. John's eyes widened with excitement as he was not expecting such a wonderful surprise. The softness of her lips was that of silk freshly woven.

"I very much like you", Jackie said in a whispered tone of voice.

John was speechless. All he could do was look at her and give her a slight smile. Jackie with a confused look on her face said to John,

"Das ist not gute?"

John with his right arm around the middle of her back gave her a small hug and said to her in a whispered tone,

"Ja das ist sehr gute!"

Mandy, Ushi, and Babette climbed into the back seat of the van and filled it to capacity. John with a raised tone in his voice asked Mike and Ray,

"So are we taking the girls to the west with us?"

The women started laughing and in unison said,

"Ja Ja take us to the west!!!"

Mike started explaining,

"They ride with us till we are almost to the checkpoint and then they get out. I like to have as much time with Jacqueline as I can."

John thought this was a bit risky but he was okay with it. He would have more time with Jackie. A few blocks away from Checkpoint Charlie, Ray parked the VW van in a dark alley where the men said good night to the women and they began to leave the van one by one. Mike giving Jacqueline a final kiss for the night, she jumped off of his lap and onto the street. Jackie being the last one to leave the van looked at John and asked,

"Will I see you soon?"

John nodding his head said,

"Yes, will see you next weekend if you are here."

With a smile, they give each other a hug and said Guten Nacht." As Jackie left the VW Van, John could sense her sadness but knew they were both looking forward to seeing each other the next weekend. Approaching Check Point Charlie they had to go through the East side checkpoint first manned by two East German border guards. Ray slowly maneuvered the VW Van through the long rectangular shaped cement blocks that were placed to create a curvy avenue of approach. Bolden noticed the East Germans guards as they waved the van across without really looking into the van. As he looked at their eyes and body movement there were no looks of concern, nor looks of anger. To Bolden it was as if the East German Border Agents wanted to have them across quickly as possible. It was a relief for all parties involved. Mike and Ray had gone through this many other times so to them it was not a big thing. Ray stopped the van at Check Point Charlie and checked them in. The NCOIC counted the heads in the van and welcomed the soldiers back into West Berlin and wished them a good night. Leaving the checkpoint Bolden said with a surprised tone of voice,

"Is that it? Is that all we have to do?"

Mike with confidence responded back,

"Yeah, pretty simple isn't it?"

Bolden chuckling said,

"Yeah, almost too simple."

The ride back to McNair Barracks was quiet as the three men did not have much to say to each other for to each his own their thoughts were assuredly upon the nights events that had unfolded for them. Their thoughts being private in nature were to be kept among themselves as it had now become a part of their treasured memories. Bolden reflecting back upon the stories Jackie had told to him was beginning to see how beautiful his own country was after being given an expression of it from someone who had never been there before. How such a small thing of candy could spark the fire of imagination in someone was astonishing to Bolden. The way Jackie described it, the way it looked, the way it smelled had started a new way of thinking for Specialist Bolden. The small intricate details of life in the United States he had missed before were starting to come to life. These were things he had taken advantage of and had never really given them any value as to how good they were to his life. How lucky he was to have them. It took a total stranger from another country, another way of life to bring this to light. In his mind he thought everyone had what he had and so it was no big deal to him. He hoped that someday Jackie would be able to see the beauty that she had described to him and wondered if she knew what such a precious gift she had given to him on that night. The ability to see things in a new light, the ability to appreciate that which you have, for to some people it is only a dream!

22
MEETING THREE

Saturday, March 22nd, 1986 it was time to go to East Berlin again. John was raving with excitement inside himself for seeing Jackie again. There was another guest that came with the usual three. It was Spec. 4 Kevin Festerman and he was eager to see Mandy. All four had obtained their East passes during the past midweek. Each of them had their own specialties to give to the ladies once they were over to the East. Ray with his Coca Cola, Mike with his Kool cigarettes, John now knowing how to work the alcohol/cigarette rations had some extra Marlboros to put on the table, and Kevin he had something special for Mandy. It was a big box of finely made mixed chocolates. John was thinking Kevin would definitely be sweetening Mandy up. A very romantic gesture, indeed! They made their way through the streets of West Berlin, through Checkpoint Charlie, through the East German checkpoint, then a right onto Alexanderplatz up to the Discos. Ray parking the white VW Van, getting as close as possible to the disco entrance, each of them jumped out without hesitation. Going up the stairs that led to the entrance of the disco Mike was in the lead followed by Ray, then Kevin with his big box of chocolates. He didn't care about hiding them for it wasn't a big deal for him to have them there. John was in the back of them holding the same excitement the rest of them had. As they topped the stairs the energy had shifted for John into a slow motion of events as if there was something around him he was supposed to notice. The door to the mens and women's bath room or as it is called, "the W.C.", were both wide open. In the men's bathroom there was a young East German male talking on the payphone that was situated in the middle of the wall. When he walked by the women's bath room, the phone, on that wall stood out to him. It illuminated brightly to him and his mind wondered on to why this made a special appearance to him. As he had noticed them from before. He shrugged his shoulders and dismissed it momentarily as he walked in through the set of double doors that led into the disco. His hopes were high and the excitement built within him as he searched the room for Jackie. John noticed that Ray, Mike, and Kevin had spotted the ladies that had a couple tables placed together for them already and they were headed in that direction. John scouting out the table hoping to see Jackie there was a bit disappointed when he did not see her at the table. His hopes ran high as he was wishing that she would show up later so they could carry on their conversation from the weekend before. Hugs and kisses were exchanged around the table as the gifts were handed out and the cigarettes were laid upon the table. Champagne and glasses were ordered and as usual John had placed an order for an extra glass for Jackie. Soon the table was occupied with the bottles of champagne. Empty glasses were quickly filled with the sparkling juice or otherwise known as the elixir of enjoyment and good tidings. The welcoming continued as the word came out "Prost" among everyone at the table. John could sense a bit of hesitation among the women and the air around them was a bit dense as he noticed that they would look at him and then look away quickly as if he was to see something he was not supposed to see. He withdrew this air of no clarity as he thought it was a possibility that he was still the new guy among them, or the incident that happened between him and Mandy the Saturday before. John sat in his chair quietly while the others were talking between themselves. He started to span the room with his eyes watching to see what was going on around him when his eye sight fell upon her. It was Jackie. She was looking right at him. John's eyes opened widely with excitement then suddenly half closed as he looked around the table she was sitting at. The table was filled with British soldiers and John knew the moment he saw them that Jackie was sitting next to one of them that had a special meaning within her life. John focused upon Jackie again and saw the expression she was conveying to him. The look that she had was not one that was afraid but of one that was hoping for understanding. John being disappointed gave Jackie a nod and a smile assuring her that everything was okay. He turned away and without hesitation drank the full glass of champagne that was sitting in front of him. Refilling the glass he downed it in its entirety. Ushi seeing what was happening came over and sat next to John. He was happy with her company but could not find solace in what she was offering to him for they had nothing in common with each other. Mandy with a concerned expression asked,

"Are you O.K. Sjahn?"

"Yes, I am", John immediately responded.

Mike intervened and stated,

"She kind of has a British boyfriend which you already know of now."

"Yeah I kind of figured that out Mike, it's all right, it's just the way it goes. Let's all have a good time, shall we?"

With that everyone filled, then lifted their glasses and yelled "PROST!!!" As the champagne was quickly consumed John started to feel the warm effects of the alcohol and the elixir of enjoyment and good tidings lived up to its name. As the good times were quickly coming to an end it was time for them to go back to the West. Everyone stood up from the table ready to leave. John glanced back over toward Jackie, as the both of them had done so many times during the evening, he gave her a slight smile in which she returned back, both of them acknowledging each other. Ushi placed her right arm around John's shoulder motioning to him that it was time to go. John in return placed his left arm around her waist and took the lead toward the door, down the stairs, then to the white VW Van where everyone piled into it. Ray in his driver's position, Mike and Jacqueline on their usual position, John in his position on the driver's side back seat with Ushi on his lap this time, Kevin in the middle with Mandy on his lap, and then Babette on the passenger's side back seat. As they were driving toward Checkpoint Charlie Ushi leaned into John and began to kiss him passionately. John responded in kind but he could not feel the passion nor, the excitement of the kiss Jackie had given him the Saturday before. Though grateful to Ushi for the compassion that she held for him all John could think about was Jackie and the evening that had unfolded before him. He knew that he was special to Jackie, but he "Was Not That Special To Her." This was something that he had to come to terms with, after all, he was a soldier dedicated to a cause much greater than oneself. The white VW van came to a halt at its usual position just before the border where the ladies were to exit the van. Babette hopped out first. Jacqueline giving Mike his final kiss for the night gave him a hug and exited the van. Kevin and Mandy as it seemed were in a deep trance kissing each other fervidly.

"She must have really liked her box of chocolate", thought John, as he chuckled inside of himself.

John and Ushi were in a passionate embrace themselves but John knew it was time to go. He looked Ushi in her eyes and said,

"Vielen Danke, Ushi."

Ushi looked a little disappointed but knew that the feeling between the two of them was not there. She gave John a tight hug and a warm smile. She was ready to leave the van. She couldn't move until Mandy and Kevin got out of the way. John looking over at them nudged Kevin in the side of his ribs gently and laughingly said,

"Hey, Heeeeyyy you guys, it is time to go. I'm getting hungry and if we have to stay here any longer I'm opening up those chocolates."

Mandy laughing slapped John on his hand and said,

"Ja Ja, we'll see you soon."

With that she jumped from Kevin's lap and they exited the van with Ushi following them. Kevin gave Mandy the final kiss goodbye and entered back in. The sliding door was quickly closed and Ray headed for the Checkpoint. Silence being the usual as they crossed over the East German Checkpoint then past Checkpoint Charlie. Once they were on Potsdamer Strasse Mike looked back at John who was staring out the window.

"Hey, you ok back there?" Mike asked.

He did not have to distinguish to whom his question was directed toward, all of them knew who it was meant for.

"Yes, I'm fine Mike. It is, what it is, and no explanation has to be given. Appreciate you asking though!"

"Next time we go back over, she'll be there for you, John." Mike said,

hoping that the confidence he was giving to John was helpful.

"Well you know as I do, it will be over a month before we go back over there. First, we have QRP coming up, which will last a couple weeks if not longer, and then off to Wildflecken, we will be there for thirty days. I'm kind of excited for that. It will give me a chance to see more of Germany than this big city buried inside a wall of concrete and barbed wire." John stated.

It was time for John to change the subject and to move on to other things.

"I wasn't kidding about being hungry. Where's the nearest Imbiss? It's Doner time!!!"

The four of them started to laugh and all agreed with John. They stopped at the Imbiss nearest McNair Barracks and placed their orders. As soon as it was filled Ray drove the white VW van through the gates and dropped them off at the Company's parking lot. Saying good night to Ray and giving him their gratitude for the transportation that he had supplied for the night's event. Mike, Kevin, and John walked up the stairs, passed the CQ desk and into their rooms. Mike hesitated upon entering his room for a moment to look at John. He was about to say something to him when John looked up at him and said,

"Good Night Mike."

"Good Night John." responded Mike.

John sat on his bunk, unraveled the foil that was wrapped around his sandwich and began to eat the delicious sandwich that he had just bought. Still warm, the herbs and spices tantalized his tongue and soon with every bite that he took, satisfied his hunger. Placing the past evening back into the farthest corners of his thoughts he began to think like a soldier and to place his training first into his mind. Wildflicken was not just another place to visit in West Germany, it was a place of training for a United States Army Soldier and it involved the "Mortar

Shoot Off" to see who was to be the best! With the mixture of the champagne that he had consumed an hour before and the Doner providing him with satisfaction of a full stomach John got up from his bunk, undressed, then turned off the lights in his room. Lying down on his bunk he soon drifted off into a somber sleep awaiting a dream of total bliss. And Then, It Happened!!!

23
THE LABELLE'S DISCO BOMBING

Saturday, April 5th, 1986 it was around 0400 hours when the four deuce mortar platoon of CSC 6/502nd Infantry heard the banging on the doors and the shouts of the CQ Runner yelling

"Q.R.P (Querp) ALERT, QRP ALERT!!!"

Q.R.P. was short for QUICK REACTION PLATOON. The mortar men had been on QRP detail for a couple of weeks and they had been used to being on alert and were getting used to the fake alerts that had been called. All personnel from the mortar platoon had been confined to the barracks. All off post mortar personnel, Officers, NCOs, and married enlisted personnel living off post had to share a room with the on post personnel which were mostly E-4s and below. No one on QRP was allowed to leave the post for any reason. Their main status was to provide a quick response of defense to any incident that constituted the emergency. They would be one of the first to set up a defensive position should any danger occur. Bolden was sharing his room with the platoon sergeant, Sergeant First Class Horton. He had chosen Bolden's room because it was big, had plenty of space, and Bolden kept it clean and orderly. It was also located at the end of the hallway which was closer to battalion headquarters. Bolden did not care for the arrangement but did not have any choice in the matter. He had been awakened with the urge to urinate around 0345 hours. Being quiet he got up, exited the door and closed it quietly behind him as he headed down the hall to the community bathroom which was located past the CQ desk which was in the middle of Combat Support Company's "T" shaped hallways that continued straight ahead about midway down the hall next to the sniper's and scout's area. The community bathroom consisted of three showers enclosed with walls, sinks on the left side, and toilet's lined up the right side not enclosed by walls. It was definitely not a place to be shy at when doing your business. Bolden walking by the CQ Desk said hi to the runner which was Russell Schmidt, a member of the mortar platoon assigned to being CQ runner as he was on light duty due to an injury he had received. Russell did not respond to Bolden's greeting as he stared at him with a hollow look in his eyes. He was worried about something but Bolden did not ask what it was. He just shrugged his shoulders and figured Schmidt was tired as it was early in the night. CQ Runner was a 24 hour duty that started at 0500 and ended at 0500 the next day. It was okay duty during the week as you received the next day off to rest. As Bolden passed by the First Sergeant's office he could hear Staff Sergeant Hines also a member of the mortar platoon who was the NCOIC of being in Charge of Quarters ask the mortar platoon leader, First LT. Pillow if they should call an alert. Lt. Pillow responding with a nervous tension in his voice said,

"This is very serious Sergeant, I think you better call it! It's up to you."

Bolden picked up his step a bit knowing there would be an alert called, headed to the bathroom. After finishing his business he walked back to his room slowing down a bit as they had not called the alert yet, thinking it was probably going to be another fake alert. He entered the room quietly as he did not want to wake his platoon sergeant in case they decided not to call the alert. He put on his BDU uniform, then his combat boots. He figured he would be ready if they should decide to call the alert. As he was lacing up his boots, the pounding and the shouts of QRP ALERT filled the hallways. SFC Horton jumped from his bunk then to the door turning the lights on. He had slept in his uniform, boots and all. Having his ruck sack on his back he turned and yelled at Bolden to hurry his ass up and get down to the truck. He knew Bolden had been up before him and exclaimed as such as he was closing the door. Bolden laced his boots up quickly, grabbed his ruck and headed for the deuce and a half truck that was in the assembly area. A few moments later the soldiers from CSC 6/502nd Mortar Platoon had jumped into the trucks and were at the ready. Most of the men still had sleep in their eyes but as the seconds passed with the chatting among the men about a fake alert you could see the readiness they had just in case the alert was not fake. The complaints were coming in full heartedly about the early morning wake up.

"Fuck, I wish they would stop calling these fake alerts!!!" one had said.

"Yeah it's getting to become annoying!" Was the response from another.

“It will only last a couple of minutes and we can all go back to bed.” One said with a hope of rest given to everyone in the deuce and a half.

A few seconds later Lt. Pillow, the platoon leader, showed up at the end of the truck.

“Break Open The Ammo, Lock And Load, They Just Blew Up A Disco Downtown And We Have To Go To Police The Area. Get Off Your Asses And Get It Done!!!”

SILENCE entered into the back of the truck as each one realized this was not a drill, it was the real thing. Each individual looking at each other, but not actually seeing that person that they were seeing. That long stare placed out into the distance of the unknowing. Not a soul moving toward anything. Bolden kneeled down before the ammo boxes and with a slight bit of hesitation took the butt of his M-16 rifle and busted the seal upon the ammo box and started to pass the rounds of the 5.56 ball ammunition out to anyone that had a rifle. His hesitation came from the grounds of having the reason for breaking the seal upon an ammo box. Everything had to be recorded and all rounds had to be accounted for. The words from the drill instructor’s voice echoed within his mind from the firing range during basic training,

“No Brass, No Ammo, Sergeant!!!

Lt. Pillow came to the back of the truck again placing his orders.

“Bolden!!! Donadio!!! Get Down To The NBC Room And Draw Your Gear Now!!!”

“Fuck!!!” Bolden said within his thoughts.

That was the last thing he wanted to hear come out of the LT's mouth. He knew what it meant and had dreaded it. They had asked for volunteers a couple months earlier to train for riot control using tear gas, CS, and Bolden was not about to volunteer for anything involving the use of gas warfare. He had seen the pictures from the effects of blood and nerve agent gas and could not picture himself using such things. He had personally gone through the Tear Gas Chamber, as so many other soldiers had gone through before him during basic training and was not impressed about being initiated into something that made his eyes water, snot running from his nose, coughing and gagging accompanied by disorientation. When no one volunteered for the duty, Bolden was pleasantly volunteered by his squad leader because he had expressed to him earlier about how he had wished he had never gone through such an experience.

"Ah, yes the joys of it all, to go through it all again." Bolden thought with a sarcastic rhythm.

It was his duty as a soldier to follow orders. Donadio, well Donadio was, John Donadio, otherwise known as Don A Dee O from everyone in the platoon. He was a comical sort of fellow and went along with the flow of everything that was wrapped up in his environment. He didn't judge anyone and lived his life with the way things went. He found comedy in all things that were around him and everyone loved being around him. Bolden and Donadio jumped off the back of the deuce and a half truck and headed for the NBC room located in the basement of the McNair barracks structure. When they reached their location their gear was already prepared for them to sign out. All they had to do was sign their names and don their equipment. They helped each other put their back pack on, which was two tanks filled with tear gas that were placed next to each other and under that was a tank that was filled with oxygen as a propellant to shoot forth the tear gas one hundred and fifty feet into a crowd should they become unruly. It looked as if they came from the series, "Buck Rogers From The 25th Century." Had the past movies made it into the future? One could only speculate at that time. With their equipment drawn and placed upon their bodies they exited the NBC room. Walking up the stairs toward the opening into the field where their fellow soldiers were awaiting them, about midway, Bolden said to Donadio,

"You do know we are the first ones to get it if things start happening, right?"

Donadio with a smile on his face and cheerful mood responded back,

"Yeah, I know. Let's make the best of it and do what we have to do. Roger That?!!"

Bolden with a smile on his face due to Donadio's uplifting comment responded back,

"Roger That!!!"

As they reached the end of the deuce and a half truck and were about to help each other in, Lt. Pillow came by and ordered everyone to

"Stand Down!"

He explained that the polizei were going to handle the situation and that they were not to enter the area. The relief that everyone felt was very calming in nature.

Normal conversations came into play as the ammunition that had been drawn from the boxes had been placed back into their proper positions and every piece accounted for. It was not until later that the platoon discovered the loss that had been accrued by such a violent act that had been placed against the United States Military. Lost that day was Sergeant Kenneth Ford, he was 21 years old, many other soldiers from the Berlin Brigade had been wounded then Sergeant James Goins, 25 years of age, was lost due to the wounds that were inflicted upon him from the bombing. It was a sad day for all Berlin Brigade soldiers as well as others serving in the Cold War that was "Hot As Hell!" Unbeknownst to many serving at this time that it would transition into a war on terrorism. President Ronald Reagan began to present the medal of "The Purple Heart" to the soldiers that were wounded from this attack. As he presented the medals to these soldiers, many other soldiers questioned the presentation of this award to these soldiers that had frequented a night club that had been bombed. The Purple Heart Medal was to be awarded to only those that had received wounds from and during an act of war. How, could such a medal with a strong voice of heroism be considered and awarded to those that were out on the town having a good time? President Ronald Reagan explained it with a clear conscience and a strong voice.

"We are living in a time where attacks against the American People and the American Military happen sporadically. This is terrorism and we will do whatever is necessary to defend against such attacks. We are at war with a known but unknown assailant. For, such attacks against the American People and our military strength we will give credit and honor to those that serve in defending our nation."

With that said, there was not much left to contemplate upon what was happening. It was clear that we were in a war that had yet to be determined by the future, for what the future holds, only one may speculate upon it until it presents itself.

24
WILDFLECKEN

With QRP being behind them, CSC 6/502nd Infantry found themselves training in Wildflecken, West Germany, a training ground for many soldiers stationed in Germany. They had already been there about a week setting things up to get ready for their training exercises. The barracks the 4.2 mortar platoon had set up in was not your regular Army barracks. It looked more like a Swiss Chalet on the outside but on the inside it reminded Specialist Bolden of basic training. The floors were made of wood and many bunk beds filled one room to occupy the enlisted soldiers. One thing was for sure in his mind though. With wood floors they wouldn't have to buff the floors to make them shine. That was a positive thing. All of their gear and equipment had been secured and everyone assigned a bunk. Their tracked vehicles and gun tubes were ready for the Battalion Mortex.

Wildflecken was located in the Bad Kissingen District that borders the northwestern part of Bavaria and the southern part of Hesse. In 1937 the German army established it as a training area for the German troops. It was built to house around 9,000 soldiers. It was primarily used by the German Wehrmacht and the Waffen SS. In 1945 troops from the U.S. 14th Armored Division took control of the camp and training area in April of that year. After 1951 its range served as a U.S. Army training base. It was the home station for many U.S. Army units that included Armored, Infantry (Mech), Military Intelligence and logistical units. It also served as a base for Bundesgrenschutz (border police) units. Called "The Top of the Rock" the small post was among the most feared and disliked of all training areas due to high altitude and extreme weather conditions. The post was home to tank ranges and artillery ranges in addition to standard training range. Now was the time for CSC 6/502nd Infantry Battalion to take its place within the training camp's history.

0500 wake up came and the Company prepared itself for the 0600 formation of PT (Physical Training). What had been plotted out for the company was a two mile road march with full ruck sack and weapon instead of the usual calisthenics of push ups, jumping jacks, and a run. As the sun was preparing itself to rise above the horizon to the east the company headed out for its road march. A quick two mile hike then back to the chalet to prepare for breakfast. A most desired meal after exercising. The road march started in a quiet fashion with the orders given. After a few minutes into the march a marching cadence was introduced giving energy to the columns of men that were involved in it. Everyone repeated the cadence with a motivated voice. A mile and a half into the march it became silent again as you heard the stepping of boots hitting the pavement. As the minutes passed all of the troops realized it was beginning to come apparent that the march was going to be more than two miles. The cobble stoned streets had left the Company awhile back and now they were on trails, dirt trails which seemed odd to the soldiers but being soldiers they shrugged it off as training and continued on with the road march. As the time and the miles continued on everyone knew that they were going to miss chow but they had confidence that sustenance would be provided to them after training. After the sixth mile the Company was ordered to halt for rest and to change their socks to keep their feet dry after such a long march. For many in the company this order came too late, for the blisters on their feet had already formed due to excessive sweat in their socks and boots with the constant rubbing on the back of their heel and front upper lobe. Specialist Bolden for one had a small blister on the back of his heel and a medium sized one forming at the frontal lobe just before the toes on the right foot. To take his boot off and change his socks was a painful experience but he knew the importance of changing his socks and continued to do so. As he looked at some of the other men changing their socks he noticed he was one of the lucky ones as many of the other soldiers had larger blisters forming on top of their toes, on their heels, and on the bottom of their feet. To continue marching on meant only one thing, a trip to the aid station once they returned. As it tried to be hidden it could no longer hide the fact that the Captain was lost. Who knew when the Company would get back to base camp? As soldiers they were trained to march on to their destination. After the rest and changing of dry socks, with boots laced up the command is given to "Forward March!" With each step you could hear the suppressed moans of those that hurt and the slightly hidden wince of pain on their faces. The road march finally concluded with it being ten miles and ending up in formation at the barracks. The Captain addressing the Company ordered the men to have their wounds looked after at the aid station and then to the chow hall once it opened up for lunch. With that he dismissed the company to assess his situation. Some soldiers headed for the aid station right away while their brothers in arms secured their gear for them and took them up to the barracks. These were the ones that had the worst of it. Some had untied their boots and laced them half way down to give them a little bit of comfort. Bolden and a few of the others grabbed their gear and hobbled up to their room to secure their gear. He did not want to unlace his boots yet even though he was in pain he thought the less movement in his boots would be best and decided he would take them off once he got to the aid station. He figured the medics would lance the wound relieving the pressure allowing the fluid to drain, apply some type of cream, and then bandage it up. It would take time to heal, that was for sure. About half of the mortar platoon did not sustain any blisters throughout the march. John Donadio had some, Kevin Festerman, Mark Tate, Tracy Long, and Bolden formed in a small group to go to the aid station. The worst of them was Gonzales, he could hardly walk and did not want to get up from his bunk. He was about to unlace his combat boots and take them off to relieve the pressure when the small group quickly advised him not to. He had to have something on his feet to get him to the aid station which was a small uphill climb on the cobble stoned streets. Tate and Donadio offered their assistance by standing on each side of Gonzales and placing his arms across the back of their necks resting on their shoulders.

They helped to lift him off of his bunk and the small group headed toward the aid station with Gonzales hopping on his left foot. He kept his right foot bent up backwards into the air as he was unable to walk on it. The small group did not walk in formation as it would have been a difficult task to complete at that time. Making their way and reaching the entrance to the aid station they opened the door and walked in. The moment they stepped foot into the aid station they heard the screams of a soldier who was receiving treatment. They stopped and looked at each other with confusion, discontentment, and wonder, on to what the treatment was about. One of the medics came by and pointed to a desk where they had to check in at, to receive treatment. After each one signed in, they found some empty chairs to sit down in and started to take off their combat boots. Tate and Donadio helped Gonzales take his boots off, which they slowly did, trying to ease the discomfort Gonzales was going through. Tate had finally removed Gonzales right boot and peeled his sock off. The small group looked in amazement at Gonzales' wounds. He had two big blisters on the front and back of his foot that was swelled with the blistery fluid. The tops of his toes had small blisters. On the back of his heel was an above average sized blister as well. His left foot had the less of his right foot but everyone knew who saw this that Gonzales was going to be out of training for quite some time to heal. Gonzales was the Assistant Gunner in Bolden's squad and Bolden knew at that point that with Gonzales out of the training, Bolden was now the Assistant Gunner for their gun squad, as this was the order of succession. Copsovic was the gunner for the squad, which Bolden could not stand his arrogant presence and avoided him as much as possible, now he had to work with him face to face. As other men were taken into the treatment room, they could hear the screams and the cussing of these soldiers as treatment was given to them but they noticed that when these soldiers walked out of the room they were walking much better. Tate, Donadio, and Long had medium sized wounds. These wounds were of minor consequence but had to be looked at to stop further infection. Bolden saw that the blisters he had on his right foot during the rest on the march had grown double their size. The fluid definitely had to be drained. Tate was the first one to ask the question that was on everyone's mind to one of the medics that was standing close by.

"What's all the screaming about in that room? Don't they just lance the blister, drain the fluid, peel the skin off, and bandage it?"

The medic replied with a chuckle and a slight smile on his face,

"No they don't do that, the possibility for infection is greater with that procedure. They insert a syringe, withdraw the fluid, then take another syringe filled with iodine solution and insert it back into the wound. It toughens up your skin so you can continue on with your training and that is what you are here for."

He concluded his statement with a smug smile upon his lips.

"Gonzales is first!!!",

said the small group in unison, that lit up the air with a laughter that followed which softened up the mood.

Everyone knew he would be first anyways because of the seriousness of his wounds. It was soon his turn as Tate and Donadio helped him into the treatment room. His screams were penetrating as the other three men sat outside the room listening. Tate and Donadio were next. Even though their wounds were less, they were the ones that would help Gonzales back to the barracks. He was placed on light duty for the rest of their stay in Wildflecken and was assigned CQ runner duty with light restriction on walking. Festerman was next. He was quieter than Gonzales and took the pain well with a few grunts and a couple of cuss words out of his mouth. As Festerman came through the door Bolden got up from his chair and met him as he was walking in the room. Looking at each other Festerman looked at him with a smile on his face and said,

"You're gonna love this!"

"Yeah I bet."

Bolden said with a chuckle in his voice. He was instructed to sit down on the exam table and with his right foot in the air the medic began to examine his wounds. The medic began to explain the procedure that was about to be performed on him.

"Yeah, I got a heads up on what is happening here, let's just get it done okay."

The medic being satisfied with Bolden's response asked him,

"Is there anything you would like to hold on to while we do the procedure?"

"Yeah I would. Bring my Captain in here so I can wrap my hands around his neck while you shoot that iodine solution in me. Maybe he'll know how to read a fucking map next time."

Laughter ensued around the room as they knew he was just joking. They worked on the blister that was on the back of his heel first. Bolden felt the needle penetrate from the syringe and as the fluid was being drained he felt the slight stinging of the old skin meeting with the fresh new raw skin that would develop. Then he saw the dark orange colored syringe filled with the iodine solution. The medic placed the needle in close to his first penetration and squeezed the iodine solution into the wound. Bolden felt the extreme pain enter into his body as his breathing became shallow and rapid holding in his screams. The other medics were holding him and he could feel his grip upon them intensify. That part was done and they waited for his breathing to return to normal before starting on the big one that was on the bottom front of his foot. After a minute or two the medic asked him if he was ready for the other one. Bolden shook his head No but then said,

"Yes, let's do it."

The needle of the syringe was placed and the watery fluid withdrawn. The same effect appeared to him. Quickly the iodine solution was injected in. The pain went through his whole body and he could not hold back his screams of what he was enduring. The cuss words followed intensifying with each wave. His breathing was shallow and rapid, more than from before. The grip he had on the medics that were holding him was stronger than ever and he felt their grip holding him back. After a couple of minutes the pain subsided and he felt much better. His breathing returned to normal and the head medic said,

"Okay you are free to go now."

Bolden looked at him and asked,

"Aren't you going to dress those wounds?"

The head medic replied,

"There is no need to. The iodine solution cauterizes the wound and makes the skin tougher. You may feel a slight discomfort for a while but you are ready to go back for training soldier."

One of the medics that had been holding Bolden down during the treatment said to him,

"It's a good thing we didn't go get your Captain, You'd probably be in the stockade by now."

The room was soon filled with laughter and a light atmosphere.

"YEAH, NO SHIT DOC!" Bolden responded.

Putting on his boots Bolden felt no pain only the slight pressure of the boots rubbing against his wounds. Getting up from the table he gave thanks to the medics for providing his care and ability to return to duty. Walking toward the door and grabbing the handle Bolden heard the head medic say,

"Hey Specialist, appreciate the laughter, you are definitely a trooper."

Bolden turned with a smile on his face and without saying a word gave the head medic a nod and walked out of the room. Feeling a bit better his thoughts were on how he was going to be able to handle Copsovic and his personality. They had an important mission to accomplish with the Mortar Shoot Off/ Mortex coming up and Bolden was wondering if they would be able to accomplish this mission with two different personalities working together. He would have to find the way to do this. Returning to the barracks he discovered that the company had been given the rest of the day off to heal up from their wounds and the chow hall was open. Not many of the men that received treatment from the aid station felt hungry due to the pain they had gone through but Bolden was hungry and proceeded to the chow hall. It is amazing what a double cheeseburger, French fries, and a cup of coffee can do for a soldier's morale. After finishing his meal he returned back to his platoon asking if there was anything he could do. They assigned him to a small group that was cleaning weapons of others that were recovering from the march.

"Dang It!, Bolden thought, I should have kept my mouth shut!"

25
SPECIAL FORCES

The CSC 6/502nd Mortar Platoon had been given 60 MM mortar tubes for training purposes. This would have been a great way to learn the smallest of the mortars however they had been given the tubes but no ammunition to train with it. They saw no use for such equipment except to keep them clean and secured within their tracked vehicles and have them displayed in a fashionable way to create them to look good for the higher ranking officers that would be inspecting them during their shoot off.

"Great, one more piece of useless equipment taking up space only to show it off when the time came."

This was in the almost silent thoughts of many from the mortar platoon, as their grumbles were kept at a whisper. Training for the day was simulated as they went through the fire missions, accomplishing each mission within an excellent time range. Bolden and Copsovic were working on their communication skills as gunner and assistant gunner. They were working well together despite the dislike of one another. This was a wonderful thing as their mission was one of great importance toward the success of winning the shoot off. With the end of the day's training each squad packed up their gear and secured the equipment. Half of the platoon headed for the chow hall, the other half headed for the cantina. The cantina had great food at reasonable prices with the plus side being, you could have a beer with your meal and then afterwards mingle among the socialites. Bolden sent most of his paycheck, each month, back home to his mother to help her pay the bills so he reserved himself to the fine cuisine of the mess hall and the camaraderie of those that would join him. After chow it was back to the barracks to write a few letters to his friends and family back home to let them know how he was doing. Around 2200 hours the men that had gone to the cantina returned in a happy and cheerful mood. Specialist Tracy Long, Tate, and Donadio were excited and talking about how they had met a few members from a Special Forces A Team at the cantina. This was exciting news for many of the mortarmen that had stayed at the barracks. All of the men listened eagerly to Long, Tate, and Donadio as they talked about their experiences with the SF. A few minutes later the order of

"AT EASE!!!"

was heard in a loud voice. Silence filled the room as everyone stood at parade rest. The Platoon Sergeant, SFC Horton stood at the entry way.

"All Right, every one of you swinging dicks listen up. We've got some good training coming up tomorrow starting at 0900 with the Special Forces Team we met tonight at the cantina. It so happens to be that they have ammo for the 60MM mortars but no tubes to shoot them out of and as all of you know here we have the tubes but no ammo. I've already acquired the range for our training with them. Get a good night's sleep and be prepared to blow some shit up tomorrow!"

The motivation was high, hearing the cheers of the men was overwhelming for anyone who was trying to catch some sleep already. To get any sleep after such excitement would be a difficult task while awaiting the anticipation of a live fire exercise on its way, and to train with a Special Forces Team was way beyond the dreams of an infantryman.

0500, Wake Up Call. Drop your cocks and grab your socks, the favorite saying from basic training. 0600, PT Formation. It was time to sing about Jody and your girlfriend having a good time together. 0700 Shower and Dress, making sure the boots were shined and the BDUs starched and pressed. 0800, Motorpool and Inspection, have to make sure you have the proper amount of elevation bubbles, one can never have too many of those. 0900 pulling onto the firing range and lining the tracked vehicles in perfect formation, there, standing in front of the mortar platoon were the Green Berets. To Bolden these men were like rock stars to a teenager. He was nervous but anxious to train with them. The introductions were quick as the orders came in from SFC Horton to move in closer to the impact area as the 60MM mortar did not have that much of a range of travel before it impacted. All of the vehicles moved out and in a few minutes they reached their destination. SFC Horton ordered his squad leaders to supply one man from each of their squad's to grab the ammo out of the 5 ton truck and one man from each squad to grab the 60MM tubes out of the tracked vehicles and prepare them for the live fire. After everything was set up it was explained that there was enough ammo to supply each man in the training exercise three live rounds. It was more than enough to make every man happy. The Special Forces Team had divided themselves up among the mortar squads and the live fire exercise had commenced. Each squad had their different ways of firing their mortars as everyone watched each other firing their rounds of ammo and looking for the impact down range. One squad, placing their mortar tube at a high angle, of an almost, straight up and down position with only a two charge ignition. As the round of ammo went down the 60MM tube everyone watched the round go up in the air. With a two charge bag that had been ignited, they all knew it would not go very far. The round peaked it's altitude and then started it's descent back down to the earth. One of the Green Berets yelled out,

"It's going to be a close one!!! Everyone take cover!!!"

Some of the men hit the ground quickly, laying flat, while others ran to the front of the tracked vehicles and took cover. When the 60MM mortar round landed, the sound of a big "THUD" is heard. Sighs of relief came from the soldiers as it became apparent that the round was a dud. After that round, all the squads fired the rest of their remaining rounds, exited the firing range, and returned back to the motorpool to clean their 60MM tubes and square away their vehicles. Everyone was in good spirits, especially the Special Forces Team. They offered a special day of training for CSC 6/502nd Mortar Platoon of how a Special Forces A Team operates, to show their gratitude for a great day of training at the firing range. This was a special treat for the mortar platoon. With all the hootin' and a hollerin' the platoon was making, anyone within a mile radius, could tell their spirit was overwhelmed with excitement and the offer was accepted for the next day. Arrangements were made to meet at the E.O.D.(Experts On Demolitions) Range the next day at 0900 hours.

26
A SPECIAL TYPE OF INFANTRYMAN

The next day arriving and after the regular company formation, P.T., and chow, all of the mortar platoon met at the motor pool and were instructed to load up onto two deuce and a half trucks that the platoon sergeant had arranged for their transportation to the range. No one hesitating to board their mode of transportation with each other helping one another hop up into the trucks. When they arrived at the E.O.D. Range all of them dismounted the vehicles, while looking around they can see an organized team of men waiting for them. The Captain of the Special Forces Team greeted their platoon sergeant with a hefty return salute and a handshake. The mortar platoon was called to formation and ordered at the position of "Attention". The Captain gave the order of,

"AT EASE"

As the men relaxed in position the Captain began to explain how the team was set up in it's organization.

"You will notice that each man is standing by a station that involves his field of expertise. Each man is trained in all of these skills, as we work as a team, however, this one man is exemplary in his skills. We excel as a team, which creates us to be a special type of infantryman. As a matter of fact, we are so special in a way, that our friendly allies, "The Soviet Union", will dedicate a whole Brigade of their own soldiers to take out one Special Forces A Team! NOW THAT'S A LOT OF LOVE IN OUR BOOK! With that much love, we feel we should reciprocate in kind. Laughter ensued among the men as the Captain continued on with his speech. Not only do we know how to blow shit up, which we really love to do, as you have seen yesterday."

The Captain paused in his speech for a moment as the men in the mortar platoon began to laugh and make small comments about the day before on the live fire exercise. The Captain continued on with his speech with a loud and clear voice.

"We also educate, inform, organize, give first aid, when necessary, build, and protect within societies to give them structure, just like a social attache' would do. So you see, we blow things up in order to rebuild things anew. All of us here are very appreciative of the training we had yesterday with each and everyone of you which is why we are here today to show you how we operate as a team. We see that you are a mighty fine mortar platoon, a highly motivated, highly dedicated group of men that respect each other and work as a team like we do. We wish you the best and are strongly confident that you will win this mortar shoot off through your great skills and determination to be number one. With this being said, enjoy your time here and feel free to ask any questions you may have of us. Sergeant First Class Horton lead your men over to the first station on the right where Donny is standing at, he is our medic."

"DONNY, THEY ARE ON THEIR WAY!" The Captain shouting out loud.

"THANK YOU JIM, I WILL TAKE IT FROM HERE!" Shouted back the SF Medic who was a Sergeant First Class in rank.

Sergeant First Class Horton yells,

"PLATOON.... ATTENTION!"

The mortar platoon came to the position of attention with the force of one snap being heard. Sergeant First Class Horton saluted the Captain and the Captain returned the salute.

"FALL OUT AND GATHER BY THE MEDIC STATION!" was the order given by the platoon sergeant. The mortarmen gathered around the station and all listened with intent on what they were being taught. After the class they were instructed to go to the next station, which was the communications specialists.

“BILL, COMING YOUR WAY!” yelled the Special Forces Medic.

“GOT 'EM DONNY!” Bill shouted back.

Bill had the rank of a Staff Sergeant. Bolden was starting to notice that these men, even though they had rank structure, were calling each other by their first names and not by their rank. This went on through all of the other expertise stations. When they arrived at the last station, which of course is every infantryman's favorite. Experts On Demolitions. The E-5 that was teaching the class shouted out,

“THAT'S RIGHT! WE GET TO BLOW MORE STUFF UP!” In this class we will teach you how to improvise with your explosive capabilities and to become an effective fighting machine. You will learn to be creative, as you scrounge the area, for any type of metal, wood, stones, that you can utilize in the functions and improvements of your explosive devices. You will learn about C-4, my favorite, on how to care for it, treat it, form it, and design it to become extremely effective for it's use. Are there any questions before we start the class?”

Bolden raised his hand and was given attention to by the E-5 of the station.

“What is your question Specialist?” asked the E-5

Bolden speaking in a firm voice,

"Sergeant, I noticed throughout the whole course that each of you call each other by your first names and not your ranks. Is there a ranking structure within your team?"

The E-5 answering back with enthusiastic expression,

"You are very observant Specialist. To answer your question, Yes we do have a ranking structure within the army, however, we are not just a team, WE ARE FAMILY! We treat each other with respect and dignity, we depend upon each other. In order to be a highly effective team we must do this in order to survive and to accomplish our mission. Does this answer your question Specialist?"

"Yes, very much so Sergeant!" answered Bolden enthusiastically.

The E.O.D. Training continued on as they were learning new ways, new techniques on the use of C-4 and other explosive devices. They came to a spot where there were some junked vehicles. APCs, tanks, and a few other tracked vehicles that could be used for demolition purposes. The E-5 looked down and picked up a perfectly round drain plug that had fallen out of one of the APC tracked vehicles.

"This will do." he said

"I will now show you how to make a platter charge out of two sticks, some wire, some C-4, and this drain plug."

In a matter of a few seconds, the platoon scrounged around the area and found what the E-5 was looking for. He positioned the two sticks in a crisscross position, took the wire and tied them together at their junction, then took some C-4 and molded it around the junction making an L-shaped form for the back and then to the front. The front looked like a shelf so the drain plug could sit on it. He then pushed the bottom ends of the sticks into the ground so that it had a solid foundation for it to be held up. He had positioned the sticks so that the explosion would go full force into an APC tracked vehicle that was positioned a few meters away. He then took the drain plug and packed more C-4 on the back of it and then around the outer edges, as if, the drain plug was sitting in a small dish. Placing the drain plug on the small shelving lip of the C-4 ledge he had made earlier on the sticks, he then placed a primer in the C-4 and rolled the wire to the back of a small burm that was built for cover where everyone followed and took cover. The E-5 hooked the two wires up to the electrodes of a claymore firing device and asked,

"IS EVERYONE READY?"

The response was unanimous, "YES!!!"

"FIRE IN THE HOLE!" yelled the E-5 as he clicked the firing device.

The sound of the explosion was loud as the earth shook and some dirt flew over the burm and landed on the mortar platoon.

The E-5 removed the wires from the firing device and yelled,

"ALL CLEAR!"

The men started to stand up and shook the dirt off of their BDU's both front and back then followed the E-5 to check out what type of damage was done to the APC tracked vehicle. To everyone's surprise, even the E-5, they saw a perfectly round hole, as if it had been drilled through the steel, right in the middle of the APC tracked vehicle. Walking to the other side of the APC tracked vehicle there was no indication of an exit hole. Looking inside the APC tracked vehicle they saw small fragments of metal everywhere inside, including into the drivers hatch.

"Whoa, that's never happened before!" Exclaimed the E-5.

He continued on,

"Usually, you would see holes where small fragments had punctured the weak points of metal on an APC, however, today, we see a fine example of how, such a small device, is able to wipe out an entire squad of men and their vehicle. NOW THAT'S GOOD TRAINING, HOOOAH!"

"HOOOAH!" replied the mortarmen of CSC 6/502nd Infantry Battalion.

With the training complete for the day, the mortar platoon headed back to the motorpool to turn in the trucks and place the final touches on their own tracked vehicles and gun tubes to be ready for the mortar shoot off the following day. With the sun setting in the west and feeling confident with their training and equipment they head for their barracks to grab some chow and finish off the day's activities at the cantina with the Special Forces A TEAM. After such a special day, no training would be complete without a couple beers and good comaraderie among soldiers. As the first beer was being downed, the infantryman's creed is heard being called,

"FOLLOW ME" is the call

"HOW FAR?" is the reply

"ALL THE WAY" is the answer

"WITH PRIDE!" is the affirmation

After a couple more beers are drank, most of the mortar platoon left the cantina to get a good night's rest to assure a successful mission for the Mortar Shootoff. Their hopes ran high.

27
THE MORTAR SHOOTOFF/MORTEX

As the mortar platoon of CSC 6/502nd began their workday, they had been excused from regular PT formation so they were able to get ready for their competition. When the time came they moved out toward the firing range. Upon arrival they are informed that they would be the last ones to fire on the range. This gave to them an advantage. They would be able to learn about the time frames they would have to beat in order to take first place, plus they would have more time to train. However, idle time is not good for a soldier as there is only a certain amount of training that can be done before boredom takes over. The time frames were coming in and in the lead was an 81 MM mortar platoon that had a record breaking time. This one was a tough one to beat. They had been the second ones to fire on the range and their time frame had set precedence on the others. The men were nervous but still had confidence. Small arguments broke out but were calmed down instantly. Then the time came for CSC 6/502nd Mortar Platoon to perform their duties. The call came in and the orders were given to move out. They had been at the ready and within seconds they were on the move. Getting close to the designated firing position they received their first fire mission. The FDC (Fire Direction Center) track pulled into it's position and set up. The gun tracks moved into their firing positions. As soon as Gun 1 turned into position, they placed their gun tube up and at the ready. The coordinates and data started to come in and within a few seconds, during which you get to hear the gunner and assistant gunner communicating between each other,

"LEVEL!"

"CHECK!"

"LEVEL!"

"CHECK!"

"GUN UP!!!!"

Everything was halted for a moment as the "Grader", a Sergeant First Class that was stationed in Wildflecken, whose only job there, was to grade these exercises by watching the performances and keeping track of times, thereby guaranteeing him to be a neutral judge of these competitions, walked up to Gun 1 to check it's status for accuracy. He checked the round of ammo, that was to be sent down range, for it's proper charge and readiness,

"AMMO ROUND IS GOOD!" He shouted out.

Then walked onto the APC to check the gun, shouting out,

"ELEVATION IS GOOD!"

He looked into the site, that was mounted on the gun, checking to make sure that the cross hairs were aligned properly with the two aiming poles a few meters down range. Looking up from the gun site he yelled,

"GUN IS UP, GOOD, AND READY TO FIRE!"

The grader exited the gun track and the order was given,

"FIRE!"

Without hesitation the ammo bearer handed the assistant gunner the round of ammo. In one swift motion the assistant gunner grabs the round of ammo and places the bottom portion of the round into the gun tube and stopped at the midsection, with half of the round inside the gun tube and half of it outside, the assistant gunner yells,

"ROUND READY!"

The gunner then instantly yelled back,

"FIRE!"

The round of ammunition is dropped into the mortar tube. The squad of GUN 1 placed their hands over their ears and took a covering position. The round hits the firing pin in the gun tube and is ignited. The shock absorbers move downward and then instantly back up into their original position. The ground could be felt shaking a little bit as the familiar sound of "VAROOOM" is heard and the reddish orange flame is seen coming out the end of the gun tube, forming into the shape of a bullet of ball ammunition, as the round of ammunition is thrust forward down range toward it's target. All of this happening within a matter of seconds. The voice of the gunner is heard,

"ROUND OUT!"

The voice on the radio is heard from the FDC TRACK alerting the FORWARD OBSERVERS that the round was headed down range.

"SHOT, OVER!"

Then came the instant response,

"SHOT, OUT!"

A few moments later the voice of the F.O.s are heard,

"SPLASH, OVER!"

The reply from FDC,

"SPLASH, OUT!"

Then the corrections started to come in from the Forward Observers,

"UP 100, RIGHT 200!"

This meant that they were close to their target but definitely had a ways to go for a direct hit. The corrections were made and the new coordinates given to GUN TRACK 2.

Bolden and Copsovic were in the last GUN TRACK, number 3, and they were eagerly awaiting their turn. The tension was mounting as their turn was getting closer. They did not say much to each other but that didn't matter as long as they did their job well then there was nothing left to say. Within a matter of seconds Gun Track 2 is up and ready to fire their round down range. The Grader moved into position to check the gun's readiness. Everyone heard the phrase they were waiting for,

"GUN IS UP, GOOD, AND READY TO FIRE!"

The Mortar Platoon of CSC6/502nd, as of that time were in a good position for time. If all went well they would not only take first place in the Mortex Shoot-off they will have set a record breaking time frame that all others would have to match or beat.

The round from Gun 2 is sent down range and the corrections came in.

“DOWN 50, LEFT 50, FIRE FOR EFFECT OVER!”

Everyone knew what that meant they were on target and it was up to Gun 3 to make it happen. Bolden and Copsovic felt the tension mount around them. In a loud, clear, mean voice Copsovic started to shout,

“BOLDEN YOU BETTER KNOW WHAT THE FUCK YOU ARE DOING ON HERE! DO NOT FUCK THIS UP!”

Bolden surprised by what he was hearing from Copsovic quickly regained his composure and fired back at him,

“I KNOW WHAT I AM DOING, YOU KEEP YOUR MIND FOCUSED ON WHAT YOU HAVE TO DO AND I WILL KEEP MY FOCUS ON WHAT I HAVE TO DO. IS THIS CLEAR ENOUGH FOR YOU? YOU ARROGANT PRICK!”

They were helmet to helmet and eye to eye, both of them leaning over the middle of the gun tube. Copsovic almost ready to shout back when all of a sudden the Grader stepped in to calm the situation down.

“ARE YOU TWO GOING TO BE OK HERE? IF NOT, THEN I WILL CLOSE THIS EXERCISE DOWN RIGHT NOW. THIS IS A TEAM EFFORT. BOTH OF YOU HAVE A CHANCE TO DO SOMETHING

SPECIAL. DON'T BLOW IT! IS THIS UNDERSTOOD?"

Both men calming down, winding down, upon the intervention between the two of them, their muscles still flexed and staring at each other replied with a hearty,

"YES, SERGEANT!"

The new coordinates came in over the radio. Copsovic and Bolden immediately went to work adjusting Gun 3. Copsovic yelling out the order,

"LEVEL!"

Bolden keeping up with Copsovics movements, knowing Copsovics movements in advance by watching him work the traversing knob, Bolden could get a sense on how to keep the bubble level for a correct gun. Bolden shouting back,

"CHECK!"

Copsovic quick with his order,

"LEVEL!"

Bolden instantly with his reply

"CHECK!"

Copsovic looking at Bolden, with a smile on his face, Bolden knowing what that meant, Copsovic quickly yells out,

"GUN UP!"

Before the words were completely out of Copsovics mouth Bolden and Copsovic had moved a short distance away from their gun so they would not bump it to throw it off. This was a very critical time and all were anxious to hear the words from the Grader.

"Great job gentlemen, if this gun is in good order then you have won the mortex and set a new record, beating the 81 mm mortar squad by three seconds. Please step aside so I am able to evaluate your gun."

Copsovic and Bolden slowly moved away from their gun being cautious not to bump into anything that could possibly offset their quick work. The excitement in their eyes carried the confidence of a job well done and knew they had won the shootoff. They looked around at the rest of the platoon and noticed the worry, but hope, the rest of their platoon members had.

The Grader stepped onto the tracked vehicle looking into the gun sight, then down to the elevation bubble, he had already inspected the ammo round from the ammo bearers as he watched them prepare the round for fire. Looking up from the gun tube he announced,

"GUN IS UP, GOOD, AND READY TO FIRE!" NOW LET'S SEE WHAT THIS ROUND DOES DOWN RANGE!"

The Grader exits the tracked vehicle, Bolden and Copsovic take their places on the gun. The order is given,

"FIRE!"

Bolden quickly grabs the round of ammo from the ammo bearer and places it half way in the tube shouting out,

"ROUND IS READY!"

Copsovic ordering,

"FIRE!"

Bolden slides the round of ammo down the tube and quickly covered his ears as the round is projected down range by the ignition of the charges that were placed on the round by the ammo bearer.

Copsovic yelling,

"ROUND OUT!"

The voice on the radio from the FDC Track is heard,

"SHOT OVER!"

The Forward Observers responding, confirming the acknowledgment, to be at the ready, to observe the round of ammo sent down range,

"SHOT OUT!"

Within a few moments the voice of the Forward Observers are heard,

"SPLASH OVER, WE HAVE A DIRECT HIT, METAL ON METAL, WE HAVE FIRE! CONGRATULATIONS MEN!"

The cheers from the men of the CSC 6/502nd Mortar Platoon were overwhelming as hand shakes and pats on the back were given out. Bolden and Copsovic smiled at each other and shook hands. Copsovic saying to Bolden,

"GREAT JOB SPECIALIST."

Bolden responding back with a smile on his face,

"YES, A JOB WELL DONE BACK TO YOU, SPECIALIST. I STILL HATE YOUR ASS, YOU ARROGANT PRICK."

Copsovic still smiling looking at Bolden replied back,

"YEAH, WELL, I STILL DON'T CARE MUCH FOR YOU EITHER, YOU SMUG BASTARD, BUT I'LL WORK WITH YOU ANYDAY, SPECIALIST."

Bolden replying back, admitting the great work they had accomplished together,

"YEAH, I'LL WORK WITH YOU TO SPECIALIST."

With that said, they had turned hatred toward each other into respect to one another. Knowing that even with wide differences between each other, personality wise, they had one main goal in common together.

"It is to be the best that you can be no matter what obstacles are in the way. You place those obstacles off to the side or you fight through them in order to accomplish your mission and to forever move forward to succeed. Their personal relationship toward each other would not improve much throughout time but their professional relationship had made great strides in their performances. Working together they were the best of the best at what they did. The energy had taken two opposing forces, placed them together, changed their polarity, and with this type of energy change, had utilized them to be an effective team that served the greater good for all. A well placed team effort from everyone involved had created the CSC 6/502nd Mortar Platoon as the best and it was time to celebrate their glorious victory through hard work and dedication of their duties. The Mortar Platoon quickly cleaned up their area of operation and packed all their equipment into their tracked vehicles and headed back to the motor pool to clean their gun tubes, track vehicles, and weapons. The weapons had to be cleaned and turned into the armory for securement. Once the gun tubes and tracked vehicles were cleaned, organized, and polished, the platoon grabbed their assigned small arms, locked up the tracked vehicles and headed for their

"Swiss Chalet" to finish cleaning and securing their small arms. As soon as they arrived to the barracks the weapons started to form in an organized pile. M-16A1's and M1911A1's were mounting up and as they were being accumulated Bolden knew what was happening. Something must have came through that placed the mortar platoon on a detail and he also knew that he would be placed on weapon's cleaning detail. He didn't mind it so much but it seemed like to him he was always being placed on this detail. Racks of German beer were being brought in to the barracks and piled up next to the weapons. Lt. Pillow, the mortar platoons platoon leader came walking through the door and the order of "ATTENTION!" was given. Everyone in the room came to the position of ATTENTION and silence instilled the room. Lt. Pillow began his speech.

"Fantastic work out there today men! Your training and dedication came forward to reward you with "EXCELLENCE" beyond measure. It is teamwork that brought you to the top level of military standards and we have set precedence for all others to set a goal to push forward and beat the time frame that we have established here in Wildflecken. It is a tough one to accomplish, with that you must realize that not only did you win the Mortex but you have instilled in others, that will come here after us, to push ahead, and strive for the same "Excellence" we have set forth here today. I am proud of each and everyone of you and with my compliments please enjoy the beer that I have provided for us. As you know, you are not to drink alcoholic beverages while on duty but I will make an exception in this case. IT IS TIME TO CELEBRATE OUR VICTORY! CARRY ON!"

The cheers and excitement of the men burst forward after the Lieutenant's speech. Bottles of beer were being opened and passed around to those that accepted them. They were cold and the outside of the bottles had the cool condensing water around them, sweating, from the warmth of the day. The men were thirsty and a cold beverage was inviting to quench their thirst. Bolden did not drink alcoholic beverages while he was on duty as he wished to keep his senses about him sharp and intact. He was thirsty and wished for something cold to drink. He went to the water buffalo that was outside of the barracks and was hoping for some cool refreshing water. He filled his empty canteen and took a drink, the water was warm and had a dense taste to it. He looked up and saw that the water buffalo had been placed in an open area where the sun had been beating down on it all day, which in turn had heated up the water inside. He looked around to see if there were any cold soda pops available that the Lt. may have bought, but there were none available. He had to have something cool to drink. The only thing available were the cool refreshing German beers, that were getting warmer by the minute sitting in the assembly area and they were going fast among the men.

Bolden looked at the Lt and asked,

“Sir, did you happen to get any cold sodas?”

“No Specialist I did not, have a cold beer and enjoy. That was one heck of a job You and Copsovic did out there today. Glad you were able to get past your differences and perform as an outstanding team. Relax and enjoy Bolden, you deserve it.”

“Yes Sir, will do Sir.” was Bolden's reply

Specialist Tracy Long already had opened one of the cold beers and handed it to Bolden.

"Here ya go Johnny, good work out there today man! Enjoy, they taste really good." stated Long

With a quick uplift of his right arm Bolden placed the open spout of the bottle to his lips and quickly chugged the beer down. He felt the coolness slide down his throat and then into his stomach. He could feel his body temperature come down slightly and was feeling comfortable. It didn't take long for the alcohol to take effect upon his empty stomach and he became quiet. He was offered another one but declined it.

Lt. Pillow piped up and said,

"Unfortunately we have been assigned to KP duty and a small detail has to be sent to the motor pool for some extra duties to be performed there. Your squad leaders have been given the orders and have assigned some of you to these details. They will tell you where to go."

The order of "Attention" was given as the lieutenant exited the room. Bolden knew in an instant what he was going to be doing and a wave of silent rage went through him. Staying quiet he waited for the order. Then the order came from his Squad Leader, Specialist Hobdy.

"Bolden, you're on weapons cleaning detail!"

"I fucking knew it! Why are you always putting me on weapons cleaning detail? Can't you pick someone else for a change?" Bolden said out loud in an angry voice.

Bolden picked up one of the empty racks that had once held the cold beer, placed it in front of the weapons, turned it upside down, then sat down upon it. Reaching for a weapon to start cleaning it he noticed the butt of an M16A1 rifle being placed in front of his face.

“Here ya go Johnny, you can do mine first if you want.”

said Specialist Long with a little chuckle to his voice.

“And how come I always have to clean this son-of-a-bitches weapon? Doesn't he know how to clean his own weapon?” I'm not doing it, I'm done with this shit!”

Bolden shouted as he got up from his homemade chair and kicked the empty rack crate across the room. He stormed through the doors that entered into the barracks and walked to his assigned bunk, slamming the door shut behind him. He paced the floor to the bunk quarters looking for solace and hoping to calm down. He knew the alcohol from the beer was talking. He was usually a very jovial personality after drinking beer but this time it had taken the opposite effect. He had always obeyed orders, however ridiculous they may have seemed to him. Pacing back and forth rapidly his demeanor was calming down and was realizing the impact of his outburst when his squad leader bursted through the door.

“BOLDEN WHAT IS GOING ON WITH YOU MAN? ARE YOU ALL RIGHT? Hobdy asking with a concerned voice.

“Yes, I'll be ok, I think.” said Bolden in a calm manner.

“Man that beer must of hit you wrong. I was surprised you took it. You usually don't drink alcohol that much! Exclaimed Hobdy.

“I was thirsty and wanted something cold to drink, I didn't want a beer but that was the only thing available. I apologize Hobdy, didn't mean to have an outburst like that against you in front of the men. Is everything okay between us? Asked Bolden with a concerned voice.

"Yes, it is fine. None of the higher ranking were around to see this happen. We'll keep this between us. It was a stressful time out there but we did good. To answer your question of why do I always pick you to clean weapons, it's because when you finish cleaning weapons they are immaculate. None of the weapons you have cleaned do not get returned to us from the armory to be cleaned again. As far as you always getting Specialists Long's weapon to clean, not sure what that's all about, seems to me he's always around you when things like that happen. You better take that up with him. Hobdy said laughing.

Laughter ensued between the both of them and the tension was relieved and of course the effect of the alcohol was going away.

"Let's get this done so we can relax. Besides I picked you for this detail again, not only because you do a great job on the weapons. We're going to get done quicker than the others and we will have more free time to relax. You get it now Specialist? Hobdy inquiring with a slight wink.

Bolden feeling a bit ashamed by his actions earlier looked at him and said,

"Yes, I Do Now."

Finishing the weapons cleaning detail, the small group headed for the chow hall to get a bite to eat. While standing in line waiting to get their food Bolden noticed Specialist Long on the other side serving green beans to the soldiers. Their eyes met and nods were given as if to say "No Harm Done." When Bolden reached the point to where Tracy Long was at serving his green beans, Bolden stretched out his open palm offering a hand shake and an apology to Long for his earlier comment about him. Long accepted both and with a chuckle in his voice with that Tennessee Gospel Southern accent of his, said,

“Hey, not a problem, ya had a lot more on ya today than we did. I like being around ya. Yuuur a lot of fun to be around, Ya know that dontcha?”

Bolden laughing and with a humorous voice responded back,

“Well if that's the case, the next time I get a premonition about being on weapons cleaning detail, I'll make sure you are no where around me.”

For those around them that knew what that phrase meant, the laughter had built up inside them so much that they could not contain it inside and from there, the good times continued onward.

When things in life can not be explained at a certain point in our life, one must have the patience to endure the time while waiting for the answer. All things that we do in our life have purpose and with that purpose it brings forth a change of character for the people involved in these circumstances. It would be a few months later for Bolden to have his questions fully answered to understand them in a way that will bring forth a solid foundation and to trust in what the surrounding circumstances were offering to him and how Specialist Tracy Long would fit into his life.

With only a few days left in Wildflecken the mortar platoon of CSC 6/502nd prepared to return to Berlin.

Their time there had many memorable events which will give to them a sense of pride throughout their life. As for Bolden, he was ready for some R&R back in West Berlin. He thought about Jackie from time to time but after his last visit over to East Berlin he wasn't to eager to go back over there anytime soon. It would soon be time to train for the 4th of July Parade, which everyone was looking forward to doing. His thoughts started to wonder and decided it was time to see what West Berlin was all about. He had only been there for a few months and with his visit to Carlstadt to see his friend John, the visits to East Berlin, and the training in Wildflecken, he really did not have much time to see West Berlin. With his mind made up on what to do he was eager to get back to West Berlin and enjoy his time there.

28
RETURN TO WEST BERLIN

With their training exercise complete in Wildflecken and with a successful victory the mortar platoon had been given a Friday off to give them a three day weekend. Bolden had already decided to discover what more West Berlin had to offer. Broadway and Williams had their East Passes approved to go over on that Saturday. They asked Bolden if he was coming with them and he had declined their offer but asked them to say hello to the women for him while they were over there. Bolden decided to take advantage of the free transportation that was provided for the American Military and hopped a bus headed North into the French Sector of West Berlin. Walking around the area he saw some old architectural buildings that he admired and looking at the surrounding areas he felt a kind of old archaic feeling to the French

Sector. Not much had been refurbished from what he could tell and the people around him seemed as if they were comfortable with their surroundings. The streets were clean and so were the buildings. The aura of the area was one of "Life is Life" or as it is stated in French, "C'est La Vie". Relaxed and content was the message that Bolden received. Like the Element of AIR, the nature of which was, vigilant, care free, with a little bit of independence to it. Wasn't much of a shine to the lifestyle their so Bolden decided to head south into the British Sector of West Berlin and see what that was all about, hoping for a bit more excitement. Upon his arrival he noticed a difference in the people who lived there compared to the French Sector. It seemed to Bolden as if these people had an air of sophistication to them. The buildings were well maintained as were the streets to that sector. The people walked the area in a confident controlled manner that showed a purpose to their daily eventful life. Kind, with an aristocratic type of behavior, when returning a greeting to Bolden whenever he would acknowledge their presence. It seemed to him like they represented the Element of Earth to him. The people there seemed to be consistent in their ways as he watched a few of them walking in and out of the stores, as if they had a daily routine schedule they followed with carefulness and punctuality. Straight and to the point with great discipline in what they were doing. After a couple of hours Bolden decided to head back to the American Sector and take a look around. Now this is what he was looking for with his youthful follies. The vibrancy of life as he stepped off the bus in the downtown area. People in a hurry with their life and getting the most out of their day. It was the hustle and bustle of everyday life. The energy was that of the Element of Fire with it's vigorous activity full of zeal and enthusiasm. The power of creativity was apparent in all directions that he looked in. There was the Europa Center with shopping centers inside and around the whole building. A display of beautiful artistry every where you looked. It was a daring display of "Boldness" on the American's part. It had to be, because the American Sector was the most visible to East Berlin. Every where you looked was a clear cut message from the Capitalists to the Communist, "WE ARE HERE TO STAY!" Bolden was placing it all together from what he had seen and heard for the day. After visiting all three sectors there was one more element to the puzzle that would complete the connection. It was the West German People. Bolden had noticed that with each sector the West Germans had adopted the influences of the people that were guarding their sectors. The West Germans were like the Element of Water, flexible, ever flowing, going in the direction where the other elements were taking it to. They were very understanding and pliant toward their guardians. With their trusting nature and compassion they had blended with their guardians and were enjoying a good life filled with a refreshing thirst for life with a harmony of healing added to it. In all the sectors there was also a mixture of different races and religious beliefs. There were Turkish People, African People, People from the West Indies, Asian People, and many others. Here, in this small capitalistic area, were people from all over the world, living together. A true melting pot of the world. It was definitely a clear message that all of us can live together in harmony and in peace. The City of West

Berlin held the secret to life, openly, in plain sight, if anyone had the vision to see it and what it represented. It is the dissimilarity of the elements to which we owe many thanks for the diversity of the world we live in and everyone has a free choice to be and to act in whatever they wish to be. West Berlin to Bolden was like “The Sword of Archangel Michael”, which was possibly the sword that was on the Berlin Brigade Patch. It represents “The Spiritual Warrior” that is within all of us who, with unconditional love in their heart, is willing to stand up for what they believe is right. It is “The Sword of Discrimination”, which cuts through illusion and lays the truth bare. The “Spiritual Warrior” is the most peaceful person in the community, because he has dedicated himself to truth at all costs. He is the champion to those who suffer and the protector of those who long to be free. This was the reason for why the Berlin Brigade was present in West Berlin. This was the purpose for every Berlin Brigade Soldier, past and present, to be “THE CHAMPION AND THE PROTECTOR, of this small great city that held such importance for the world.” Bolden had to have more, his quest for knowledge was yearning deep inside of him. He was beginning to see more in life and about life than he had ever known before. He was beginning to feel stronger, more confident in his being. He was grateful to himself for having had the courage to take the time, on his own, and to see what was around him. His thoughts were on how he would be able to see more of this wonderful city without being confined to the public transportation that was provided to him. His answer came swiftly and unexpectedly when he was returning back to his room at the barracks. The deal he was about to make would serve very useful to his near future.

29
BERLIN WALL PATROL

Bolden was returning back to the barracks close to the end of business for the day. Scurrying up the steps and reaching the top floor a few of the scouts had assembled by the CQ Desk. Their platoon sergeant was giving out the orders of whom had to perform Wall Patrol for the weekend duties. As he called out one of the names, the soldier who he called started to plead to his platoon sergeant to give him the weekend off as he had some personal business to take care of with his family on that Saturday. His platoon sergeant told him it was his turn to do Wall Patrol and to make his plans for at home at another time, unless he could find someone to volunteer to take his place. Bolden saw his opening moment and seized it quickly by intervening and asking the scout platoon sergeant,

"Excuse me Sergeant, does it have to be a scout to take his place?"

"Not necessarily Bolden. Why are you asking? Do you want to take his place on Saturday?" asked the scout platoon sergeant.

"Yes, I would, if it is ok with you and your men sergeant?" said Bolden in a hopeful tone of voice.

"Are you familiar with the M60? Can you disassemble, clean, and reassemble this weapon? Are you capable of loading, if necessary, firing this weapon and hitting your target, Specialist Bolden? Asked the scout platoon sergeant.

Bolden went into the position of "PARADE REST". With his feet slightly spread apart and his hands behind his back, he stated with a firm tone,

"YES SERGEANT! The M60 Machine Gun is my favorite weapon and if I had a choice I would choose that weapon as my main source of defense. I AM, able to disassemble, clean, and reassemble that weapon in a reasonable amount of time. I may be slower than a few others but I am quicker than most at this task. I AM, able to load and, if necessary, fire this weapon, not only hitting my target but am able to cut it in half like I did during basic training. I AM, surgical with this weapon SERGEANT!"

The scout platoon sergeant started to laugh a bit and said to Bolden,

"At Ease Specialist. You didn't have to go through all that. You got the job, if you want it, that is, if it is okay with your platoon sergeant. You better check with him first."

"He is gone for the weekend sergeant. Our whole platoon has three days off and all of our NCOs are gone until Monday. I'm sure Sergeant Horton will be okay with this." Bolden stating with confidence.

"Okay then Bolden, meet your squad here at the CQ Desk at 0600 hours. Sergeant Gannon will be your squad leader and Specialist Hall is the driver. If you have any questions ask them. They will help you with everything you need to know. Keep active and stay alert while on this patrol. Your main duty is to protect your squad leader at all times as he will be gathering intelligence close to the Wall. He knows how close he can get to it without being fired upon. You keep your eyes on those towers on the East side for any suspicious movements. You got it!?" asked the scout platoon sergeant with a firm voice.

"Yes sergeant, I got it. Appreciate you giving me this opportunity sergeant. I will be here at 0600 hours." Bolden stated earnestly.

Bolden was excited about being accepted to this new position. He knew Sergeant Gannon and Specialist Hall from quick conversations he had with them from before. He didn't know them personally well but he was comfortable with them. He went to his room and immediately prepared his uniform and equipment for the next day. There was a knock on his door and wondered who it was. Opening the door he saw Broadway standing in the hallway. He asked Bolden with excitement in his voice that was filled with a little bit of hope,

"Johnny, are you sure you don't want to come to the East with us? There is still some time to get your East pass in. Festerman and Copsovic are going this time. Come along, we will make it a whole group of us and it will be a lot of fun."

Bolden was quick with his response,

"No Mike, I've already volunteered to do Wall Patrol with the scouts. I'm really excited about it. You guys go ahead and have some fun. When you get back you can tell me about anything exciting that happened."

Broadway surprised at what Bolden had just told him asked,

"Wall Patrol? With the scouts? Man, you do more things with the scouts than you do with us mortarmen. You should have been a scout. You know, Jackie is going to be there looking for you and she is going to be asking where you are. What am I supposed to tell her?"

Bolden answering back with a little bit of wonderment in his voice,

"Yeah, come to think of it, I should have been a scout. They do all the fun stuff that we don't get to do. As for Jackie, after the last time I was over, I really doubt she will be looking for me. If she asks about me then tell her the truth, that I'm on duty. Tell her I said hello and will see her soon. I'm sure I will see her again. It isn't that big of a deal Mike."

Broadway being persistent with his persuasion,

"Johnny, Come On Man, it's not going to be the same over there without you. That British soldier she was with, the last time you were over there, is a good friend of her's and she really likes him. It's not the first time she didn't come over to our table to say hello when he was there. Don't take it to personally, she really likes you to. Besides he probably won't be there this time. I've rarely seen him over there and I go over there every weekend, you know that."

Bolden answered back with a stern voice,

"Mike, I'm not taking it personally. This Wall Patrol with the scouts is something I feel I have to do, actually, as a matter of fact, this is something that I wish to do and I am very excited about it. Now let me be so I can finish getting prepared for this patrol. I have to get up early. Thanks for asking me again though. When I feel it is right, I'll go back over there with you soon okay?"

Broadway with a disappointed look in his eyes, nodded his head and walked out the door closing it behind him. Bolden finished laying out his uniform and equipment then called it a day.

0545 hours, Bolden is standing at the CQ Desk waiting the arrival of his new squad. A few minutes later he sees them walking up the hallway to the desk. Sgt. Gannon started giving out the orders once they arrived.

"Hall go get the jeep from the motor pool, sign it out, and meet Bolden by the armory door and help him carry the ammo and secure the M60 on the stand in the jeep. Bolden get down to the armory, sign out the M60 and the ammo. Remember to do your checks and make sure everything is efficient. I want to roll by 0630 hours. I'll have a case of MREs for us and will meet you at the assembly area where the company formation gathers in the parking lot."

Both Bolden and Hall affirmed their orders with a hearty,

"Yes, Sergeant."

Then headed out to perform their assigned task. Once complete they met Sgt. Gannon in the assembly area along with the other patrol jeep. Bolden was very excited on this mission. Standing up in the jeep, holding onto the M60, with his Kevlar helmet on and his LBE gear wrapped around him, the patrol jeeps took off down the road in formation with Sgt. Gannon's squad in the lead. Bolden had a hard time maintaining a serious face at the beginning of the patrol. He felt like a little kid, sort of antsy in a way. He remembered watching the old series of "The Rat Patrol" when he was a young man and in his heart he was wishing to do this type of activity and now here it was. His wish had come true. They hit the cobble stoned streets and with every turn Hall had made with the jeep, Bolden kept switching his weight from side to side to maintain his balance while standing in the moving vehicle. As they passed the people on the street, some of them stared at them and some of the people just ignored, or tried to ignore them , as they drove by them. In all actuality, these men and their equipment were very hard to ignore. They looked impressive with their starched BDUs and clean equipment. There was a certain air of distinction around them, one that had a definite sense of purpose to what they were doing. They were not looking for attention but the attention was there, none the less. Sgt. Gannon knew all the checkpoints the wall patrol had to scout out, twenty minutes later they arrived at the first checkpoint. Bolden looked around scouting the area out noticing there was not that much activity in the area. He watched Sgt Gannon dismount from the jeep and walk over to a man made stand that could oversee the wall while standing up. The height of this stand was designed for a purpose as it would have been easy for one to crouch down and take cover if fired upon from the East Side of the wall. Bolden was doing his job watching the East German guard towers and quickly came to the decision that no one was in the guard tower from what he could detect as there was no movement from the inside. Sgt. Gannon, reaching the top of the stand, placed his binoculars up to his eyes and quickly scanned the area.

After jotting something down on his notepad he returned back to the jeep and said,

“There's nothing going on here, but it's early. I have a feeling we will be coming up on something later today. Both of you keep your eyes and ears open. They know where our small stands are but that doesn't mean we'll see any movement in those areas. They might be working in an area that is hard for us to see, so stay alert! Anyone up for some chow? I was able to get two cases of MREs so we have plenty to eat and the choice is yours on what you want.”

Hall and Bolden declined the offer stating they weren't that hungry but the other squad decided to grab a bite to eat. They headed off into a shaded area and concealed the jeeps to stop for a brief rest. Sgt. Gannon said with a chuckle in his voice,

“I think for lunch, we'll all drive over to the Air Force base and get some good grub to eat.”

Everyone had a smile on their face except for Bolden. He didn't know what they were talking about and wondered why everyone was smiling.

Specialist Hall looked at him and said,

“Bolden you're gonna love it man. The Air Force has some great chow. They hate it when we show up there because they don't expect us. We don't go there all the time but when we do, it's a feast!”

Bolden nodded his head a bit and put on a small smile as to say he was good with it all. After the second squad was finished with their breakfast the two jeep squads headed out stopping at all the small checkpoints. There was no activity going on in these small sectors so the surveillance time was quick, the only thing that held the patrol up was the small passages they encountered between the wall and buildings where they had to stop and pull in the side mirrors in order to be allowed passage onto their route. They were coming up to an area that Bolden was becoming familiar with and soon recognized it to be Check Point Charlie. There was always much activity surrounding this check point as it was the main area where traffic was coming in and out between the East and West parts of Berlin. The patrol jeeps took their tactical positions and the two NCOs got out and walked up to the watch stands that peered over to the East side of the wall. Bolden watched as two tour buses pulled up. They were close to the patrol jeep he was in. The tourists began exiting the buses and the sound of cameras clicking could be heard in the air. Two of the male passengers were brave enough to come up to the patrol jeep. They did not speak English but their indication was clear, with their cameras in their hand, motioning back and forth to take a picture. Specialist Hall gave them permission with a nod of his head and the cameras started clicking. One of the men sat on the hood of the jeep as his friend started taking pictures of him. The other tourists noticed what was going on and decided to come over and take their pictures with the patrol jeeps. Bolden quickly placed his boots up against the ammo that was sitting on the floor of the jeep and took a firm position up against the M60 machine gun wrapping his hand around the pistol grip and his trigger finger held tightly around the trigger. He was guarding Sgt. Gannon, his squad leader, as he was ordered to do. Bolden watched the tourists divide themselves as some of them started to walk up the watch stands to get a picture with the NCOs. The excitement was turning into chaos as the tourists were surrounding Sgt Gannon on top of the watch stand, the tourists on the ground were beginning to jump in and on the patrol jeeps, some of them laying on top of the jeep hood in funny poses as their pictures were being taken. Specialist Hall started yelling at the tourists to get off of the jeep. His words were going unheeded. Sgt Gannon was beginning to become overwhelmed by the picture taking crowd as women and men had their arms and hands around him. With his right hand over his pistol harness that was covering his M1911A1 .45 caliber pistol and his left hand over the pouches that carried his ammo on his LBE, (Low Bearing Equipment), he barked his orders out to Bolden,

"WATCH THE AMMO, WATCH THE AMMO!"

Bolden immediately responded back,

"I'VE GOT IT SERGEANT!"

Specialist Hall exited the jeep. Firmly but politely he began pulling the tourists off and away from the jeep. With a quick motion one of the male tourists jumped into Specialist Hall's drivers seat and acted like he was driving the jeep. Bolden quickly yelled out,

"HALL!!!"

Specialists Hall was no longer polite with his gestures, with two quick steps he arrived at his driver position, with both hands, he wrapped his fingers into the male tourist's shirt and with a firm grip lifted the tourist up in to the air and quickly through him to the ground, saying in a loud voice,

"UNASS MY A.O.!!!"

Taking back his driver's position he quickly started the patrol jeep up. Chaos in the air had presented fear within all of the soldiers that were present, East and West. The East German soldiers standing in the guard towers were on alert and watching how the American soldiers were going to react to this situation. The M.P.'s at Checkpoint Charlie were standing outside of their small building with their hands placed upon their holstered pistols. The observers had turned into the observed and it was up to them to take control of the situation. They had to take the fear and turn it into courage. Specialist Hall had taken the first step with his actions and claimed his rightful position as the driver of the patrol jeep. Bolden quickly racked the slide of the M60 machine gun as if he was loading a live round of ammunition into it's chamber. The weapon was no longer being pointed in the air as he brought the barrel of the weapon down with intent, then pointed it into the crowd that was surrounding Sgt. Gannon. The M60 machine gun was not loaded with a live round but the crowd nor the East German Border Guards knew that, these actions had to look real in order for them to be taken seriously. From the pit of his stomach Bolden could feel the churning of his nervousness, from fear, being formed into nerves of steel. Moving upward from his stomach, past his heart, into his throat, then out of his mouth, the thunderous explosion of the words came forth as he barked out his orders with absolute authority, to the crowd,

"CLEAR THE WAY FOR THE SERGEANT NOW OR I WILL FIRE UPON YOU!!! MOVE AWAY FROM THE JEEP, NOW!!!"

The words echoed in the air as the wave of intent magnified with each echo. The second squad gunner had followed suit simultaneously with Bolden as he was protecting his squad leader. The area was silent as the crowd of tourists stared in awe at the two gunners. The sound of the engines are heard running at the ready from the two gun squad jeeps. With the two M60 Machine Guns aiming at their first initial targets that were the closets to their squad leaders the crowd surrounding them slowly started to disperse and clear a way for the Sergeants allowing them safe passage back to their vehicles. Sgt. Gannon arrived safely to the jeep and took his leadership position on the passenger side. Making sure everyone was safe and all equipment accounted for, he gave the silent order to "Move Out" with the hand signal. The two jeeps formed in a tactical travel formation and moved out. Clearing the way, the crowd began to applaud and yell cheers to them as they continued on with their mission. Finding a secluded area Sgt. Gannon, with his hand signals, gave the order to form and assemble. With quick cover available they formed in a tactical defensive position. Sgt. Gannon began giving the orders,

"Everyone o.k.? Anyone hurt? Make a thorough inspection of your equipment and make sure everything is accounted for, then report back to me. Bolden, did you put a live round in that chamber? If you did, then clear that weapon and make it safe! Is that clear?"

Bolden responded back,

"No Sergeant, this weapon is not loaded and is cleared for your inspection."

Bolden pulled the bolt back of the M60 machine gun to show that it was clear and safe. Sgt. Gannon climbed up next to him to inspect the chamber, found it to be clear, then motioned to Bolden to close the bolt. Looking at Bolden he asked,

"How did you do that? I watched you and from what I could see it looked like you loaded a live round into that chamber with the feed belt attached to it. That was quick, so how did you do that?"

Bolden looked at Sgt. Gannon and started to explain his actions,

"In basic training when we were given instructions on how to fire the M60 machine gun I was lucky enough to have this E-5 as my instructor, Sgt Gannon. He knew I saw the capabilities of this fine weapon right away and gave me extra training on it. This Sergeant showed me many secrets and short cuts to the M60 and to become very efficient with it. Loading it quickly just happened to be one of those secrets. The other part of not actually loading a live round in the chamber then hiding it to make it look real, well, Sgt. Gannon, I had to improvise on that one, hoping that it would pass. Lucky for us, it did!"

Sgt. Gannon looking at Bolden with eyes of amazement, a slight smile, and a hmmph to his voice said back,

"Yes, you ain't joking there, lucky for us! Where in the world did that command voice of yours come from anyways? You put that crowd into a slight shock when you put that order out to them. Well, that, plus the M60 action you provided. Why the heck are you a mortarman and not a scout? You fit in great with us. With that voice of yours you would make a fine NCO, matter of fact, I'm thinking Drill Sergeant Position!"

"Bolden blushing from the statement and compliment he received from Sgt. Gannon started to shy away from him. Looking at the ground he stated back to the sergeant,

"Thank you Sarge but I don't feel that I am ready for a leadership position just yet. I just made E-4 a few months ago. As for my voice and what I said to the crowd, it just came out the way it did. There wasn't time to think about it and acted accordingly to the way I felt the situation had to be handled. Specialist Hall started it with picking that guy up by his shirt and then slamming him to the ground the way he did. I was amazed to see him do that as skinny as he is. I wish I was a scout instead of a mortar man. You guys get to do a lot of the fun stuff we don't ever get to do."

Sergeant Gannon picking up on the shifting of attention Bolden was putting out to him toward Hall, started laughing hysterically, and said in a clear voice,

"WHAT AN ASS!!! Ah Huh, I get it! What we have here is a thrill seeker with modesty. That's a new one on me Bolden. Usually your type have an arrogant attitude, which is a character trait I definitely do not admire. You sure are different than anyone I have ever come across, I'll give you that Specialist. It's time for lunch. If anyone is up for some Air Force Chow I better start getting those reports in on your equipment men!"

The attention was definitely shifted and it went to where it was to appropriately go and that was to the leader of both gun squads, SGT. Gannon! The reports came in quickly from each man on the patrol and all was cleared as Sgt. Gannon hollered out,

“MOVE 'EM OUT!”

Specialist Hall placed the jeep in gear, popped the clutch, pressed the accelerator and started moving forward. Quickly looking up at Bolden to grab his attention, with a smile on his face, he glanced back down to the road to continue his driving and said,

“Hey, be on special alert for bikini watch as we will be passing by the Wannsee. It' still early in the year but there will be plenty to look at as we are passing by.”

Bolden with a smile on his face nodded his head in affirmation to what Specialist Hall was saying to him. They cruised through the streets of the American Sector in West Berlin swiftly. Passing by the Wannsee, which is located in the southwestern borough of Steglitz-Zehlendorf district of West Berlin and is part of the River, Havel. The two lakes are named, “The Greater Wannsee and the Little Wannsee which were separated only by the Wannsee Bridge.” The Wannsee Lake was well known as the number one bathing and recreation spot for West Berliners, as well as a popular nudist area, where American soldiers were not allowed to go and interact with the West German Culture. However, the Wannsee was known, to a few well informed American soldiers, whom had read up on the history of World War II and the Nazi Regime, of which, at the beginning of 1942, senior Nazi officials met at the Wannsee Villa to plan the “Final Solution” to the “Jewish Question” - The extermination of the Jews from Europe. This event, that was presided over by Adolf Eichmann has become known as "The Wannsee Conference". The building where the meeting was held serves as a memorial and education center for anyone who wishes to learn from history and progress toward a future of greater being within society. The Wall Patrol passed by this building and had one more stop before the Air Force Chow was to be presented to them for their lunch meal. It was the Gleinecke Bridge, better known as "Freedom Bridge." The Americans and the Soviets used this bridge to exchange captured spies. There were not that many people laying out by the Wannsee and the special "Bikini Patrol" drove through the area with a little bit of disappointment with their observation, but their was always "Air Force Chow" to look forward to. The two patrol jeeps pulled up to "Freedom Bridge". With one jeep on the left and the other jeep on the right side of the bridge, they quickly scouted out the area. The only activity in the surrounding area were a handful of tourists and a few West German Citizens going about their daily lives. The patrol moved out in tactical formation toward the Air Force Base, Tempelhof. Upon arriving, Sgt. Gannon checked the two gun squads in with the entrance security and then headed for the chow hall or as the Air Force would have us call it, "The Dining Facility." Sgt Gannon ordered one man from the second squad gun jeep to stay with the vehicles and equipment for security assuring him that he would be relieved for chow as soon as one of them came available after eating. Walking in to the Air Force Dining Facility there was an array of food on display unlike the Army Mess Hall where there was only a few items to choose from. The Air Force Sergeant was none to pleased to see the arrival of Army Grunts enter into his facility, like it or not he followed proper protocol and asked each member to present their green military I.D. Card so he was able to account for the extra food he had to serve to them. The small line that formed around the food moved swiftly until it was Bolden's turn. He didn't know what he could get as he was used to whatever food was available and served on his plate. The Air Force Sergeant looked at him and said,

“All right, what will you have Specialist?”

Bolden looking at him confused asked,

“What do you have Sergeant?”

The Air Force Sergeant replied back with a huff in his voice,

“Anything you want, tell me what you want. If we don't have it here in the display case, we'll go find it and cook it for you!”

Bolden surprised and still unsure of what he had just heard asked for clarification,

“Are you serious Sergeant? I'm not used to this. Not sure what I really want, I guess.”

The Air Force Sergeant growing tired of Bolden's indecision barked at him,

“Yes I'm serious! Hurry up and tell me what you want! You're holding up the line! I've got other soldiers I have to feed here!”

Bolden looked around. He saw steaks, pork chops, hamburgers, cheeseburgers, spaghetti dishes and much more. There was an assortment of vegetables of all kinds, even stuff he had never tried before. All kinds of side dishes, mashed potatoes, baked potatoes, augratin potatoes, rice, macaroni salads, a salad bar to create your own salad with all fresh ingredients and then there were the deserts. Pies and cakes of different kinds and different styles were lined up within the display case. Bolden quickly made up his mind on what he wanted and put his order in,

“I'll take some steak.”

Air Force Sergeant asking,

“One or Two?”

Bolden didn't hesitate to answer back,

“I'll take two, mashed potatoes and gravy, green beans. Let me get a cheeseburger on the side please. For desert I'll have two slices of blueberry pie and some of that lemon cake you have sitting there. It all looks very good Sergeant!

The Air Force Sergeant kept up the pace with Bolden's order then asked him,

“Would you like a small lobster tail with those steaks?”

Bolden chuckling answered back,

“No thanks sarge, not much for seafood. If you guys eat like this all the time, I'm thinking, I should have joined the Air Force.”

Bolden slid his tray of food off of the rail, picked it up and joined the rest of his squad at the table where they were sitting at. He ate his meal quickly. It may have been Air Force Chow but it was Army Time and he was trained to eat fast. He was the first one to complete his meal and stated he would go relieve the soldier that was guarding the jeeps and equipment. In less than an hour the two patrol squads were on the move again heading back to patrol the wall. Cruising through a quiet residential area the sound of heavy machinery could be heard on the East side of the wall. Sgt. Gannon made the hand signals to form and assemble. There was very little cover available to hide the jeeps so they took up a defensive position. This was not a planned stop and there were no man made structures to climb up on and peer over the wall. The two sergeants saw a small tree that was big enough to climb up on and take a look but it was very close to the wall. Sgt. Gannon in a low voice gave his orders to Bolden on the M60,

"We're going to climb up that tree and see what is going on over there. It sounds like they are building something new. Keep your guard up, stay alert, and watch those guards in that tower. That tree is to close to the wall and with us climbing up on it, it may look as if we are trying to breech the wall. If those guards look like they are going to fire on us, you definitely let me know. if we get fired upon you have my permission to fire back. Do not be the first to engage them. Is this clear Specialist Bolden? I've seen how fast you are.

Bolden responded back displaying confidence in his voice,

"Yes, Sergeant your orders are clear. I've got you covered Sarge!"

The two sergeants walked over to the small tree. Moving cautiously Sgt. Gannon is hoisted up into the tree and climbed into a somewhat comfortable position in the crotch of the tree where he was able to observe over the wall. From where he was sitting he could have easily jumped on top of the rounded edge of the wall and throw himself over to the other side. His binoculars were lifted up to his eyes and after a few minutes he began writing in his tablet. Bolden watched the movement of the guards in the guard tower. They were watching Sgt. Gannon but made no aggressive movements to indicate any type of threat against him. Sgt. Gannon climbed down from the tree then hoisted the other squad leader up where he climbed into the position Sgt. Gannon had been a few moments earlier. Sgt. Gannon walked toward the jeep. Upon his arrival he started giving his orders,

"Hall, get up on that M60 and cover us. I'm going to take Bolden over there so he can see what is going on. We'll see if he is scout material."

The two men proceeded over to the tree as Specialist Hall took his position on the M60. The second patrol squad leader climbed down from the tree. Sgt. Gannon began stating the task that he wanted Bolden to do,

"I want you to climb that tree, observe what is happening, and then report back to me with what you've seen. You got it?"

Specialist Bolden, excited, responded back,

"Got it, Sergeant!"

The two NCOs hoisted him up in the tree then Bolden took his position. He saw two bulldozers that were manned and working quickly, opposite of each other. One was pushing dirt out of the way and the other one was leveling the ground. There were eight men on the ground, unarmed, but each were carrying shovels. They were matched in teams of two which made four teams. The area they were working on was a mixture of dirt and sand. There was a troop transport truck located on the cement area close to the dirt area where the men were working. He saw two motorcycles with side cars and an East German soldier standing by each one, they were armed with automatic rifles. There was a Trabant Field Car located a few hundred feet away from the motorcycles indicating a high ranking officer was present to oversee the construction project. Possibly more than one officer present due to the side cars that were attached to the motorcycles. There were two East German Border Guards armed with pistols in their holsters, holding their barking German Shepard Dogs back on their leashes. He saw two stacks of rifles up on the cement, four in each stack, indicating that the working men with shovels were also soldiers, low ranking of course, but nonetheless, soldiers. After making his assessment Bolden climbed down from the tree and gave his report to Sgt. Gannon. With a smile on his face Sgt. Gannon said,

"That's pretty good for a quick observation. What do you think they are building over there?"

Bolden stating inquisitively,

"I don't know Sergeant. Could be a few things. Possibly fixing some damage from an attempted escape, maybe. What do you think they are doing Sarge?"

Sgt. Gannon responded,

"I'm thinking they are either building or rebuilding a mine field. There were some wooden cases built up next to that transport troop truck that could possibly carry some small mines. With those bulldozers there working fast I'm thinking it is a new mine field. I'll finish this report and we will head out. We are just about done for the day. Go ahead and get back on that 60."

Bolden followed the order and took back his position from Hall, who took back his driver position. A few minutes later the patrol jeeps were on their way again. The areas and the check points were becoming denser with no activity being present, civilian or military. They drove up to their last checkpoint of the day. With a few abandoned buildings in the area it felt as if this area was forgotten, like nobody cared it existed. With a cool wind picking up in the air, the dirt on the ground was being lifted up, getting into the eyes of the soldiers that were present. Every movement echoed in the air with a hollowness of being alone in the midst of nothing. Bolden looked at the wall and saw a space that was open, it was big enough to slip a human body through. He thought it odd that it had caught his attention. He thought it even more mysterious that there would be an open gap in the wall big enough for someone to slip through. This stayed in his thoughts but did not ask any questions about it. When the last observation post was complete the patrol jeeps headed back to McNair Barracks. Upon returning, the two patrol squads went to work cleaning their equipment then securing them to their proper places. With everything complete Sgt. Gannon dismissed everyone into off duty status. Before walking away Sgt. Gannon says to Bolden,

"Nice work today Specialist! You can come along with us at anytime. I will definitely put in a good word for you to your platoon sergeant and mine. Have a good rest of the weekend!"

Bolden smiled and with excitement in his voice responded,

"Appreciate it Sergeant! It was a great day and I just might take you up on that. It is a whole lot better than sitting in my room. You have a good rest of the weekend as well."

Bolden called it a day and went up to his room to relax. His thoughts were still on that gap in the wall but dismissed it after a few minutes. He went on Wall Patrol again that next weekend but it did not compare to his first encounter. There were no unruly tourists to deal with or some good Air Force Chow to gobble down. He had went on a patrol with a different squad leader who had went on to other check points, as each patrol was different. Bolden decided it was time to go have some fun for a little bit and made it a point to get a pass to East Berlin for the next weekend that was coming up. He didn't have to ask Mike or Ray if they were going over because he knew they had their passes already approved. Besides, according to Broadway, Bolden was cool enough to go with them now.

30
MEETING 4

Saturday evening, Bolden is informed that Kevin Festerman is going with them to see his girl Mandy. The three soldiers are dressed in their Class A uniforms and ready to go. Ray pulled up in his white VW van and without hesitation everyone jumped in and took their seats. Festerman, this time around brought Mandy some flowers. Mike brought his usual gifts for Jacqueline. Ray brought some extra coca cola. John brought his extra packs of Marlboros with him. He didn't worry about anyone else wanting his cigarettes because they all wanted Mike's Kool Menthol cigarettes. They made their way through the streets, presented their passes to the military police at Checkpoint Charlie, swerved around the concrete blocks, passed the East German guards, traveled to Alexanderplatz, then parked in front of the disco buildings. Piling out of the VW van they entered the building, ran up the stairs, and met their ladies for the evening. Bolden looked around and saw Jackie sitting at a table by herself. He walked over to her, hoping to surprise her, because she had not seen him yet. When he was a couple feet away from her she turned around and saw him. With a big leap she wrapped her arms around him and gave him a big hug. Her arms were so tight around him he could hardly move. She was delighted to see him and after a couple of minutes she loosened her embrace and asked him sternly,

"Where have you been? I look for you every weekend and no John, no John, no John! How have you been doing? What have you been doing? I bet you have a girlfriend in the West, that's why you haven't been here. I am correct, Yes?"

John looking at her with a little dazzle in his eyes and recovering from her extraordinary hug, said,

"Whoa, Lady, slow down a bit, will you? It's good to see you to. I've been busy with many things lately and putting in some extra duty. I have been doing good and to answer your other question, No, I do not have a girlfriend in the West. I'm too busy to have a girlfriend. Have to tell you the truth. I'm quite surprised that you are this excited to see me after the last time I saw you."

Jackie looking a little embarrassed was quick to answer him back, but John being a bit quicker, interrupted her before she could get a word out,

"It's okay, you don't have to say anything. I heard the story and I understand. We are good friends and I like it this way."

Jackie, feeling like she had to give John an explanation to what happened, said,

"Ja, I feel we are good friends to but the British soldier I was with that night is very special to me and..."

John really didn't want to hear anymore about it and interrupted her again,

"Jackie, that's your business. I really came over here to have some fun and loosen up a bit. If you would care to join me then I will be most delighted with your company. I know you and Jacqueline don't get along but will you join us at our table?"

Her response was quick and precise,

"JA, I WILL!"

The both of them walked over to the table where the group was sitting. Everyone said their greetings, with champagne glasses filled, they raised their glasses in the air and yelled,

"PROST!"

After a couple glasses of champagne the table was in their merriment. Even Jacqueline was being nice to

Jackie which quite surprised everyone at the table. Glasses of champagne were being quickly drained and filled back up again. There were more bottles of champagne on the table than ever before. The mood was cheery and talkative, it may have been the champagne but it seemed as if the ladies at the table were speaking better English or the men were understanding more German. Either way it didn't matter. Everyone was having a great time. It was a good enough time to have someone forget where they were at for the moment and to go with the flow. The dance floor was filled with many couples dancing even a few singles were out on the dance floor getting lost to the music and moving with the rythym. All of a sudden the sound of Bruce Springsteen filled the air with his song, "Born In The U.S.A.". Jackie grabbed John's hand and jerked him off of his chair, claiming in a loud voice,

"GET UP AND DANCE WITH ME! I WANT TO DANCE TO THIS SONG WITH YOU!"

John forgetting where he was and what he was wearing, hopped up from his chair and yelled,

"YEAH, LET'S GO!"

They hit the dance floor with a fury. Not missing a beat their bodies moved with a parallel motion toward each other. Without intending it, they had taken over the dance floor. Other couples and even the few singles were leaving the dance floor, one by one, only to stand on the outer sides of the dance floor to gaze at the highly active couple. Bolden with his John Travolta moves was singing at the top of his lungs,

"BORN IN THE U.S.A., YEAH, I WAS, BORN IN THE U.S.A."

Jackie singing along with him, laughing and having a wonderful time. When the song was finished, John and Jackie did the appropriate manners of bow and curtsy, in a comical, sort of laphsodasical way. John offering his right elbow for Jackie to take, which she readily accepted, then both of them started hopping off the dance floor. They were laughing and kissing together when they both felt the stares of the crowd upon them. John suddenly realized where he was and that he was wearing his Class A Uniform. He looked at the people around him and looked them in the eyes. Most of the crowd was gazing at them in astonishment. Some of them had a mean look in their eyes. John looked at the table and saw Broadway and Williams staring at him, shaking their head at him with utter disappointment. Festerman and Mandy were to busy kissing each other from the moment they sat down at the table together, so they didn't really give John and Jackie the same attention as everyone else was doing. Then John felt Jackie's movements. With her arm still in the pocket of John's escorting elbow, John felt her hands come up to her face to cover her grief and sadness, possibly embarrassment. John was feeling the flush of embarrassment running through his body because of their actions on the dance floor. Their actions were unintentional but it had set off a different type of mood within the whole disco. John looking at her could see her tears running down her face. Looking at Jackie he begins to offer solace to her,

"Hey, hey Jackie, it's okay. We didn't mean anything by what we did on the dance floor. We just got caught up in the moment. Cheer up! It will pass!"

The DJ, after a small moment of pause, put on some Technik disco music and soon the dance floor was filled again. The party mode had returned and all was almost forgotten of what had transpired earlier. Jackie's body began to tremble as the tears were flowing from her eyes more than before. John feeling compassion for her, wrapped his arms around her as if shielding her from any unwanted attention. The brace of compassion from John gave very little solace to Jackie and John felt that an apology to her was in order,

"I apologize to you Jackie. I did not mean to place you in that situation due to my actions. I forgot where I was. I told you before, you do that to me. When I am with you, I feel free, I feel happy, and I feel good!"

Jackie softly put her arms around John, it was a weak hug because most of her energy was placed into sadness, her words were muffled a bit from her crying but John could understand them.

"No, No, No..., It is not you. I feel good around you to. It is this place. Why was I born here? I don't belong here! I don't want to be here! I WANT MY FREEDOM! I WANT TO TRAVEL! I WANT TO SEE THE UNITED STATES!"

Her body was trembling more than ever and the tears kept flowing. John could feel that her tears were not one of embarrassment but of healing. The many years of tension living in East Berlin, the Stasi watching your every move, the persuasion of those political parties, and many other facets, had caught up with her and it was time to let her emotions be brought forward to heal her physically and mentally. John thought that it might be best for them to leave the disco for a little while, then said to Jackie,

“I don't think I can help you with any of that Jackie. Let's stop drinking the champagne and go outside to get some fresh air. We will take a walk and talk about some things, maybe it will help the both of us to relax.”

Jackie accepted his proposal and they walked over to the table. Mike was the first one to say something to John,

“Johnny..., why did you do that? Look at Jackie she is crying now!”

Ray put in his words as well,

“Yeah Man, why did you? You do realize where we are, don't you?”

Festerman and Mandy came up for a breath of fresh air from their kissing activity. Festerman moved the fresh flowers out of the way that he had given to Mandy and asked,

“What is going on? Oh hey, why is Jackie crying?

Broadway was quick to respond to Festerman's question,

“What..., you mean to tell me you didn't see what they did?”

Festerman, inquisitively answered,

“No..., Mandy and I have been busy. What is more important than that? What was I supposed to see?”

Broadway answered him back in his usual sarcastic voice,

"John took Jackie out on the dance floor to dance to Bruce Sprinsteen's song, "Born In The U.S.A. and he is wearing his Class A uniform.

Festerman asking,

"So...., What's wrong with that?"

Broadway being sarcastic again,

"WE'RE IN EAST BERLIN! YOU IDIOT!"

Festerman bounced back with his response,

So what..., there's nothing wrong with that. Hey, as a matter of fact, play that song again, Mandy and I will go out there and dance to it."

Mandy laughing, backs up Kevin by saying,

"JA, JA, Do It!!!

With Mandy's comical personality she had brought laughter to the whole group sitting at the table. Bolden was calm in his response to Mike and Ray,

"I know what I did men and I have already apologized to Jackie for it. I just got caught up in the moment and forgot where I am. Jackie and I are going to go outside and grab some fresh air. We will be back in a moment."

Ray politely reminded John of the time they had to be back through Checkpoint Charlie and John reassured Ray that they would be back in time to head out. John and Jackie headed toward the open double doors then descended down the steps. With each step down John could feel the pressure easing up on Jackie as her breathing was becoming more calm. When they opened the doors to exit the stuffy building they could feel the cool air gently sweeping across their face. It was a fresh sensation that relaxed their whole being. As they began their walk John was the first to say something,

"How are you doing? Are you feeling better?"

Jackie answering in a calm manner,

"Ja I am okay. I am happy we came outside."

John, creating a conversation, started with his questions,

"So... you really wish to see America? I have to tell you, ever since our first conversation, I see my country in a different way now, more than ever before. Why do you want to see the United States?"

Jackie answered him back,

"I told you, it is a dream of mine,ever since my Uncle gave me that candy from the West. I have seen pictures of the different states and they are beautiful. They are filled with exciting life. The trees and the flowers look so wonderful. The water looks so clean and blue. It is beautiful there, everywhere, I know it, I feel it!" It looks so relaxing and free. It looks like you can do anything you want to do and you will be happy. I don't trust anyone here. The girls at the disco are not my friends, I do not trust them. I have to be very careful what I say to anyone. I have to be on my toes all the time."

John, trying to put some humor into their conversation butted in with a little chuckle in his voice,

"Yeah, you should try being a soldier."

Jackie sensed his humor and came forth with a bit of laughter. John continued on,

"I know what you are saying Jackie. I look around here in East Berlin and it is so gray and dismal. I really don't like being over here but I come here because you help me to forget about the surroundings and you make my time here very enjoyable. I listen to everything you tell me and I see how lucky I am to have been born in America. You see Jackie, the way I think, is that, if I have it, then everyone else has it. When I talk with you, I see, that is not the way things are. I wish I could help you but I don't think there is any way I am able to."

Jackie with a slightly sad undertone to her voice said,

"Ja I know. I am happy that you talk with me about this. I know it is safe to talk with you about it. I can not talk to anyone here about it. I feel like you do when I am around you. How can I say this?"

Jackie paused for a moment, searching for the words to state her expression,

"You bring the Spirit of America with you when you are here because I feel so free around you. I am filled with much life and happiness."

John looked into Jackie's eyes, they were wide open with surprise and excitement in them. It was as if she had found the perfect expression to state what was on her mind and she felt free to say it.

John felt the same way. He did not expect that from her. He was waiting for her, to ask him, if he would help her escape into West Berlin. John was overwhelmed with what Jackie was saying to him. He searched his thoughts and his soul for an answer back to her. He had quit making decisions with his heart a long time ago. His decisions had to come from his way of thinking, being logical and practical, and above all other things his beliefs. He found what he was going to say to her. His decision was based on the facts that, Jackie did not ask him to help her escape, she gave to him a different way of looking at his own life and to be happy with what he has because others may not have it. The energy between the two of them, when they were together, had such veracity that it filled an entire disco, which was evident from what had happened earlier. There was something special about these two people and they knew it. They just didn't know how special it was supposed to be. John stopped their walking activity and looked at Jackie,

“Jackie, look, I'm not promising you anything here but I will see what I can do. I'm new here in Berlin. I don't know too many people. So...., really I don't know if there is anything I can do for you. If something should come up then I will let you know, other than that, we will not talk about this anymore. Do you understand me? Do you know what I am saying to you?”

Jackie, with hope filled in her eyes said,

“Yes, I understand you.”

John looked at his army watch and saw the time was getting close to leave and go back to West Berlin and said,

“We better head back to the disco. By the time we get back there we will have to leave right away and go back to the West. Are you feeling better now?”

“Ja, I am much better than before. Let's hurry!”, she said with happiness in her voice.

As they were approaching the disco building they could see the whole group coming out of the doorway and heading toward the white VW van. Ray was the first one to notice them as he said,

“Right on time you two. We better get going. It's going to be a close call.”

When they arrived at the van everyone took their usual positions. Jackie was sitting on John's lap and they were embraced through passionate kissing. Mandy was sitting on Kevin's lap and of course, they to, were still enjoying each others company. Babette took the place in the backseat behind Mike and Jacqueline. Mandy holding the fresh flowers in her hand was unknowingly brushing them against John and Jackie. When they arrived at their secret drop off point Babette exited the van. Mandy, climbing off of Kevin's lap, accidentally swished her flowers across John's face. John adding some humor to the situation said,

“Hey Mandy, watch where you're swinging those flowers will you? You know what might happen to those at this time of night, with that candy you got the other time.”

Mandy laughingly responded back,

Ja, Sjahn, I thought you might be hungry. You might like these.”

With Mandy's cute little giggle everyone couldn't help but laugh about the situation. John whispered into Jackie's ear,

“I don't know when I will see you next. It might be a long time. I will let you know when I see you again okay?”

Jackie didn't answer back with her voice. She gave John a wink of her right eye and a long passionate kiss good bye. Ray growing impatient blurted out,

“Okay you two, it's time to say good night. We have to go and we have to go now!”

Jackie exited the van and stared at John with her loving eyes. Ray placed the white VW van into gear and headed for the checkpoint. Once they reported back in, the white VW Van headed down Potsdamer Strasse. Mike turned and looked back at John,

“What did you and Jackie talk about when you went for your walk? She looked a lot better when you two came back, than when you left the disco.”

John being pervasive with Mike's question,

“We didn't talk about much of anything. I think the fresh air did us both some good. She calmed down once we got outside. I think she was just embarrassed about what happened on the dance floor. Which, by the way, I don't want to talk about that anymore. I still feel a little bit out of sorts about it. I'm usually in much better control of my self.”

Mike with his usual sarcastic tone of voice said,

“Yes, you should be. That was not a smart move on your part. You two weren't the only one's embarrassed by it.”

John offering a way out of the conversation said,

“Whatever Mike, I'm hungry! Is everyone up for some Doner ke bobs?”

The answer was unanimous and went without saying as Ray pulled the white VW Van close to the imbiss where everyone piled out and stocked up on their favorite meal of the evening. With sandwiches in hand they hopped into the van for a short ride to McNair barracks. After exiting the van everyone said their good byes to Ray and thanked him for the transportation. Bolden, Broadway, and Festerman walked the steps to the top floor without saying a word to each other and went into their separate rooms. Bolden put his sandwiches in the small refrigerator then moved over to his wall locker opening it up, taking his Class A Uniform off he placed it on a hanger on the right side of his wall locker, indicating to him, to take it to the dry cleaners when he had time. He sat down on his bunk after putting on his PT shorts and thought about grabbing one of the sandwiches he had just placed in the refrigerator. He really wasn't that hungry. He decided to get up from his bunk and sit on the window ledge to look up into the night's sky. Being unusually dark out for the night he could see the small stars shining brightly. His thoughts were on what he had said to Jackie. He had no idea of how he could help her and thought maybe he should not have mentioned anything to her about it. He thought about the tour he took with the Iron School of Standards and looking at the wall. Being so high with rounded edges, barbed wire, guard towers, mine fields, guard dogs, armed guards, everything that he saw on Wall Patrol, including the gap he saw in the wall in that desolate area. Even if he could bring her to that area how would he get them past all of that. No ideas were coming to him at the moment. He shrugged his shoulders and thought,

"Well, if it is meant to be, then something will present itself to him."

He was confident with that, then allowed that thought to leave his mind and enter into the night sky. John was getting tired. Getting up from the window sill he walked over to his bunk and laid down for a good night's sleep. The next few weeks training will be to prepare for the Berlin Brigade Parade that was to be presented on July 4th, America's Independence Day.

“How appropriate is that?”, John thought.

With a chuckle from his lips, he closed his eyes and fell fast asleep.

31

TWO IDEAS COMING TOGETHER

Almost three weeks had passed by since his last visit to East Berlin and the conversation he had with Jackie. The soldiers had been preparing for the Berlin Brigade Parade six days out of the week. No passes were given out to anyone that was involved with the parade. Practicing Drill and Ceremony was a fun activity for most soldiers but the constant training in the summer heat was taking it's toll upon many of the soldiers that would be in the parade. Bolden, every now and then, would try to think of ways to help Jackie but nothing was presenting itself. Every idea he came up with was shot down with the, “What If This Happens”, so on and so forth. Bolden was never much of a chess player but he knew that a good chess player had to think of at least ten moves in advance in order to win the game. So few possibilities came up, so many barricades got in the way of those possibilities.

Sunday, June 29, 1986, Bolden is pacing the floor in his room. It was supposed to be a day of relaxation for the parade soldiers. The Berlin Brigade Parade was coming up soon and the commander was making sure the soldier's had some rest. These parade soldiers, had shown to the commander, their excellence, in Drill and Ceremony. The commander had felt confident with his men that they will perform in an excellent manner. Bolden couldn't rest that day. For some reason he was feeling antsy. His thoughts were upon Jackie and trying to help her, trying to find a way to get her into West Berlin. He knew that after the parade was over with, on that Friday, that Williams and Broadway were going to go to the East. Their passes were already completed and approved. Bolden was hesitant about placing his pass in because he wished to be able to give something to Jackie, a possibility for her, anything that would help, but nothing was there. He wasn't going to go back to the East and see Jackie unless he had something to give to her. He continued pacing the floor, fumbling with small items in his room, placing them from one area to another, then back to their original position. There is a knock on his door, as he opened it, he sees it is Michael Broadway. Mike was the first to speak,

"Do you mind if I come in?"

John opened the door fully and motioned with his hand giving Mike permission to enter his room. After the door was closed Mike continued on with an explanation of his visit. He was being unusually polite, quiet, and cautious with his movements, which Bolden thought was odd. The mannerisms of his voice and words were of not being sure if he should say them.

“I have something I want to talk with you about. I don't know if you will like what I am going to say to you.”

Bolden calmed down a bit. He stopped being figity with his movements and pacing. He was ready to listen to what Mike had to say and he wished for Mike to know what was on his mind as well, when he said,

Mike, I have something I wish to talk to you about also. I don't know if you are going to like what I have to say either. Go ahead with yours then I will let you know mine.”

Bolden said this to him not in a distrusting way of Michael but of concern for Mike because Bolden knew of Broadway's personality by now and knew Mike was different this time because of something important on his mind. Mike needed a friend and John was there for him. Mike reciprocated back to John,

“Go ahead, what's on your mind?”

John stating back with a little humor,

“It can wait Mike. Go ahead with yours. I know it's important to you because you're acting weird. What's Up? Vie Gehts, as the German's would say.”

Broadway, without a smile on his face, said,

“Okay, but you have to promise me that you will keep this secret, even if you don't agree with it. You can't say a word to anyone. Promise?”

John, being serious,

“I Promise You Mike? What's going on?”

Broadway with a relaxed breath brings forth his desire,

"I want to bring Jacqueline and her baby over to the West. I want to marry her. I Love Her And Her Son! Will you help me?"

John sighs, releasing the tension from his body and entered into a calm relaxed state. Looking at Mike, Bolden opens up to him with his thoughts,

"Well Now, This sure is something because what I was going to ask you is along the same lines. Jackie wants to come over to the West. I have no idea of how I can do this by myself. I have been thinking about this since our last visit over to the East. I would like to do this for her Mike but everything I have thought of doesn't seem to work at this time. You have been here longer than I. I was going to ask you if you had any ideas, any way that we could bring her across. Do you have a plan for anything yet?"

Mike was relaxed at this point with what John had expressed to him. He was beginning to become his usual self,

"No, I don't have a plan right now, you idiot. That's why I came to see you, to see if you could come up with something. Get it right Johnny! Let's start thinking of something."

Broadway showed a quick smile on his face as if a light bulb was turned on in his brain,

"Oh..., I get it now. That's why you went on Wall Patrol, isn't it? That's what You and Jackie were talking about when you left the disco the last time. I'm right, I know I am."

Bolden didn't take offense when Mike called him an idiot. He was actually getting used to Mike's different personality and came to accept him for his non-thoughtful expressions. John began to blush a little and with a chuckle said to Mike,

“Well you are half right with that Mike. I went on Wall Patrol with the Scouts because I wished to do something exciting, more training, to learn about what we are here for, so I am able to make sense out of all of this. To see my purpose here Mike. That is my reason for that. I did not know at that time Jackie wanted to come to the West. I can tell you this Mike, when I was on my first patrol, the last observation post we went to, is close to the line where the American Sector and the British Sector meet. It is a desolated area there. There is only one East German Guard Tower at that position and it was unmanned at the time we were there. There was no activity at all on either side of the wall, no civilians, no military. There is a gap in the wall, big enough to fit a human body through it. It caught my attention and I still think about it. This may be the way to bring them across but I don't know what is on the East side of the wall there. It is possible that a heavy mine field is laid there which would account for the gap and no East German Guards or dogs. Now your other question about Jackie is a Yes. We did talk about her coming over to the West. I did not promise anything to her Mike. I only told her that if I was able to help her then I will. Does Jacqueline know you want her to come to the West with you?”

Mike being serious with his answer stated,

“No, she doesn't know anything about what I said to you but I am sure she and her son will come over here with me. Did Jackie ask you to help her escape?”

John was quick with his response,

"No Mike, she did not ask me to help her escape or for anything else. That is one of the reasons why I decided to see what I was able to do for her. Like I said, I didn't promise her anything. All that I told her was that I will see what I can do. I have to tell you what is on my mind with Jacqueline and her baby. It will, for sure, be a task to bring them over. We will have to try and keep the baby quiet when we bring both of them over. You do realize that, don't you?"

Mike answered him back with a slow tone at first but then picked up his words,

"Yes, I realize that, but we will come up with something. I have an idea. Let's concentrate on bringing Jackie over first, if we are successful, then we will bring Jacqueline and her son over. AGREED!?"

John with a big smile on his face, shook Mike's hand and said,

"AGREED!"

John continued on as he was a bit curious about something,

"Mike, does Ray know anything about this? Have you said anything to him about what you were thinking? I know we can trust him if you did."

Broadway answered Bolden earnestly,

"No, you are the only one, I've said anything to, about what I wanted to do. I was a little nervous about bringing it up to you, but I had to talk with someone about it. I feel you are my best friend here and I trust you."

Bolden started laughing a little bit,"

“You know Mike, at the beginning of our conversation, I'm pretty sure we both acted like two East German Border Patrol Guards wanting to escape into the West, not knowing if they could trust each other. Hmm..., this sure is something, it's the same thing only different. How are we ever going to figure this one out?” The feeling is mutual here Mike. I feel I can trust you to. You are the only one I have talked with about this.

Mike said to John just before exiting his room,

“We don't have to figure that part out, all we have to do is come up with a good plan. If you come up with anything then let me know and I will do the same with you, okay?”

John with a serious tone of voice replied,

“Yes, I will let you know if anything comes up. I don't know if I will being do anymore Wall Patrols with the scouts but if the opportunity arises I will see if I can go. From what I have seen each patrol is different.”

Mike nodded his head and asked,

“Are you going with Ray and I to the East this coming Saturday? We have our passes already in.”

Bolden shaking his head,

“No..., The next time I go over there with you guys will be if I have something to offer to Jackie. If something does come into play I don't want to arouse any type of suspicion. Matter of fact, I don't want Jackie to know much of anything if we do come up with something. The less she knows, the better off she will be at this point, and for us.”

Mike agreed with John and walked out of his room closing the door behind him. John was more relaxed now knowing that he had an ally to help him with his ideas but he had more to think about now. Instead of just one person he had three people to think about now. His thoughts were on Jacqueline's infant son and how to safely bring both of them over, without either one of them being harmed in the process. It was becoming a more difficult task than what he had to think about before but he was confident that with Michael Broadway by his side all will be well and a plan would soon come to bring all three of them safely over to the West. Bolden continued on with his daily activity more relaxed than before. The day turning into night, as the sun settled in the west, he prepared his uniform for Monday's training on the Berlin Brigade Parade. With everything completed and in it's place, he examined his uniform making sure that all of his brass and his boots were highly shined. Taking the ruler examining precise placements of everything. He was satisfied with his work and felt the desire to relax, putting the events of the day behind him and prepare for the near future. He sat upon his window ledge and stared, again, into the night's sky. It was densely illuminated by the waning half moon that was apparent, with it's half glitter, progressing forward in a slow motion toward a new moon. The portal for wishes to be granted was closed for the moment, from the darkening of the moon. With each day that passes, from there on, was a step forward to seeing visions that will bring hope and faith for goodness to come. Decisions will be made easily as these visions come forth and clarity is given. All that had to be done was to let go of his thoughts and release them into the universe. Soon, after the new moon appears, the portal for wishes to be granted will open once again, bringing forth the magic of your deepest desires. Bolden closed his eyes, released his thoughts, then allowed his body to enter into a deep relaxation. Relaxing too much, he had fallen asleep on the shallow width window sill only to be awakened by his sudden quick fall to the floor next to his bed. The concrete floor offered no soft landing to his body. Half awake and startled Bolden looked at his alarm clock and discovered he had been asleep for three hours on the window sill. Rubbing his elbow and grunting a few words of displeasure, he grabbed one of the metal bed posts on his bunk, pulled himself up then flopped onto his bunk. The only thing left to do was to have patience.

CHAPTER 32

THE COLONEL'S SPEECH

Tuesday, July 1st, 1986, three days away from the annual 4th of July parade for the Berlin Brigade soldiers who had been training for this event for the past four weeks. They had been given the shiny Berlin Brigade black helmets with the emblem in the middle of it, the white belt that went around the middle of their torso across their uniforms, and the thin white gloves that covered their hands. Their standing order was that no one was allowed to pass out from the heat during training for the parade and especially during the actual parade. If you passed out from the heat while standing at the position of attention for such a long time meant only one thing, you locked your knees while standing, which cut off the circulation of blood flow to the lower legs and feet and that was grounds for an Article 15, disobeying a direct order. Their boots had to be shined every day as the heat from the sun melted the wax on their boots. The brass insignia that they brandished on their uniforms had to be highly shined with no scratches visible on the brass. It was delicate and intricate right down to the finest detail of the uniform. All of it had to be perfect as it represented some of the finest soldiers America had to offer in the defense of liberty for West Berlin. The rulers had been handed out and uniforms inspected every day for any flaws that were in them. CSC 6/502nd Infantry had been chosen as the Honor Group to carry the flags of each individual state of the United States of America for a Salute to the States ceremony during the parade. Bolden had been given the honor and the privilege of carrying the Colorado State Flag. He felt the pride of carrying it while holding onto the long shaft that it was attached to. The slight breeze of the wind would whisk its way by the flag giving life to it while it waved so freely in the air causing the long shaft to move in his hands. Bolden would grip his hands tighter around the shaft to provide a strong base. This was their job for the whole month of June. Marching up and down the 4th of July Platz, which was located next to McNair Barracks and The Clock Tower. They were finishing up their marching training for the day when the battalion commander, Lt Colonel Hutchinson came front and center to the podium that was located on the center sidewalk of the 4th of July Platz. The battalion was ordered to

"Attention".

You heard one large click as the battalion clicked their heels together and stood at

“Attention”.

The clicking noise came from the steel taps that were nailed to the bottom of the soldier’s boots. While marching during the parade, these taps would click in unison with each other, front and back. The taps that were nailed to the back of the boots had a rim that went slightly above the rear heel of the boot. When the combat boots came together side by side, when ordered to the position of

“Attention”,

it created a more distinct hallowed sound than what was presented from the marching tap. The Colonel then ordered the battalion to

“Parade Rest”.

In unison you could hear the tinny sound of the taps as they came to rest on the pavement as the soldiers set their boots back down after separating them for a short distance and the slap of their hands as they came to rest with each other in the small pocket of the lower back area. The Colonel began his speech with the Battalion.

Soon, we will be celebrating the 210th Anniversary of our Nation’s freedom. By way of The Constitution of the United States, of which, our forefathers have given us as a guide to live as free and honorable men. We have sworn an oath to defend this freedom and to uphold the dignity that our Declaration of Independence has to offer to all free people. Standing here before me today I have seen the achievements of what you men have done that has earned you a place within the Berlin Brigade. Your dedication and devotion to your country and your military service has instilled confidence in your superior officers and we have no doubt that when called upon to defend this freedom, that you will act, without hesitation, to do so. We have been called upon to defend this great city of West Berlin Germany against communist aggression and we stand together with a wall of cement that surrounds us. I have spoken with many West Berliners here and my conclusion is this. They are as much Americans as we are and they are willing to defend their freedom along with us. This wonderful city and its citizens are sovereign territory. We are not alone in this silent fight to uphold this city's independence. This is a time where we are reliving history. A city that is surrounded by authoritarianism is waiting on the outskirts of its borders to claim victory over its spirit. This cannot and will not happen as long as we have the heart of a lion that will fight to the end, if necessary, to remain free and independent. We have a duty to each other to protect that which we value the most and that is the freedom of our future generation. All of us have the right to a life of liberty and the pursuit of happiness, may it always be so!

As the troops were called to

"Attention"

and then to

"Present, Arms".

Lt. Colonel Hutchinson departed from the podium then stood at Attention from his place of command. The loud speaker crackled as a familiar tune carried its way through the air waves. It was a song by Lee Greenwood,

"God Bless the U.S.A."

Bolden standing at Attention had felt so much pride of being a soldier in the United States Army than at any other moment, since his enlistment, after hearing the Colonel's speech, his chest could not protrude out any further to show his gratitude for being a part of such a special event that was making history. Then as the notes of the music came to his ears, it took all he could muster to withhold the tears from his eyes while in formation and standing at Attention. When the words from the song came to him,

"And I won't forget the men who died who gave this life to me, and I'll gladly stand up........next to you to defend her still today. For there ain't no doubt I love this land...... God Bless the U.S.A.".

His body trembled slightly and his heart beating strong, he had made up his mind to help Jackie obtain her freedom from the East. Nothing would stand in his way and he would give everything that he was to secure the freedom of one individual who desired it the most! Mike and John had discussed the possibility of bringing Mike's girlfriend Jacqueline and her baby over to the West and had decided to bring Jackie over first. They did not know how they were going to do this as the plan had not been formulated yet.

33

THE PLAN COMES TOGETHER

Saturday, July 12th, 1986. Laying on the bunk in his room, Bolden was in a deep sleep. He is awakened by the loud, hard, quick, continuous wraps on his door. He drowsily looked at his alarm clock and discovered it was 2330 Hours. Half awake, he slowly raised from his bunk and started walking to the door to open it up. The knocking on the door continued. He was getting irritated with it and wondered who it could be, as he yelled,

“I'm coming! Stop knocking on the door!”

The continuous hard wrapping had ceased. John opened the door to see Mike standing in front of him with his Class A Uniform on. His eyes were wide open with excitement and he was sporting a big smile on his face. He pushed his way through the open door. With his strong entry he had moved Bolden off to the side and closed the door behind him with one quick movement. Bolden was wondering why Mike was back so early from the East. They usually didn't return until 0030 hours or later depending on if they decided to go to the Ku'Dorf. Mike being way to excited for being Mike blurted out his reason for waking Bolden up,

“I've got it, Johnny! I've got it, Man! You are going to love this!”

Bolden confused, as he was still waking up from his deep sleep, asked Mike,

“What did you get? Did you get promoted to Sergeant or something?” This better be good for waking my ass up like this Michael! I've had a busy day today! Hey, why are you back so early from the East?”

“No, I didn't get promoted to Sergeant. I just got my promotable status. You know that, you idiot! I know how we can bring them over to the West. It is so simple. I don't know why I didn't see it before”.

John hearing the exciting news started to perk up a bit,

“What do you got, Mike?”

Mike answering in a low voice,

“We got back early because Ray has to be on duty on Sunday, something about loading his van up with some equipment for supply. Any how, I remembered there is an empty spot underneath the back seat. I helped him put some small things in there, from the back of the van, so he had enough room to fit the supply things, he is supposed to haul tomorrow. It is a very small place but I know we can fit Jackie in there, and.... I think we can fit Jacqueline and her son in there later. This will work, I know it will!!!”

John, not trying to be pessimistic, but being cautious, reminded Mike of one thing he may have forgotten,

“Mike, that sounds like a good plan and I am all for it, but you know, they might have those infrared heat seeking sensors planted around the area. They might detect a human body, in the van, laying in a conspicuous position, especially if I am sitting on top of that body. Did you think about that?”

Broadway with a big grin on his face, looked at John, nodded his head and said,

“YES I DID! This is, what is, so perfect about this. Even if they do have those devices there and think something is up, they can't touch us Johnny! They are East German Border Guards and they are the enemy. They can't touch us! They can't detain us! Do you get it?”

Bolden's aura began to glow with excitement. He was wide awake now and filled with happiness from what Mike had expressed to him. He knew, right then and there, Mike was correct and had come up with the perfect plan for the escape. It was BRILLIANT! Then he calmed himself down for the moment. John realized that there was going to have to be another party involved in order to make this happen, Sergeant Ray Williams, after all, he owned and drove the van. Bolden knew very little about Williams but was hopeful that he could be trusted. Bolden had to know for sure and asked Mike,

" Does Ray know anything about what we have been talking about? He is going to have to know what we plan on doing, Mike?"

Mike calmed down a little and said,

"No, not yet. I plan on talking with him about it soon. I am sure he will go along with it. We can trust him Johnny. I've known Ray for awhile now. Don't worry about anything. I have this under control. Next time I see him, I will bring it up to him and see what he says, okay?"

John being confident with everything said,

"Okay Mike, it's your plan and I like it a lot. It will work if he goes along with it. If he does jump on board with us then all three of us will have to talk about this and make plans. You know, "The What Ifs" and so on. We will have to be prepared for anything and everything."

Mike with a knowing look on his face said,

"Yeah, I know this. Go back to sleep and get some rest. You know, sleep on it. That's what I'm going to do within the next few minutes."

John having a delightful smirk on his face, laughingly said,

"Are you joking? I'm wide awake now. It will take awhile for me to get back to sleep. I'll think about this some more and see what I can come up with. I'm going to have to look at that empty space under the backseat to give me an idea of what you are talking about."

Mike opened up the door and said,

"Yeah, you do that. When you see it then you will know what I'm talking about. Have a good night Johnny!"

Bolden pushing the door shut said,

"You to Michael. We'll talk soon."

Being alone in his room and filled with excitement, Bolden walked over to the window ledge and perched himself upon it. This, it had dawned on him, was his thinking spot. Looking up into the night sky he spotted the waxing crescent moon. The portal for wishes was open and he could see that the plan was coming together slowly, however, his thoughts, on the other hand, were coming in rapidly. As each thought came to him, he was keeping track of them, one by one.

"I hope Ray goes along with this. He will, I am sure of it. How comfortable will Jackie be in that space under the back seat? How are we going to be able to get Jacqueline and her son under there? Will either of them go along with it? How will we get them away from the group to hide them? How will we explain why they left once they were hidden? How are we going to react if we get caught on the East side of the wall? How are we going to react if we get caught on the West side of the wall? What will either of them say to the four powers once they are in the West in order to get clearance to stay in the West? How are we going to take care of them when they are in the West? All of these questions kept coming up in Bolden's thoughts and many more followed. The answers to those questions had to come from the three soldiers and it was not time for them to be answered yet. The best part of the whole thing was that progress was being made. To move forward with any event is a true blessing, for it brings with it, hope and faith toward a brighter future.

The answers came that next Sunday, July 20th, 1986. There is a repeated knock on Bolden's door. Opening the door he sees Mike and Ray standing in the hallway, both of them wearing sheepish grins upon their faces. Bolden knew what they were there for as he invited them in. He closed the door behind them and he was the first to speak,

"By the look on both of your faces I can tell Ray is in, right?"

Ray spoke next,

"You bet I'm in! I've been wanting to do this for a long time. I didn't know how you guys felt about it. That's why I didn't say anything."

Mike was next to speak,

"The van is down in the parking lot. Do you want to go with us to check it out?"

John, excited, said,

"Yep, let's go!"

They exited the room and walked down the stairs into the parking lot. Looking around the parking lot there was very little traffic going in and out of the barracks. Ray opened the side door of the van then lifted the top of the backseat up. John looked down and saw the very narrow space that was available. It looked like it would be wider than what he had expected from the top view with the seat down. The boards that were used to make the frame of the backseat were wider than what he thought they would be. True, there was enough space available, to put one human body inside, but it would be very cramped. John put his right hand around his chin and expressed his thoughts,

“Jackie can fit in there but we are going to have to be quick on getting her over here. I'm not sure how long she will be able to stand being in there. Mike, I don't think Jacqueline and her son will both fit in here together.”

Mike being sarcastic and fast to reply,

“He's a baby, John! How much room do you think he is going to take up, you dumb ass!?”

John was able to come back with a quick response in his own defense,

“Mike, think about this, the baby has to be quiet. In order for him to be this way he is going to have to feel comfortable in his environment, he has to feel secure. The only way that is going to happen is if he is in his mother's arms. Think about this, is there enough room in there for her to hold him in her arms?”

Mike dropping his shoulders was beginning to see the reality of it,

“Yes, I see what you are saying, but we aren't going to have that much time left, after we bring Jackie over, to come up with another plan, once they discover she is gone, and that's even if we are able to bring her over here."

Ray was hopeful as he intervened between the two of them,

"Hey, we aren't going to stop with just those three. We are going to bring over as many as we are able to, who ever wants to. This white VW Van is, "The Freedom Van!" I told you guys, I've been wanting to do this for a very long time. Seeing that we are going to go through with this then we are going to push forward and keep it going until we can't do it anymore."

John and Mike were surprised, very surprised, to hear those words come from Sergeant Ray Williams. He was their leader for their visits to the East. Always being responsible, always watching out for them, making sure they were on time going back across, how they acted in the East, and much more. Now, Bolden and Broadway, could see they had a rebel on their hands. A rebel that despised what the Berlin Wall stood for, a rebel against oppression and tyranny for many people that lived on the Eastern side of that wall. The words that Ray expressed had pressed motivation and dedication into John and Mike. There was no longer a trust issue involved with anyone. These three men, these three soldiers, were dedicated to a cause. The past events of fun and folly, due to the wide range of East Mark to American dollar exchange, creating the American soldier to be wealthy enough to afford bottles of champagne, many bottles of champagne, other alcoholic beverages, coca cola, Kool cigarettes, Marlboro cigarettes, and other western gifts, given to the East Berlin Women, fancy dinners that were expensive to some people but affordable to them, were beginning to become more defined, more refined, as to why those events had occurred. Their youthful actions were beginning to take shape, to unite as one, with their personalities and character coming together to serve a purpose that was greater than either one of them. They knew, in their thoughts, they could not do this task alone, but together, they will be able to accomplish their dreams. John spoke up,

“I'm in with that Ray. Let's make that happen.”

Mike was next,

“I'm in with it also. Let's get Jackie, Jacqueline and her son over here first and then we will go from there.”

John was curious as to how long someone was able to stay inside that hidden compartment. He was going to place himself in there for a few minutes and expressed his thoughts to Mike and Ray,

“All right, this is what I'm going to do. Help me in there and close the lid. Give me five minutes and we will see what happens.”

John stepped inside the van and placed his feet in the small boxed in area. He had to shift onto his left side. Kneeling down he braced himself with his left arm while Mike balanced him holding his right arm. Crouching into an infant position he was tightly snugged into the small hidden compartment. His arms were tight up against his ribs. There was very little room to move around. Mike was being comical but sincere,

“You wouldn't happen to be claustrophobic there, would ya, Johnny? If you are, it's too late now.”

John smiling said,

"I wouldn't be doing this if I was, you smart ass! Close the lid and start the time."

As Mike closed the lid, the darkness set in. The first few minutes went by easily. A few seconds after, John could feel his legs start to tingle from lack of blood circulation. He tried moving them slightly. It took extra effort and the small movement from his legs helped. His breathing was still good and his heart rate was at an even pace. His arms and upper body were doing well but the tingling in his legs was starting to intensify. The five minutes were up as the back seat lid was lifted upward and daylight presented itself into the previous darkened area. With a little help from Mike, John was able to lift himself up and out of the hiding area with ease. The blood circulation was beginning to flow back into his legs. While standing, he begins to bring his feet up and down, one at a time, to increase the circulation. It only took a few minutes to get his legs back to normal. Mike being curious stated his question,

"Well..., What do you think? Will they be okay under there?"

John was optimistic but with a slight pessimism in his voice , answered Mike's question,

"Yes, I think they will be okay under there, however, we are going to have to be quick in getting them over here to the West. Both of you seen how I reacted after five minutes in there. My guess, will be, that they will have fifteen, maybe twenty minutes in the hiding spot before anything serious begins to happen to them physically.

Maybe a little more time than that but that will be pushing it."

Mike was uneasy with John's answer and spouted back,

"No, they should have more time than that! I'm bigger and taller than you are! Let me get in there for ten minutes and see what happens."

John and Ray were all for it, even though John thought Mike was measuring manly hood sizes, the extra minutes that Mike would be in there could possibly give them a few more minutes, for the, just in case something happens time, that might arise. It was an insurance, to be safe, for what could happen. Mike entered the white VW van and John followed in after him,

"What do you think you are doing?" Mike asking sarcastically.

John was surprised with Mike's question. Looking at him with concern in his eyes said,

"I'm going to help you get in there. You know, like you helped me. Why...?, Is this a problem?"

Mike, being sarcastic, said,

"I can do it myself. I don't need your help!"

John shrugged his shoulders and exited the van as he said,

"All right you asshole, do it yourself. I'm trying to be realistic. You know, the women might need some help getting in there. I'm being a gentleman, is all, and I'm treating this situation as if it is real. You go ahead and do your thing. Ray and I will let you out in ten minutes.

Laughingly, John added... and don't be calling us to let you out of there any earlier. You Da Man!!!"

Mike responding back,

"Yeah, yeah, yeah... close the lid, will ya? This way I can get some rest from you, Johnny!"

John and Ray started laughing, then John said,

"Nope, I'm not closing the lid".

John looked at Ray, with a smile and a circling wave of his right hand, imitating a British accent, John asked Ray,

"Will you do the honor, Sir, of allowing, Sir Michael, Lord of Rector, Arkansas, King... of the Arkansas Nation, to be entertained within his own solitude, so that the answers to his manly questions, be answered to him, with precise knowing, giving him his dignity, to be justified within the realms of his own mind?"

Ray looked at John with a little confusion on his face and then with a smile, he said,

"Yeah..., Okay..., Whatever..."

Ray entered the van then closed the backseat lid. Time was ticking by slowly. After five minutes, John and Ray could here Mike moving a little inside the hidden compartment. John knew Mike's legs were tingling from the slow blood circulation. In a few more minutes they would have the answers to their questions. As the ten minutes came to an end, Ray went to step into the van but was stopped suddenly by John grabbing his arm. Ray looked at John with a confused look on his face. John looking at Ray and with a loud voice said,

“Hey, let's give Mike a few more minutes to show up before we head out. He's been wanting to go on this trip for a long time.”

Then with a louder voice, John yelled,

“ATTENTION!”

Both Ray and John went into the Position of Attention as Ray noticed Lt. Pillow, their platoon leader, walking up to them. Ray gave his salute to him and Lt. Pillow gave him the return salute. Lt. Pillow gave the order of “At Ease”, then asked,

“What are you men doing out here? Plan on going somewhere today?”

Ray and John being in the “At Ease” order, that Lt. Pillow had given them, became relaxed. Though being concerned for Mike in the hidden compartment, as time kept ticking forward, neither one showed any suspicion with their actions. Bolden's voice was loud enough when he shouted out the order of, “ATTENTION”, that they knew Mike heard it and was aware of what was going on. The small movements of his legs had stopped and Mike was being quiet. Ray answered the Lieutenant,

“Hello Sir, we are waiting for Broadway to show up. He is a little late and I want to get going. We are going to the Wansee and take in the sights. That is, if Mike ever shows up.”

Lt. Pillow answering back,

“You guys sure did pick a good day for going to the Wansee. It's hot out here. Take in a good swim to cool you down.”

Bolden wishing to add his comments with a comical tone and a smile on his face said,

"I can't swim Sir. That's why I joined the Army instead of the Navy. I'm going along for bikini patrol, as the scouts call it. Maybe do a little F.B.I. work while I'm at it."

Lt. Pillow looking a little bit confused asked Bolden,

"F.B.I. work? Do you plan on going into law enforcement after the Army, Specialist?"

Bolden being at ease with his platoon leader, started to laugh and said,

"No, Sir..., you know, Female Body Inspector. I have to make sure those bikinis are properly fitted and in general proportion to the female's body. It is to give them character and uplift our morale. I'd love to have a future career in that."

Lt. Pillow rolling his eyes and with a slight smile on his face said,

"Oh jeez, Specialist. Leave it to you to come up with something like that. All right, you men have fun at the Wansee and stay away from the nudist area over there. You know it is off limits to us. Besides that, Bolden wouldn't have a future career, to train for, if you men go there. I've got to get back to my duties. I'm the Officer of the Day again. If I see Specialist Broadway then I will tell him you two are looking for him."

Williams and Bolden went into the position of Attention. Ray saluting the Lt. for his departure. Lt. Pillow returned the salute and said,

"Carry On, Men!"

The two men watched the Lieutenant walk away, then he disappeared through the steel door, as it closed behind him. Both Ray and John were very concerned for Mike. Ray looked at his watch and said,

“We've got to get him out of there. He's been in there for fifteen minutes already.”

Ray stepped into the white VW Van and lifted the backseat lid. Mike placed his right arm up into the air, as if, asking for help to get out of the small hidden compartment. Ray grabs Mike's right arm and helped him up. Mike was slow in lifting his legs out of the box. Ray continued to steady Mike as he helped him exit the van. John watched carefully for Mike's actions, then said,

“We couldn't get you out of there Mike. I'm sure you heard our voices out here. Ray said you were in there for about fifteen minutes. What do you think Mike? Can we add some more time from what my estimate was?”

Mike moving his legs up and down, one at a time, like John had done previously, winced a little in his face, showing that he was in some pain,

“I know. I heard that loud voice of yours when you yelled, Attention. Figured it was an officer in the area but I didn't know it was our platoon leader until I heard his voice. Yes, I think we can add a few more minutes. Maybe thirty minutes. I agree with you, we will have to be quick to go once they are inside. Everything else on my body is fine except for my legs. If the compartment was wider, then we wouldn't really have a problem.”

The three of them were satisfied and all agreed that this was to be the mode of escape. They had other details to talk about in order for the plan to come together with perfection. John began with his suggestion,

"Mike if you are okay to walk then let's go up to my room and discuss how we are going to get some other things accomplished.

Ray locked up the "White VW Freedom Van", then the three soldiers walked up to Bolden's room. Upon entering the room and closing the door behind them, Ray was the first one to speak,

"Do you two have other plans made out yet, as in..., how are we going to get them inside of the compartment without drawing any suspicion from anyone, including all of the cameras along Alexanderplatz?"

John was next to bring forth his ideas,

"Ever since I talked to Mike about this, waking me up from a deep sleep, this is all I can think about. Ray I notice that when you park the van over there, you park it in a somewhat desolate area. At night it is dimly lit and I've always seen that the nearest camera has a good distance between us."

Ray with a smile on his face said,

"Yes, I do and I do that for a reason. You're very observant!"

John smiled back at him and said,

"Yes, I can be. This is just something that I noticed. If the two of you can keep the other girls busy, then I will take Jackie out for a walk again. This shouldn't be too suspicious since we've done this before, the last time I was over there. Once I get her outside I will take her to the van and explain everything to her and see if she is agreeable with everything. If she is, then I will help her into the hiding spot, then come up and get you two. If you see me without her, then you know it is time to go, and you have to hurry, we all know this now.

Mike curiously asking, in a somewhat sarcastic tone,

"The girls are going to want to know where Jackie is. How are you going to explain that?"

"That's easy Mike. I'll have Jackie slap me and I will have her slap me hard enough to leave some red marks. You know, as if, I made a move on her she didn't care for. They will know it is real enough, so that, they will not question it. The time frame with that will fit perfectly. I've known Jackie for a short time to know her, but not know her that well. So..., to make an advance toward her that she is not agreeable with, will work fine.

Mike being concerned about Jackie asked,

"What are you going to tell her? She will most likely want to call her Mom and Dad. She may want to go get some extra clothes and other things. Are you going to tell her about the plan before doing it?"

John being hard, stern, and with a serious tone to his voice answered Mike's question,

"No, Mike, she will not have the luxury of doing all that. I won't tell her anything until the exact time comes. I will tell her we have a plan, when we are at the disco, and if she is agreeable to it, then she will not leave my side for any reason. If she has to go to the bathroom, then I will go with her. If I lose sight of her at anytime, after I tell her we have a plan, while in the disco, then I will abort it! If I feel we have been compromised at any time, then we will not go through with it. There are many things we have to consider here. No one but the four of us, especially us three, are to know of what we plan on doing!?

Ray stepped in with his comments,

"John is right, Mike. We have to take into consideration that we may get shot dead doing this. That would be the easy part. If we get caught doing this in the East then the East Germans could say we were kidnapping her. This is an international incident, you know. We are going to have to take every precaution necessary to assure success. We have to be prepared for the worst but hope for the best. It is possible that we could be giving up our freedom to give someone their freedom. This is going to be a serious incident, even here, in the West. They are going to want to know how Jackie, Jacqueline, and her son, got here. They are going to push them, interrogate them, to get an answer that they will be satisfied with. Hopefully, Jackie and Jacqueline will be able to come up with a good story that is believable to them. Are all of us willing to go through with this? I know I am!

Mike and John assured Ray that they knew the possible consequences, if they were to be caught on either side, Mike spoke first,

"I'm in love with Jacqueline! I will marry her when we get her and her son over here. I am ready and willing to do this!"

John was next to speak,

"That's what being a soldier in the United States Military is about Ray. We defend our right to be free and we defend those that wish to be free. There are many other soldiers that have given the ultimate sacrifice for this. I wish to do this for Jackie. She has given me so much to look at within my life. She has defined my purpose for being here and being an American soldier. You both know she is different than any other person we have met over there. She has the strength to oppose and rise above the tyranny and oppression she is living there in East Berlin. She hates the East German Government with a passion. She doesn't belong there, with her free spirit, and you guys know this. That's why I am ready and willing to do this for her!"

Ray being satisfied with John and Mike's answer, started to chuckle, this little laugh that was coming from him, was one of healing, as the tension was being released from his shoulders, he was more comfortable with the situation than ever before,

"Bolden, you know, you are an over-achiever, don't you? You didn't have to go through all of that. All you had to say was, "I'm In", and I would have been happy with that."

Bolden looked at Ray and said,

"I've been told that before. Let's get back to planning. We have a lot of things to discuss."

Mike came in with more concerned questions about Jackie,

"When we get her over here, where are we going to take her? Do we have any money to get her a hotel room until Monday where she can turn herself in to the proper authorities? Are we able to bring her some food and something to drink? I send some money home to my

Mom every month in an allotment that comes out of my check. What I have left over is very little. I will do what I can.

John was concerned with those issues as well and said,

"Yes, I know. I have thought about those things to. Like you Mike, I send some money to my Mother back home in the States. It is an allotment that comes out of my check at the beginning of the month. I will try to save up as much as I can to help out with this.

With John and Mike looking at Ray, he was quick to add his comments,

"Don't know what to tell you there, men. My wife handles all of the finances for the household. I don't even see my paycheck when it comes in. When the time comes, I will see what I can do though. You two should know this, I heard, that when an East German escapes into the West, The West Germans provide them with a place to live, a job, a car, and $5,000 West Marks to start a new life. Jackie will be fine when she gets here, the West Germans will take care of her. We have to make sure she will be okay until that happens."

John and Mike already knew of the story Ray had just told them. They've heard it before from others. They did not know if it was true or not, however, they were hopeful that, that was the case. John, being a bit comical, said,

"Well one thing is for sure, we can't bring her back to the barracks. Without an I.D., they won't let her through the gate, let alone, allowing her to stay in one of our rooms."

Mike had a light bulb turned on in his head, as his eyes widened, he expressed with excitement,

“I've got it! The Ku'dorf is open twenty four hours. Jackie is always talking about wanting to go to the Ku'dorf and seeing it. One of us can stay with her at all times until Monday comes along for her, to turn herself in to the proper authorities. When I say us, I mean Johnny and I. Ray, I don't think you will be able to do that, being married and all.”

The three soldiers were in agreement with everything that was being brought up with the plan. There were more remaining questions that had to be answered, John being curious asked Ray,

“When it comes time to go through the checkpoints, how good are you at maneuvering around those concrete barriers? I know you do it well going slow when we come across, but if they try to stop us on the East side for any reason, how fast do you think you can get around them? We won't have any weapons on us to fire back if we get fired upon. So..., in all actuality, we will have to take the flight, in the fight or flight situation.”

Ray being confident with his answer said,

“I don't think we will have any problems with the East German Border Guards on the East side. They are not supposed to detain us for any reason. However, I thought about this before. If that situation arises, be assured, that I can maneuver around those concrete barriers quickly. We might bounce back and forth up against them but I will get us through them. If this should happen, we are not stopping for anybody, not even the Military Police at Checkpoint Charlie. You guard Jackie as much as possible. That's your job, John! Mike and I will get us through both checkpoints.”

John accepted the position of being the guardian for Jackie through the time of the escape. With his shoulders lifted up and his chest held high, he said,

"I will do whatever it takes to get Jackie over here and I will do the same for Jacqueline and her son, Mike. The both of you can count on me for this!" I think we all know what we should do if we should get caught on the East Side. What do you think we should do if we get caught on the West side? Anyone have any suggestions?"

Mike began with his suggestions,

"When the time comes, ask Jackie if she has any ideas for that. I would say, that they could say, a friend from the West brought them over and they wish to keep their identity safe. There isn't much that we can tell them what to say. They are going to have to come up with something on their own. We don't know how the four powers are going to interrogate them or how far they are going to push them. In my opinion, I don't think they are going to ask them too many questions on how they got over here. They'll just be happy they are here." If they catch us on this side of the wall, they'll think of us as heroes and won't push it too far. I think we will be okay on this side. They will want to keep it quiet. They won't want to stir up a hornet's nest."

John was next with his suggestions,

"That is very possible Mike. They are going to want to know names though. Yes, I agree with you. Jackie and Jacqueline are going to have to come up with an explanation on their own and hopefully it will be good enough to pass them. They might treat us as heroes if they find out it was us that helped them. That will be a desirable thing for us but being practical about this, I'm not sure if that will happen. I agree with you that they will want to keep this quiet, as much as possible. What do you think Ray?"

"I'm listening to the both of you and with what you are saying, there isn't going to be much of an explanation that Jackie or Jacqueline will be able to come up with, unless they have a great imagination, we are going to have to come up with something on our own in order to save our asses here in the West. Jackie and Jacqueline will be fine here, no matter what they tell them, of how they got here. The four powers are not going to send them back to the East. Once they are here, they will stay here. I've come up with something and I hope the both of you will agree to it. Once they have turned themselves in to the Western Powers, should our names come up with anything, then we will have to say that they did it all on their own. We had no idea they were hiding in the van until it was too late. All of us were surprised to see them in the van once we crossed back over into West Berlin. John felt something move under his seat but thought the muffler was falling off from under the van. He didn't know there was an empty space under the backseat until he heard someone cry out to let them out. I had forgotten to lock the van up, leaving it unsecured, while we were in the disco, therefore creating the possibility for someone to hide themselves under the back seat. When we discovered them in the hiding place, we didn't know what to do, then let them out of the van, so they could find a place to turn themselves in to the proper authorities. If we get caught doing this in the West, gentlemen, do not kid yourself here, we will not go unscathed here. At least, with this story, we were not active participants in the escape. This will lessen the punishment on our end. No disrespect meant toward Jackie or Jacqueline, but we must keep our best interest in mind also. I agree with both of you. We do not know how their interrogation will be on them, or as far as that goes, how it will be on us. If we all agree to this story, and stick to it, they will go very lightly on us. I agree also, they will want to keep this as quiet as possible. Are we in agreement with this story?"

John and Mike readily agreed with Ray's story and swore to stick with it, should that scenario come to be. They went on to other matters that were of concern and as they talked the time flew by. Ray looking at his watch, said,

"I've got to get going. Barbara should have dinner ready soon, that is, if she hasn't finished it already. I think we have a great plan here. I'm sure we will have other questions come up in the future. We can discuss those at another time. Do we know when we are going to do this? Do you guys have a date in mind yet?"

Bolden was getting hungry to and was ready to head downstairs to the mess hall to get something to eat. Answering Ray's question, he says,

"No, I don't have a date for this to happen yet. I don't want to go back over to the East again until I have something to give to Jackie. The less she knows about this, the better she will be, and the better we will be. I know Jackie wants to come over, but Mike and I don't know yet if Jacqueline is ready."

Mike bursts in with his comment,

“She will come over. I haven't said anything to her at all, but I know she loves me too. I know she will want to come to the West!”

Ray was getting antsy,

“All right, I've got to go. You guys pick a date and I will be there. I will have to be there. I've got “The Freedom Van!”

The three men shook each others hands. It was their bond between them. Each of them carried the trust from one individual onto the next, uniting them as one being. The will, each one possessed, was now intensified threefold, bringing with it, a strong possibility of success to their ideas and beliefs. Mike and John bid Ray to have a great evening, as they both expressed it was getting close to the time that the mess hall would be closing soon. They walked with Ray down the stairs until it was time to separate and descend down the steps to the mess hall. John and Mike were quiet during their meal and had decided to have the rest of the evening to themselves, to rest and relax, after a long hard day of thinking. They were satisfied with the days activities and were confident that more of the escape plan would unfold with ease. Times come and times go, there is no time to think of the past as those events have faded away. There is only time now to envision a future, created by the imagination, to bring forth the power of their wills combined. The three powers of energy, when joined together, created from the ethereal mist, what is to be manifested upon the earthly plane. All three of them hoping for their wishes to be granted.

34
GENESIS

Tuesday morning, August 5th, 1986, the mortar platoon of CSC 6th/502nd Infantry Battalion is given a secret order by their platoon sergeant, SFC Horton. They are informed that Specialist 4th Class Copsovic is graduating from his Genesis Class and the secret order is, for the whole platoon to attend his graduation. Copsovic was sent on a special duty assignment so that he would not know that his platoon would be there to see him graduate. This was to be a special occasion for this man. The platoon sergeant had decided that Copsovic would have the backing of the men he worked with and it would be a surprise for him. Every one was happy with the order as it was a special event for a member of their platoon, not only that, it was a chance to, let's say, get off of duty, sooner than, what was to be the expected normal situation. “Genesis”, was the equivalent to “Alcoholic's Anonymous”, in the civilian world. Bolden could only figure out, that the new name, for such an event, given the definition of the word, was to mean, “A New Beginning”, “A Rebirth”, into a new and different life than what a person had lived through. In other words, with new knowledge granted upon that individual person, they have become learned in a new lifestyle, a new way to live, to advance them forward into a better life. Bolden could see the progress that Copsovic had made and was very proud of him, though given the circumstances, that was presented between the both of them, during the Mortex in Wildflecken, Bolden was not about to back away, from what he had expressed to him, the day, they won the Shoot-Off. Bolden was, none the less, happy to be a part of Copsovic's new life. Copsovic had shown commitment and dedication to what he had learned about the effects of alcohol, upon the body and upon the mental health of those that drank alcohol in excess. He was now becoming a "Mentor" for others, a leader, to help others, into a better way of thinking about themselves to create a better life for all that were around him. The mortar platoon went about their duties for the day at the motor pool, when it was time they closed everything up and headed for the assembly area. The building where the "Genesis" was to take place was in marching distance from McNair Barracks. The mortar platoon of CSC 6th of the 502nd Infantry marched proudly that day. When they entered the building, then into the room, where the event was being held, members of the "Genesis Group" had to find more chairs to accommodate the mortar platoon. The event began with a prayer, then afterwards the members of the graduating class, one by one, stood up at the podium and told their stories. Each one beginning with, "Hi, my name is …., and I'm an alcoholic." The group would respond back saying, "Hi, ...", after the fourth one, came a beautiful young woman, her age of around thirty. She stood up at the podium and said,

"Hello, My name is Jane and I am an alcoholic."

Everyone in the group responded back,

"Hi, Jane!"

Jane continued on with her story, talking about how she felt insecure about herself and the only way she could be secure with herself was to find someone that would accept her, even if it was for only one night then she would be happy with herself, only to discover that when she woke up the next day, that she was with a total stranger she didn't even know.

Bolden was sitting next to John Donadio. Now, Don a dee o, being his comical self, quietly said to Bolden,

“Hey, she's pretty fricking hot! Where was I when she was doing this?”

Bolden couldn't help but give a chuckle to his comment, from the way Donadio had said it. In all essence, Bolden was thinking the same thing, but he could relate to Jane about her story and was feeling very compassionate toward her. With the movement from his elbow, Bolden slightly nudge Donadio in his arm and whispered back,

“Hey, cut that non-sense out! She's serious, man! Can't you see she has regrets about doing those things. Think about this, she's an American civilian, which means she's married, and she is married to an American soldier. If her husband is still with her, and I am sure he is, then I know he is in this crowd, can you imagine what he is going through right now? We should give both of them respect for being able to carry on John!”

Donadio didn't say a word about what Bolden had expressed to him. He pushed himself upward in his chair and began to listen to what Jane had to say. After Jane was finished it was Copsovic's turn at the podium, he began his story,

“Hi, my name is Tim and I'm an alcoholic.”

The response was unanimous as the mortar platoon yelled,

“Hi, Tim!”

He was surprised to see the whole mortar platoon there, which gave to him a glow in his aura and a big smile on his face. He paused for a moment, took a deep breath in, looking at the sheet of paper in front of him, tossed it to the side, and began with his story,

"Worthiness?!, this is what I wish to talk about while I am up here. The reason why I am here, speaking to you today, is because of this question. I was a driver for our Battalion Colonel. This isn't the only reason why I am here. It is a small part, that is very important, that I wish to express to you. I held an important duty, it was so important, that I failed to see the cause/purpose of this duty. My job was to be on call twenty four hours a day, seven days a week. I was to make sure that my leader, our leader, was to be able to make his appointment times, on time. I felt that I was unworthy of this position because I was thinking of how others thought about me in this position. They thought, is what I was thinking at the time, that I had a cushy assignment, driving the Colonel to Balls and fancy engagements. How was I worthy, to the men of my platoon, to have this position? This was my thought. I drank alcohol heavily to cover up my insecurities with this. So much, in fact, that I failed to pick up the Colonel, to make his appointments on time. True, I drove him to officer's balls and parties, but I also drove him to many, and I mean many, important meetings. I did not give any value to these important meetings that the Colonel was supposed to attend, only that I had to drive him there. I felt like, I was a warrior without a battle, and when you think this, you feel a warrior has no value unless he has a battle to fight. I was fighting a battle against myself to give me a false value.

My pride got in the way of my worthiness. The Colonel saw this, where as I did not, and he fired me as his driver. Blaming the Colonel, for my problems, I proceeded to drink heavily. I found his jeep and with my hatred, I damaged his vehicle. I was forced to come here and take assessment of my life, which has come to be the best thing that ever happened to me. The Colonel saw more potential in me than I did. For this, I am very grateful to him. The mortar platoon, that I am assigned to, are all here today, to see me graduate. They see more potential in me. I am grateful to them as well. With my faith and continued support from everyone here, I feel positive, that my prayers will be answered, to see the potential value of everything that I do. From here on forward, all things great and small, shall be given importance, for I know now that everything that we do, holds a purpose in life. Those things that we do not know at the time are given clearer definition later in to our future, where clarity is given, as if, a bright light bulb has been turned on and the knowing of such purpose brings with it a new life, a new beginning, a genesis! As I look around me, I see myself, not as an individual anymore, but as part of a team. All of us combined together to accomplish similar goals. This is the new light that I see in my life and I see it shining brightly to bring forth a greater future for us all!"

As Copsovic began to exit the podium, from where he was speaking, applause filled the room. One by one the audience rose to their feet to give a standing ovation from what they had just heard. The CSC 6/502nd Mortar Platoon began hooping and hollering, with dog howls following after. The dog howl was representative of the alpha male dog, whom is the leader of his pack. The leader who makes all the decisions. To a soldier, it is a great honor to hear the sound, for it notes worthiness among his peers. Copsovic was feeling that honor, while shaking hands with his attentive audience, as he walked up the aisle to greet his platoon members. Coffee and sweets were available for the small party that was being held in the lobby area. Within an hour the commencements were finished and the mortar platoon began their formation for the march back to McNair Barracks. Copsovic, calling the cadence, loud and proud, keeping the rhythm of the march. When the mortar platoon arrived back at the parking lot of CSC 6/502nd Infantry Battalion, they were being dismissed for the day, except for the chosen few who were called out to perform flag detail. SFC Horton called out the names,

"Bolden, Broadway, Tate, Donadio, Long, and Gonzalez... You're all on "Flag Detail!" Get upstairs and change in to your best pressed B.D.U.s. Pick up your helmets, white gloves, and white belts at the CQ Desk. Sergeant Green will be your NCOIC of this detail. You will meet him at the CQ Desk at 1630 hours. MAKE SURE YOUR BOOTS ARE SHINED!!!"

In unison, all of the names that were called out, yelled back,

"YES, SERGEANT!"

They scrambled up the stairs and ran to their rooms. There wasn't much time available to be ready for "Flag Detail". This was a detail that came with much honor and considered a privilege to be called upon to do this. "Flag Detail" was a simple task but a heavy discipline of silence came with it and it was strictly adhered to. The detail was to march to where the flag was at, being centered in the middle of the post, where it flew proudly in the wind, during the work day. At the end of the work day, being at 1700 hours, "RETREAT" is played, for it notes, to turn back and rest, in order to regroup and prepare for the next day's affairs, it is also a symbol of "Respect" for those who gave the ultimate "Sacrifice" for defending our "Freedom", and as the music is playing, the detail slowly lowers the flag, with each member taking their position, grabbing the flag, ensuring that it does not touch the ground. Once all members of the detail have the flag in hand they begin to fold the flag in a triangle formation. When the flag is folded properly, making sure no red is visible, for red represents the blood of all veterans that was spilled upon a battle field, then all that is visible is the blue portion of the flag, with the white stars in perfect formation. The flag is then handed to the NCOIC, before taking the flag, the NCOIC salutes the flag, then after receiving the flag, the flag detail, march with the flag , to it's resting place, for the evening, which was located in the museum at McNair Barracks, where it is highly secured. The "Flag Detail" assembled in the parking lot of CSC 6/502nd Infantry Battalion, then began their march to the flag pole. Looking sharp and proud, soldiers and civilians cleared the way for them. Sergeant Green leading the detail with Specialist Tate and Specialist Donadio being in the forefront of the detail. Specialist Bolden and Specialist Broadway being in the middle. Specialist Gonzalez and Specialist Long at the tail end. Upon arrival to the flag pole, Sergeant Green takes his position to the right of the flag pole. He comes to the position of "Attention" and gives his order for Specialist Tate and Specialist Donadio to take their position along side of the flag pole. Specialist Donadio was assigned to handle the lanyard, on the left side, to lower the flag. Specialist Tate was assigned to the right side of the flag pole to grip the the flag as it came within his grasp and then disperse it to the other members of the detail to prepare the flag for proper folding. When Specialist Donadio and Specialist Tate were in position, Sergeant Green gave the order of,

"PARADE REST!"

Each member of the "Flag Detail" came to the position of "Parade Rest". As the seconds ticked away, the "Flag Detail" gave their moment of "Respect" with "Silence", staring into the air with only their thoughts, showing silence and gratitude for having the honor of the duty that they had been chosen to perform. With only a couple minutes left before the ceremony was to commence, Specialist Donadio, being his comical self, stated in a comical tone, above a whisper, that only the "Flag Detail" could hear, stated,

"Hi, My name is John and I'm on flag detail."

With those words being expressed with such free expression, the members of the "Flag Detail" looked at Specialist Donadio with serious eyes of discontent upon his verbal expression. His demeanor, was such, that the detail could not contain their discipline of silence. As Specialist Donadio kept his air of sophistication for the order of "Parade Rest", the others could not. The serious eyes for the rest of the "Flag Detail" changed to silent chuckles as they knew what Specialist Donadio was referring to. All of a sudden a familiar voice is heard in the air that came from behind them,

"SILENCE!!!, YOU MEN REMAIN AT THE POSITION OF PARADE REST! MAINTAIN YOUR DISCIPLINE AND SHOW RESPECT!"

The harsh order was coming from their platoon leader, Lieutenant Pillow, who was, once again, the O.I.C, for the day. With the way the order was given and the reminder of what the men were there for, the silence was adhered to! A few seconds later the boom from the cannon, being fired, and the first note from the tune of "RETREAT" began ringing out in to the sky. The order from Sergeant Green is given,

"DETAIL, ATTENTION!!!"

The "Flag Detail" immediately followed the order and as "RETREAT" was being played, Specialist Donadio, slowly began lowering the flag as Specialist Tate prepared for the flags appearance. The "Flag Detail" performed their duty with outstanding performance and secured the flag within the museum, where it was to rest for the night. After the ceremony was complete, Specialist Donadio received the feedback from his previous comments. Sergeant Green began with his disciplinary action,

"Donadio, you are going to be lucky if the LT., doesn't write you up for that comment you made. You better make amends with him later and by that, I mean, you better apologize to him for that!"

Specialist Bolden began with his comments,

"That was good John, really good! I got the humor of it. Know, that I am hoping for the best for you!"

Specialist Broadway came in with his,

“Don A Dee O! Have to tell you, that was right on time, but..., well I don't have to explain it to you. GOOD LUCK!!!”

Specialist Long was next, with his southern drawl accent,

“John, One for all and all for one, but I have a feeling you're going to be alone on this one buddy. You'll be okay. The LT., does, have a sense of humor, I think?”

Specialist Gonzalez shook his head and with a smile waved at Specialist Donadio as in saying,

“Good Luck With That Mon!”

Specialist Donadio, looking a little dumbfounded and with a smile on his face, said,

“Oh, come on now! I was just trying to lighten up the situation a bit. I didn't mean any harm or disrespect. You guys know that!”

The men of the “Flag Detail” knew what Specialist Donadio was trying to express to them, but they also knew, the importance of the symbolism, from the duty they had previously performed, had meaning and definition to so many, past and present. There was no harm intended from Specialist Donadio but strict discipline had to be maintained in order for a successful mission to be accomplished. This is the code that all American Military Soldiers must follow in order for chaos to be restrained in to order. This was a lesson to be learned from a couple members of that “Flag Detail”, who thought they were exempt from such discipline. It is a lesson in life that will stay with them for the rest of their life!

35

FIRST ATTEMPT

Saturday, August 9th, 1986. The plan was in motion with everything agreed upon. The only one left to give their acceptance of the plan, was Jackie. The East Berlin passes had already been approved for Bolden, Williams, and Broadway. Their motivation and dedication was set high for the task that they had planned and nothing was to get in their way. Specialist Bolden placed his Class B uniform on, making sure everything was in proper placement and that his shoes and brass were highly shined. This was to be a special occasion. Approaching close to 1900 hours, he was anxious to get moving forward. A knock on the door, with it's continuing rapping movement, indicated Specialist Broadway's signature at the door. Bolden opened the door then proceeded to step out. Broadway blocking his way, slowly moved Bolden back in to his room with his body, then closed the door behind him. Bolden being surprised looked at Broadway with wonderment in his eyes then said,

"Okay Michael. What's going on?"

Broadway with a disappointed look in his eyes, responded back immediately,

"We have a problem! You're not going to like it!"

Specialist Bolden placed his shoulders down then prepared to listen to what Specialist Broadway had to tell him. Bolden didn't ask what was going on. He looked at Broadway with concerned eyes. Broadway went forward with his explanation,

“Copsovic is going with us. He's ready and waiting downstairs in the parking lot for us. Are you going to be okay with this?”

Bolden erupted in a fit of anger with his response,

“MIKE!!! YOU KNOW TONIGHT IS THE NIGHT!!! WHY DID YOU INVITE HIM TO COME WITH US? DON'T TELL ME YOU DIDN'T KNOW ABOUT THIS BEFOREHAND. I KNOW YOU TWO ARE KIND OF TIGHT!!! YOU SHOULD HAVE TOLD ME EARLIER WHAT WAS GOING ON!!! YOU KNOW I WASN'T GOING BACK TO EAST BERLIN UNLESS I HAD SOMETHING TO GIVE TO JACKIE ABOUT BRINGING HER OVER HERE TO WEST BERLIN!!!”

Specialist Broadway looking down at the floor and with regret in his eye's, responded,

“Johnny, I didn't know he was coming with us. I just found out. He put his East Pass in a few hours ago and well he's still pretty tight with the Colonel, so the Colonel signed his pass right away. John it's not my fault. I can't tell him No, he cant come with us. That would bring more suspicion. We are just going to have to either abandon the plan for tonight and try again next weekend or figure out something to go ahead with tonight's plans. I don't know what to do or what to tell you. Ray doesn't even know about this yet!”

Bolden, being persistent, to move forward with their plan, expressed with a harsh tone,

“I don't care what you have to do Mike but you avert Copsovic's attention away from what we are about to do. I plan on moving ahead with this! We have planned too hard and too long for this moment and he is not going to mess it up! He's feeling righteous, right now, and with good cause. We can not include him in our plan! He will screw it up for sure! You make sure you have his full, undivided attention and I will do what I have to, to complete this task! Are you hearing me? Do you got that!?"

Broadway, looking away from Bolden, said,

"Johnny, he's got a thing for Jackie. I know that's why he is going over there. He is going to show her how different he is now. I don't think, I'm going to be able to take his attention away from her. Those two have history together Johnny! I will do what I can do but I am telling you, right now, how it is going to go!"

Bolden without losing hope, expressed his opinion,

"Okay Michael, let's just go with the flow and see how things will go. I will kind of let Jackie know what we have in mind but I won't tell her the full details. I want this to happen tonight Mike! I really do, but I am not going to jeopardize our safety over this! Ray is going to figure it out, once he sees Tim, and us, standing there, waiting for him. He is intelligent. He will figure it out without either one of us saying anything to him. Let's get going!"

Bolden and Broadway exited the room then proceeded down the hallway, to the stairs, then arrived in the parking lot, where Copsovic was awaiting them. He looked at Bolden and said,

"Hope you don't mind me going with you tonight. It was a last minute decision on my part. I'm looking forward to seeing Jackie and the other girls. Haven't seen them in awhile and would actually like to get reacquainted with them."

Bolden disguising his disappointment, said with a little bit of enthusiasm,

"Oh, heck no Tim! Glad you are coming with us. It will give you a new change from what you've been going through. Mike just told me you were going with. I was surprised but a good surprised."

Copsovic looked relieved from what Bolden had expressed to him. In a few minutes Ray pulled up with his White VW Van, ready to pick up his colleagues. Bolden and Broadway saw the gleaming smile that Williams had, diminish, upon seeing Copsovic standing with them. All of their eyes met with concern, even Copsovics. Mike took his position on the front passenger side. Bolden opened the back door to let Copsovic in first. As they took their seating in the back seat, Copsovic said,

"Ray, I hope you don't mind me going with you guys tonight. It was a last minute decision on my part."

Sergeant Williams had no choice but to accept Copsovic's presence. Ray put the van in gear and headed for the front gate, saying,

"Hey, the more the merrier! I know you and I won't be drinking champagne tonight. Can't speak for Broadway or Bolden though. Hope you can handle those two."

Laughter ensued among them all, however, it was a disguised laughter with everyone. Silence took it's place as they headed for Checkpoint Charlie. After being cleared, Ray drove the van onto Alexander Platz then parked the White VW Van in it's usual discretionary parking spot. All of them exiting the van with Copsovic in the lead. They entered the disco and scanned the room. All of the ladies were there waiting for them, even Jackie. Copsovic immediately went up to her and gave her a big hug. They kissed each other upon their cheeks, excited to be reunited. Jackie looked at John with concern in her eyes. John looking back at her, gave her a wink and a smile, then embraced passionately with a kiss upon the lips. Jackie whispered in to John's ear,

"Do you have a plan? Are we going tonight?"

John whispered back,

"Yes, I have figured something out for us. I don't know if we are going to be able to do this tonight Jackie. You stay by my side where I can keep my eyes on you. If you leave my side for any reason and I don't see you then we will not go through with this. If you have to go to the bathroom then I will escort you there. You will not call anyone. Do you understand what I am saying to you?"

Jackie, with a look that contained a mixture of happiness and sadness together, with confusion, whispered back,

"Yes, I understand."

Jackie and John released their passionate embrace then stepped back to view the table where they were going to be sitting at for the evening. Copsovic was still making his rounds among the ladies. When he was finished getting reacquainted with them he returned back to Jackie and pulled a chair out from under the table, offering her a seat, which she accepted. Copsovic sat down in the chair next to her on her left. Bolden followed suit pulling the chair out from under the table and sitting down on the right side of Jackie. Packs of cigarettes were being placed on the table from Broadway and Bolden. Ray brought his Coca-Cola and offered one to Tim which he accepted. Broadway looking at Bolden said,

“Well, what do you think Johnny? How many bottles of champagne should we order? I'm thinking, we should get five right away and then go from there. What do you think?”

John looked at Mike then said,

“That's fine Mike. I will get the first round. I don't plan on drinking too much tonight but we will see how things go.”

Mike ordered the five bottles of champagne which were brought to the table immediately with the accompaniment of nine glasses. Tim grabbed his glass to give it back to the waitress, saying,

“I don't need this! I don't drink alcohol anymore!”

Ray butted in quickly saying,

“Tim, use the glass for your Coca-Cola. It may be a champagne glass but you can still use it.

Copsovic nodded his head in agreement then placed the champagne glass back down on the table in front of him. The waitress looked at Mike, who then, pointed his finger at John, to indicate who was paying for the champagne. John gave the waitress the appropriate amount plus a good sized tip. Then asked the waitress,

“Verschtain English?”

She responded back,

"Ja, I speak and understand English."

Bolden looked at her and said,

"Please keep an eye on this table. If you see the bottles of champagne empty then bring five more. That guy that ordered the first five bottles is buying the next five."

The waitress understood what John had said to her and said,

"Ja, I will do this."

The evening went forward with the festivities at hand. Copsovic gave all his attention to Jackie. Mike trying to intervene, at intervals, where it seemed appropriate, could not get his attention away from Jackie. Bolden sat quietly next to Jackie as there was nothing he could do to take her away from Copsovic's attention toward her. He began to drink heavily upon the champagne that was available at the table. Jackie saw what John was doing and began to get a worried look upon her face. She to, began to drink more than usual. John picking up a champagne bottle began to fill her glass then his. They "Prosted" each other, clicked their glasses together, then in one swift movement, Bolden downed the alcoholic liquid quickly, which emptied the glass he had just previously filled. Copsovic watching him said,

"Hey John, take it easy man! Is anything wrong? Anything that I can do to help? I hope you are okay! I know you don't drink that much but you are drinking like I used to do. I know You and Jackie are kind of an item. I've heard the stories about you two. We're just talking. I haven't been here in a long time and it is good to talk with her again. She's special. I know you know that!"

Bolden feeling the full effects of the extra alcohol he had been drinking that night knew Copsovic was sincere in what he was expressing to him. Bolden caught on to that when Copsovic called him by his first name, John. He never called him by his first name before. Looking at Copsovic, Bolden, responded back in a calm manner,

“Everything is fine Tim. I'm just going along with the celebration here. You are right, I usually don't drink that much alcohol but it's feeling pretty good to me right now. Jackie and I are good friends and yes, you are right, she is very special and I'm glad you two are catching up on things. It's all good Tim! Hey, I appreciate you asking and your concern for my well being. Enjoy and have a good time. This is what I am going to do.”

Bolden filled his champagne glass back up, along with Jackie's and emptied the bottle. The waitress seeing the empty bottles on the table proceeded to bring five more bottles of champagne over. After placing them on the table she walked over to Mike, who gave her the appropriate amount and a good sized tip then pointed at Bolden saying,

“At the rate Johnny is going on this, he's buying the next round. You might want to take it easy on these Johnny and share some with the rest of us.”

The excessive alcohol Bolden was drinking, kicked in, at that exact moment. With his speech still in full force and without slurring any words, he responded back to Mike in a huff tone of voice,

“Don't you worry about me, Michael! I'm having a great time and feeling good! Matter of fact, if you are worried about how many bottles of champagne are going to be left, then have her bring us five more bottles! I'll pay for it right now so we have that out of the way!"

Broadway responded back with a worried look on his face, said,

"John, I'm not worried about five more bottles of champagne. I'm just looking out after you, making sure you are going to be okay. We will wait on ordering anymore champagne!"

Jackie stepped in with her comment after downing her half glass of champagne that she had left, with a giggle she said,

"Michael, I'm feeling very good now! We better get some more champagne!"

John, after hearing what Jackie had said, filled her glass back up and then his. Both of them raising their glasses and in unison yelled,

"PROST!"

As John and Jackie drank to the toast, Mike with a disgusted, submissive, look on his face, said to the waitress,

"All Right, Damm It! Bring us five more bottles of champagne! Johnny and I are splitting the cost!"

Mandy, Ushi, Babette, Jackie, and John began laughing out loud in agreement with Michael's decision. Jacqueline, Mike's fiance showed a disgusted look on her face, as well as, Ray and Tim. Broadway finishing up his statement, added,

"I might as well join you assholes in the celebration!"

Mike was getting back to his usual sarcastic self and Bolden didn't mind it at all. They both knew that their plan was not going to go through that night. Jackie knew it also, but she still had hope for her freedom. She looked at John and said,

“I have to go to the bathroom. Will you please escort me?”

John picked up on what she was asking and obliged her query. Standing up from his chair he placed his elbow out which Jackie accepted. They both excused themselves from the table, then proceeded to walk toward the exit of the disco toward the bathrooms, that were located out in the hallway, before descending down the stairs to the exit. Bolden began to think, that this, was now the moment, to make his move and take her down to the van, and explain the plan to her. When they were away from hearing distance of the table, Jackie whispered in to John's ear,

“Are we going to do this tonight or not?”

John, being reluctant to answer her, said,

“I don't know Jackie. It is going to be very risky at this point. As much as I would love to, I have to tell you, it might not happen tonight. Let's see how things go tonight and go from there, okay?”

Jackie nodded her head in agreement. They arrive at the ladies W.C. (Wash Closet), where she released John's escorting elbow, then entered the room to do her personal business. John stood outside the open entry way keeping his eye on the pay phone that was clearly visible from his sight. A few moments later Jackie appeared. John escorted her back to the table where the group's festivities were in full force. Looking at the table, John could see the five, newly arrived, fresh bottles of champagne sitting among the other bottles. The sweat on the outside of the bottles glistened in the dimmed lighting of the disco. John looked at Mike and said,

"How much do I owe you?"

Broadway, looking at John with a smile and a bit of discontent, said,

"Don't worry about it! We will settle up later!"

John shrugged his shoulders and said,

"Whatever, Mike! You just enjoy the evening! I will make it right with you! You know that!"

Broadway knew that Bolden would square things away with him on the monetary situation, but he also knew, the plan wasn't going to go through for the evening. He had a worried look on his face, then began to drink more champagne, hoping, like Bolden and Williams, were doing, that their plan would progress on another date, without their plan being discovered by anyone. The air of celebration was being felt more freely as Mandy came over and sat on John's lap, whom was being more quiet than usual. Upon sitting on his lap, she gripped John, with her left hand, by his lower chin and on both cheeks, then gave him a long passionate french kiss. John accepted the invitation, though a little bit reluctant about it, he began to enjoy such passion being given by Mandy. It didn't take long for Jackie to notice what Mandy was doing, as she nudged Mandy in her ribs, with a striking force from her elbow. Mandy instantly released her passionate embraced, from John, as harsh words of

German descent were exchanged between them. Mandy stood up from John's lap and as she did so, Jackie replaced Mandy's position, then proceeded to give John her passionate french kisses. Bolden was not reluctant to receive such goodness, as he immediately accepted Jackie's feelings of emotion toward him. The air around them filled with a glow of light, that was felt by everyone that was around them. Copsovic noticed the glow, then looked at his watch, stating,

“Ray, it is getting close to get back over to West Berlin. If we are going to be on time with our curfew, then we better leave now.”

Sergeant Williams was in total agreement with Copsovic, then made his intentions heard to Bolden and Broadway,

“ALL ABOARD THAT'S GOING ABOARD! WE'VE GOT TO HEAD OUT!”

Bolden was way to drunk to keep track of the time, neither was Broadway, with keeping in tune with the time frame, so they were relying upon their leader, Sergeant Williams, to let them know when it was time to go. All of them knew, including Jackie, that tonight, would not be their night, for their dreams to come true. Neither one could find solace with what was happening that night. They had to play the part and hope for a better future, enabling them to progress with their plan of freedom. Looking at the table, everyone could see there were three full bottles of champagne left on the table. There was nothing to worry about as Mandy, Ushi, and Babette grabbed each bottle, off of the table, then prepared to exit the disco, waiting for the others to follow suit. Jackie and John stood up from the table. John placed his right elbow out for escorting Jackie, which she accepted. They led the way out of the disco, then down the steps in to the Alexander Platz Market Area. Their walk was interrupted with a couple of stumbles from each one of them, laughing through their mistakes of accepted etiquette. Everyone arrived at the White VW VAN at the same moment, with each of them waiting for Ray to unlock the van so they could gain entryway. Ray took his position as driver. Mike and Jacqueline took their position on the front passenger side, as usual. John entered in to the back seat with Jackie immediately following after him. He sat down, then Jackie took her place upon his lap. They proceeded with their passionate french kissing as Copsovic followed in after them, then Ushi sitting upon Copsovic's lap, Mandy was next to fill up the back seat. Laughing and speaking in German she offered Babette a place on her lap, with both of them embracing in a passionate french kiss, laughing hysterically afterward, they close the back door behind them. Ray placed the White VW Van in to gear and headed for their private secluded area, just before the checkpoint, to let the ladies out. He parked the White VW Van and ordered the women out of the van. Time was close to their check in time and it was no time to be playing around with it. Mandy and Babette exited quickly, as they threw the back door open. Tim quickly threw Ushi off of his lap and on to the street. Mike and Jacqueline were still kissing with a passionate embrace, so were John and Jackie. Copsovic began speaking in a harsh tone,

"All right you guys, let your women go. We have to get across Checkpoint Charlie."

His words went unheeded, with his knowing of such things, he grabbed Jackie by her waist and pried her from John's embrace, tossing her out of the van, saying in a rough tone of voice,

“THAT'S IT! WE'VE GOT TO GO! MIKE GET JACQUELINE OUT OF THE VAN AND LET'S GO!”

The excessive alcohol John had drank, that evening, was in full force, as he was beginning to feel dizzy. His vision was doubled coming in and out of focus. He could taste the saltiness of his saliva. He knew what would be coming soon after that. The muscles of his body were becoming weak and were slow to respond to his thoughts of movement for his arms and legs. He slouched down in the back seat waiting for Ray to put the van in gear and go. From the right side of him came a flash of vision. It was Jackie. With desperation, she rushed by Copsovic, moving him, pushing him, out of her way. She threw herself on John's lap giving him a big hug and a passionate kiss. John's lips could not respond properly to her passionate kissing. He was way too drunk and he knew it. Jackie leaning into him with her lips approaching his left ear, pleading desperately to John in a whisper,

“Take me with you! Please, take me with you!”

John was heart broken to hear her pleading words, for he knew, there was nothing he could do for her at that time. He whispered back into her ear,

“I can't take you with me right now Jackie! You have to go! You have to get out of the van!”

The secret conversation lasted only a few seconds between them for they felt the swift harsh movement from Copsovic grabbing Jackie around her waist, once again, throwing her out of the van, this time, with so much force, she flew through the air. When she landed on the cement sidewalk, next to the White VW Van, her body rolled with the swift movement. She quickly gained her composure. As she began to stand up, Copsovic closed, then locked the back door, saying,

"What the heck is up with her? She knows we have to go!"

Ray quickly put the white VW Van into gear and proceeded down the road to Checkpoint Charlie. John sitting up in the back seat. Looking back at Jackie, he saw the tears streaming down her face with the sadness that accompanied them. John's vision was still focusing in and out but he could see clearly what tonight's event had brought forward. He looked at the other ladies that were standing close to Jackie consoling her, then he looked at what was coming up behind the women. The familiar bright green and grayish green uniform, of an East German Border Guard, was slowly coming up behind the women, they were unaware of his approach. John could see this soldier had a slight smile on his face and hoped that the women would be okay. John thought the soldier was possibly on his way to report to duty and hoped he would leave the women alone. The White VW Van quickly gained distance away from the women as John kept looking at Jackie hoping she would be okay. The possibility of the women being hauled in for questioning to the Stasi was very strong after what just happened so close to the Checkpoints. The cameras had to have been focused on all of them, as it, was a far more unusually bizarre event, from their other departures. Ray turned the corner and with that, Jackie was gone from John's vision. He moved his eyes forward to look out of the windshield to see where they were at. Ray began the curvy maneuvers through the concrete barriers and then onto Checkpoint Charlie where they stopped to check in with the Military Police. Ray was being apologetic to the NCOIC of Checkpoint Charlie,

“Apologies there Sergeant. We know it is getting close to midnight.”

The NCOIC of Checkpoint Charlie was in a carefree state for the moment. He looked in the van and saw Specialist Bolden with his head down in the back seat indicating his overindulgence of alcohol. He looked at Sergeant Williams and said,

“Nothing to worry about there sergeant. You've got another ten minutes. By the looks of him in the backseat, you better get him back to the barracks right away before doing anything else tonight. Welcome Back! Have a good evening!”

Sergeant Williams nodded his head in agreement then placed the white VW Van into gear then slowly proceeded down the road. Bolden in the backseat with his eyes closed could taste the saltiness of his saliva coming through again. He knew this time he wasn't going to make it back to the barracks to calm his senses. He opened his eyes trying to focus them. The double vision was going in and out with a bit more frequency than usual. He picked himself up, climbed over Copsovic, pushing him out of the way to get to the back door handle to open it, so he could, “woof his cookies”, as his best friend, Jim Conant, from Wisconsin, had used this expression to others, back in the day of their youthful follies. Bolden slurred his words, saying to Ray,

“Stop the van! I have to throw up!”

Ray calmly stated back,

“I'm not stopping the van! You do what you got to do! I'm getting you guys back to the barracks then I'm going home. That's what you get for drinking so much. We told you to watch what you were doing. You're a grown man. Maybe next time you'll listen to us!”

Bolden, without hesitation, answered back,

“All right! You keep the van moving. I'll do what I got to do!

At the end of his words, Bolden grabbed the handle of the back door then opened it up. Looking down he could see the pavement below him moving quickly. He looked up to see a few prostitutes standing along the wall of a building on Potsdamer Strasse. They were staring at Bolden to see what he was going to do. There was nothing he could do but hold onto the inside of the van as he could no longer contain himself. His evening meal had come up to the surface, out of his mouth and onto the moving pavement. Bolden felt his shirt tighten around him as Copsovic's forceful grab gripped the back of his shirt, hanging onto Bolden, so he would not fall out of the moving van. Bolden could hear Ray's voice,

“You got a hold of him Tim?”

Copsovic answered back immediately,

“Yeah I got his drunken ass! I'm so glad I quit drinking. I don't have to go through this type of thing anymore. Bolden I told you to slow it down a bit but you didn't listen. Maybe you should go through the Genesis class yourself and get straightened out!”

Bolden finishing up with his activity, wiped his mouth, then answered Copsovic back,

“Tim, you didn't have to do that to Jackie! She would have got out of the van herself! You didn't have to throw her out!”

Copsovic defended his position with a harsh tone in his voice, saying,

“We had to get going and you know that! I don't know what is wrong with her. She never did that before! I did what I thought best for all of us and we made it on time! What was your problem tonight anyways? I told you Jackie and I were just talking and you had to blow it way out of proportion. Slamming down that champagne like it wasn't going to effect you. I can tell you what that alcohol is doing to your mind and body right now....!”

Copsovic was still in full force with his lecture to Bolden when he interrupted him,

“Tim, look I don't want to hear it. You have no idea what was on my mind tonight, or any other night, for that matter. I'm glad you went through what you went through. I'm proud of you for making the change into a better life, I Really Am! But, for right now, please just let me be, so I can get through this on my own and think things over. Can you do that for me?”

Copsovic continued on with his lecture as if he didn't hear a word Bolden had just said to him. Bolden sat down in the back seat where Copsovic had been earlier then closed the back door. Looking at Copsovic, sitting where Bolden was a few moments ago, still had blurry double vision, trying to maintain a focus, he said,

"Ray can you get us back to the barracks soon? I'm tired of hearing this and I really want to get to my bunk."

Ray was melancholy with his answer,

"We're almost there John. Don't pass out back there. Maintain your focus. Tomorrow is another day."

Bolden nodded his head in agreement and felt at solace with what Ray was telling him. He knew the meaning of what Ray was telling him,

"Tomorrow is another day!"

The plan that they had come up with would have to be performed at another time.

They checked in with the guards at McNair Barracks, gained access, then proceeded to the parking lot of CSC 6/502nd Infantry Battalion. Once they arrived, Williams bid each one a good night. Bolden was beginning to get his focus back as he opened up the back door then exited the van. Copsovic and Broadway followed after him. Maintaining his balance, Bolden walked up the stairs to the top level, then to his room, without saying a word to anyone. His thoughts were upon Jackie and the other ladies, hoping that everything was going good for them, and that the East German Border Guard, that had passed by them, did not cause any problems. He laid down on his bunk. Listening to his thoughts, he kept hearing the words, over and over again, that Sergeant Ray Williams had said earlier, to him in the van. With that thought he slipped into a deep sleep, for,

"Tomorrow Is Truly Another Day!"

36
THE TIME HAS COME

August 16th 1986, was a beautiful day with the sun shining brightly and the temperatures being moderate. Bolden, Williams, and Broadway had the plan of escape ready to execute for the day. They would spend the whole day in East Berlin with the ladies that were available. Mike had already called his girlfriend Jacqueline to let her know they were coming early and to invite anyone else that wish to come along. They were to meet everyone at Jacqueline's apartment and go from there. The time to meet was 10:00 A.M. By 0900 the men were meeting at 6/502nd parking lot, breathing a sigh of relief from the night before because the Colonel had not signed their East Passes that they had put in on Monday after the last weekend. At the close of business on Friday Broadway had approached Bolden and franticly told him that the Colonel had left for the day without signing the passes to give them permission to go to the East. Broadway made the decision to go to the Colonel's office and see if his secretary was still around, a Spec.4 that Mike knew had signed the Colonel's signature before on East Passes when the Colonel was too busy to take care of the small things like that. Broadway left and after a few minutes returned with the three East Passes signed and officially authorizing permission for the three of them to enter East Berlin. Bolden did not ask any questions of how they got signed. He was ready for one of the biggest achievements of his life and was in high hopes that their mission would be a success. Jackie knew that they were going to try and bring her over to the West but was not sure about it. Bolden had not given her a clear indication of his decision and he wished to keep it that way.

With their Class B uniforms on, short sleeved shirts, highly spit shined shoes, and caps. Bolden, Williams, and Broadway jumped into the van, with Ray at the wheel, they headed out to East Berlin. They were silent during the trip over there, while their thoughts were on how the plan was going to be played into action and if it would ever happen. They checked in at Checkpoint Charlie then passed through the East side checkpoint as they were waved through like always. Promptly arriving at Jacqueline's apartment at 1000 hours Bolden was observing the building structure and the surrounding area. The housing area was old and not kept up very well. For a beautiful day no one was out enjoying the clear sun shine, there was no activity. Could be the earliness of the day for a Saturday, people could be sleeping in taking advantage of the relaxation that was offered at the end of the work week was Bolden's thoughts. He looked around for any cameras mounted on the top of buildings or light posts and could not see any. The whole area was clean but very old and he was reminded in his thoughts that it took years for someone to get an apartment there possibly winning it through a lottery type system, or being provided by the Stasi in exchange for information by being a spy. Yes, that thought was in his mind. He did not care for Jacqueline or her attitude and she did not care for him because he and Jackie had something special going on between them. It was not a boyfriend girlfriend type relationship. It was the way they connected with each other. The van was parked facing toward the apartment complex to the right of them was another apartment complex, the street between them seemed to be narrow as if it were an alley way but big enough for a car to fit through to the left of them it was more open the street widened and did not seem very stuffy. Broadway leading the way, he opened the door to an entrance that led into a small alley walking a few feet then taking a left into another small alley which led to the door of Jacqueline's apartment. He knocked on her door and as she opened Broadway handed her a carton of Kool cigarettes then a bag with some baby food and diapers in it for her child. They kissed and hugged each other and welcomed everyone into her home. Mandy and Ushi were there waiting for their arrival ready to go have some fun for the day. Bolden looking around the living room of the apartment he noticed the grayish white of the walls and a few old photos Jacqueline had on her wall. She had made it a comfortable place with what she had to work with and he complimented her on the warm setting of her home. She looked at him and being polite said, "Thank You." She had a sofa that was full length placed at the right of the entrance and straight forward was a love seat that would seat about three people, she had a rocking chair close to the sofa on the right with a small wooden coffee table next to it. He saw a few other doors that probably led to the bedrooms, bathroom, and kitchen but he did not explore anymore of her place as he was not invited to. Everyone sat down for a moment to decide on what the activity was going to be for the day. Mike, Jacqueline, Ray, and Ushi sat on the long sofa. John and Mandy took up the love seat and while sitting down to get comfortable, Mandy sitting down placed her legs over the arm rest and then rested her head in John's lap gazing up at him she said something in German, seemed pretty sexy to Bolden the way she said it, and then started laughing. Bolden not taking offense of what she said, because he did not know what she said, but her laugh made him feel as if she was joking around, like she always did, the feeling of trying to be romantic. He could not help but laugh with her as did the others following suit. It was a good way to bring everyone into being comfortable as they all knew that it was forbidden for either of them to be there. American soldiers were not allowed to enter into East German's Quarters and the East German's were not allowed to have American soldiers into their home. American soldiers were not allowed to provide transportation to East German's as well. If they got caught doing this it would have definitely been an Article 15 or a court martial. As for the East German's inviting an American into their home or accepting transportation from them: it was definitely going to be an interrogation on their part. All was put to ease as all of them decided to have fun together and put all those differences aside and enjoy one another's company. After about an hour they all decided to go to lunch, then to the zoo, and after that to the beach, then return to the apartment till it was time to go to the disco and have some champagne. Jacqueline called Babette to inform her of their plans and Babette decided to join them at the beach later on during the day as she had some things to do before. Leaving the apartment all of them got settled in the van with Williams driving, Jacqueline in the passenger seat to give Ray directions on where they were going. Mike, John, Mandy, and Ushi sat on the backseat. They went to a nice restaurant that was filled with people and close to the zoo. When they walked into the restaurant all eyes were upon the American soldiers and the girls that accompanied them. It was a strange feeling as they were the center of attention. The waitress pulled two tables together to accommodate the seating for their group. The menus were handed out among them, Mandy helping John with his choice of food which really was not that big of a help with the way she joked around John was not sure of what she was going to order for him. He knew he wished to have a steak with potatoes and an order of that Krauterbutter. Jacqueline with her serious nature pointed out what Bolden was looking for and he ordered two of them for himself. The girls looked at him in a weird sort of way and he said, "I know the portions are small here and I like to have something that fills me up." They shrugged their shoulders in a manner of, whatever pleases you and continued to indulge in what their order was going to be. Mandy being her usual funny self said something smart assish in German and the girls began to giggle. Mandy looking at John from the corner of her eye being delightfully smug to sense a reaction from him. John looking at her playfully said, "Mind your own business, woman." Mandy responding with, "Ja Ja Ja," laughing after saying it. After all the orders were placed everyone started talking about the day's events they had planned and how lucky they were to have a nice day to go along with it. About thirty minutes later the meals started to arrive. After all of them had been dished out to their appropriate diner, Bolden started to cut his steaks into small edible pieces. Completing the first steak he started on the second one and he heard the silence around him and the glares from everyone at the table. As he looked up he saw everyone at the table and a few of the other guests close by looking at him as if he had done something wrong. Even Mike and Ray were looking at him. A little embarrassed and self-conscious he dropped his shoulders and said "WHAT?" Jacqueline was the first one to say something, arrogantly and with a look of disgust on her face, she said,

"John das ist not gute!!!"

John responding back, lifted his shoulders back up and said, "Yes, I know, it's this etiquette thing that I've been told about before. I have always cut my meat first before eating it. To me, you get your work done first and then enjoy your meal." By the look on Jacqueline's face, with her nose crinkled up and her upper lip in a tense position, he could tell she did not like his response and he did not care. He was a bit ticked off at the way she reacted and to gain his pride back, he spouted out without even thinking,

"I'm an American, I can do anything I want, now let me be so I can enjoy my food!!!"

He knew it was not the right thing to say in a place like that but he did not regret saying it even though it set an awkward mood at the table. Jacqueline slouched back down in her chair as her eyes averted away from John. Mike and Ray were not very pleased with what John had said but John was not going to let anyone push their attitude on him. The diners at the other tables that were close by got the message as well as they did not look over at the table where the Americans were anymore. Mandy lifting the tension of the mood at the table lifted up John's roll and with the big butter knife split the roll in half and applied the Krauterbutter on to it offering it to John saying,

"Das is gute Ja?

John with a slight smile and with kindness said to Mandy,

"Ja, sehr gute, danke."

When the meal was finished and the after lunch coffees had been drank by those who ordered them. The three soldiers split the tab together and left a big tip for the waitress. The whole crew walked over to the zoo and after a few minutes met up with Babette. After a couple hours walking through the zoo, looking at the animals, they arrived back to the VW van, jumped in and went to the beach. The three American soldiers in their Class B uniforms stood out among the crowd as they walked with the women on the sandy front trying to find a good place to lie down and catch a few rays of sunshine. Bolden was bored because all he could think about was how the plan was going to be placed into action later on that night with Jackie. Would she even be at the disco? He did not know. There were a couple times where he was with Mike and Ray at the disco and she was not there for the night. He envisioned how he would ask Jackie to go out to the van with him and have a talk, getting her away from the crowd at the disco hoping no one would follow them. Ray would have to find a dark area to park the van without any cameras around. This was going to be a difficult task for him to try and do this without being obvious of what he was trying to do. John and Mike were going to have to try and keep the girls attention away from what Ray was going to do. Would Jackie even go with the plan of hiding her under the backseat with the small space available? His thoughts were interrupted as Mandy asked him a question in German and then started laughing sheepishly as her face was turning red from blushing. Bolden, not knowing what she said was interested and turned to Jacqueline for her to interpret what Mandy had asked. Jacqueline was hesitant in interpreting it but Bolden insisted. Jacqueline being cautious said,

"Mandy would like to know if you would like to sunbathe nude?"

"It's ok here you know people do it all the time, it's not such a big deal."

Bolden started to blush and said coy fully with a slight grin on his face,

"Tell her I will if she will."

Mandy declined the offer as did John. Ray joined in on the conversation saying,

"It's probably a good thing you don't do that, even though it is legal here to sunbathe nude by the time we got back someone at the company would have to talk to you about it and would most likely end up as an Article 15. We are to keep our uniforms on at all times here and to keep up our respectable image. You never know who is watching us over here."

In his thoughts Bolden agreed with Ray. Their uniforms were like shields. The East German Polizei, Border Guards, or Stasi could not touch them while their uniforms were on. Their uniforms represented the defense of freedom in all things. It was a subliminal message of strength, courage, and dedication to the cause of individual rights. This message had the force of the United States Military backing it up. It was best to keep the uniform on and respect the honor that it upheld. The time was going by quickly as they chatted among themselves, sometimes there were quiet times between them as they would close their eyes and take in the essence of the day feeling the warm wind coming off the water carrying a slight mist with it that was cooling them down. It was peaceful and relaxing, so much that it was easy to forget the place they were in. As the sun was approaching the end of its duty for the day Jacqueline suggested getting some refreshments for the evening and head back to her place to enjoy each others company. Bolden was all for that and he was getting anxious as the time was quickly approaching. They arrived at Jacqueline's apartment, with her being a good hostess she offered everyone a cool beverage and prepared them for each of her guests. Bolden decided he was not going to drink very much alcohol so that he could keep his senses about him in case anything should happen later on that night. Everyone was having a great time together. Mike, Jacqueline, Ray, and Babette were sitting next to each other on the long sofa couch. John, Mandy, and Ushi were snug, fitted together in the small sofa love seat that was against the wall. After a while Mike got up and sat in the rocking chair saying it was too tight of a fit and was too warm sitting there. Jacqueline got up and grabbed Mike's hand and led him into her bedroom. Ray stating,

"That's fine with me, we got the whole couch to us now. You two have fun, don't do anything that I wouldn't do, but if you do, make sure you enjoy it."

Ushi got up and headed for the rocking chair while Mandy assumed her earlier position of throwing her legs over the side of the love seat and resting her head on John's lap asking him if it was ok? John looking at Mandy admiring her sense of humor and beautiful character, smiled and said,

"It is definitely okay!"

Placing his left arm over her stomach then behind her back giving her a gentle squeeze upward their eyes met as they started to bond in a passionate way. Bolden could sense the warm tender loving feeling between the two of them. The blood rushing through his veins like a raging river, the inside of his neck was beginning to swell, and he was starting to lose focus. He wished to bend over and kiss her lips as she was anxiously awaiting him to do so. As much as he wished to do so, he couldn't, as she was kind of designated to be Kevin's girl. Though there was no clear indication that any of the American soldiers had a definite relationship with any of the ladies, it was like an imaginary line that should not be crossed in order to keep the respect among them. The only exception was Mike and Jacqueline's relationship. Everyone knew they were definitely an item together and it was clear that Mike was in love with her. Bringing her gifts from the west and providing her with some necessities she had to have. Her son was almost a year old, he was not Mike's son, but he cared for her infant child as much as he cared for her. Ray and Babette sitting on the big sofa were having a great time together. Ushi sitting in the rocking chair by herself got up and headed for the door when Bolden asked her,

"And just where do you think you are going, young lady?"

Ushi pointing at John and Mandy then at Ray and Babette, then at herself, put her arms up in the air and shrugged her shoulders as in a gesture of

"Who am I to be with?"

John, pointing his finger at the chair, told her to sit down because she was with us and we enjoyed her company. Ushi took his demand joyfully and with a smile sat back down in the rocking chair. Mandy interpreting as much as she could to Ushi so that the three of them could have a sensible time together. They were having fun between the three of them talking about anything and everything even though the language barrier was a bit difficult at times.

It was getting close to 8:00 P.M. when Mike and Jacqueline emerged from the bedroom into the living room to join the rest of them. The three soldiers knew it was time to go and place the plan into action. Bolden was the first to say something.

"Everybody ready to go to the disco?", he asked.

Mandy and Ushi were overly excited, nodding there head yes, and getting up headed for the door. Mike, Jacqueline, Ray and Babette, looking disappointed were all shaking their head No! Bolden totally surprised and disappointed at Mike and Ray glared at them with confusion in his eyes. They all agreed that this night was the night to bring Jackie across The Wall. After what had happened the Saturday prior to this one, they could not afford to put the plan on hold again. If it was not going to happen this night, it would never happen, as it would be too risky to try and do it again. Mike looked at John and said,

"Man we are having a lot of fun here. Let's stay here for the night till we have to go."

Ray backing Mike up said,

"Yeah John we are having a great time here. We can go to the disco anytime."

Bolden was insistent as his voice was loud, clear, and straight to the point,

"WE MADE PLANS TO GO TO THE DISCO EARLIER AND IT IS NOW TIME TO STICK TO THAT PLAN GENTLEMAN!!! NOW GET UP OFF YOUR ASSES AND LET'S GO!!!"

Bolden was hoping that the word PLAN meant something to Ray and Mike as they would get the subliminal message attached to his wording. Jacqueline and Babette both insisted on staying at the apartment. Jacqueline said,

"John, you don't have to stay here, you go to the disco with Mandy and Ushi."

She wanted him to leave and Bolden could sense that she tolerated him being at her apartment because he was with Mike and Ray. He was okay with that as he really did not want to be at her apartment. John replied to her comment abruptly and said,

“I would but it is a long distance to walk and I don’t really know how to get there.”

Ray immediately offered the keys to his VW van to Bolden which Bolden was hesitant to take because his driver’s license had been revoked in the state of Wisconsin and the driver’s license he had from the state of Texas was expired. The only license he had that was valid was to drive an APC. Explaining this to Ray so that he knew that what he was offering, should Bolden accept the keys to the van. Ray said,

“John you are in East Berlin, no one is going to stop you here. Hope you can drive a stick.”

Bolden quickly grabbed the keys from Ray looked at Mandy and said,

“Show me the way and we are off to the disco.”

Mandy and Ushi were both excited, Mandy saying,

“Ja Let’s go!!!”

The two women were out the door headed for the van. Before leaving, Bolden turned, looked at Mike and Ray then said,

“I will be back in time to pick you both up to head back to the West. Be ready to go the moment we get back!!!”

Mike and Ray both knew what John was stating and they agreed that they would be ready. They knew that time was of the essence once Jackie was placed into that small hidden compartment under the back seat. It was a cramped space that would cut the circulation of blood flowing through the legs. Bolden had placed himself inside that small box for five minutes to see what it was like and if it was able to hold a body inside it. Within those five minutes his legs began to tingle and cramp up. Broadway did the same thing as he followed suit. Bolden walked out and closed the door behind him,when he arrived at the van the two women were jumping up and down waving him to hurry up. Bolden took his position in the driver's seat with Mandy on the passenger side to navigate and Ushi sitting in the back, she did not actually sit on the back seat as she kneeled down in the middle of the open space between the back seat and the two front seats. She wished to see where they were going and keep John and Mandy company while traveling. Driving a van with a stick shift was not new to John but it had been some time since he actually drove a vehicle. All of his transportation was provided for and he was a little timid about driving in a foreign country. He did not know the traffic laws very well but he did figure out the traffic lights were the opposite of the states. The yellow light followed the red light in Germany then it would turn to green instead of the yellow light following the green light then to red in the states signifying to be ready to stop and allow the other traffic to go through. It was funny to Bolden that they would do that with the lights, it was as if the yellow light was a signal to press on the accelerator and be ready to go once it turned green. Must be big fans of NASCAR he thought chuckling inside. He could see where it had a purpose for that in the races. Mandy navigating through town instructing John on where to turn, his concentration was on driving and not giving attention to the street signs, putting his trust into Mandy to get them there and back safely. As he would down shift the van coming into the corners he would always grind the gears popping it into place. He was tense driving the van in the East but thought if Ray could do it, he could do it, and hoped he could bring Ray's vehicle back to him in one piece. Mandy looking at John in a weird sort of way, kind of a mix between being worried and not too sure about John's driving abilities spoke up with her accent intact,

"Shjahn, do you know how to drive, sheesh?"

John looked at her and said,

"Yeah I do, you just sit there and tell me where to go, you'll be okay, I think?"

The laughter filled the van from the three of them as the tension began to fade away. Bolden could see The Pope's Revenge Tower coming closer and knew they were coming into range of the disco. John asking Mandy where a nice dark place was to hide the van and keep it safe hoping to be conspicuous as to what he was about to do.

"You can park it anywhere here they have cameras all over the place, it will be safe", she said jokingly.

John with his quick wit said,

"Yes I know there are cameras everywhere here but what I am actually looking for is a nice dark quiet place so that I can talk with Jackie, if she comes tonight. Do you know what I am saying?", giving her a wink, hoping she would catch his drift.

"Ahhh, ok Shahn, I know," responding with her giggly laughter.

She found a spot, it was perfect. Dimly lit, one camera that Bolden noticed but it would not be able to get an angle to look down toward the van.

"Hmmm, have you done this before Mandy?" John asked with a smile.

She returned the smile and did not answer the question as she started to laugh she opened her door and headed toward the disco. The two girls were running to get up the stairs with Bolden right behind them.

"What is the big hurry, ladies? Slow down we will get there soon enough."

Mandy without looking back said,

"Come, come we have to hurry to get a good table."

They found one in the center of the Disco close to the dance floor. The lighting seem to be brightly lit at that table as they sat down Mandy asked if John was going to have champagne for the table and he said,

"Why of course we are going to have champagne here, order us four bottles right away and if we have to have more we will get them later."

Mandy commenting quickly,

"Ja we will have to have more to take back with us."

John looked around the room of the disco about four tables down to the left of him he saw Jackie. She was sitting with a group of British soldiers that were there visiting for the night. He had seen them at that disco before remembering the night that he came to the East with Mike, Ray, and Kevin Festerman. Jackie had stayed at their table that night only to come over to the American's table to say hello quickly and then she was gone. She saw John with Mandy and Ushi and had a confused look on her face, most likely wondering where Mike and Ray were. Bolden was wondering how he was going to be able to get her away from those British soldiers, then the solution came to him from the right side. It was Mandy, as she placed her hands on his shoulders she leaned over and whispered in his ear.

"Do you want me to go get Jackie for you?" she asked.

"Yes, please, if you will, I would be so very grateful to you." was his response.

He watched her as she walked over to get Jackie. The British Soldiers were busy in conversation with each other and did not notice her until she reached the table and started talking to Jackie. Jackie got up and walked back to the table with her. John was watching the British soldiers as they stopped talking with each other and glared at John for having taken away Jackie from their table. John glared back giving no indication of submission to their hearty stares. He remembered what Ivey told him about the British and how to act around them. When Jackie and Mandy arrived at the table John stood up and pulled a chair out from under the table and offered it to Jackie which she accepted. Mandy giggling put her arms around the both of them and said,

"kiss, kiss"

and blew a kiss into the air between the two of them. The champagne and the glasses arrived at the table and Mandy opened a couple bottles right away. She loved to drink and had no qualms about it. She filled the glasses for everyone at the table and held her glass up in the air and said

"Prost"

which everyone at the table followed suit. Mandy then grabbed Ushi and they walked away saying they would be back soon. This was a good thing because John had to talk with Jackie and see where she stood about going to the West. As soon as the two women were out of ear shot distance Jackie leaned over and said,

"Is tonight the night?"

John nodding his head in acknowledgment but saying words of an opposite notation, said

"Could be, may be".

He then started to lay down the ground rules to her in a strict and orderly voice so that she understood everything he was saying to her.

"You will not leave my side for any reason. If you go to talk with someone I will be there with you. If you have to go to the bathroom, I will go with you. She was not laughing because as she looked into his eyes she knew he was serious and had every intent of helping her escape. He continued on with his demands. If I see you on the phone, I will walk away from you. If you talk to someone and I don't know what you are saying to them, I will not take you with me."

She asked him if she could go get some clothes from her apartment and he could go with her. He told her NO, if she wished to go to the west she would go with what she had on her. There were no if's, and's, or but's about this. He did not tell her this to be mean as the safety of everyone that was involved was in his hands. He was going to make sure that he had a tight grip on the situation at hand so that their crossing would be a safe one and that no one would be harmed. She asked where Mike and Ray were and if they knew what was going to happen. John shaking his head No, said

"Yes, they are over to Jacqueline's apartment and we will have to go back and pick them up later."

She asked,

"How do we do this?"

John responded back with,

"All will be explained to you when the time comes, we won't talk about it anymore." Then he burst into laughter as he was throwing his body language into a different mode as if he had finished telling a joke. Jackie figuring out what he was doing followed suit and started to laugh with him. He could still feel the stares from the British soldiers every so often as they were curious as to what made Jackie get up and leave their table to join the American soldier. Mandy and Ushi returned and sat down at the table with Jackie and John. Jackie did not talk much in German to the two women at the table but she spoke enough not to be to suspicious. Jackie and John got up a few times to go dance to some popular American songs. They would occasionally have a sip of champagne from their glasses to be sociable. They spent most of their time at the table. Jackie did not leave his side at all. Mandy and Ushi stayed at the table with John and Jackie which did not give John the opportunity to ask Jackie out to the van. He thought about just taking her out there and hiding her under the back seat then returning stating that Jackie had left but he thought the travel time involved getting back to the apartment to pick up Mike and Ray and then the drive to the checkpoint and getting through would be too long for Jackie to stay in that cramped position. Besides that it would most likely arouse suspicion with the other girls and that, he had to avoid. It was 10:00 P.M. and time to go pick up Mike and Ray. Mandy asked John if he would order some champagne to take back to the apartment. John said,

"Yes, we definitely have to have some champagne, order us three bottles please."

He then thought that while back at the apartment Jackie and John would stay in the van and the women would think it was their private time together. He would then ask Jackie to slap him as if he had made an advance toward her so that when he went into the apartment with a red face they would think Jackie had left then place Jackie under the back seat and then go retrieve Mike and Ray. He figured two of the bottles would go into the apartment and one would stay in the van with Jackie and John so that the four of them could open it once they got across the checkpoint to celebrate the success of the mission and welcome Jackie into West Berlin. The moment the three bottles arrived at the table, John gave the waitress the appropriate amount for payment plus a good size tip telling the waitress to keep the change. Mandy grabbing two bottles and Ushi the other headed toward the exit laughing and giggling all the way. John, with a smile on his face, looked at Jackie and offered his bent right elbow to her which she accepted by placing her left arm through it and clenched him tightly. They followed the two women out to the van. John being cautious looked around to make sure they were not being followed. When they arrived at the van, Mandy and Ushi were already sitting on the back seat. John opened the front passenger door for Jackie and as she settled on the seat he closed the door behind her. John could tell she was a bit nervous and so was he. Walking around to the driver's side he searched the area making sure they had not been followed. The dimly lit area and the solitude it offered easily shown they had not been followed. Mandy jumping off the backseat and kneeling down in the middle of the open space between the driver's seat and passenger's seat laughingly said,

"Shjahn, let's see if you are any better at driving."

Ushi burst into laughter as did John while Jackie had a confused look on her face wondering what Mandy was talking about. Mandy navigated back to the apartment and John drove much better this time, still grinding a few gears along the way. By the time the four of them arrived at Jacqueline's apartment it was a little after 1030 P.M. John had parked the VW Van in the same spot Ray had done earlier. Mandy and Ushi jumped out of the van then noticing Jackie and John not getting out quickly turned and looked at them suspiciously. Mandy asking,

"Was ist das? Are you coming?"

John responding back said,

"No, I wish to talk with Jackie for a moment. Leave a bottle of champagne with us, we will be there in a little bit."

Mandy and Ushi snatched the three bottles of champagne up and headed for the apartment laughing. Mandy said,

"No, when you are done you come join the party, kuss, kuss."

John wanted one of those champagne bottles to open in the west for the celebration but he was not about to make a scene over it. He wished to be alone with Jackie. When Mandy and Ushi disappeared into the alley way leading to the apartment, Jackie and John went to the back seat and sat down. John looked Jackie directly into her eyes and asked her,

"Are you sure you wish to do this?

Her response was immediate and direct, looking back into John's eyes saying,

"Yes, I do."

John cautioning her said,

"When you get across the Wall there is no turning back Jackie, you will have no friends there."

She quickly responded back,

"I have no friends here, all of my friends are American G.I.'s and they are over on the other side of the Wall."

John continued on cautioning her on what will and may happen when she was safely in the West.

"You will be interrogated by all four powers, The Americans, British, French, and West Germans, once you turn yourself in to the proper authorities. They are going to ask you who helped you escape. What will you tell them?"

She responded like she had rehearsed this over and over again.

“I will tell them a diplomat helped me to escape.”

John stating that it was a thin explanation, very thin, but it just might work.

“Ja, it will work!!!” she said with confidence in her voice.

John stating in a heavy and serious tone of voice,

“They can not know that we helped you escape. If they find out American soldiers helped you escape it could start something that will be way out of our control, do you understand what I am saying?”

“Ja, I do.”, she said sadly.

John hesitantly said to her,

“One other thing, we wish we had some money to make sure you will be okay before turning yourself in on Monday, get you a hotel for the weekend and some food but Mike and I both send money home to our family in the States and Ray is married, we will do what we are able to do to make sure you will be all right. One of the three of us will be with you at all times over the weekend. The Ku’dorf is open twenty four hours. Mike and I will stay with you all night tonight and Ray will pick us up on Sunday. His wife will be gone on Sunday so you can stay at his place Sunday night. Are you okay with this?”

Enthusiastic and with a positive tone she exclaimed,

“Ja, I am!”

Looking at John she grabbed his hand and asked him,

"Why do you do this?"

John blushing and looking away from her said,

"Because you wish to have your freedom and we are able to do this. John Wayne is my hero. Ever heard of John Wayne?"

"Ja, John Wayne the Cowboy!" she said in an upbeat tone.

John explaining said.

"I'm not much a cowboy but I love his character."

"I wish to see America!" Jackie exclaimed with a shine in her eyes and a brightly lit smile on her face.

"I can get you to the West but you will have to find your own way to the States. You have to know this, I am not in love with you and I will not marry you. I'm a soldier and plan on being one for the rest of my life." John stated in a calm manner.

He told her this for a couple of reasons. He did not wish to give her any false hopes of his intentions. He knew that he would not be able to be there for her at times and if they got caught on either side he would most likely not see her at all. The reality of it all was way too serious to be playing games with anyone. The possibility of being shot or imprisoned was something to take into consideration should the plan go wrong. She had to know that she would be starting a brand new way of life and it was something she was going to have to do on her own. She would be in a world of hope and faith that would carry her to the dreams she had envisioned within her thoughts while growing up in East Berlin. He admired her strength and courage and willingness to change her life. To jump into a new world without knowing what it is like is a great achievement for anyone willing to take that first step. With the dreams of her imagination of what her life would be like in the West, to have her freedom to do which ever it is she wished to do and go to any where she wished to go, this energy had set into motion the series of events that was about to happen to make that dream come true. John with his pride of being a soldier defending the right of freedom for everyone was ready to have his dream fulfilled of proving that not only did he believe in this inalienable right for everyone but that he was willing to do whatever it took to give this to someone who desired it. With his thoughts and power of his imagination the energy had put him in a place to make it all happen. It was as if he was behind enemy lines in the heat of battle carrying a wounded soldier back to safety. Their union was perfect! The path of their life's journey had paralleled and it was now or never to make this dream come true. The Eagle, with its talons gripping tightly around the Berlin Wall and a stern look within his eyes has spread its wings for a freedom flight that would carry them safely to the West.

37

THE HIDING PLACE

It was now time to put the plan into action and to let Jackie know how things were going to go. As John was about to explain it to her she asked,

"How are we going to do this?"

John stood up from the backseat of the van and grabbed Jackie's hand for her to follow his lead. He then bent over slightly and with the fingertips of both his hands gripped the extended lip of the seat and lifted it up. As he looked at Jackie he saw her eyes widen with a little bit of concern in them. She gasped and said,

"Bohhh, are you sure about this?"

John assured her that even though it looked very small that she would fit in there. It was a very tight fit and explained to her that Him and Mike had fitted themselves snug in the small hidden compartment. John said to her,

"You won't be in there for very long, about ten minutes at the most. As soon as you get in there I will go in to the apartment and say to Mike and Ray that it is time to go. They already know the moment I knock on Jacqueline's door that it is the signal for us to go right away. While you are in there try moving your legs slightly to keep the blood flowing through your legs. I was in there for five minutes and they started to tingle on me. Mike and Ray had to help me out of the compartment."

Jackie started to giggle a little bit and placed her right hand over her mouth. She seemed a little nervous about what he was explaining to her and John started to become concerned over her reaction.

"Are you okay Jackie?" John asked worriedly.

"Yes, I am fine she said but there is no window seat!"

John appreciated her sense of humor as both of them began laughing simultaneously. It was a breath of fresh air for the both of them to lighten up the situation. John continued on with his instructions to Jackie.

"Before you get in there, there is something you are going to have to do first."

"What is this?, Jackie asked cautiously.

John not hesitating in his words making sure his communication was clear enough for her said,

"You are going to have to slap me across the face and you will have to do it hard enough to leave a hand print or at least leave a good red imprint. I will tell them that I made a pass at you and being insulted by this, you slapped me and left. There can be no question that you actually left. The girls in the apartment have to believe that you went somewhere else."

"NO, I CAN NOT, I WILL NOT DO THIS!" was Jackie's immediate response.

Pleading with John she continued on,

"PLEASE DO NOT ASK ME TO DO THIS!"

"Jackie if you don't do this then I am going to have to, and if I do it, I know it's going to hurt, I'm not much for pain you know, so you will be doing me a favor. If you do it I know it will be tolerable and can get by with it." John said hoping she would be able to see his point.

Jackie with compassion and tears in her eyes said

"No, I cannot John."

John conceding to her plea and with a smile on his face said,

"Okay, I will do it myself, it's not going to be any fun though you know?"

With Jackie wiping the tears from her eyes the both of them had a worried laugh between them. Each of them hoping all will be well as they both knew the dangers that were involved with what was about to take place. John looking at his OD Green Army style wristwatch that glowed in the dark saw the time as 2315. Looking at Jackie he said,

"It's time, are you ready?"

Jackie looking at him with much affection replied

"Yes, I am ready."

Giving each other a tender kiss and a tight hug John said,

"Good Luck, the next time I shall see you will be in West Berlin!"

"Jaaaaa, In West Berlin! She responded with a nervous but confident tone in her voice.

John grabbing her right hand with his left hand helped her get into the small compartment under the backseat. Her head laid toward the driver's side while her knees were brought up to her stomach and her feet pointing toward the passenger side. It was a very tight fit and John knew this. He was very concerned for her welfare and as she settled into the fetal position John looked upon her with pride for the courage she carried to accomplish such a wonderful feat. She would become like a new born infant entering into a world of unknown possibilities having only a trusting soul hoping that whomever she would come into contact within this new life would provide her with the knowledge she must have to learn how to cope into a new society, a new way of living life as a free and independent human being with the right to make mistakes and to learn from them without being subject to questioning on every little detail of such a facet of learning or to become whatever you wish to be without being told what you are supposed to be. The journey she was to embark upon has endless possibilities and John knew in his heart that if she was given the chance Jackie would grasp those opportunities and create a better life for herself. John asked Jackie if she was okay and she responded,

“Yes, hurry please.”

John responded back,

“I Will!”

He closed the lid of the backseat and hurriedly exited the sliding side door of the van closing it quickly. He knew the time available to them was quite short. His task now was to make the story that Jackie had left the area and to create it to be credible as to not draw any suspicion. He quickly surveyed the area to see if anyone had been watching and saw that it was clear. He next entered into the small alley way that entered toward Jacqueline’s apartment. Midway into the alley he stopped and prepared himself. Breathing in deep and then exhaling he mustered up the power and then struck his right cheek with the palm of his right hand. The tingling sensation of pain went from his right cheek to the top of his head. Gritting his teeth he prepared himself for another strike upon the right cheek. Without thinking he struck himself twice and then twice again with his left hand against his left cheek. As the pain subsided he could feel both sides of his face swell up as the flow of blood began to warm both cheeks on the sides of his face. He wasn’t ready to knock on the door yet. The tears started to form from his eyes and as they began to have a steady flow to them he knew it was time to knock on Jacqueline's door asking permission to enter. That was Mike and Ray's signal. Once John entered into the apartment and explained what happened they were to get up right away and go. They both knew that time was of the essence and that Jackie was under the back seat of the van. John walked up to the door and knocked upon it. He heard Jacqueline say,

"Come In."

As soon as he opened the door and walked into the apartment he heard Jacqueline say,

"Jackie cannot come!!!"

John looked at her with tears flowing from his eyes and red puffy cheeks said,

"What?, Oh I don't think you have to worry about that, Jackie is gone. She just slapped me and left."

Mike knowing what was happening began to laugh out loud. Jacqueline right away turned around and smacked Mike in his face. John thought to himself,

"Damn, Now why can't Jackie have done that to me? It would have made things much easier."

John kept his composure through it all and played his non-chivalrous part in the matter. Jacqueline grabbed Mike's hand and yanked him from the couch they were sitting on and headed toward the door where John was standing. John being surprised with such an action asked,

"Where are you two going?"

Jacqueline's response was immediate,

"TO FIND JACKIE!"

"Oh No", John thought, this isn't part of the plan."

Mandy and Ushi at the same time came over to John and flowered him with kisses on each cheek and then on the lips.

"It is okay John, are you okay?",

Mandy asking with a concerned tone of voice. With John having two women on him at one time it was hard to concentrate on the plan. John thinking intently,

"What a dream come true for a man, does it have to happen right now?"

The two women pulled John onto the couch that Mike and Jacqueline had left previously. They were still kissing and hugging on John, comforting him with his discomfort and supposed inconvenience. John looked at Ray and Babette motioning his head for Ray to head out the door. Ray and Babette were laughing at what was happening between John, Mandy, and Ushi. Ray could not push forward with the plan; neither could John without drawing suspicion among the ladies that were present. All they could do was to hope that Mike and Jacqueline would come through the door confirming that Jackie had left. Time started to creep by slowly and it seemed like forever to John. Mandy offered John some champagne to comfort him but John refused. He wished to have all of his senses about him when it came time to cross over to West Berlin through Checkpoint Charlie in case something was to happen. He glanced at his watch quickly and noticed Jackie had been under that back seat for ten minutes, double the time he had been in there himself. He knew it would take another ten minutes just to get to the border. He was worried about Jackie and how her legs were feeling. He prayed that she would have the strength to be able to hold out until they made it across. Still no sign of Mike or Jacqueline, John had to think Jacqueline was making sure that Jackie was gone.

"Could Jacqueline be a spy for the Stasi?" He thought.

If she was and discovered Jackie under the back seat then all would be over. John could not go outside and see where Mike and Jacqueline were without drawing suspicion. He could not allow any doubt that Jackie had left. John expressed his appreciation to Mandy and Ushi for helping him through his time of discomfort and was rewarded with a loving kiss from each one of them. The second hand on his watch was still ticking away as the anticipation grew inside of him to go. He looked at Ray and saw the concern that was starting to build in his eyes as well. Ray was the one that would have to say it was time to go. John looked at his watch it was 2345, they had to be back to Checkpoint Charlie before midnight and register in. Then he heard Ray say,

"It's time to go, Mike better be in that van!"

The girls knew it was time as well. All of them headed out the door and walked through the alley way leading to Ray's white VW van. John noticed that Mike and Jacqueline were sitting on the back seat on top of Jackie. He knew Jackie had to move her legs to keep the circulation flowing in her legs. She had been under that backseat for over twenty five minutes already and most of that time with Mike and Jacqueline sitting on top of her. John would have to read the signs from Jacqueline to see if she found out if Jackie was under that back seat, if she did and was keeping quiet about it, then they would have to abandon the plan and let Jackie out of the van before crossing. Ray walking over to his driver's side had left Babette standing by Mandy, Ushi, and John. John slid open the sliding side door and said to Mike and Jacqueline,

"Hey, it's time to go. There isn't much time left so it's going to have to be a quick good bye once we get close to the checkpoints."

Mike stepped out from the back seat grabbing Jacqueline's hand quickly; he knew it had been quite a while since Jackie had been placed under the back seat. Mike took his place on the front passenger side and Jacqueline jumped onto his lap. John entering the van slid all the way over to the driver's side back seat with Mandy holding his hand. Once he took his position Mandy jumped onto his lap. Ushi sat next to them followed by Babette. When all the doors were closed Ray put the van in gear and headed for the checkpoint. Mandy began to kiss John passionately. John responded in kind but kept his eyes on Jacqueline and how she was acting. John saw the embrace Jacqueline had on Mike and knew instantly that all was in the clear. Looking up at Mandy he saw that her eyes were closed then glanced back over to Jacqueline. He was confident that everything was still in play as she was affectionately kissing Mike. Ray pulled the van into the usual hiding spot just before crossing over.

"We'll have to make this quick, we only have a few minutes left, "Ray shouted."

Babette slid the side door of the van open and jumped out followed by Ushi. Mandy clinging tightly onto John did not want to exit the van. She looked at John and said,

"I'm sorry things did not work out between you and Jackie. I like you very much John!"

With those words she leaned into him and affectionately gave him a kiss.

"I'll see you next weekend okay?"

John answering back,

"I like you to Mandy. Hopefully we will see each other again soon."

He did like Mandy very much. She was always so cheerful and loved her sense of humor. It seemed, to John, as if she was happy anywhere she was. She always had a bright side to her and looked toward the positive side of things. If the present moment was not positive for her she would shrug it off and wait patiently for the good times that would definitely come to her. With their final quick kiss good night she exited the van. Ray placed the white VW van into gear and headed toward the Checkpoint. Mike and John were looking back and seeing the ladies waving good bye to them, they both waved back wondering if they would ever see them again. The energy soon shifted from the party essence into a more serious toned environment. The three men were silent as they soon came up to the wavy concrete barriers that were placed in front of them on the east side of the checkpoint. John had already shifted his position in the backseat from the driver's side to the middle with his arms stretched out across the top of the backseat. The silence in the van was heavy and thick like the smoke from a fire about ready to ignite and burst into flames. What was going to happen? Were they ready to have the courage of their convictions enacted if the plan went wrong? Were they willing to sacrifice everything and anything for what they believe in? Were they willing to give their life if it was necessary? The questions kept mounting up with the intensity of each heartbeat from these three men as the white VW van came closer to the East German Border Guards. Time slowed down to a trickle as the energy sped up within their thoughts. Seconds seemed like minutes! Shock was imminent as it displayed itself in full fashion, sharply dressed and keen to the senses. John looked first at Ray and then at Mike, the stare in their eyes was straightforward in achieving their objective. Ray steered the van passed the first curve to the left then straightened out the front wheels to negotiate the curve to the right. During the middle section of the S-curved concrete barriers was the East German checkpoint. John looked to the left with his eyes glancing upward he saw the two East German Border Guards looking into the van and then noticed, standing in the middle of those two guards, was a tall well-dressed uniformed, what looked like to be a, Soviet Officer!

"Damn It",

John said to himself in his thoughts.

"There were never any Soviet Officers present before when they had crossed over from West to East or East to West."

John became very concerned because he knew that the East German Border Guards could not search the vehicle, they were considered to be, "The Enemy" but if this was a Soviet Officer, then he would be considered to be "An Ally" and could detain them or search the vehicle. There was no time available for this, should that possible Soviet Officer deem it to be necessary. Time was running short and there were only a few minutes to make it to Checkpoint Charlie. The proper protocol for a U.S. Soldier was for the highest military ranking of the group to salute this possible Soviet Officer. Ray was the highest ranking being a Sergeant. He was the driver of the van, his attention was on driving a few more yards to Checkpoint Charlie. He did not notice the possible Soviet Officer. John kept his eyes upon him to watch for his reaction as the possible Soviet Officer kept his eye on John. They were fixated upon each other. John, not being able to salute this officer, watched this man for his reaction to the current situation. The officer possibly thinking, that John was the highest ranking man in the group because he was sitting in the backseat while having a driver transport him places, was looking for the respect due an officer of an allied force. A mixture of emotions were going through the both of them not knowing what to do. The numbness John felt that surrounded him seemed to last an eternity. If anything was going to happen at that exact moment it was going to be initiated by that soldier. Ray, keeping his calm while driving the white VW van idled by and then entered the border line crossing it with pure precision. They were not in the clear yet. They had to stop by Checkpoint Charlie and announce their crossing. Coming up to the Checkpoint, Ray stopped the van by the window where immediately the NCOIC of the evening commenced to chew Ray's ass.

“It’s about fucking time you guys came across! Do you realize what time it is? It is two minutes before midnight!!! You had about one minute before we sent a search party out for you men! You do realize what that fucking means don’t you? Sergeant Williams, you are the highest ranking one of your group. You are their leader! You should have more concern and respect for your men! DO YOU UNDERSTAND WHAT I AM SAYING TO YOU!!!”

Ray took all of it in stride. He had performed his duty as Sergeant and highest ranking member to the best of his ability and unbeknownst to the NCOIC of Checkpoint Charlie it was perfection according to the plan. Sergeant Williams responded back,

“Yes I know Sergeant, but we have made it back before midnight. I apologize to you for making you overly concerned about our welfare and appreciate you looking out for us. We lost track of time for a moment and made a hurried effort to get here on time.”

With that said the NCOIC of Checkpoint Charlie welcomed them back and said,

“Have a good night men!”

Ray thanked him and said,

“Have a good night as well, Sergeant!”

Ray placed the van into gear and moved forward. They were in the clear and had made it safely into West Berlin. To follow the plan they would have had to wait one mile before letting Jackie out from under the backseat of the van but she had been in there, crouched in a tight position close to forty five minutes. Going down Potsdamer

Strasse they were one hundred yards past Checkpoint Charlie. John said,

"I have to let her out of there!"

Mike and Ray both agreed and as Ray started to turn the white VW van to the right, onto a side street, John immediately jumped up off of the backseat and lifted the lid offering his right hand to Jackie to assist her out from under the tight compartment that she had been placed in for such a long time.

"I cannot feel my legs." Jackie said.

Listening to what she had just said John knelt down in the middle of the backseat placed his right arm under the midsection of her back as his left arm went around the top midsection of her back and lifted her up from the compartment trying to help her stand up. She could not keep this standing position without the help of John and as the lid of the backseat came back down John placed Jackie into a seating position on top of it.

"My Legs, My Legs!" Jackie cried but she had laughter within the tone of her voice.

She knew she had made it safely into the freedom she had so wished for. So many have tried this and only a few had succeeded. John knelt before her onto the floor of the van and began vigorously rubbing her legs to get the circulation of blood flowing through her veins. In unison, John, Mike, and Ray shouted out loud,

"WELCOME TO WEST BERLIN!"

38
THE KU'DORF MEETING

The excitement was running high, with all four of them, as the plan was successful, providing Jackie with safe transportation into the West. Ray pulled the van over to the side of the road and parked "The White VW Freedom Van". John still rubbing her legs to help Jackie get the feeling back into her legs. John opened the back door and helped Jackie get out of the van. Her right arm was over John's shoulders and around the back of his neck. With his left arm around her waist and his right hand holding her right hand, he began the therapeutic walking with her in a straight line, back and forth. She relied on his assistance as she limped slowly with each step. After a few minutes she stopped and said,

"I think I will be okay now. I will be right back."

John being concerned said,

"Are you sure? Where are you going?"

Jackie, with a mean look in her eyes said,

"There is something I have to do. I hate them so much, John!"

John being confused,

"What are you going to do? You can't go back there Jackie! I will go with you to make sure you are okay."

John continued to help Jackie walk over to the corner where Ray had turned the van earlier. They were not that far away from Checkpoint Charlie. Jackie looked at John and said,

"You stay right here. I will not be very far away. When I am done then we can go."

John thought that her actions were much too bold after having gone through such a daring escape, still being so close to the East Side of Berlin, it created him to feel uneasy as he did not know what Jackie was going to do. Jackie let go of John's arm, walked out onto the street corner, then stood underneath the highly lit lamp post. At the top of her lungs she began yelling obscenities in English and German. The middle finger of her right hand was raised high in the air and pointed in the direction of the East German Border Guards and the East German Guard Towers. Jackie kept screaming at them,

"I HATE YOU, I HATE YOU, I HATE YOU!!! I AM FREE NOW!!!"

She repeated this phrase a few more times, then giving one last middle finger flip off to the East Germans, she walked over to John and said,

"There, we can go now."

John, though being uneasy with what she had done, looked at her with a glow in his eyes. He was amazed with her. He was proud of her and felt honored being around her. He knew he had done the right thing. With a slight laughing chuckle, he said.

“Good! Do you feel better now? Are you happy with that?”

Jackie, with an extreme glow of comfort, laughingly expressed,

“Ja, I do... Ja, I am. I am free, John! Let's go!”

She gave John a hug and a kiss, then wrapping her left arm around his right arm, she began to take control of the walking back to the van, still limping slightly along the way. When they returned back to the van, Broadway began with his question of curiosity,

“What was that all about?”

John answered him back,

“It was just something Jackie had to do, to get it off of her chest. Hey, I'm good with it. She gave me a hug and a kiss. I'm happy.”

Mike answered back being sarcastic, but in a joking way, said,

“Yeah, Yeah... Get in the van and lets get out of here.”

John and Jackie entered the van then John closed the door behind them. As they were sitting down on the back seat, Ray and Mike asked the same question simultaneously,

"Where do you want to go first Jackie?"

Jackie laughingly responded,

"That's a silly question, THE KU'DORF!"

Everyone was delighted with her response. They knew though, that they had to stop at McNair Barracks in order for Mike and John to change their clothes. They had to get out of their Class B Uniforms and change into civilian clothing. Upon arriving to McNair barracks, Ray had to stop "The Freedom Van" a few blocks away from the guard shack entry instead of driving into the compound because Jackie was with them. As John and Mike were exiting the van, Jackie stated that she was getting cold. John assured her that when he returned he would bring her his black leather jacket to keep her warm. John and Mike rushed out of the van and ran toward the guards at the entry way. The guards on duty recognized the both of them and without asking for their identification waved them through as they seen they were in a hurry. They did not stop running till they reached the doors to their rooms. Within minutes they were changed and ready to go. John was carrying his black leather jacket for Jackie. They rushed back down to the van and took their usual spots. Ray placed the van in gear and headed out. John helped Jackie put his jacket on. She was beginning to warm up. Jackie placed her hands in the pockets of the black leather jacket and said,

"What is this? The pockets are ripped and they have holes in them."

John was a little embarrassed by her comment but offered her an explanation,

“Yes, it is an old jacket but it will keep you warm. Besides that, you look good in it. Better than I do actually!”

Jackie snuggled up against John and said,

“I don't care if it has holes in the pockets. I am very happy you let me use it. Ja, it is very warm. Put your arm around me and keep me warm too, please.”

John was more than happy to oblige her. Along the way to the Ku'Dorf, Ray and Mike were showing Jackie the different things that were in West Berlin. John wasn't much help in that area as he was still new in West Berlin. They arrived at the Ku'Dorf where Jackie, John and Mike exited the van. Ray bid them to have a great evening and reminded Mike and John that he would pick them up at the Ku'Dorf around 1100 hours. Everyone waved good bye to Ray as he placed the van in gear then took off for home. Walking down the steps to the Ku'Dorf they stopped to pay the entry fee then proceeded further inward, took a left, walked down the dimly lit section. They were coming up to the S-curve in the middle of the Ku'Dorf, where the mens bathroom was located on the right, they hooked a left. Walking toward the curve to the right, they suddenly stopped. All three of them recognized someone that they knew, straight ahead of them. It was Specialist Tracy Guill. He had his back to them for the moment. They saw him lean forward to pick up a full glass of beer that had just been served to him. Turning around, he placed his left elbow up on the bar. With the full beer in his right hand he raised the glass up to his mouth to take a drink. It was too late for Jackie, John, or Mike to turn back. They saw Guill's eyes move back and forth, then he spotted them. His mouth was wide opened. His right hand lessened the grip he had on his glass of beer, without taking a drink from the glass, it had slipped through his fingers and with a loud thud hit the floor and smashed into pieces. He was speechless, as he was figuring out for sure what he was seeing. Walking clear of his spilled drink, Guill approached the three of them and said,

"Is this true what I am seeing here? What did you guys do?"

He gave Jackie a hug and welcomed her to West Berlin, as he was speaking to her in German, Mike interrupted him and said,

"You didn't see anything tonight Guill! You got that!"

Guill was still in shock as he said,

"No, I don't see anything here tonight. Congratulations Men! You are heroes in my book!"

Everyone of them decided to take a seat, at the small round table, that was in the small corridor, at the quiet little bar that, John had always enjoyed going to. Though quiet, there was enough traffic in that route to keep bumping elbows with people passing by on both sides.

Two gentleman appeared along Jackie's side, then started to speak to her. Jackie got up from her chair and gave them both hugs. They were about Bolden's height of around five foot eight inches tall, maybe a little shorter. They were dark complected with curly black hair that leveled at the top of their shoulders. They were not Turkish from what Bolden could figure out, as they did not have the characteristics of being from Turkish descent. Bolden had seen them in the discos in East Berlin. They stood out enough to be noticed by him but Bolden didn't give it much thought back then. Now, he was seeing them in West Berlin and wondered why and what they were doing in West Berlin. As Jackie and the two dark complected gentlemen were talking in German, Bolden was watching the two men, when they spoke to each other in their native language Bolden picked up on it. They were Yugoslavian! John had heard this language being spoke before from his best friend's, mother, Marie Conant, who was Yugoslavian. She would speak her native language to her sisters, whenever they came over for a visit.

Bolden picked up on a few words they were talking about but did not realize the full extent of their conversation. A round of drinks had been bought from Guill for everyone around the table. Bolden had chosen to drink Pepsi with a splash of lemon to it. He still wished to have his senses about him all night, seeing that, they would be staying up all night with Jackie at the Ku'Dorf. Jackie had a look of concern in her eyes, as her and the Yugoslavian gentlemen were talking. John and Mike were very curious and concerned to what they were talking about.

Jackie leaned back into Mike and John and drew them in closer to her, then said to them,

"The both of them offered me a place in their home tonight to sleep. If it is okay with both of you, then I will go with them tonight. Will you meet me back here in a few hours?"

John and Mike were both very concerned. They did not know these two men. Even though they seen them in East Berlin, at the discos, neither one of them had really talked to them to get to know them. John asked Jackie, with a stern look in his eyes,

"Are you sure you want to go with these two guys? Do you know them well? Are you going to be okay? I told you, Mike and I will stay with you all night till Ray picks us up in the morning. If you think you will be safe with these men, then of course, stay with them, but if you are unsure about any of this, then don't go. We wish to know that you will be safe here Jackie!"

Jackie was confidant with her answer back to John,

"Ja, I will be okay with them. I know them well. You and Mike, tell Ray, to meet us here at ten in the morning. I will be here in the same spot to meet you."

Even though John felt insecure with her answer, he agreed to her terms and hoped for the best. Mike felt the insecurity of it, as well, but was submissive to her desires. Both, John and Mike, felt they had an obligation toward Jackie, but, with Jackie being at ease with her new company, reluctantly gave in to her request. John, reassuring her, said,

“Okay, if that is what you wish to do, then go for it. We will be here to pick you up at ten! If you aren't here, we're coming to look for you! You got that!?”

She laughed and said,

“Ja, I got that! I will be here.”

The next round of drinks was ordered and the Yugoslavian gentlemen were buying. John and Mike feeling a bit more secure with Jackie's decision, this time ordered a golden Weissen beer. Jackie ordered a glass of wine and started to relax a bit more. The feeling of being in West Berlin was beginning to set in with her. She was feeling a little more free than usual but she still had her cautious side to her. A couple more drinks came onto the table, after a few moments, the group at the table decided to move further into the Ku'Dorf. They were headed to the disco at the end of the Ku'Dorf when all of a sudden they heard the sound of the song from Lynyrd Skynyrd, “Free Bird”. John was in total bliss, it was a sign from above, that he had made the correct decision in helping someone, to obtain, what this song was actually describing. Bolden was a complete fan of this song when he first heard it as a teenager. He felt like he was at home and lost all consciousness of where he was at. He went straight to the dance floor by himself and started to place his expression in a dance. He moved to the music like never before, not caring who was watching or what they were thinking of him. He was free in spirit, free in soul, to do whatever he wished to do. In the middle of the song, on the dance floor, he felt two hands grab him gently around his waste. He knew it was Jackie, coming from behind him, to dance with him. He closed his eyes and grabbed those two hands to pull them closer to him, then wrapped those arms around him. He turned around, opened his eyes, then discovered it was one of the Yugoslavian men that offered Jackie safe shelter for the evening. John was shocked, in total amazement, he was caught off guard while being in his fantasy. He quickly threw the two hands, that were gripped around him earlier, away from him. Showing his feeling of disgust, for being caught off guard, thinking, at first, that those hands were from Jackie, embracing him around his waist. The Yugoslavian gentleman placed his arms and hands up to his face in a guarding position, thinking that Bolden was going to hit him. John, seeing this man's reaction, was quick to calm him down, with both of his hands up in the air and his palm's facing outward with a slow back and forth movement, said,

“It's okay, it's okay! I thought you were Jackie.”

The Yugoslavian gentleman cautiously placed his arms downward. Beginning to feel comfortable around Bolden's presence he said,

“Thank you for bringing Jackie to West Berlin. You are a true American. If there is anything we can do for you, please let us know. We will be happy to do it for you.”

He opened his arms to offer Bolden a hug. It was not a hug of a loving nature, but of one for brotherly love. Bolden accepted his offer. As they embraced, Bolden said to him,

“There are two things that I ask of you. One is, that you keep Jackie safe, I wish for you to treat her with dignity and honor. The other thing is, that you keep this secret. You did not see any of us here tonight. Do you understand what I am asking of you?”

As they were easing up on their embrace together, he said to Bolden,

“I understand what you are asking. You're wishes will be granted. Please be assured that Jackie will be safe with us. She will be back here for you to pick her up in a few hours.

Bolden felt comfortable with what the Yugoslavian gentleman was telling him. He went to kiss Bolden on his cheeks as if sealing a deal the old fashion way. Bolden stopped him before he could get close to John's cheek and with a smile on his face said,

“Whoa..., hold on, I know what you are doing and I can respect that, but..., how about we just shake hands on this? I'm American, you know that. I'm good with a hand shake.”

The Yugoslavian gentleman started laughing. He placed his right hand out and said,

"Yes, I am good with this. We are so proud of you!"

The hand shake took place and the deal was sealed with confidence in both men. The two walked up to the end of the Ku'Dorf, to where the disco was. They found Jackie, Mike, and the other Yugoslavian gentleman. All of them were showing signs of being tired as the time was getting late. Guill had left the disco awhile back, claiming that it was getting too late for him to stay. John and Mike were aware of the time and how the public buses were running according to those times. They both made sure that Jackie was confidant, in being safe, with the two Yugoslavian gentlemen. With the atmosphere of satisfaction around for everyone involved, Mike and John assured Jackie that they will be back at 1000 hours. Jackie assured John and Mike that she would be there waiting for them. Jackie gave Mike and John a big hug and a kiss, then told them,

"I LOVE YOU GUYS! ALL OF YOU! I AM FREE NOW! I WILL MAKE YOU PROUD OF ME!"

Mike and John in unexpected unison said,

"YOU ALREADY DID!"

Mike being sarcastic to John said,

"Hey I said it first, you asshole!"

John, laughing, blew Mike's sarcasm off and said,

“Whatever Mike, just be happy, would ya?”

The laughter ensued among everyone in their small circle. It was time to depart company. John and Mike waved goodbye to Jackie and her gentlemen friends then walked to the other end of the Ku'Dorf. Walking up the steps to the public streets, the Doner Ke Bob stand was close by where both of them grabbed a couple sandwiches for their meal home. They walked over to the bus stop stand just in time as the bus pulled up to take them back to McNair Barracks. Hopping onto the bus, they found a couple seats that were free then sat down. The bus diesel engine roared as it took off down the road. After a few minutes of silence Broadway was the first one to speak,

“We did good tonight Johnny! It was successful! I can't wait till Jacqueline and her son get here next weekend!”

John was quiet as he responded back to Mike,

“Yes we did good Mike and it was very successful. I have to tell you what is on my mind though. There are too many people, right now, that know what we have done. Guill, being one of us, has a duty to report what he has seen tonight. The two Yugoslavian men, that were at the Ku'Dorf tonight..., well I've seen them in the East and I know you have to. What is saying, that they are not double agents? Even though we were successful tonight in bringing Jackie over here, we still have a few more days to go, to know if we are able to bring Jacqueline and her son over here. I don't want to discourage you Mike but we do have to take into consideration what happened tonight."

Broadway with a look of reality setting in was still hopeful saying,

"Yes, I know, but everything is going to be fine. Next weekend we are going to bring Jacqueline and her son over here to the West and I will marry her! Oh, by the way, Jackie wants to go to the German-American Volksfest when we pick her up in a few hours. I told her we would take her there. Are you okay with that?"

John was astounded to hear what Mike was telling him. His thoughts were going in every direction. John knew that, if they went to the Volksfest, they would surely come across someone else that they knew and would figure out what they did. Bolden could voice his opinion but knew it would not change the circumstances that were going to come up in a few hours. He expressed them anyways, saying,

"Now Mike, that is extremely risky. I will go with you, of course, but I have my doubts on this. I have to take over CQ Runner from Schmidt in the afternoon, so I will have to be back before then. You and Ray take care of Jackie. I know she will be with you two at Ray's house Sunday night. Monday, after you get off of duty, both You and I will meet her at the Ku'Dorf to see how things went, as far as her turning herself in to the proper authorities. Is that okay with you?"

Mike being extremely happy and hopeful said,

“Yes, that's okay with me. We will call you Sunday night and let you know how things are going. You have to answer the phone anyways, so I will know it is you. You're thinking too much Johnny! Everything is going to go good. We will keep to our plan and everything will be fine! You'll see!”

Bolden shrugged his shoulders then lifted his arms into the air and said,

“Yes, we will see!”

The bus pulled up to the stop for McNairs Barracks. John and Mike, with Doner Ke Bob sandwiches in their hands, exited the bus and walked to the gate. They didn't have to present their identification, due to the guards working the shift, knew of them already and waved them through the gate. They were silent as the both of them walked up to their room, then bid each other a good night. Bolden entered his room and placed the sandwiches in his small refrigerator. He was overly tired and in being so he was not able to go to sleep right away. He perched himself up upon his window ledge. The place where he did all of his wishing and thinking. He knew his dream, his wish, had come true. He was happy, very happy, but deep down in his heart, he felt the uneasiness of something that was unknown to him for the time being. He wondered what it could be, but in all essence, he knew. Looking up into the night sky he saw the moon, waxing three quarters and headed full force into a full moon. The waxing of the moon was climbing upwards and soon the portal would be closed for wishes to be granted. Bolden had to wait for the near future to unfold before him. He knew that by the next weekend the portal would be closed for wishes to be granted and that the possibility to bring Mike's fiance and her son over to the West would not be granted. There were other things in the ether mist that had to be answered for, which laid in the essence of dreams brought forward. There was a price attached to the deed they had done, that previous evening, and it would be up to them in how to handle that debt. Bolden lifted his head and then his chest. Standing up and looking at the moon, shining brightly in the sky, he prayed for everyone's safety and hoped that all who were involved with such a great deed would go unscathed from such an incident. He laid down on his bunk, placed his head on his pillow. It did not take long for him to go to sleep. Though anxious and delighted with such a success, that evening's event had taken a toll upon him, enough so, that his body placed itself into full rest, preparing itself for the next days adventure.

39
GERMAN-AMERICAN VOLKSFEST

Sunday, August 17th, 1986. Bolden is awakened by the continuous raps upon his door. He knew it was Broadway. His continuous rapping knock was beginning to become his signature for announcing his presence. Bolden opened the door and let him in. Broadway was filled with excitement as he said,

“Come on Johnny! It's almost time to get going. I couldn't sleep last night. How about you?”

Bolden, yawning, answered Broadways question,

“I was doing just fine until you knocked on my door! Give me a few minutes to wake up and get dressed, then we can go. Is that okay with you?”

Broadway being sarcastic said,

“Yeah, yeah, get your ass moving! Ray is going to be here in about thirty minutes. We will meet you downstairs in the parking lot. Be ready to go or we're leaving without you. We told Jackie we would meet her at 1000 hours, so Ray and I are going to be there, with or without you! You got that!?”

Bolden looked at him with half opened eyes and an uncaring look, then said,

“I will be there. If you have to wait for me, then you are going to wait till I come down there. The two of you are not leaving without me! You got that!?”

Broadway started laughing, then said,

“Yeah, come on! Let's get going. We are going to go have some fun at the Volksfest. All of us Johnny!”

Bolden, becoming more awakened from his deep sleep, said,

“I will be there Michael. You can count on it!”

With those words said, Broadway exited the room, then proceeded downstairs to the parking lot. Bolden was dressed within a couple minutes, then headed down to the parking lot/formation area. Throwing open one of the double doors he noticed Ray and "The White VW Freedom Van" pulling into the parking lot. Mike opened the side door for Bolden to enter. The moment Bolden entered that van and before he was able to take his seating place on the back seat, Broadway had the side door closed and running for his place in the front seat. Broadway and Bolden said their greetings to Williams and as soon as Broadway closed his door on the front passenger side, Ray had the van in gear and headed toward the guard gate at McNair Barracks. They exited the compound then headed directly to the Ku'Dorf. Arriving at 0950 hours, ten minutes earlier than what the plan was, they notice Jackie exiting a black BMW. Inside the BMW were the two Yugoslavian gentlemen that Mike and John had personally met a few hours prior. There was no need to enter the Ku'dorf, for all parties involved had precise timing. Greetings were given among everyone, then soon after were the blessings of departure. Jackie entered "The Freedom Van", into the back seat with John following behind her immediately after. Ray took his driver's position, then Mike with his. Ray did not know what the plans were of Mike and Jackie from the previous night and asked,

"Where are we going?"

Bolden was silent but Mike and Jackie were instant in answering the question, in unison they said,

“To the GERMAN-AMERICAN VOLKSFEST!”

Ray was very cautious in what they had said, then asked,

“Are we sure we want to do this? Most likely we are going to meet someone there that, not only knows us, but knows Jackie too. If they see her with us, they will most definitely put two and two together I don't think this is a very smart move on our part, but if everyone wants to do this then we will go.”

Jackie and Mike were quick with their answers,

“Yes, let's go!”

John was hesitant. He really didn't want to answer what Ray was asking. Ray looking in the rear view mirror, positioned it in a way that he was looking at John directly,

“John, what do you think? Do you want to go or not?”

Bolden looked into the mirror staring into Ray's eyes and said,

“Well.., I don't think it's the smartest move on our part, but if they want to go, then let's go.”

Ray being uneasy, placed the “Freedom Van” in gear and proceeded onward to the GERMAN-AMERICAN VOLKSFEST. Ray found a parking spot close to one of the entrances. Before he was able to place the “Freedom

Van" into park, Broadway opened his door and exited the vehicle. Opening the side door and with happiness in his voice, said,

"Come on, Let's go!" This is Jackie's first GERMAN-AMERICAN VOLKSFEST! Let's Celebrate!"

Bolden exited the van, then Jackie followed after him. Waiting for Ray to secure the van, they walked slowly toward the entrance. John and Mike took a stand on each side of Jackie, then Ray followed behind them. They were all close together, as if they were shielding Jackie for her safety. A few steps inward they noticed three of their platoon members. One of them stood out among them and was in the lead of his companionship. It was Copsovic. Of all the members of their platoon, Bolden did not want to meet Copsovic, as he knew who Jackie was. The other two were, Specialist Tracy Long and Specialist Mark Tate, neither one knew who Jackie was. It wouldn't be long for their discovery. Copsovic looked in their direction and stopped in his tracks. His other two companions stopped with him. All three were astonished at what they were seeing. As Jackie, John, Mike and Ray were approaching them, Copsovic shouted out,

"What did you guys do??? This isn't right! Take her back, Take her back over there now!!!"

Jackie, John, Mike, and Ray were astounded by what Copsovic had expressed. They didn't expect what had come from his words. John looked at Jackie and discovered from her eyes that she was in a daze, a shock of some sort. It was as if she heard what Copsovic had said but chose to place it in the back of her mind. Then John looked at Mike. From what John could figure out, Mike had a look of disgust on his face and was searching for the words to respond back to Copsovic. John looked at Ray. From what John saw, it was a look of worry upon Ray's face. Ray was searching for a response back to Copsovic as well. John took the lead in the situation to respond back to Copsovic. He wished to protect his group of “Freedom Fighters” so they were able to keep their pride. Looking back at Copsovic, John saw the strength of Copsovic's convictions. Specialist Long and Specialist Tate had a look of shock on their face. John knew they were putting everything together by what Copsovic had stated. They had a glow about their aura that displayed happiness from an unknown source, but with happiness in abundance, that surrounds your soul, no one really questions it, they enjoy it's presence. Bolden could hold back no further and without thinking, stared Copsovic in his eyes,

“What do you mean take her back? You know the repercussions of such an act, if she goes back there! What a selfish prick you are, you arrogant piece of shit! You're lucky! We were going to bring her over last weekend but you had to come along with us and spoil the whole plan! She's here now and she is here to stay, whether you like it or not!”

Bolden knew, the moment his words left his mouth, that he had given out the secret of their activities. His pride got in the way but he couldn't help himself, to defend, his friends, from such a sarcastic, arrogant remark, from the one person that he had disliked, with a passion, from the moment he first met him. Tim with his haughtiness, responded back,

"You're damn right, you didn't do it last weekend when I was with you. I would have thrown her ass out of the van!"

Bolden could not stop in his responses,

"YOU DID!!! YOU PRICK!!! YOU PUT YOUR TWO HANDS AROUND HER WAIST AND THREW HER OUT OF THE VAN!!! SHE WAS BEGGING ME, PLEADING WITH ME, TO TAKE HER TO THE WEST WITH US AND YOU THREW HER OUT OF THE VAN!!! WHAT YOU DIDN'T SEE OR CARED NOT TO SEE, WAS THAT, AS YOU DID THAT, THERE WAS AN EAST GERMAN BORDER GUARD PASSING BY TO REPORT TO HIS POST!!! I MAY HAVE BEEN PUKING DRUNK THAT NIGHT TIM BUT I WAS AWARE OF MY SURROUNDINGS!!! THAT'S WHY I WAS DRUNK THAT NIGHT. IT WAS BECAUSE I KNEW WE WEREN"T GOING TO BE ABLE TO DO THIS WITHOUT INCLUDING YOU AND THE WAY THINGS ARE, RIGHT NOW, IT WASN'T GOING TO HAPPEN!!! DO YOU HAVE ANY IDEA WHAT HAPPENED TO HER THAT NIGHT, WHEN YOU THREW HER OUT OF THE VAN, WITH THAT BORDER GUARD PASSING BY? DO YOU EVEN CARE?"

Copsovic stopped his complaining. Bolden had hit a nerve in him. Tim opened his arms to Jackie to give her a hug. She accepted and as they embraced, Tim welcomed her to West Berlin. Specialist Long was still in shock as to what was going on. Bolden introduced Specialist Tracy Long to Jackie. After Copsovic, Tracy Long extended his arms out to Jackie to welcome her saying to Bolden,

“I know who she is. I don't go to East Berlin with you guys but I have heard good stories about her.”

Then Specialist Mark Tate extended his right hand out to shake Jackie's hand and to welcome her to West Berlin. He wasn't a huggy type of person, so therefore, Jackie extended her hand out, shaking hands with him. Specialist Tate did not go over to East Berlin too much either, but him and Jackie had known each other from before. It was a silent type of reunion between the two of them.

Ray, taking the leadership role, looked at Copsovic, then said,

“With what you know now, Tim, we trust that you will not say anything about what you have seen and heard here today. Tracy?, Mark?, The same goes for you two as well! Do we have the confidence of your discretion?”

Copsovic, being hesitant with his answer, gave Ray his assurance of being quiet. Specialist Tate was quiet with his response in giving a thumbs up for his approval of secrecy. Specialist Tracy Long, on the other hand, was not quiet with his gestures, as he began stating his opinion,

"ARE YOU GUYS JOKING? ALL OF YOU ARE FRICKING HEROES!!! YOU CAN COUNT ON ME!!! IF YOU NEED ANYTHING, I MEAN ANYTHING, THEN ASK AND I AM THERE FOR ALL OF YOU!!!"

With what was transpiring among the group everyone seemed confident with the incident that had just occurred and the secrecy would be upheld. There was still a small air of distrust lingering that everyone could feel but was placed off to the side for comforts sake. Copsovic began his comments,

"We can't be seen with neither of you. Good Luck To All Of You!"

He gave Jackie another hug. After that, he took his companions and headed in an opposite direction from the "Freedom Fighters". The next few hours continued on as Jackie, John, Mike, and Ray enjoyed each others company, frolicking upon the rides that were available at the German-American Volksfest. The roller coaster and the tilt-o-whirl being there favorites. All of them grabbed a couple of hotdogs mit pomme frits for their afternoon meal. The time soon came when Bolden said,

"I hate to say it, you guys, but I have to head back to the barracks and take over CQ Runner duty for Schmidt. Ray could you give me a ride?"

Ray was quick with his response,

“Yes, I will give you a ride back. We have to get out of here soon anyways. There will most likely be a lot more people, who know us, coming here. Right now, there are too many people who know what has happened. Let's get moving.”

The group walked back to the “Freedom Van”, took their spots, then headed down the cobble stone street roads toward McNair Barracks. Bolden was the first one to break the silence,

“I know Long and Tate will be quiet about this and I hope Tim will keep his mouth shut about today. You guys know they have an actual duty of reporting what they have seen here today, don't you?”

Mike bounced out his response quickly,

“Johnny, Tim is good to go, man! So are the other two men. They won't say a word!”

Then being sarcastic, he said,

“Why did you have to tell him what you did, you idiot? You could have kept quiet like the rest of us. All that they would have had was, guessing at what happened, now they know the real story.”

John, feeling somewhat uneasy about what Mike had said, hesitated with his response,

"I know, Mike and I apologize to all of you for saying what I did, to Tim. I really do not like that guy and the way he thinks, he is so much better than anyone else. I despise him! My pride got in the way and I felt I had to defend us against his wordy attack on what we believe to be right. I will take your word on it Mike, that he will be quiet about what he saw today."

Ray, driving the van and listening to the conversation, put in his words,

"Tim will be quiet about it. I trust him. He may have gone through his Genesis and is on a straight path now but he knows what is right and what isn't. He cares for Jackie and would not do anything to harm her. Whatever comes our way we are going to have to hit it straight forward and all of us are going to have to stick to our story in order for all of us to walk away from this. Like the Three Musketeers, "All For One And One For All!" We have Jackie with us now so she is like the Fourth Musketeer."

Jackie began to giggle then said,

"JA! All For One And One For All!"

Her cute comment and funny little giggle lifted the spirit in the air and provided the comaraderie among them all. The ride went by quickly as they arrived at McNair Barracks. Ray, stopping the van on the corner of Fourth of July Platz to let John out. Exiting the van John said,

“Give me a call later on and let me know how things are going, will you?”

Mike, being in a gleeful mood, said,

“I told you, last night, we will call you. You just make sure you're the one answering the phone.”

John didn't respond back. He waved good bye then started walking to the entrance of the compound. Making his way pass the guards, to almost the end of the compound, then through the parking lot of the formation area, and up the steps, arriving at the CQ Desk, where Russell Schmidt was waiting for him. He looked at Russell and said,

“Give me a few minutes to change into my BDUs and I will be right back to relieve you of duty. I know it's a little early yet but this will give you some extra time at home.”

Schmidt didn't say a word. He stared at Bolden then just nodded his head. Bolden thought it was kind of strange for Russell to be acting that way. Schmidt was usually very jovial and seeing that he was going to be going home soon, in Bolden's thoughts, Russell should have been a bit more happier. Bolden shrugged it off then went to his room to change his clothes. He returned to the CQ Desk and relieved Specialist Schmidt from his duty. Russell thanked him and without hesitation, he was out the door, walking down the steps to go home. All was quiet for a Sunday afternoon and then into the evening.

The phone rang a few times. As Bolden answered the rings of the telephone, he was discovering the usual calls from some of the soldier's girlfriends calling them. He would go knock on their doors to see if they were in. Most of the soldiers that were in their rooms would take their call and some of them would not, giving an explanation that they had some things to accomplish soon and were unavailable to take the call. It was 2030 hours when the phone rang. Bolden picked up the phone and presented his usual greeting,

"Hello, Sir or Ma'am, Thank You for calling CSC 6/502nd Infantry. You are speaking on an unsecured line. Specialist Bolden speaking, how may I help you?"

As the voice started speaking, Bolden knew it was Michael,

"Yeah, Yeah, I know it is you. Stop speaking so formal would ya? How are things going on CQ Duty, Johnny?"

Bolden was delighted to hear Broadway's voice. It was the phone call he was waiting for. He began speaking,

"Kind of quiet and boring here for a Sunday night, Mike. Schmidt seemed a bit out of sorts when I relieved him of his duties earlier. I kind of figured maybe it was something going on at his home. How is it going for you guys?"

Bolden could hear Ray and Jackie laughing in the background then Mike following with his laughter soon after. His voice sounded a little faint as Bolden heard Broadway say,

“Will you guys knock it off over there. I'm on the phone with Johnny!”

Mike's voice became more clear as he said,

“We're having a great time here, Johnny. Wish you could be with us. We picked up some beer and wine earlier. We aren't drunk yet, but we're working on it. I've got something I have to tell you. Hold on a moment. I have to go into the bedroom for some privacy.”

A few seconds pass then Bolden could hear a door close, through the receiver of the phone. Mike lowering his voice, says,

“Johnny, she called her British boyfriend from Ray's phone here. I didn't know who she was calling or who she was talking to until she hung up the phone and told me. I think we may have a problem!

John was quiet on the phone. He was in a bit of shock, then he became furious, then he calmed down. With a stern voice he said,

“You think we have a problem? No Mike, from what you just told me now, on this unsecured line, I'm pretty sure we have a problem! You know better Mike! You should have watched her the whole time. You and Ray, BOTH!

What did the British boyfriend have to say? Did she tell you?"

"Mike, with a little uncertainty in his voice, said,

"She told me she wanted to let him know that she was here. Johnny, you know how special he is to her. Once she told him she was here, he told her that he didn't want anything to do with her, then hung up the phone on her. I think we will be okay. Don't worry about it Johnny. Tell you what, I will have a couple beers for you to help you to relax. How's that for you?"

Bolden had to contain himself. With a calm voice he said,

"Mike, you go ahead and do that. I better let you go for now so we can keep an open line. You guys have a good night and I will see you tomorrow. Out here!"

Bolden didn't wait for Mike's response, quickly hanging up the phone, so their conversation could go no further than what had already transpired. He knew that too many people already know what they have done. First it was Guill, then the two Yugoslavian Gentlemen at the Ku'Dorf. Copsovic, Long, and Tate at the Volksfest. Now, Jackie's, British Soldier Boyfriend. He had a duty to report the phone call he received from Jackie telling him she was in the West. John's thoughts began to go in every direction,

"That British Soldier will undoubtedly report this to his commander. Specialist Ivey told me how the British are sticklers for following the rules. They are strong willed for sure. And with Saturday night, as it went, taking Jackie away from his side, from the table they were sitting at, he has to know it was us, that brought her over here. Mike telling me about this on an unsecured line, where anyone could be listening. If anyone was listening, they know it now to. What about Schmidt? He was acting odd!"

Deep into thought, Bolden kept thinking, adding things up and producing possibilities. The accounting columns of debit were beginning to become much longer than the credit side. John heard a door open up a couple doors down from the CQ Desk. The noise interrupted his thinking, as he looked down the hall to see Specialist Long coming out of his room. Long with a big hearty voice said,

"HEY, JOHN..., HOW ARE YOU DOING THERE, HERO?!!!"

John, standing up from his chair and with a low stern voice said,

"You stow those words, right now Tracy, and lower your voice! Schmidt was acting weird when I relieved him from his duty. Did you guys tell him anything?"

Specialist Long walked cautiously to the CQ Desk, stopped, then answered Bolden's question,

"Well..., It kind of came out. Copsovic couldn't stop his complaining about you guys. He kept on and on about it. He was becoming annoying and boring. We decided to come back here. Russell overheard him when we walked by the desk here and asked what was going on? So, we told him. Don't worry about it John! He will keep quiet about it. To us, you guys are definitely heroes..., well Tim might not talk about how he thinks you guys are heroes, but he thinks you are anyways. You have to give him time to cool down because you didn't include him in what you were going to do on that weekend he went with you. Man..., Johnny, you guys are GREAT!!!"

Bolden's suspicions were confirmed by what Tracy had just told him. He sat back down on his chair, placed his elbows on the desk, leaned forward and placed his face into his open palms. It was too much, too many people were finding out about their activities, and there would be more. It had gone way out of control. Bolden rambled in his thoughts,

"WHY? WHY DID I HAVE TO SAY, WHAT I SAID, TO COPSOVIC! My pride got in the way. If I could only take back what I said to him. We are going to have to stick to our story. It is the only thing that is going to save us right now. I know we aren't going to be able to bring Jacqueline and her son over now. Mike is going to have to realize this soon. I don't know what to tell him. It's my fault, saying what I said to Tim. I hope Mike will forgive me. There is hope though. If we all stay faithful to our story. If we all come together as one. We might be able to bring Jacqueline and her son over!"

Bolden was immersed in his thoughts when he felt the touch of Specialist Tracy Long's hand, embrace his left shoulder, as Tracy said,

"John, everything is going to be okay. Be at ease with all of this. John, they are going to give you a medal for doing this! I will tell you, it took balls to do what you men did. I believe it is everyone's dream to do this. You will be okay! I told you before, if there is anything I can do for you, then let me know and I am there for you!"

Bolden, hiding his insecurity, moved his head upward. With a smile on his face and a small chuckle of laughter from his voice, said,

"Tracy..., You know what I would like you to do? Clean my fucking weapon the next time we come out of the field. As many times as I have done that for you, I think you owe me that."

Specialist Long was laughing so hard from Bolden's comment that it drew the attention from Sgt. Heinz who was resting in the First Sergeant's office. Walking up to the CQ Desk, Bolden noticed his movement and yelled,

"AT EASE!"

Both Bolden and Long came into the position of, "Parade Rest". To understand the differences of a command, is to be a soldier. When an officer walks into your area of operation, the senior ranking, yells the command of,

"ATTENTION"

Therefore, all soldiers, of inferior rank, come to a position, where their feet come together, chest and head held high, with their arms being straight along each side of them, the enlisted men, or inferior ranking, wait for the order of,

"AT EASE!"

To continue on with whatever it is to what they were doing previous, or to listen to any orders that must be carried out from their superior officer. When an NCO, (Non-Commissioned Officer/Sergeant, of any class, enters your area of operation, the senior under ranking of that NCO gives the men the order of,

"AT EASE!"

When this order is given, then the inferior ranking come to the position of "Parade Rest", which is, feet spread evenly out, to maintain balance, and both hands held behind their back. In this position they wait for the orders to be carried out, or to hear the words,

"CARRY ON!"

This is the distinguishing characteristics to know who you are to be addressing at the time of their presence.

Sgt. Heinz gave the order to "Carry On", then asked Specialist Long,

“Don't you have something you have to do right now, Long?”

Tracy, understanding what Sgt. Heinz was asking said,

“Yes Sergeant, I was headed to the latrine to take care of business!”

Sgt. Heinz responded back saying,

“Then go take care of your business and leave my CQ Runner be for the night. He's got some thing far more better to do than listen to what you are talking about. You got that?”

Specialist Long understood what Sgt. Heinz was saying to him then simply said,

“Yes Sergeant.”

Tracy headed for the latrine without saying good bye. Both Sergeant Heinz and Specialist Bolden watched as Specialist Long entered the community latrine. After that, Sgt. Heinz looked at Bolden and said,

“Is there anything you want to tell me Specialist Bolden?”

Bolden's response was simple and direct,

“No Sergeant! It has been a peaceful and quiet evening, therefore all is going well.”

Sergeant Heinz, with his quick and clever wit responded back,

"That's not what I am talking about and you know it. I heard the discussions earlier from Specialist Schmidt, Copsovic, Long, and Tate. Is there something you want to tell me?"

Specialist Bolden came into the position of "Parade Rest", he knew what Sergeant Heinz was inferring to but gave no expression to what he was asking for from Specialist Bolden,

"Sgt. Heinz, I do not know what you are talking about. All that I can tell you is that everything has been quiet and all is well, SERGEANT!"

Sgt. Heinz, with a stern look in his eyes said to Bolden,

"You keep playing that line and you will be fine! There isn't going to be much that I will be able to do for either one of you. I suspect that I won't be seeing you around here much longer but I wish for you to know this. "I THINK YOU ARE A FUCKING HERO AND ONE OF THE FINEST SOLDIERS THAT I WILL EVER KNOW! GODSPEED, TO YOU JOHN! IF YOU NEED ANYTHING, YOU LET ME KNOW! I'VE GOT TO GO MAKE MY ROUNDS. I WILL BE BACK IN A FEW MINUTES! YOU ARE IN CHARGE HERE UNTIL I GET BACK, YOU GOT THAT? CARRY ON!"

Before coming out of the position of "Parade Rest" Bolden responded back,

"Yes Sergeant! I got this!"

Bolden watched Sgt. Heinz exit through the front double doors then heard the sound of his boots as he took each step downward. A few minutes later Specialist Long came out of the community latrine, walked up to the CQ Desk, then said,

"I heard what Sgt. Heinz said to you. I apologize, to you, for not keeping quiet about this. He did say though, that he thought you guys were heroes, just like I told you. See, everything is going to be fine."

Bolden looked at Long and said,

"It's too late now. Too many people know and there will be more Tracy. I've got to do some thinking here on what to do. If you will excuse me I have some things I must attend to. Have a good night Trace!"

Specialist Long responded back saying,

"You have a good night as well. I will see you in the morning."

Tracy turned then walked to his room. Bolden watched him as he entered his room. It was quiet, very quiet, in Bolden's area of operation. He placed his face into his open palms again to relax from his stress. He prayed that everything would be fine and that everyone involved would be okay. Deep down in his intuitive thoughts, he knew, that all of them were going to have to go through a gauntlet of what was to come. He didn't know for sure yet of how all these things were going to play out. Jackie was to turn herself in to the proper authorities early in the morning and hopefully she would be accepted into West Berlin. John would have to wait, to find out from Jackie, of how her meeting went with those authorities, in order for him to know if all was going to be safe, if they were still going to be able to bring Jacqueline and her son over to the West. Everything at this point in time was dependent upon Jackie's meeting. Bolden would have to draw up his patience and wait for the answers that would come from Jackie from their meeting at the Ku'Dorf on Monday night. For right now he was safe and chose to live in the presence of NOW and to relax within the comfort of the peace and stillness that was with him!

40
MONDAY AUGUST 18TH, 1986

Specialist Bolden had missed company formation because he did a half day of CQ Runner for Specialist Schmidt who had to take care of some personal things at home that Sunday night. Him and Bolden had made a deal a week prior to the arrangement and it had already been approved by the platoon sergeant. Schmidt due to his light duty status was considered almost permanent CQ Runner Status. The arrangement had been established that Schmidt would start his regular duty hours at 0500 Sunday and work till 1700 then Bolden would take over till the end of the shift and have the full day off on Monday. This suited Bolden just fine as he had planned to meet Jackie at the Ku'dorf later that evening to see how things went as far as turning herself in to the proper authorities. After his duty was complete he went to his room and fell asleep. He is awake at 1500 hours and heads to the community bathroom to take care of business and shower to get ready to go downtown. He was feeling anxious and wanted to know if Jackie made it through and that everything was going to be okay with her. He decided to skip the chow hall with plans to grab a doner ke bob on the way to the Ku'dorf. It was a little after 1710 hours when there was a knock on his door. It was Broadway, feeling excited he asked,

"Hey, are you ready man?"

Bolden answered back,

"Yeah, hurry up and get ready!"

"I'll get these B.D.U.s off and we'll head out." responded Broadway.

Bolden shut the door to his room then in a few minutes he looked at his clock, it was 1730 hours. He grabbed his coat and started to put it on. He heard the two bay doors that were located next to his room, that led to the staircase, which led to the Battalion Headquarters the next floor down, slam open, then heard the loud angry voice of the Captain, his company commander, shouting with full force. With perfect clarity he barked out his order to the CQ Runner Schmidt.

"YOU GET BOLDEN, WILLIAMS, AND BROADWAY IN MY OFFICE RIGHT FUCKING NOW!!!"

Bolden knew in an instant, as the feeling of excitement turned into anxiety, what those words had meant. His thoughts were simple as the words kept repeating themselves over and over in his thoughts.

"FUCK, FUCK, FUCK",

then he couldn't keep it in as the word came pass his lips and out of his mouth. He was carrying his keys in his right hand as he was about to exit his room. His keys were on a key ring that had a blue plastic clasp that clasped around his belt loop when he carried them. His BDU shirt was long enough to cover them up when he was on duty so they were not noticeable. In his fit of anger and with all his might the keys and key ring came flying out of his right hand as the word came out of his mouth,

"FUCK!!!!!!"

As the keys hit the wall, by the door, the blue clasp shattered into pieces as a freshly made hole appeared on the wall. He dropped to his knees and put his hands over his face to cover up the sadness he was feeling and praying that Jackie was okay. Hearing the soft knock upon his door, he knew who it was. He gained his composure, stood up, walked to the door, and opened it. It was Russell Schmidt with a sad look on his face.

"I guess you heard that." he stated.

Bolden looking at him said,

"Yes I'm on my way."

Schmidt knew what they were being called into the C.O.'s office for, as word of the escape was already out, by that Saturday night. Schmidt looking at Bolden said in a whispered voice,

"You can run, go out these doors and get downstairs, I will tell them I couldn't find you."

Bolden looking back at Schmidt said in a low voice,

"Where am I going to go Russell?"

With a stern look in his eyes, his chest up high, his shoulders lifted back said with pride,

"I'll face the music of what is to be."

As he walked out the door and began to be escorted by Specialist Schmidt he looked toward the CQ Desk and saw two military policemen standing at the desk. Broadway was coming out of his room as they approached his door. Bolden and Broadway both winked at each other at the same time. It was, as if, they both had said to each other,

"Stick with the story."

without ever having to say a word to each other. They walked into the Captain's office and saw three more military policemen standing in the C.O.'s office. The Captain yelling loud,

"GET THESE MEN OUT OF MY OFFICE, THEY DON'T DESERVE TO BE IN HERE!!!"

First Sergeant Dean immediately ordered Bolden and Broadway into his office, which was next door. The M.P.'s followed, then Bolden felt his left hand being pulled backward and the cold feel of metal as the hand cuffs were being wrapped around his wrist, then the right hand. He heard the voice of the M.P.,

"You are under arrest for violation of the Uniform Code of Military Justice by unlawfully transporting an unauthorized personnel through Check Point Charlie in the American Sector of West Berlin Germany."

Then he heard the M.P. give him his military rights, which were not very much. Bolden heard the muffled sound of the M.P.'s voice that was arresting Broadway stating the same thing. The M.P. standing next to Bolden asked him in a calm voice, his words filled with sincerity,

"Are the hand cuffs too tight, Specialist Bolden?"

"No, Sergeant, they are fine." replied Bolden in a soft tone holding back his distress.

As Bolden and Broadway were being escorted out in hand cuffs, the Captain came out of his office screaming,

"WHERE THE FUCK IS WILLIAMS, I WANT HIM HERE NOW!!! IS THAT CLEAR LT. PILLOW?!"

Lt. Pillow was the officer of the day (OD), who was in charge of the CQ Sergeant, who was Sergeant Hayes, who was in charge of the CQ Runner, Specialist Schmidt. Before the order came down through the chain of command, Specialist Schmidt answered the Captain immediately, in a loud clear voice he could be heard saying,

"SIR, I CALLED HIS PLATOON SERGEANT WHO TOLD ME HE HAD WENT HOME ALREADY AND I CALLED HIS HOME, THERE IS NO ANSWER. HIS WIFE IS OUT OF BERLIN, AT THE MOMENT, FOR HER JOB. I WAS UNABLE TO LEAVE A MESSAGE, SIR!"

"YOU FIND HIM AND YOU FIND HIM NOW! IS THAT CLEAR SPECIALST SCHMIDT!?", piped the Captain.

"YES SIR!" WAS SCHMIDTS REPLY.

Everyone was silent as Bolden and Broadway were being escorted down the steps and into the Company Formation Area where the squad cars were sitting to provide transportation to the holding cells of the M.P. Station. Bolden felt embarrassed and ashamed as he had never been in that type of situation before. He thought he had done the right thing, a noble thing. He didn't expect, nor could he accept what was happening to him at that moment, he felt like crying but held his tears back. He lifted his head up and looked at his best friend Mike Broadway, sitting in the next squad car, and saw the tears streaming down his face.

"OH NO",

thought John as he felt his friends feelings, as he knew what Mike was thinking. He wouldn't be able to see his fiance, Jacqueline, or her infant son, ever again. It took Bolden all he could muster to keep his tears from flowing. With a big gulp to take the knot away that was beginning to form in his throat, looking at each other John nodded to his friend Mike, and gave him a tight lipped smile. Then they looked away from each other as the squad cars began to roll.

Upon arriving at the M.P. Station, Bolden and Broadway were helped out of the squad cars and escorted down the stairs of the M.P. Station and into the holding cell areas. Their hand cuffs were removed and both started to rub their wrists at the same time. The M.P. Sergeant asked again,

“The hand cuffs weren't too tight on you, were they men?”

Bolden replied with a bit of humor in his voice,

“I don't know about Mike here but I've never had a set of handcuffs on before. It's just a strange feeling Sergeant.”

Broadway piping back with his usual sarcastic tone but in a humorous way said,

“What do you mean, you don't know about Mike here, as if I've had them on before, I don't make a living out of wearing them ya know?”

Broadway was in a much better mood with that humorous undertone to his voice. The laughter ensued among everyone and the M.P. Sergeant with a calm voice said,

“Please take a seat there. We are waiting for Sergeant Williams to arrive. He has called us and is coming in on his own accord.”

Bolden and Broadway took a seat next to each other in the open area. They looked around and saw three open cell blocks. There were no other prisoners in the area. With the time going by, waiting for Williams to show up, Bolden and Broadway talked with each other about other things than the escape. They already knew the story to tell them and both felt confident they would stick to it. Bolden asked Broadway,

“Hey, you're in a much better mood. What happened?”

“On the way here the M.P. said to me, “Specialist Broadway, it's okay, I think you're a hero.”, That lightened things up a bit.” was Mike's reply.

Bolden didn't mention anything about Jacqueline, as he wished for Mike to stay in a good mood. Just then Williams started walking down the stairs toward the M.P. desk. The three men looked at each other. The confidence was high that all three would adhere to the story they had rehearsed so many times before. The desk sergeant led Williams into the interrogation room where C.I.D. (Criminal Investigations Division) awaited him for questioning.

“Looks like they are going to take us in order of rank.”, said Bolden to Broadway.

“Yeah, you know what that means, don't ya? You're the last one Johnny.” was Broadways response.

With a chuckle Bolden said,

“Yep, hopefully they won't take too long and we can get back to the barracks. I'm hungry, I got to get some chow in me.”

Thirty minutes went by and a loud voice was heard,

“ATTENTION!”,

Within an instant everyone was on their feet standing at the position of ATTENTION. A full bird Colonel walked down the stairs. His loud thunderous voice is clearly heard,

“What are these two prisoners doing sitting next to each other? Get them separated, put them in separate cells, no talking, do it now Sergeant!” was his order.

The order was carried out as the two men were led to their concrete cells. The doors were left open, then silence ensued the room. Bolden sat down on the concrete bunk and braced his back up against the cold wall and awaited his turn. He wasn't tired as he had slept most of the day after his CQ Runner duty status from the night before.

Hours later Williams came out of the interrogation room and said good bye to Bolden and Broadway. They didn't speak a word to him and just waved good bye to him. After some time went by they called for Specialist Broadway to come in to the C.I.D. Investigation room. Bolden's confidence ran high as he was sure they would stick to the story. He knew interrogation could be tough on a person. He thought about Jackie and hoped she had made it through in good shape. Hours went by and Bolden was getting anxious as well as hungry. Then Broadway exited from the C.I.D. Interrogation room. He looked at Bolden with a concerned look in his eyes and said,

"Hopefully I'll see you back at the barracks, John."

Bolden didn't know how to interpret the meaning of that, but he knew it would soon be his turn. Bolden didn't say a word and waved good bye to Broadway. He knew it was getting late but wasn't worried about the time as he thought that when he returned back to the barracks he could catch a quick bite to eat and get some sleep. What would follow next would catch him completely off guard. They called his name and ordered him into the interrogation room. He was equipped to provide short uninformative answers to the questions that he was about to be asked. Walking in to the room he viewed the interrogator up and down as much as he could. The interrogator was sitting in his chair behind a desk stacked with papers. He looked more like a civilian than he did military. His hair was longer than the usual military type haircut. He had wavy brown hair that covered and flowed over his ears, and he was wearing a civilian suit, not a professional type business suit, but a casual suit that was a bit wrinkled, not creased or pressed that would show any evidence of any military type discipline.

"This is going to be a piece of cake.", Bolden thought, "He looks tired, probably from interrogating Ray and Mike. Hopefully I will be out of here soon."

Bolden stopped at the middle of his desk, stood at the position of ATTENTION and announced,

"Sir, Specialist Bolden reporting as ordered!"

Bolden didn't salute him as he could not tell if he was an officer or not, but he treated him with respect as he was trained to do.

The first words out of the interrogators mouth and with a chuckle in his voice that had great confidence in what he was expressing said,

"Well Specialist Bolden, you might as well go ahead and admit to everything right now. All three of them gave you up to save their own asses. Jackie told us you were with her the whole time. Williams and Broadway said you must have planned the whole thing out by yourself as you were not with them the whole night you were in East Berlin together. Williams and Broadway said they were both surprised to find Jackie in the back of the van when you crossed Check Point Charlie after you lifted the backseat up to help her out. Jackie even stated all three of you gave her cigarettes. Have a seat Specialist Bolden, be at ease, speak freely, and we can get this statement typed up. The both of us will sign it and you can get back to your room at the barracks to get whatever sleep you are able to, before your company formation gathers, which is only a few hours away. I know you're tired and probably hungry to. Come on ,let's hurry and get this completed so we both can relax.

Bolden relaxed as he came out of the position of ATTENTION and took the seat that was offered to him. While standing in front of the interrogators desk and listening to him talk his opening statement, Bolden was also watching his body movements and mannerisms. Bolden had always been interested in the study of kinesics, the language of body movements, and handwriting analysis. The way to the truth is to know the soul, for the soul is bonded to purity, and as soul energy we are all one. This was a study he had done on his own, through reading books, and observing people and their mannerisms. Though he wasn't a professional at either one, this type of skill had helped him in the past to determine what type of individual he was dealing with and how to act or react with that type of person. He noticed the basics of kinesics on the interrogator, the movements of his eyes that would half close, close, or look away when the half truths and the non truths presented themselves as he spoke, the constant rubbing of both wrists, indicating his nervousness/anxiousness to finish up the interrogations. The leaning forward on his desk and tapping his finger upon it meant that he was authoritative and confident he would get an admission from Bolden based on the answers that were given to him from Jackie, Mike, and Ray. Then the big one at the end of his statement, the leaning backwards in his chair with his arms up, palms open. This communicates acceptance, openness, and trustworthiness with the individual you intend it for, but there was the last movement that he did that caught Bolden's attention, as he leaned back into the chair he had taken his open palms, clasped them together, then placed them behind his head along with moving his chair backward from the desk crossing his right leg over and laying it on top of his left knee.

Bolden picked up on the subliminal message that the interrogator was giving to him, either it was intentional or unintentional, it was clear. Bolden could see that he was the main targeted suspect, in their investigation, to place blame upon should it come to that point, after all, he was the lowest ranking of everyone involved. He also knew that the interrogator wanted some type of truth to the story that he was about to tell him. The interrogator did not want the whole truth to the story and hoped that, what Bolden was going to tell him was somewhat believable. It didn't have to be believable but it had to be possible. The story that was agreed upon with Jackie, John, Mike, and Ray would work if they all stuck to it. Bolden had to be confident, a little smug, but also respectful. He wasn't nervous or afraid of his interrogation but curious in a way of learning how the interrogation was being performed. Bolden wanted to be a military policeman when he was choosing career choices before his enlistment but was denied the position because he was a half inch too short in height. The requirements were to be five feet, eight inches tall or taller and he had measured in at five feet, seven and one half inches, so therefore he had chosen the infantry to be his career.

Sitting comfortably in the chair that was provided for him, Bolden put a smile on his face and with a hardy laugh looked at the interrogator and stated,

"Sir, I doubt anyone gave up anybody. There is no one to place blame upon here."

The interrogator lurched forward, dropping his leg back down to the ground and sliding his chair forward toward the desk, grabbing a piece of paper off the top of one stack of papers that had cluttered the desk top. Handing it to Bolden, the interrogator quickly snapped his words,

"Do you think I'm joking with you Specialist Bolden? I am not joking! Here are their statements. These are just partial statements but they will easily tell you what you need to know. You did this all on your own, didn't you Specialist? Not only that, but you involved two innocent men, that are mighty fine soldiers I may add, to your plot and now you are going to ruin their military careers with this ridiculous incident. Go ahead and read this then make your decision on what you would like to tell me next. Go On Take It!"

Bolden slowly got up from his chair reached over and grabbed the piece of paper the interrogator was offering him. Looking at the piece of paper he saw the three statements of Jackie, Ray, and Mike. They were small in length with only a few sentences each, vague in nature, which left open many possibilities. Sitting back down in the chair he began to read the paper that was given to him.

Jackie's proposed statement said, John helped her out of the place where she was hiding, under the back seat of the van, and rubbed her legs for her, then she received cigarettes from all three of them and that they welcomed her to West Berlin. From what John could figure out, from reading the proposed small statement, was that, Jackie had stayed with the story they had agreed upon. There was no mention of what had transpired earlier from that evening in question. All of it, was to some point, true, except for Ray giving her a cigarette as he didn't smoke.

Then John moved on to Williams' proposed statement and read it. It said, he saw Bolden in his rear view mirror get up from the back seat of the van, lifted the top seat, and helped someone out from the storage space that was beneath the seat. He was surprised to see Jackie in the van and had no idea she was in the van when crossing through Checkpoint Charlie. The statement also read he was the least culpable to be involved in the incident. John was starting to put it all together, so far, the scenario of the story had been adhered to, as the statements only had to do with after the crossing of Checkpoint Charlie.

Then on to Broadway's proposed statement. It said that he was in the front seat talking to Bolden when he seen Bolden get up and opened the top cover from the backseat and helped someone out from underneath it. He said he was surprised to see that it was Jackie. He said Bolden was rubbing her legs because she was complaining about her legs being numb and offered her a Kool cigarette, which she accepted. Then welcomed her to West Berlin. It further read that he was possibly culpable to have aided in the incident.

Then Bolden noticed his name on the piece of paper. The only thing it said was, Specialist Bolden is the most culpable in planning and aiding Jackie into West Berlin.

After reading all of it, Bolden looked at the interrogator and said,

"So, what do you want to know? From what I've read here all of it seems to be true. There is nothing here indicating that anyone of them gave me up on anything, as it was a surprise for all three of us to see Jackie when we crossed through Checkpoint Charlie.

"How about you start from the beginning Specialist? How you planned the whole thing from start to finish. How you tricked Williams into using his van to aid in Jackie's escape. How you helped Jackie get underneath the back seat. What was your plan after you got her through Checkpoint Charlie? What was your plan if they had caught you on the Eastern side of Berlin?"

The interrogator was not finished stating what he wanted to know and Bolden had to stop him in order to gain control of the situation and hopefully throw him off with his questioning. Bolden intervened quickly,

"Sir, there is nothing to tell you. There was no plan at all. There was no trickery involved anywhere at anytime on my part with anyone. All I can tell you is that I was as much surprised as Ray and Mike were to see Jackie once we crossed over in to West Berlin!"

"Did you borrow Sergeant Williams' van to escort two women to the disco in East Berlin?" asked the interrogator.

"Yes, I did.", admitted Bolden

"Did you meet Jackie at the disco in East Berlin when you arrived there with the other two women?" He asked.

"Yes, I did.", answered Bolden.

"Did you drive and escort these women, including Jackie, back to Specialist's Broadway's girlfriend's apartment, which by the way, is an unauthorized and illegal place to convene at?", was the interrogator's question.

Bolden realized the impact of that question and knew what the interrogator was doing. If he admitted to it, it could be another charge laid upon him. If he denied it, and the interrogator knew better, because more information had been given to him other than what was shown to Bolden earlier, then he may set himself up for providing a false statement. Bolden knew he had to take the lesser of the two evils and said,

"Yes, I did."

"When you arrived at the apartment, did you and the three women enter the apartment together?"

"No, I did not. The other two women left the van and went into the apartment because I asked them to leave Jackie and I alone together, as I wished to have some time together with Jackie." Bolden answered.

"And this is when you helped Jackie under the back seat of the van, on your "alone time" together, wasn't it Specialist Bolden?" asked the interrogator.

"No Sir, I did no such thing?" piped Bolden

"Then what was your intent, Specialist?"

"Well what do you think it was, Sir? Jackie is a beautiful woman, no doubt, and I thought I may be able to persuade her to have a little fun together. So, I put my suave and debonair, Broadway and I call it Swayve and Deboner, moves on her to see if I could get a little bit of that. Now, Sir, You can't fault a man for trying, can you? Bolden said with a chuckle in his voice trying to loosen the mood up in the room that had become tightened by the questioning.

The interrogator replying back with a little bit of sly laughter in his voice,

"Nope, can't blame a man for trying. So, Specialist Bolden, did she accept? Did you have sex with Jackie?"

Bolden knew where the interrogator was going with that question and knew, that the truth, to the answer of his question, was going to disappoint the interrogator.

"Noooo, she slapped me a good one across the face and stormed out of the van. She was pissed! I thought she liked me." replied Bolden.

The interrogator, laughing, asked,

"So, where did she go?"

"I don't know. I was too busy rubbing the cheek on my face to get the stinging to stop. She hit me a good one!" replied Bolden.

"You don't know where she went?" asked the interrogator.

"No, Sir. By the time I could get my senses about me she was gone. Couldn't tell you what direction she went to. Didn't matter, I didn't know the area that well anyways.", was Bolden's reply.

"Then what did you do after that?" asked the interrogator.

"After I gained my senses back I knocked on Mike's girlfriend's apartment door and they let me in. They asked where Jackie was and I told them what happened. It was all good, because the two women you asked about, that went with me to the disco, Mandy and Ushi, they were unaccompanied and quickly came to my rescue, giving me hugs and kisses and loving up on me and everything.", Bolden replied with a happy tone in his voice.

"I see, so did you have sex with these two women, this Mandy and Ushi, that you called by name?" asked the interrogator.

"No, there wasn't too much time left before we had to head back to West Berlin. Believe you me Sir, if there had been time enough for that I would have taken them up on it. Never had two women at the same time before. I think that would be kind of fun." Bolden said in a jovial manner hoping to get the interrogator to lighten up a bit on his questioning.

"So, you have no idea where Jackie went to?", asked the interrogator again but in a different manner.

"Nope, didn't care where she went. I was having a great time with Mandy and Ushi." Bolden said with a smile.

" So, the van was left unattended while you were in the apartment?" asked the interrogator.

"Yes, Sir. As far as I know. Mike and Ray were in the apartment with me." replied Bolden.

"Was the van secured? Did you lock up the van before leaving it to go to the apartment?" asked the interrogator.

"No Sir. The van was unsecured and I didn't think about locking it up.", replied Bolden.

“Then it is possible Jackie returned to the van that was left unattended and unsecured, entered the vehicle, closed the door and hid herself under the back seat of the van without being detected by either one of you? Is this what you are telling me Specialist Bolden?”, asked the interrogator, who seemed to be offering a way out from being blamed for anything that arose from the incident in question.

“Yes Sir, it sure seems to be that way, seeing that she is here on the West side of Berlin now.”, Bolden replying with a bit of smugness to his voice.

“Answer me this Specialist Bolden, at what point did you realize Jackie was hiding under the back seat of the van?”, asked the interrogator curiously.

“It wasn't too far away from Checkpoint Charlie on the West side. We were only a few minutes away from the midnight curfew and we had gotten our asses chewed by the NCOIC at Checkpoint Charlie. He wasn't quiet about it either Sir. After that I felt something move under the seat, I thought, at first, that Ray had hit a pothole or something, then I felt it again a few moments later. Broadway and I had been talking to each other as he was asking me about what happened between Jackie and I in the van earlier that evening. I picked myself up from the backseat and lifted the lid and there was Jackie. We were all very surprised!”, answered Bolden in a confident expression.

“Then that's it? Jackie did this all on her own? Neither You, Sergeant Ray Williams, nor Specialist Michael Broadway, planned or aided Jackie with her escape from East Berlin into West Berlin?”, asked the interrogator, as he sounded like he was ready to rap up the interrogation.

“Yes Sir, that's it! No Sir, neither one of us helped her. As I stated we were all very surprised to see her in the van on the west side. Actually Sir, I was a little nervous when I first saw her. I thought she was going to hit me again. She's a strong woman you know!”, Bolden stating with a little concern in his voice.

The interrogator laughing boldly, looked at Bolden, then his tone turned serious and said,

“Well Specialist that about raps it up. There will be others that will be asking you more questions later on. Make sure you are available for them. A couple more hours the sun will be coming up. Go back to the barracks and get some rest. There will soon be an appointment made for you to go see J.A.G. There will be an attorney appointed to you and I suggest you be honest with them as your fate will depend on it. This is a serious matter and it is going to get tougher for you. You are free to go!”

Bolden responding with an assured tone,

“Where am I going to go Sir?, I'm over 4,000 miles away from home in a country I hardly know, in a city surrounded by the Soviet Army. I have no choice but to stay where I am at.”

“Yes, that's the beauty of this whole situation, Specialist.” was all the interrogator had to say.

“Can I get a ride back to McNair Barracks, Sir? Got a ride here in those fancy squad cars.” Bolden stated with a humorous voice.

“No Specialist. There is free public transportation provided for us here in Berlin. I suggest you use it as it is quite a hike back to McNair Barracks, but your an infantryman you should be used to those type of hikes. If you start now you might make it on time for your company's formation. I suggest you get moving out now.”, said the interrogator with a stern voice.

There was no more humor left in Specialist Bolden as he responded in a simple tone of voice,

“Yes Sir.”

Specialist Bolden lifted himself up from the chair, walked over to the door and opened it up. He was about to exit the room when he heard the interrogator's voice.

“Specialist Bolden!”

Bolden turning his head to look at him,

“Yes Sir?”

With a nod and wink from his right eye, the interrogator said in a low voice,

"You did a fine job here on the interview."

Bolden, with a nod and a wink back at him with confirmation in his voice, only said,

"Sir."

With that, he walked out of the interrogation room, up the stairs that he had previously walked down on, through the doors and out into the open fresh air, where he took a deep breath in and exhaled it. Looking at the night's sky and seeing the stars twinkling in the heavenly dark blue open space, his imagination and thoughts burst wide open like water coming forth from a dam that had held it's water flood gates closed for too long. His prayers were strong, filled with the wishes for safety and that all will be well for everyone that was involved. He recited "The Lord's Prayer", over and over again until he felt the warm, calm peace come over his entire body, like a breath of fresh air in his lungs. He was at solace for the moment and walked over to the bus station to look at the schedule for the next bus to arrive to take him back to McNair Barracks. It would be another thirty minutes for the next arrival then departure. He sat down on the bench and closed his eyes for a minute. The next thing he heard was the squealing of brakes as the bus came to a stop next to the bench he was sitting on. The bus driver opened the doors. Bolden, tired from his quick unexpected nap, got up and entered onto the bus. He took the first seat in the front row and asked the driver to take him to McNair Barracks. The driver nodded and took off down the road to his next stop. Bolden was the only one on the bus as it was still too early for anyone to begin their day, but it wouldn't be too long before the city would be at full throttle, bringing to life a new day of adventures. The bus arrived at the bus stop designated for McNair barracks and Bolden quickly hopped off the bus, saying “DANKE”, to the bus driver. Walking up the stairs he passed by a few soldiers wearing their BDUs and getting ready for their formations. Reaching the top floor and arriving at CSC 6/502nd Area of Operations he walked by the CQ Desk where Specialist Schmidt was sitting. With a smile on his face and a gleam of happiness in his eyes Specialist Schmidt said,

“JOHN, IT'S GOOD TO SEE YOU MAN. I THOUGHT FOR SURE THEY WERE GOING TO KEEP YOU!”

“No, it's all good Russell. Hey, appreciate you wanting to cover for me, I really do! I'm going to head to my room and get some sleep. See you later.”, Bolden said slowly with a hint of small exhaustion in his voice.

“Sure thing John. I'll let Sergeant Horton know you just got in and not to expect you at formation.”, said Schmidt.

Bolden didn't say a word. He nodded with affirmation and walked to his room. He started to get undressed to get ready to lay down on his bunk and get some rest when there was a knock on his door. He walked over and opened the door. Pushing his way forward into Bolden's room, was his Platoon Sergeant, Sergeant First Class Horton. Looking at Bolden he calmly asked him,

"Why are you still in civilian clothes? Why aren't you getting ready for company formation, Specialist?"

"I just got back from being interrogated by C.I.D., at the M.P. Station, Sergeant. I was there from the time we left here yesterday till just a few minutes ago. Thought I would get some rest before joining the platoon down at the motor pool, if that's okay with you Sergeant?", Bolden replying with a tired, hopeful, and respectful voice.

Bolden didn't expect to hear, what he was about to hear, from his platoon sergeant. With an angry voice he snapped at Bolden,

"YOU STAND AT THE POSITION OF PARADE REST WHEN AN NCO WALKS INTO YOUR ROOM AND WHEN YOU ADDRESS ME, IS THIS UNDERSTOOD, SPECIALIST BOLDEN?"

Immediately Bolden went into the position of parade rest with his hands behind his back and his eyes looking straight forward. Sergeant Horton wasn't finished yet as his voice kept thundering on,

"DO YOU ACTUALLY THINK I'M GOING TO GIVE YOU A DAY OFF FOR THIS BULLSHIT? NO, HELL NO, THAT WAS ON YOUR TIME SPECIALIST AND RIGHT NOW, THIS IS OUR TIME, THIS IS ARMY TIME SOLDIER. NOW YOU GET YOUR ASS DRESSED FOR COMPANY PT FORMATION AND I EXPECT YOU TO BE ON TIME. YOU GOT THAT SPECIALIST!? NOW GET MOVING!"

"YES, SERGEANT!!!", Bolden hollered out, without moving a muscle.

Sergeant Horton grabbed the door knob and while exiting Bolden's room slammed the door behind him. Bolden feeling exhausted and confused at what just happened was stunned for the moment. He didn't have that much time to think about it and hurriedly got dressed with the Company PT Uniform. Once he was fully dressed he bolted out the door, ran down the three flights of steps, and took his place in company formation.

"Whoa, he thought, this is definitely going to be a day."

He was going to have to muster up the energy to get through it. He was tired and hungry and all he could think about was the chow hall and how good his bunk would feel once he laid down upon it. He was anxious to meet up with Jackie to see if she was doing okay and wanted to ask her about her interrogation. For the moment he would have to first get some rest to regain his energy.

The company started with their warm up exercises and then soon afterward they were on their two mile run. Half way complete with the run his squad leader nudged him in the side and quietly said to him,

"Don't worry about it Bolden. We've got you covered for the day. Sergeant Horton will more than likely be on you all day. In between those times you can get some rest down at the motor pool and we will keep watch for you. You'll be fine."

Bolden nodded at him but didn't say a word back to him. His squad leader knew he was grateful for covering him even though he didn't express it to him. After Company PT Bolden went up to his room, skipped his shower, donned his BDUs, and went straight to the mess hall to get some chow. He had it down his stomach in less than a minute, after all, it was an infantryman's breakfast, put it all together, then down it. After that, he immediately went back up to his room and laid down on his bunk. It didn't take much and he was off to sleep, where he would remain for the next three hours, thanks to his squad leader for sending him on a fake errand that would require the same exact time frame.

The future had yet to be unfolded before them. As for their fate, well..., that was in the hands of the All Mighty and it had yet to be determined. Like the hands of the Clock Tower at McNair Barracks, time, keeps moving forward.

41
GREPO

Wednesday, August 20th, 1986. Bolden and Broadway, after being relieved from duty, for the end of the day, hurried to their rooms to change into civilian clothing. They were hoping that Jackie was able to meet them at the Ku'dorf. They could not make their appointment with her that previous Monday night. On Tuesday night, Bolden and Broadway went to the Ku'Dorf, hoping to find her there waiting for them. After a few hours of waiting, they returned back to the barracks, hoping that she was doing well. Both of them were anxious to see her. They wished to know how her meetings went and that she was cleared for West German Citizenship. Tonight, Wednesday night, they hoped to receive an answer. They hopped the bus, arrived at the Ku'Dorf, then descended down the steps in a hurry. They paid the entrance fee then proceeded to their designated seating area. When they turned the corner in the middle of the Ku'Dorf, by the men's bathroom, they saw her sitting in a chair at the designated table. All of them were relieved to see each other doing well. Jackie gave both of them a big hug and a kiss, then sat down in the chairs that surrounded the table, with John and Mike sitting at both sides of Jackie, she was the first to speak,

“I didn't tell them anything. There is so much I have to tell the both of You and to Ray. Is he coming tonight?”

John and Mike shook their head, to say “No, that Ray wasn't going to be with them that night”. Mike took the lead with his comments,

“Has everything been okay with you? Did they treat you well? Are you a West German Citizen now? Did they give you a place to stay? Do you have enough food? Johnny and I have been worried about you. We have something to tell you too. Are you thirsty? I will go get us something to drink. What would you two like to drink?”

Jackie placed her order,

"I'll have a coke."

John was next with his order,

"I will have a coke also Mike, with a twist of lemon in it. It's tastes great with lemon. You should try it Jackie!"

Jackie with a smile on her face, giggled, then said,

"Ja Mike, I will try that twist of lemon."

Mike proceeded up to the bar to order the drinks. When he arrived at the bar, Jackie reached her arms out and then around John giving him a big hug. She whispered in to his ear,

"I Love You, So Very Much, For What You Have Done For Me! I Have Something Very Important To Tell You!"

She released her embrace from John, held his hands firmly with both of hers, looked him in the eyes, then said with much concern for his well being,

"I called Tanye, in East Berlin, she said the Stasi is looking for me and they know, now, that I am in West Berlin. They know that it was three American soldiers who helped me to escape. They don't know for sure if it was you guys and are asking a lot of questions. The Stasi have brought in Tanye, Jacqueline, Mandy, Ushi, and Babette for questioning. You guys did so well doing this that they do not know anything about it. The Stasi already know who Mike and Ray are because they have been over there so many times but they don't know who you are. All they know is that your name is John. You are new to them and have not been over to East Berlin very much. They want to know your last name and many other details that no one else knows about. The Stasi wants to build a profile on you John! They will try to find you here in West Berlin! You must be very careful who you talk to!"

Mike walked up to the table carrying the three cokes with a lemon wedge on the side of the tall thin glasses, so they could all twist their own lemon juice into the fabulous concoction, that would quench their desire of thirst. When he placed the drinks on the table, before he could sit down in his chair, Jackie sprung up and gave Mike a great big hug then said to him with excitement in her voice,

"I LOVE YOU SO VERY MUCH MICHAEL, FOR WHAT YOU HAVE DONE FOR ME!"

Mike taking in the warm heartfelt embrace, said,

"Well, we love you to Jackie, very much! We are all glad you are here with us! What were You and John talking about while I was gone?

Jackie looked at Mike with a bit of concern in her eyes. John stepped in, to explain,

"Mike, I will tell you later on. Jackie has more important things to tell the both of us right now. Have a seat and let's hear what she has to tell us."

Mike and Jackie took their seats, then Jackie began to tell them about her experiences with the four powers of West Berlin,

"The first ones that I saw were the West Germans. They asked me how did I escape? I told them that a diplomat brought me across Checkpoint Charlie. They asked me a few more questions but nothing to serious. They were okay with the diplomat story and granted me asylum in to West Berlin. Then they took me to see The Americans. They to, asked me how I escaped. I told them the same thing, that a diplomat brought me across. To The Americans, it was no big deal, so they cleared me. Then I went to see the French and it was the same question. How did I escape and who helped me. I told the French the same answer that a diplomat helped me to escape and brought me through Checkpoint Charlie. They were easy to and did not show much concern when they cleared me. Those three were very easy. Then they took me to see The British. They were not so easy. They asked me how did I escape and who helped me? I told them that a diplomat helped me to escape and brought me through Checkpoint Charlie. They said that I lie to them and they know that three American soldiers brought me across Checkpoint Charlie and demanded that I tell them who they were. I told them nothing! I stayed with my story about the diplomat! I was very scared and asked them if they were going to send me back to East Berlin? They said they would not send me back to East Berlin. They said they wanted to know the names of the three American soldiers who helped me to escape. I told them nothing and still stayed with my story about the diplomat. I was there for a couple of hours until they cleared me to stay in West Berlin. I have my own apartment now in the French Sector. Yes Michael, I have food and some money, West Deutsche Marks, Yay! Everything is okay, but I am very scared, you guys have to be careful. I know I am being watched. I look out of the window, from my apartment, and see the same car with two men in it. When I go to do my shopping, they follow me, and they are probably here now watching us. I was scared to come out of my apartment, to come here and meet you, because I know they follow me. You guys have to be very careful!"

John and Mike listened intently. They already knew that they were under surveillance after what had happened that previous Monday night. It was their turn to explain to Jackie what was going on with them. John took the lead,

"Yes, we all have to be very careful Jackie. Monday night, the three of us were taken in for questioning. This is the story we have given to them, please be patient with me, seeing that we are not able to deny this whole thing happening and not getting us involved. Mike, Ray, and I are going to have to go through something we haven't gone through before. I can't tell you how much time we have left, to be together, as we don't know yet, what they are going to do. They, for the most part, have a strong idea, that we helped you, so instead of denying the whole thing, we have to give them some truth, to the matter, not the whole thing. In all actuality, "THEY", don't want to know the whole story, so, with all of us, including, "THEY", the least they know, the better off, ALL OF US ARE! This is what we told them and I hope you will agree with it. I don't think they will bring you back in for questioning, however, if they do, please go along with what we have, at this time. "We were unaware that you had hidden, yourself, underneath the back seat of the van. Once we crossed over from East Berlin to West Berlin, through Checkpoint Charlie, we discovered that you were hiding underneath the backseat of the van. You were discovered, by me, because you kept moving your legs to keep the blood flowing into your legs, as they were getting numb. Your movements were so loud that I lifted up the backseat of the van and discovered that you were hiding underneath the seat. All of us were surprised, and astonished that you did this. We did not help you to escape, you went outside of the disco, discovered that the van was unlocked and hid yourself, into the tight compartment, then waited for the ride across Checkpoint Charlie. You heard the voices of Ray and the man he was talking to, which you were thinking, was an American soldier, at Checkpoint Charlie, then decided, that it was time, to let us know, that you were in your hiding spot, because your legs were getting numb. I hate to ask this of you Jackie, but we are going to be lucky, to get out of this situation! If they feel, that you acted alone, without our participation, they may let us go, without being punished. Like I said, I very much doubt that they will bring you back in for questioning. You are here in West Berlin and you are going to stay here! Will you do this for us, if they continue to ask you questions?"

Jackie was amazed at what John was saying to her. She looked at Mike, with concerned eyes, looking for confirmation from him with what John had asked of her. Mike answered her question with a nod of his head confirming what John was saying to her. She looked back at John with loving eyes and said,

“Ja, of course, I will do this for you guys! You are my heroes!!!”

With the three of them being in agreement with their stories, it had placed a bit of confidence among them, which provided hope that everything will be okay. All of them knew, in the bottom of their hearts, that soon, it would be a time, to go on their own. All of their wishes had been granted, for the time being, and it was time, to separate the parallel energy, that had brought them together. There were only two questions, that were left to be answered. That was, how were they going to part each others company and when will they be able to see each other again? Questions, that may be left unanswered, for the quest, they were to embark upon remained uncertain, for the time being.
They talked about small things after that and they knew it was getting late. Jackie, John, and Mike made arrangements to see each other again, at the same place that , they had designated, for each other, the first night Jackie gained her freedom. Jackie wrote down her new address and gave it to Mike. Finishing their coca-cola drinks with the lemon twist, leaving them on the table for the waitress to pick up. After their departure, they soon

made their way around the Ku'Dorf, to the stairs that led them upstairs, out the doors, and into the market place. John and Mike stood with Jackie till her bus arrived to take her to her new home. Jackie, giving Mike and then John a kiss and a hug, boarded her transportation. John and Mike waited for their bus. It was a brief moment for waiting till their bus arrived. Without getting their favorite nightly meal, the Doner Ke Bobs, they boarded the bus. On the way back to McNair Barracks, Broadway was the first one to begin the conversation,

“So, Johnny, What do you think? What were You and Jackie talking about when I went up and got the cokes?”

John could sense the jealousy, curiosity, and concern, that Mike had in asking the questions he did, from the tone of his voice. John responded back carefully,

“Well, Michael. We are definitely in a situation, that is above us! I don't know if we are going to get out of this at all! You have to know, by now, and if you don't, I'm just going to tell you. I'm pretty sure we are not going to be able to bring Jacqueline and her son over here to West Berlin, or any others for that matter. I wish we could do that for you Mike, I really do! What Jackie told me tonight, was that, the Stasi are going to be looking for us, not so much, You or Ray, because they already know who you two are, seeing that, the both of you frequent East Berlin so much. They already have a profile on both of you. Seeing that I'm new, the only thing they know about me is my first name. Now, they want to know more, so they can build a profile on me. Jackie said, to expect the Stasi to be here, in West Berlin, and to be very careful who I talk to. The Stasi have already hauled in Jacqueline, Mandy, Ushi, Babette, and Tanye, which is who, Jackie got this information from, for questioning. Jackie said that, we did such a great job, that none of them were aware of what we did. This is a plus for us Mike, they think we were involved but there is no concrete evidence, saying that we did this. Like I said to Jackie..., Mike, we are going to have to give them something, but not the whole thing. If we leave a speculative window open then we should be okay. This is what she told me Mike when you went up to get us our drinks. She is very concerned for all of us! I'm not going to pull any punches against you Mike! You have to believe that! We are all in this together and if we don't stick by each other, then I hate to say, what I think could happen. Some way, some how, we are going to have to get in contact with Ray and let him know what is going on. If we stay together on this, I think we will all be okay! What do you think?"

Broadway sat in total silence for a moment taking in the realization of what Bolden had just expressed to him. He had a look of concern on his face, then said,

"I have to call Jacqueline to see if she is okay. I have a few coins on me for the payphone. Do you have any extras?"

John reached into his pockets and produced some coins for the payphone, which he gave to Mike. He produced a small smile on his face then said to John,

"Thanks Man! We are going to be all right Johnny! With what we have done, WE ARE HEROS! We can go public with it and get favoritism on our side."

Bolden was happy to hear the hope in his friend's voice. It provided the confidence John had to have to know that Mike was going to stay by his side, but he had to bring his friend to the reality of what was happening,

"Mike, it is good to hear you talk positive, but favoritism of the public, has nothing to do with military protocol and that is what we are dealing with here. I know you are concerned about Jacqueline. When you call her please keep in mind that you will be talking on a payphone connected to East Berlin and for sure, the Stasi, have her phone tapped right now. Keep your conversation personal and to the point. After what I just told you, what Jackie said to me earlier, this is not a smart move on your part right now. But..., I know you wish to know if Jacqueline is okay. So go ahead and make your call. I hope you don't mind me standing next to you. I'm actually interested in what she has to say."

Mike nodded his head in agreement. The bus arrived at it's stop next to McNair Barracks. Mike and John took their departure then headed straight to the public pay phone, located a few feet away from the imbiss stand. The lighting was dim as a couple of the street lamps had burned out. Having not being replaced yet, the burned out street lamps, provided an eerie dark presence to the area, but also a good place for cover. Mike threw the coins in to the payphone then dialed Jacqueline's number. She answered with the usual German greeting of, "Hallo!"

When she heard Mike's voice, she interrupted him on the phone. Her voice was loud and held concern for his well being, she was loud enough that her voice carried over to hearing distance where John was standing next to Mike, a couple feet away from him,

“Michael! Are you okay? What did you do Michael? The Stasi are asking us a lot of questions about You, Ray, and John, especially John, and Jackie to. Is Jackie in West Berlin? Did you guys help her escape? Michael, I Love You! I miss you very much! Am I going to be able to see you again?”

Her questions kept coming and then stopped abruptly as Mike interrupted her,

“Everything is fine. I am doing good. I am worried about you. I Love You Too! Are you doing okay? Yes Jackie is over here in West Berlin. I don't know how she got over here. No, we didn't help her escape!” She just showed up over here.”

Mike was interrupted by Jacqueline once again, this time with anger in her voice,

“IT WAS JOHN!!! I KNOW IT WAS HIM!!! IS HE THERE WITH YOU NOW?”

Mike looked at John. John with a heavy concerned look in his eyes was shaking his head and moving his lips to express to Mike to tell her “NO, he was not with him!” Mike turned back to the phone, then said,

"No, he is not here with me right now. He is up in his room. No, I don't think he had anything to do with Jackie being here in West Berlin. If he did, then I would know this."

Jacqueline lowered her voice but John could still hear what she was saying to Mike,

"Michael, I know it was him! I hate him so very much! I'm not going to be able to see you anymore! I hate him for doing that to us. Michael, the Stasi are going to find you in West Berlin! If you come back over here, and if they know you are here, they are going to take you in for questioning, saying you took Jackie away! Be careful Michael!"

Mike responded back, assuring her that they would meet again,

"Jacqueline I will see you again! I Love You And Wish To Marry You! Everything is going to be all right! I have to go for now. I will call you again soon!"

There was enough time left from the coins in the payphone to say their good byes to one another, a click was heard from the pay phone indicating the call had ended. Mike hung up the phone and turned toward John. With tears in his eyes, he said,

"I don't care what I have to do John! I am bringing Jacqueline and her son over here as soon as possible! With or without your help!"

John showing his friend compassion, said,

I will try to come up with something. If you have any ideas then let me know. I'm with you, please know that!

They walked together through the gates of McNair Barracks then up to their rooms. Without saying a word to each other, their silence indicated the heavy thoughts that were present in their mind. Entering into their separate rooms, to be in a world of their own, they looked for the peace and the solace they had to have in order to think things through, which would ultimately create a better world around them!

Saturday, August 23rd, 1986, John and Mike, had not yet, a chance to talk to Ray, about what was decided upon, between Jackie, John, and Mike. It was still, up in the air, hoping that Ray would stick to the stories, that were agreed upon, with the three liberators, prior to the successful escape of Jackie, giving her, her freedom. In some way, Mike and John had to relay the information to him, that Jackie agreed to, of being her own liberator. This would relieve them from any blame. This would allow them, to return to East Berlin, to help Mike's fiance' Jacqueline and her infant son, to escape in to West Berlin, granting Michael's wishes, for the marriage between them. It would be a higher risk than Jackie's escape, however, Mike and John were willing to do this, as long as Ray would accept it. John and Mike wondered when they would be able to talk to Ray, but placed it in the back of their thoughts for the moment. They had a date with Jackie at the Ku'Dorf tonight and they were motivated to see that this date was met. They were ready to go at 1800 hours so they would be able to arrive by 1900 hours. As they were walking out of their individual rooms, to unite together, they spotted Specialist 4th Class Festerman, who spotted them in return. By the look on his face, it was easy to tell what he was going to ask,

"Hey, you guys are going to go see Jackie, aren't you?"

Mike and John looked at him with a knowing look on their faces. Mike was the first to respond, being his sarcastic self,

"Yes, we are! What's it to you?"

Festerman drew a big smile on his face and then said,

"So, it's true! You guys did bring her over here! You guys are my fucking heroes!!! I so, have been wanting to do this with Mandy, wish you guys would have let me in on this! Can I go with you to see Jackie? Will you let me go with you? If I can help you guys in anyway, know that I am there with you!!!"

Bolden and Broadway had a look of amazement and confusion upon their faces, with what Festerman had just expressed to them, they had to squelch Kevin's excitement. Bolden was next to respond,

"Will you lower your voice? The answer to your question is , "No, we didn't help Jackie in any way, DO YOU GOT THAT!!!?"

Bolden was hoping that Kevin caught on to what he had just expressed to him. Festerman put his left hand over his mouth then nodded his head in affirmation to what Bolden had expressed to him. Bolden continued on with his expressions to Festerman,

“Yes, you can come along with us, if you want to. Say, do you have some West German Marks on you? You can buy the drinks tonight at the Ku'Dorf!”

Kevin, with a concerned, but hopeful look, in his eyes, said,

“YEAH!!!, I've got plenty of West Deutsche Marks! Let's go Party!!!”

Bolden responded back,

“Kevin, I'm just playing around with you. We won't be drinking any alcohol tonight. We have to keep our senses about us, at this time. At the most, we are going to be drinking coca-cola with a lemon twist in it, fifty cents a pop, one German Deutsche Mark per drink. Can you handle it?”

Kevin, hysterically laughing, responded back,

“YEAH, I CAN HANDLE IT! Give me ten minutes and I will be ready.”

Bolden responded back,

"Kevin, You Know The Deal! We Are Infantry!!! You Got Five Minutes Or We Are Leaving Without You!!!"

Festerman, without responding, ran to his room to change his clothes. He presented himself in civilian clothing in exactly five minutes. The three of them headed for the Ku'Dorf together. With the bus arriving in the market place, the three of them hopped off the bus then headed for the arranged meeting place. When they arrived, they saw Jackie sitting in her chair at the designated table. She had a very surprised, but delightful smile upon her face when she saw Kevin Festerman being with Mike and John. Greetings with hugs and kisses were given, then Festerman took everyone's drink order, leaving the table, approaching the bar, to fill the orders. Mike was the first to ask his questions to Jackie,

"How have you been doing? Is everything going good for you?"

Jackie responded calmly,

"I am doing good Michael. All is good, but those two men watching me all the time. I know they are here tonight but I don't know where they are. I talked with my Mommy and Daddy to let them know that I am here in West Berlin and that I am doing okay. They are sad, but happy, that I am safe and being treated good. The Stasi have already questioned them, asking them, "Why did I leave their beloved country?" I hate the Stasi so much!!! I HATE THE GERMAN DEUTSCE REPUBLIC!!! I am afraid for my Mommy and Daddy!!! I hope they will be okay!!!

Mike came in to console Jackie's feelings, with compassion, he was hoping to give her comfort,

“Jackie, things are the way they are now. Your Mom and Dad will be fine. You are in West Berlin now! You are Free! Your Mom and Dad know you will be okay! You have to give this some time and everything will be fine!

Jackie heard Mike's words as he was speaking them, but it offered no solace to her as her tears began to stream from her eyes down her cheeks. Festerman showed up with the three coca colas, with the lemon twists, and a Golden Weissen Beer, for himself. He looked at Jackie and seen she was crying, then said, in an uncouth, nonchalant way,

“Hey, what's her problem? She's got a whole new world in front of her and she looks sad. What's going on?”

John and Mike looked at Festerman with a little bit of confusion on their face with the way Kevin asked his question. Mike immediately, with his sarcasm, answered his question,

“Well..., If you really want to fucking know! Her Mom and Dad were questioned by the Stasi, asking them, why Jackie left their beloved fucking country. Not..., That you seemed too concerned about this, I thought, you should fucking know!”

Kevin shrugged his shoulders, without thinking too much about what was expressed to him from Mike, he responded back haughtily,

"Yeah, so what did you three expect, what was going to happen afterwards? Did you think all was going to be peachy keen and the enemy will forgive you? Toughen your asses up and move forward, there's a new agenda coming up for all of you and you better be prepared for it!"

Jackie, John, and Mike were not prepared, at the moment, to hear what was coming from Kevin. All of them looked at him with astonishment. He didn't stop there, as he kept on with his opinion, he handed his Golden Weissen Beer over to Jackie, then said,

"Here, this will help you get by. I'm going up to get me one."

He looked at Mike and John, then asked,

"Did you guys change your mind? It just might help you too! I'm going up to get me one, like I said earlier, I'm buying, so speak now or forever hold your peace!"

With the three, still being astonished at what Kevin had expressed, looked at him with amazement. Bolden was the first to speak,

"No Man, I'm good with the coca cola. You do what you got to do."

Broadway was next, without his sarcasm, stated,

“Ahhh, I'm good with the coca cola Kevin.”

Jackie didn't say a word as she took a drink from the Golden Weissen Beer that Kevin had given her. They could tell that it wasn't her favorite drink of choice but..., it would suffice for the time being. Kevin left the table and went back up to the bar to order his beer. Jackie, John, and Mike continued on with a light conversation between themselves. By the time Festerman arrived back to the table with his beer he noticed that Jackie had over half of her non-deliberate order of drink finished. Kevin shook his head, handed his newly ordered glass of Golden Weissen Beer over to Jackie, then said,

“All right, I'm going back up for another one. Matter of fact, I'm going to bring four of them, just in case you guys change your mind. Geez, I haven't had a drink of beer yet! Will you guys let me relax!? This is supposed to be a happy occasion you know!”

The laughter ensued among them at the table. Jackie quickly finished her beer, handed it over to Kevin, and said,

“Danke, Kevin! I am feeling much better now!”

Festerman swirled his eyes up in the air, in a joking, uncaring way, then said,

"Yeah, Yeah! Drink the next one and you will be feeling a lot better, only this time, slow it down a bit, will ya? At least, until I get back with another one."

His comical tone set an atmosphere of relaxation among friends. It was what everyone had to have for the time being. He lifted up her empty glass to retrieve it back to the bar where it had once came, then left the table to place another order. Jackie, John, and Mike continued on with their small talk. In a few minutes Festerman returned to the table with four Golden Weissen Beers. He placed each one, on the table, in front of his company. The three of them looked at Kevin's glass of beer that looked almost empty. Jackie, John, and Mike started laughing then moved the beer that had been placed in front of them back over to Kevin. He shook his head and started to laugh, then said,

"All right then, I will take care of these if you guys don't want them."

He finished the first glass, that was almost empty before his arrival at the table, took another one, then quickly drank it down without coming up for air. He set the next one in front of him. Looking at the three of them he asked,

"Are you sure you guys don't want these because I'm ready for another one!?"

Jackie, John, and Mike, in unison, without saying a word, motioned with their hands, a swift movement with the open palms of their right hands, saying silently together,

"Go ahead! Knock yourself out, Man!"

With their swift silent permission, Kevin lifted up another glass of beer and downed it quickly. Jackie, John, and Mike looked at him with amazement, actually astonishment! The laughter among them had created a wonderful atmosphere that had replaced the serious tone of the previous environment. It created such a loving nature around all of them, for the moment, that was care free. They were enjoying the time that they had together, without a care in the world. It was truly, "SAN SOUCI", as the French would call it,

"WITHOUT A CARE IN THE WORLD!"

John was inquisitive to Jackie about how the Yugoslavian Gentlemen treated her while providing her comfort, for her first night in West Berlin. He was always concerned about her welfare and knew that Mike was concerned for her as well. John asked Jackie,

"How did those Yugoslavian guys treat you Saturday Night, Sunday Morning? Were they good to you?"

Jackie expressed herself with heartfelt concern to John and Mike,

"Yes, they were very good to me! One of them gave me his bed to sleep in while he slept on the floor next to me, guarding me. They were very much, GENTLEMEN!"

John, Mike, and Kevin were very happy to hear about this. John wanted to find these men and show his gratitude to them for their kindness. He knew that the Yugoslavian gentlemen had a thing for the new Teknik, Disco type of music and thought that if they were at the Ku'Dorf that night, that he would find them at the end of the Ku'Dorf where they played that type of music. John finished up his coca-cola with the lemon twist, then put the one that was in front of Jackie in front of him, and with a smile on his face said,

"I've got this one! Don't any of you guys touch it! I'm going up to the disco and find those guys. If they are here, then I will bring them back to join us. I will be right back!"

Festerman was on his toes. He looked at Bolden and said,

"I'm going with you! You should be protected right now!"

Given the light atmosphere that was surrounding the table at the time, Bolden responded back with a happy tone in his voice,

"Kevin, everything is all right! I will be back in a couple of minutes. You and Mike stay here and keep Jackie company. Make sure she is okay! All right?"

Festerman sat back down in his seat complying with Bolden's request. Being concerned, but having a smile on his face, he responded back,

"I don't think that's a good idea, but screw you! I will stay here with Jackie then. She's a lot better looking than you are anyways!"

The hearty laughter continued among the table then Bolden took his leave to find the Yugoslavian Gentlemen, to give them his Appreciation, and to offer them a spot at their table. Before leaving, Bolden gave Jackie a hug and a kiss affirming to her that he would be right back. Bolden rounded the right hand curve, of the "S" curve, that was in the middle of the Ku'Dorf, located not very far away from where the designated table was at. He was stopped by a young West German female that he had known from before, that "Don A Dee O", had introduced him to, many months ago. She spoke English fluently, and as Bolden engaged her in conversation, the traffic of human party goers began increasing. The area that Bolden was standing in was quickly filled with people. He tried looking over at the designated table where Jackie, Mike, and Kevin, were at, to see if everyone was doing okay. With the many people standing around him, talking in loud conversation, drinking their beverage of choice, and with the music that had just started to play, Bolden could no longer see, nor hear, his original company. It was only a few moments later that he had felt a tug on his left forearm. Bolden, not thinking anything unusual about the tug he felt on his arm, dismissed it as, people walking by him. A couple seconds later he felt a stronger tug and then a grip upon his left forearm. Bolden disengaged his conversation from the known West German woman to look at who had a grip of his forearm. Bolden's focus went straight to a man that was a couple inches shorter than him, about five feet six inches tall, skinny, but muscular. He had curly, long, blondish, brown type hair, that touched his shoulders. The man was being forceful in his demands, speaking in German, a word, that Bolden had been trained to translate quite well into English. What seemed to be like slow motion, Bolden looked into this German man's eyes, interrupting his determination, then looked down at what this German man had presented in his right hand, waving it up and down. It stood still for a moment, enough time for Bolden to check what this man was showing him. It looked like some type of West German Credential that represented the West German Polizei. Being light green in essence, without a photo, the black small print, displayed a name that could not be read. At the top of the credentials, was the display of a copper coated symbol, that resembled a United States Army Officer, that being a Major, of clustered oak leaves. This did not phase Bolden's emotions. After looking at the credentials, Bolden looked back up into the German man's eyes, who was still saying the same words, of,

"AUS WEISS!!! AUS WEISS!!!"

Bolden's chest immediately sprouted forward, his shoulders lifted back, his muscles in full display, then with a hefty, hearty voice, said,

"LET ME GET THIS STRAIGHT! YOU WANT TO SEE MY I.D.? MEINE AUS WEISS?"

The German man kept up his demanding temperament,

"JA, JA, SCHNELL BITTE, AUS WEISS!!!"

Bolden forcefully withdrew the grip of, his German counterpart, from his left forearm, by quickly bringing it down to his side, then back upward, ready to do battle! With both hands, palms open, Bolden, pushed forward such a fierce, forceful thrust in to the German mans chest, forcing him backward, losing his balance. As Bolden quickly went forward to continue to disable his combatant, he noticed a much taller and bigger man, standing about six feet, three inches tall, standing behind the short German man. This big German man had muscles protruding from his body that made the clothes he was wearing, skin tight, as if, the stitches from his clothing would burst at their seams, at any given moment. He was bald and from the look in his eyes, Bolden could tell that this big German man did not like what Bolden had just done to his friend. Catching his partner with both hands, to brace his fall, he helped his partner regain his balance and composure by standing him back up. In a flash Bolden stopped his forward advancement, as he knew he was outmatched for the time being. The shorter German man recovering his balance, from his taller friend, was shaken, from what just occurred. Bolden had to keep his front advantage, his voice was loud and clear when he expressed to both the German men, stopping their advancement,

"I'M AN AMERICAN SOLDIER!!! AND YOU WANT TO SEE MY I.D.? MEINE, AUS WEISS? I WILL TURN YOUR ASSES IN FOR THIS KIND OF SHIT!!!

WHO THE FUCK, DO YOU THINK YOU ARE DEALING WITH?"

Bolden could tell the big guy was the muscle and the little guy was the intelligence. What he couldn't tell about them, was if they were West German or East German. It would have made a big difference to him if he had the knowledge of where they were coming from. The only thing he could think of, for the moment, was to ask the West German young woman, who spoke English well, to translate for him. Bolden immediately turned to her, still keeping his eye on the two men, he demanded from her to translate,

"YOU ASK THEM WHY THEY WANT TO SEE MY IDENTIFICATION AND IF THEY KNOW WHAT THEY ARE DEALING WITH HERE? ASK THEM NOW!

Nervously, she began speaking to them in German. Bolden watched each of them as they talked among themselves. Bolden could tell by their body language that the two German men had overstepped their boundaries. They had taken a chance against someone, to enact their will upon him, and found the opposite of what they had expected. The short German man was nervous in his actions. His hands were shaking, as he folded up his identification, then placed it in his right back pocket of his trousers. Though, speaking in German, answering the West German woman's questions, that Bolden had asked her to relay to him, Bolden could tell that he was stammering his voice, not sure what to tell her. Bolden cut to the chase. With his voice being strong, he asked his translator,

“What is he saying?”

She responded back to Bolden with a worried expression on her face of not being sure what to tell him. Being nervous her eyes went to the floor, becoming submissive to Bolden's demands. She paused for a brief second, then with a nervous voice, she translated,

“I am not to sure what he is talking about. Did you bring someone from East Berlin over here to West Berlin? If you did, then I don't want to be involved. You should go party and leave this alone!”

Bolden was hoping for an answer to help him identify who these German men were. With what his translator had relayed to him, there was no answer to figure out for the time being. He did not want to get the young woman more involved than what she was. The short German man hearing the word, “Party”, from her, pushed his way in to their conversation, saying,

“JA, JA, GO PARTY, GO PARTY!”

Bolden took this as an insult to his intelligence, hearing the short German man's words. He looked at his translator and said,

"I apologize to you for getting you involved with this. You better go for now and, "Thank You", for telling me what he said."

She immediately left the area, then disappeared in to the crowd of people. Bolden wasn't finished with his counterparts just yet. He looked at the two German men with a half cocked smile, then with a haughtiness in his voice said sarcastically,

"Jaaa, Jaaa, Go Fucking Party!"

Then Bolden, pointing his right index finger at the two German men, intimidatingly said,

"I'm sure we are not done with each other here. I will be seeing the both of you later!"

The short German man, though he may have not understood what Bolden was saying to him, picked up on Bolden's intent. The taller, bigger, German Man, remained silent through the whole transaction, standing emotionless. In a motion of not caring, the short German Man, placed his back right hand up in the air, waving it back and forth, then calmly said,

"Go Party, Go Party."

Bolden had to have the last word of the incident. With strength and confidence in his voice, he stated firmly,

"Oh, we'll party! That's for sure!"

Bolden's thoughts, were on obtaining this man's identification to give to military intelligence so they could decipher who this man was, who was, being so bold and brazen, in trying to get an American soldier to show his military identification to him. Bolden thought of this man as either, “Having A Set Of Balls On Him”, or the possibility, “That He Was Just Plain Ignorant”, either way, an answer had to be found out. Instead of going forward to the end of the Ku'Dorf, where the Disco was located, to find the two Yugoslavian Gentleman, Bolden decided to go back to the designated table to relay to Mike, Kevin, and Jackie, what had just occurred with him and to warn them to watch out for these two men. He arrived at the table where all three of them looked at him with confusion, trying to decide, if he found the two men he was looking for. Bolden began his explanation,

“I think it is time for us to get back to the barracks. I just had a run in with two German guys. I don't know if they are East or West Germans, but they asked me for my identification.”

Festerman, taking a drink of his last Golden Weissen Beer, swallowed what he had in his mouth, then slammed the glass back down on the table. He was furious with his response,

“I TOLD YOU, YOU HAD TO HAVE PROTECTION!!! YOU SHOULD HAVE LET ME GO WITH YOU!!! WHERE ARE THESE GUYS AT RIGHT NOW? WE'RE GOING TO GO KICK THEIR ASS!!!”

Bolden was calm when he answered Kevin's questions,

"Look Kevin, I don't know if they are West German or East German. Jackie told me a few days ago that the Stasi are looking for me. They don't have any information on me, other than my first name, and to be careful who I talk to."

Jackie, with a worried look upon her face, nodded her head in agreement with John. Kevin noticed her affirmation, then sternly said,

"I don't care who they are, what side their on, or anything like that! John, you know the West Germans would not ask you for your military identification. I say, we find these assholes, right now, and put them in their place!"

John being concerned for Jackie, backed down, away from his goal of obtaining the German man's identification, then said to Kevin, with much concern in his voice,

"Kevin, right now, we have to protect Jackie! If they are coming after Me, Mike, or Ray, then that's a different story. We have to make sure Jackie will be okay! Are you with us on this?"

Festerman did not like what Bolden had just said to him, but he understood what Bolden was asking of him. Calming himself down he replied,

"Yes, I am with you. Let's get Jackie out of here then come back down here and kick some serious German Ass, so they don't follow her!!! I don't care if they are East German or West German, they don't ask us to identify ourselves, those fuckers already know we are United States Military!!!"

Bolden answered Festerman, being in total agreement with him,

"All Right Kevin! If you want to do this then I'm with you. Mike, how about you? You in on this?"

Broadway was a bit shaken up but was unsure of what Bolden had expressed, to them, what happened to him. His main concern was for Jackie. He looked undecided on what to do, but answered back,

"Yes, I'm with you guys. Let's make sure Jackie gets out of here okay before we do anything.

The three men were in agreement with what they were about to do. Standing up from the table, Bolden said,

"Before we go, I've got to take a leak. I will be right back then we will head out."

Kevin and Mike took a stand next to Jackie. Bolden did an about face, as the men's bathroom was behind him, then walked to the entrance, pushing open the door. He discovered a long line of men waiting for their chance at the urinal. He looked to his left and seen the old German

man that took care of cleansing the bathroom. The front line soldier that was in charge of disease control, keeping everyone healthy and in good spirits. It was the unrecognized, important job, that kept a society in good health and in good cheer. He recognized Bolden, came up to him, gave him a hug, and asked,

"Alles Gute?"

Bolden responded back saying in German,

Ja, Ja, Alles Gute!!!"

The old German man talked to Bolden in German, hoping that he would be understood. Bolden, nodded his head, but shrugged his shoulders to him, with interested eyes, out of respect, for the old German man, to say, "I don't understand what you are saying..., I wish I did!" The old German man picked up on Bolden's body language, became silent, then shook his hand. The line of men waiting for their chance at the urinal shortened quickly. When it was Bolden's turn he quickly took the open spot and finished his business. Bolden walked over to the wash basins and washed his hands. The Old German Man, personally handed him a dry, clean towel, for Bolden to dry his hands with. Bolden accepted his kindness and dried his hands with the fresh clean cloth that the Old German Man had offered him. Bolden placed the dampened cloth into the laundry hamper, that was located by the entrance/exit door of the men's wash closet. He reached into his pocket and produced a Five Deutsche Mark Coin, equivalent to about two dollars and fifty cents in American currency. Bolden placed it into the Old German Man's Tip Dish located on his table, which Bolden had done many times before. The Old German Man gave Bolden a hug then shook his hand. Looking into Bolden's eyes with gratitude, but also with concern from his eyes, said to Bolden,

“Danke, Danke! Veilen Danke!

Bolden bowed his head to the Old German Man and said,

“Danke Schon!”

Their eyes met with sadness and knowing that it would be the last night that they would ever see each other again. They shook hands then Bolden took his departure. Opening the door, exiting the mans bathroom, with sadness, looking down toward the floor. The door closed behind him making such a loud click, which forced Bolden to lose his deep, penetrating, thoughts and enter into the present. He looked up to see the short German Man, that had asked him for his identification earlier. He had Mike close up against the wall. Demanding from Broadway, his identification. Bolden was furious from seeing this and moved quickly into action. His previous goal of obtaining this man's identification was fully intact. He thrust forward with a smooth momentum. His eyes were fully focused with intent on grabbing the short German man's identification. Bolden yelled out to his friend Mike,

“THAT'S THEM MIKE!!! DON'T GIVE THEM ANYTHING!!!”

The intense conversation that Mike and the short German man had going, was broken off immediately, as Bolden came between the two men, grabbing the short German man's identification, placing it into his right hand. In the quick instant that Bolden had acquired the identification, of his now again counterpart, his counterpart used Bolden's swift momentum, by grabbing him and throwing him up against the wall, trying to retrieve back, his identification. Broadway, immediately went into action, grabbing the short German man, to protect his friend John. Within a split second, the bald, muscular, Big German Man, grabbed Broadway by his shirt, trying to throw him off of his friend. This attempt failed as Kevin Festerman threw, four, quick hard thrusts into the much bigger, muscular, bald German Man's back, where his kidneys were located. Bolden was pinned against the wall from the weight of the three men, pressed against him. His main goal, his main objective, was in obtaining, the short German man's identification. Bolden looked at the big German man's eyes and seen him wince with excruciating pain from Festermans forceful punches into the man's kidneys. Then watched Kevin jump into the air with his left arm and place it in a choke hold around the big German Man's neck to cut off the circulation of his oxygen supply to render him useless. Bolden thought that if Kevin was successful with what he was doing, then he would be free to help win the battle that was ensuing. A few seconds passed by quickly, then Bolden noticed the Big German Man's eyes roll to the back of his head. It was only a matter of a few more seconds to win their battle. From the right of Bolden, which was the entry way into the Ku'dorf, came three big muscular men. They were the bouncers of the Ku'Dorf. One of them immediately tackled Festerman, throwing the both of them into the middle of the S curve. It had forced Festermans grip on the Big German Man's neck to be released, which allowed him to be able to breath and recover his consciousness, however one of the other bouncers tackled him throwing him down to the ground. The third one grabbed Mike and pulled him away from the short German man. With the weight of all the men that were against Bolden, pinning him up against the wall, being off of him, he was able to thrust forward and push the short German man away from him. He stood in a defensive position waiting for the short German Man to come back against him and ensue the battle but withdrew his advance. The three bouncers from the Ku'Dorf controlled the situation. The bigger of them shouted out,

“WHAT IS GOING ON HERE?”

Bolden took the lead, shouting back,

“ASK THIS MAN WHY HE WANTS TO SEE OUR IDENTIFICATIONS? HE KNOWS THAT WE ARE UNITED STATES MILITARY AND HE HAS BEEN ON US ABOUT SHOWING HIM OUR IDENTIFICATION! THIS IS NOT RIGHT! YOU ASK HIM AND YOU ASK HIM NOW!!!”

The lead bouncer of the Ku'Dorf knew exactly what Bolden was asking and immediately started talking German to the short German Man. Bolden watched with intensity as they conversed with each other. The short

German man was very nervous explaining his situation with the lead bouncer. Festerman recovered from his tackle and was up against the big, bald, muscular, German Man, staring him eye to eye. Broadway was a bit shaken from the incident but was on guard for what might happen next. His focus was on the short German man. Jackie had went back to their designated table and had tears streaming down her cheek. She was very worried about what might happen. Bolden looked at the lead bouncer, looked into his eyes and discovered that his look of intent had changed to a look of worry. Bolden was curious about this and asked,

"Okay, what did he say?"

The lead bouncer had a look of submission in his eyes when he turned to Bolden and said,

"Look, why don't you just give him his identification back and you guys go about and party, like nothing happened here. We will let you do this. Give him back his identification. Everything is okay. Everything is good. They are going to leave now."

Bolden knew that the situation was way too serious than what had been relayed to him from the lead bouncer. The usual protocol for whenever a fight broke out in the Ku'Dorf was that who ever was involved in the fight was forced to leave the Ku'Dorf. It did not matter who started the fight. They did this to keep a safe environment from anything further happening. Bolden knew that what the bouncer said was not right and responded back with a hefty voice,

“Well if that is all you are going to tell me then I will have to keep his identification and hand it over to military intelligence, explaining to them what just happened here. He knows he should not be asking any U.S. Military members to show their identifications to him. This isn't right!”

The lead bouncer of the Ku'Dorf was becoming nervous and had much concern in his eyes. He looked at Bolden and asked him nicely,

“Please give him back his identification. In Germany, all of us must have our identifications on us at all times, just like you Military Service Men. Please give it back to him. We will make sure the both of them leave here. You guys can stay here and continue partying.”

Bolden granted the lead bouncer of the Ku'Dorf request and handed the short German Man his identification back. The short German Man's hand was shaking as he took his identification back and placed it in the rear pocket of his trousers again, as he did this he looked at Bolden and said,

“Danke Schon!”

Even though the short German Man's tone had changed to being nice, Bolden was not about to go easy on him after what he had done to them. Bolden, pointing at the lead bouncer of the Ku'Dorf and with stern voice said,

"You're lucky this man talked me into giving you your identification back! I don't want to see you following us around again! VERSCHTAIN?!!!"

Bolden already knew the short German Man didn't understand what he was saying to him but his body actions relayed the definition he was putting forth to the short German Man. As the short German Man was about to turn and exit the Ku'Dorf, Bolden waited to see if this man was going to wave the back of his right hand at him again, a sign of disrespect, like before. This type of motion from the body relays to the intended party, "Go Away, I Don't Care What You Are Saying or Who You Are!" The short German Man motioned to the Bigger, Bald, Muscular German Man to follow him in leaving the building. Bolden had to have the last word again as he said in a loud voice,

"Wave The Back Of Your Right Hand At Me Again And See What Happens Next! I Dare You!!!"

Bolden was trying to provoke them into another fight but it didn't work as the two men turned and walked away from them. The lead bouncer of the Ku'Dorf looked at him and asked,

"Are you guys going to stay here and party some more?"

Bolden replied back,

"No, we are going to head out. There has been enough excitement for tonight. Besides that, you guys should keep up your standards by keeping this place safe."

The lead bouncer of the Ku'Dorf laughed a little then with a smile on his face said,

“Will you let us escort you out? We will make sure that you are safe.”

Bolden agreed to the lead bouncer's request. Mike and Kevin were standing by Jackie at the designated table. They had calmed her down a bit but she still had a worried look on her face. Bolden motioned to the three of them to indicate that it was time to go. Jackie was in the middle of the small ring that circled her from John, Mike, and Kevin. The three bouncers of the Ku'Dorf circled around the four of them, like the seven main planets of the solar system, they moved in their own way but huddled together to provide an atmosphere of protection. As they walked through the hallway, people began clearing the way for them, looking in awe at them as they passed by the crowd. They arrived at the bottom of the steps then ascended upward out into the open marketplace. The lead bouncer shook Bolden's hand and said,

“This is as far as we go. We have to get back down there. You guys have a good night.”

The three bouncers of the Ku'Dorf turned and walked away descending back down the steps from where they once came. Mike, John, and Kevin stood with Jackie by the bus stand waiting for her bus to arrive to take her back to her new home. She began crying again then said,

"I am very scared for us. I hope you guys will be okay."

Mike gave her a hug and began to console her. With compassion he said,

"We will be okay. We are worried about you. You have to stay strong right now and soon this will all be over. We can live our lives back to normal again."

Her bus was arriving at the bus stop. She gave Mike a kiss and then a great big hug. Festerman was next to receive a hug and a kiss from Jackie. Then she turned toward John, looked him in his eyes, with sadness in hers. She moved forward pressing her lips against his and passionately gave him a kiss. She held her arms around him tightly not wanting to let go. John did the same, not knowing if they would ever see each other again. She whispered into his ear,

"I Love You John!"

John responded back,

"I Love You Too Jackie! We Will See Each Other Again! I Promise You That!"

They released their passionate embrace from each other. With tears in her eyes she boarded her bus that would take her to her new home. She took her seat, looked out the window and stared at John and Mike with the tears and sadness in her eyes. The bus closed the doors and began to travel down the cobble stoned street of the market place. Jackie placed her opened right hand up to her mouth, kissed it, then blew a kiss to John, Mike, and Kevin. The three of them waved back to her as she disappeared from their vision as the bus went down the street. Unbeknownst to them, it would be the last time, that John and Mike would ever see Jackie again! The three of them stood in silent thought next to each other for a brief moment. Then the silence was broken as Festerman said,

“Hey, I'm getting hungry! You guys want a Doner Ke Bob? I'm buying!!!”

Mike and John looked at Kevin as if they wanted to kick his ass for interrupting their thoughts, being of the serious nature that they were. Kevin looked at both of them and said,

“What??? I'm going up to get a sandwich. You guys want one or not?”

Bolden and Broadway shook their heads and with a swift, but silent motion wafted their hands in the air to say,

“Go ahead! Knock yourself out man!”

Festerman shook his head then turned to walk up toward the Imbiss stand to get his Doner Ke Bob. All three of them looked in the same direction at the same time. They discovered the two German men they had encountered earlier next to the Imbiss stand. The two German Men, saw them at the same time. The short German man was on the payphone talking and the big German Man was guarding him. They both had a worried look upon their faces when the three Americans noticed them but when they noticed the Three Americans their worried look turned in to concern. Festerman was the first to say something. With a smile on his face he looked at John and Mike and said,

"There they are!!! Let's go finish what they started!!!"

Mike had a worried look upon his face, so did John. Bolden had to bring the situation under control. Looked at Festerman and said,

"Kevin let those guys be for now. We are at a neutral stance with them for the moment. I think we should turn this in to OPSEC and let them figure out who those guys are. Like I said before I don't know if they are East German or West German. If they are East German and we kick their asses then we will be okay but if they are West German and kick their asses then we will have something else to deal with besides Jackie's escape. It is best right now to get back to the barracks and report this."

Kevin didn't like what John was saying to him but he knew what Bolden was talking about. The bus to take them back to McNair Barracks was coming up to the bus stop. Bolden continued on with his conversation with Kevin,

"It's too late to get a Doner Ke Bob here anyhow. You can get one when we get back to the barracks at the

Imbiss Stand outside of the gate. Come on, let's get going!"

Festerman, jokingly picked up his right leg then slammed it down on the ground acting like he was angered about not getting his desired Doner Ke Bob. He was the first one to get on the bus. Bolden followed next, then Broadway. They took their seats quietly. Bolden had to say something to relax Kevin's demeanor. With his right hand clenched in a light fist he tapped Kevin lightly with it on his left shoulder. Bolden with a big smile on his face and admiration in his eyes looked at Kevin and said,

"Look At You! Check You Out, Man!!! Being the warrior that you are. Giving those love taps, of yours, to that big, tall, muscular German guy. He enjoyed everyone of them, I could tell.

Festerman rolled his eyes up in the air and started laughing,

"Love Taps? Where are you coming from with that non-sense? That man felt every bit of that love that I gave him. I would have had him to if that bouncer hadn't of tackled me.

Bolden nodded his head in agreement with Kevin, then said,

"Yes, you did. It was only a matter of a few more seconds. I was watching the both of you."

Bolden looked at Mike with admiration in his eyes for him, then said,

"And you Mike! Coming to my rescue like that. That was brave Man. I know you got my back and appreciate the both of you very much!

Mike was quiet with a sad, concerned look on his face, he said,

"We aren't going to be able to bring Jacqueline and her son over here, are we?

The light mood around them changed to a serious tone. John looked at Mike to confirm to him what he expressed,

"No Mike. I don't think we are going to be able to do that. I Apologize to you Sir!"

The rest of the ride on the bus was silent going to McNair Barracks. The bus arrived at it's stop and the three men took their exit. Festerman went to the Imbiss Stand and got his Doner Ke Bob for the evening. The three of them walked together up to the CQ Desk of CSC 6/502nd Infantry Battalion. John and Kevin stopped at the CQ Desk where as Mike continued walking to his room. John looked at Mike and said,

Hey Mike, where are you going? We have to report this to OPERATIONS SECURITY! They might want to ask you some questions."

Mike turned to John and sarcastically said,

“Johnny, don't report this man! It's better off that we keep this quiet!”

Bolden was confused with Broadways response but he was determined to do his duty. His intuition told him he had to report it and relayed this back to Mike,

“Mike, I have to do this! I will let you know what they say, okay?”

Mike nodded his head, waved his hand good night, then entered his room.

Specialist Russell Schmidt was the CQ Runner for the night, as always, seeing that he was still on light duty. He didn't ask any questions about what was going on. He picked up the phone and handed it to Bolden. Looking in his wallet he found the OPSEC card then started dialing the number. After a couple of beeps, the European ring tone, a voice is heard on the other end of the phone,

“Operations Security, Specialist Donovan speaking. How may I help you Sir or Ma'am?”

Bolden began his conversation with Specialist Donovan,

“This is Specialist Bolden from CSC 6/502nd Infantry Battalion. I have an incident to report that happened to us at the Ku'Dorf tonight that I thought you guys should know about. I am one of them men that is allegedly involved with...."

Specialist Donovan quickly interrupted Bolden,

"Yes, we know who you are Specialist Bolden. This incident has already been reported and they are looking in to it right now. You guys did good tonight! You guys did the right thing!"

Bolden wanted to know who they were. He asked his question,

"Who were those guys? Were they East or West Germans?"

Specialist Donovan reported back,

"It was GREPO, East German Undercover Agents, trying to get information from you. Like I said, you guys did the right thing tonight. It is best if we don't say anything more over the phone. We will take it from here! Oh, By The Way, just to let you know, all of us here think you guys are heroes. Have a good night Specialist Bolden and Good Luck To You!"

Bolden Thanked the man for giving him the information that he was looking for, then hung up the phone. Festerman was looking at him anxiously to know what they had said,

Bolden looked at him and said,

"Well Kevin, we could have kicked their asses and got away with it. The man just told me they were East German GREPO, looking for information from us. They also said that we did good tonight. There, now we have our answer.

Festerman slammed his clenched fist down upon the CQ Desk and said in a low voice,

"I told you we should have kicked some serious German Ass! You should have listened to me!"

Bolden smiled at Kevin then said,

"Kevin we did good man. Intelligence is handling this now. They know much more than we do about this and how to handle it. It is best left up to them. Appreciate you backing me up tonight!"

Festerman shook Bolden's hand and wished him a good night then headed off down the hall and into his room. Bolden turned, then walked down the hall toward his room. He stopped in front of Mike's door ready to knock upon his door and tell him what he had found out from OPSEC. He stopped the forward movement from his right hand, thought for a moment, then decided that it would be best if he told Mike another time the information he wished to relay to him. He knew Mike had to have his time with his thoughts and respected it. John turned to his left and walked down the hall to his room. He opened the door, walked in, closed it, undressed, throwing his dirty clothes of the day into the laundry bag attached to the end of his bunk. He put on his PT shorts, his nightly wear for sleep, then laid down on his bunk. He was too tired too think about the night's events, that had occurred. John found the answer that he was looking for and so did Mike. For the rest of their time in West Berlin, they would not see Jackie ever again, or help Jacqueline and her son to escape into West Berlin. The both of them would be Lucky to be able to stay in the Army to receive an Honorable Discharge. The dream that Bolden had of being a United States Army Infantry Soldier for the rest of his life deteriorated within his thoughts. He gave, what he thought, to be the best of his beliefs, to everyone involved. He was unsure of himself, thinking that it may have not been enough, to continue on, being a part of a team. The veil of uncertainty had to be lifted in order to provide a knowledge of light to move forward with a new plan. He had to let his family know, especially, his mother, of what he had done and the possibility of what may happen to him. Bolden also had to have some type of advice to help him decide on what to do. The only one that he could think of, for the moment, was a true family friend, that had retired as a Lt. Colonel from the United States Army, who served during the Korean War. As a youth, Bolden would listen to him tell his stories, which were not very often, of his exploits, during such a time. Bolden admired this man so much that he wished to be able to live up to his standards. The first thing that Bolden had to do was to write this man, ask him for his advice, and hope that he would receive an answer from him in a timely manner, that would enable him to move forward with his decisions. With a little bit of solace placed within his thoughts, he laid down on his bunk. Without knowing it his body went into action and immediately went to sleep.

42
MEETING WITH THE GENERAL

Sunday, August 24th, 1986. Bolden awoke from his night of rest. It was early enough that he decided to take a quick shower then head down to the chow hall for a relaxing breakfast. He placed in his thoughts that, Sunday is to be a day of rest and relaxation, so therefore, he would enjoy the food that was presented to him in a calm and joyful atmosphere. He used this time to think of what he was to write to the dear family friend he had thought of, the previous night, for his advice on what to do. Before he finished his breakfast, while being in deep thought, he felt a nudge on his right side. Looking up, he knew instantly who was sitting next to him, it was Micheal. Bolden was delighted to have him for his company. He was anxious to relay to him what he had found out from Military Intelligence and waited for the moment to tell him. Broadway began the conversation first, apologizing for his actions from the previous night,

"Hey Johnny! How are you doing? I want to apologize to you for how I acted last night. It was not anything against you. I think you know that already."

Bolden was compassionate toward his friend and relayed back,

"Mike, the way things went down last night, you have nothing to apologize to me about! You protected me! I am forever grateful to you for that. I wish for you to know this! You had a lot to think about last night! When you are ready I will let you know what I found out about those two German men from last night."

Broadway didn't hesitate,

"Go ahead! Who were they?"

Bolden was at the ready and conveyed his information quickly,

"Intelligence told me they were GREPO! You know, the kind that attend the Humboldt University in East Berlin, the one that's pretty close to those goose stepping East German Soldiers at that Memorial over there. They look good at the ceremonial for, "The Changing of the Guard", I got to give them that. Well anyways, Intelligence told me they were here undercover looking to get information from us. Intelligence also told me that we did good by what we did to them, or I should say, what You and Kevin did to them, as I was pinned up against the wall. They also told me, and I really think you should know this Mike, that all of them there, think, we are heroes!"

Broadway had a smile on his face from hearing what Bolden had expressed to him, but then he showed a serious expression in his face, when he said,

"That's all good and fine but I think we are going to have to have a plan, on a way to get out of the situation, we are in, right now!"

Bolden knew exactly what Mike was talking about and offered the plan that he came up with from the previous night,

"Mike, I placed a lot of thought into this and this is what I've come up with. I'm going to give my family a call later on today. My mother, especially, has to know what is going on. I suggest you do the same. When I get done with breakfast here I'm going up to my room and write a letter to an old family friend of ours and ask him for his advice. He is a retired Lieutenant Colonel from the Army. I know him very well. He is hard core and will let me know what we have to do. I will let you know what he says, if he is able to get back to us, before, they decide what to do to us. Are you okay with that?"

Broadway, with his sarcastic attitude, answered back,

"What fucking choice do we have, right now, at this time, Johnny? Let me know what he says! I'm with you! We have to stay by each others side right now! It's the only strength that we have left for the moment!!!"

Bolden finished up his breakfast, stood up, and then took his tray of empty dishes, he said with confidence,

"I'm on it Mike!!! I will let you know!!!"

With what Bolden had just said, he took his leave from his friend and went up to his room. He sat down at his desk and started writing his letter to the family friend,

"To Lt. Colonel Richard "Dick" Morahn, United States Army, Retired:

Sir, this letter, that I write to you is between a soldier to a soldier. Though, you are a true family friend, that I love with earnest from my heart. I must ask your advice, soldier to soldier, to an Officer from an Enlisted Man, on what to do with my current situation. As you already know, I am currently stationed in West Berlin, Germany. What you do not know, is that I have been involved with a successful escape of an East German female into West Berlin, providing her safe passage through Checkpoint Charlie. As of the current time I am under scrutiny of such a bold and daring act, that I feel I am justified in being part of, only to think, that I am being wrongly accused of breaking the very act of freedom that we truly defend. I feel that I have gone way above and beyond the call of duty that us as soldiers are called upon to defend and that is the right of every individual to have their freedom to be whoever they wish to be. I am lost on knowing what to do, at this time, and am asking for your advice, on what to do. As a young man, I listened to the stories you told about how you were a platoon leader, a young silver bar Lieutenant, who led his platoon into battle during the Korean War. How your men had very little clothing, to protect them from the cold harsh winters of Korea and very little ammo to fight the battles that you and your men ensued. How you wished you were able to provide for them, MORE, of what they had to have to win the battles and how with so little you and your men won those battles! I so admire You, Sir!!!, for telling me those stories as others slept through them. I

Respect You Very Much! You are the pillar of my strength! Though I could not be an officer in our military, your essence has given me the goal, to obtain the honor that you hold within yourself! No Sir, I am not, as some would say, kissing your ass, I am explaining to you how I feel and where I am coming from, of what I believe, and how you have helped me to achieve this belief, that I feel to be true and correct for right livelihood! I believe, that your advice to me, about this current situation, that I am in, will provide me, with the correct decision to make. Whatever your answer is, I will know it to be true and correct in making my decision on how to move forward, for the greater good, of all involved in this. I anxiously await your answer and pray that it will be delivered to me, in a timely fashion, so that it may be considered, to take part, in my further actions. Soldier to Soldier, Family to Family, You will always be a part of my life, my heart, that led another younger soldier into battle and unto victory!

With Much Respect,
John A. Bolden
Specialist 4th Class
Untied States Army, Infantry

Bolden folded the letter, placed it in the envelope, then sealed it. He went up to the CQ Desk and handed it to Specialist Russel Schmidt to place in the outgoing mailbox, hoping for a return letter that would soon arrive to help him make his decision. He walked back to his room and laid down upon his bunk, thinking of what he should express to his family about what he had done and what might happen. It wasn't a call that he was excited to make but he knew it had to be done. He called home about once maybe twice a month on a Sunday, as it was the least expensive time to call, because the call, that he made home, had to be placed as a burden onto his family, as a collect call, and when the charges were accepted, on the other end, the dollar amount began to quickly gather up. This is where most of the allotment of $400 a month went to, that he was sending home to his Mother. Their time on the phone had to be limited. Bolden waited for the time to call home and calculated the least inexpensive way to do this, optimizing his air time for a connection to his family back in the United States. When the time came he exited his room then took a quick left to the double set of glass doors, that was located next to his room. Opening the doors he went down the two flights of stairs to where the phones were at. He located an available booth, sat down, picked up the phone then dialed the number to his Mother's home in Tomah, Wisconsin. After a couple of beeps he heard the familiar voice of his Mother on the other end. They began their conversation with the usual of asking how each one was doing. His Mother explained to him that his sister Lea Ann had some important news to give to him that he would be happy to hear. She also told him that his Father was there to talk with him as well. Bolden was excited and anxious to hear the good news from his sister, he thought it might cheer him up a bit but he also knew he had to tell them what was going on and was happy that all of them were there so he could talk to them. He decided that he should begin his explanation then proceeded on,

“Mom, I have something I have to tell you. It's not good news but I think you should know.”

His Mother became silent on the other end. She always had a sixth sense about things and from her silence Bolden knew that she already knew something had happened. She had a worried tone in her voice when she asked,

“Oh, John B. I know something happened, are you okay?”

Bolden began his story,

“Mom, I don't know yet. I am fine for now. Myself and two other soldiers have been involved in helping an East German woman escape from East Berlin into West Berlin. I thought we did the right thing but I am finding out different here on this end. I'm not really sure how they found out about us being involved. I have an idea of what may have happened but there are so many possibilities. They are deciding on what to do to us. I may be home sooner than you think, or it might be quite a long time before I get to see you again. I will let you know what they decide on once I find out. I Love You Mom!!! I wish for you to know that!”

His Mother was strong giving her response to her son,

“John B. You did good. You did the right thing. Everything will be fine. You will see that. I know in your heart you did this out of love and caring. This will protect you in what you have to go through. Be strong through all of this. I will pray for you and you better do some praying on your end, cause we are going to need a lot of help getting you through this!"

Receiving the healing from his Mother's words, Bolden began to laugh from the way she had expressed about how he needed a lot of help to get him through his situation. Her upbeat personality always expressed a positiveness in her voice that was soothing and relaxing. Bolden's tension from worry began to fade away from his shoulders and then out of his body. She laughed with him for a moment then said,

"Here, you better tell your Father what you told me. I will talk with you again before we hang up. I Love You Too!!! And You Already Know That!!!"

She handed the phone over to his Father, who was very inquisitive, straight and to the point, he came with his question,

"Okay, Son, What did you do? Your Mother doesn't talk like that unless something happened. What is going on? And don't bullshit me because whatever you did or are thinking about doing, I've already thought about doing it."

Bolden had a slight chuckle in his voice the way his Father had expressed his question. He relayed to him what he had told his Mother. He also told him that he had written a letter to Dick Morahn asking him for his advice. With silence on the phone, Bolden could tell his Father was thinking about what to tell him. Then the silence was broken, when his Father spoke,

“Hmmm, Got to tell you, that's an original one. I never thought about doing that. My Son? My Son, did this? You're Mother is right. You did good Bucher! They should give you guys a medal for this. There is nothing to worry about. You will be fine! I'm proud of you Son!!! Writing to Dick is a good move on your part. He will tell you like it is and you better take his advice. He's a good man and you already know that. You stay strong and the three of you stay together on this! We will see you when you come home. I'm going to hand the phone over to your sister, she has something important to tell you. Love You Son!!! We will talk with you again soon!”

Bolden relayed his same feelings back to his Father and could tell that his Father wasn't done in voicing his opinion as Bolden could hear him talking to his Mother in a loud voice,

“Can you believe what your kid, did, Mary!? What are we going to do with him Bridgey?”

That was all Bolden heard clearly as the phone was handed over to his sister, though his Father's voice could still be heard in the background. Bolden was astonished, some what amazed, from the conversation he had with his Father. He called him by a nickname that his Father's Father, Bolden's Grandfather had given him when he was a young man, “Bucher”. His Grandfather was full Romanian and spoke the language fluently. “Bucher, as

Bolden found out, meant, "Joy", in Romanian. His Father used to call him that many times when he was younger but as Bolden grew older he hardly ever heard it from his Dad, unless he did something good. Then he heard him call his Mother by her middle name, which was "Bridget". When Bolden's Father was in a happy mood he would call her "Bridgey". So to Bolden, the only thing he could figure out was that his Father was actually very proud of him, which is a good thing for a young man to know. His deep thoughts were brought into the moment as he heard Lea Ann's, his sister's, voice on the phone.

"Hey John B., what is all the fuss about? Mom and Dad aren't saying anything about it. They are talking but can't be for sure what they are talking about."

Bolden relayed his information to her quickly and then changed the subject over to her,

"So what is the good news that you wish to tell me?"

His sister was worried but she relayed her story over to her brother,

"David and I are getting married. He asked me last week and I accepted but I told him we had to wait until you returned home so you could be in the wedding. So, what are we going to do now, Mr. Hero?!"

They both started laughing. Bolden had to give her an answer that he was unsure about answering,

“I don't know what to tell you Sis. You two might want to get married without me being there because I can't tell you when I will be back home now. It might be sooner or it might be later. I will let you know as soon as I find out anything. And “STOP” with that hero thing, will you? By The Way, CONGRATULATIONS, To You and David!!!”

His sister was adamant when she responded back,

“No, it doesn't matter. We are going to wait till you come home. You will be fine. I know you will be. David wants to talk with you for a little bit then he will hand the phone over to Mom again. I know we only have a little bit of time on the phone here. I Love You John B.! Be Strong My Bro! My Hero!

They laughed together for a brief moment then the phone was handed over to her fiance' David. Bolden knew him briefly from high school. David was a tall, strong, muscular man. He was a comical type of man but had a serious side to him as well. Bolden liked him very much and knew that David and his sister were a good match for each other. His loud strong voice came over the phone,

“Hey, what's this hero shit I'm hearing from your sister? You ain't that type, you little featherweight. This better be good or I'm coming over there and bring your ass back here so I can marry your sister!”

Bolden expected that type of comment from David. The laughter was hearty between them on the phone. Bolden explained his story to him. Again there was silence on the phone for a moment, Then Bolden heard the strong voice of David,

"Yeah, that's a good one! So, is this gal pretty good looking? And did you get any of that?"

Another expected comment from David. Bolden was on his toes with him. Chuckling on the phone he answered David's questions,

"Yes David. She is very good looking. The answer to your other question is, "NO". That's not why I did it David. She could have been a man and I would have done the same thing. She is a strong, brave woman Dave!"

David kept up his comical tone,

"So, are you telling me you are gay or what?"

They continued laughing together for a brief moment. Bolden knew they had to cut their conversation off as the time was coming near to hang up the phone. Still laughing Bolden said,

"Knock it off David, but I know it is all in good fun. Seriously, now, CONGRATULATIONS! To You and Lea Ann. You two are good together and I wish the both of you many happy years together."

David became serious with his tone of voice,

“Yes, I'm just having some fun with you. You know that. I wished to talk to you and ask you for your blessing to marry your sister. It is very important to us to have your blessing.”

Bolden being serious replied,

“Yes! Of course you two have my blessing. You had it a long time ago! You might not want to wait for me though. Who knows when I will return home.

David responded back,

“We will wait until you get here! Be safe over there! Here is your Mother again. We will see you soon, Mr. Hero!”

Bolden heard his Mother's voice again on the phone, She was calm, cool, and collected when she said,

“John B.!,What is the name of the woman you helped to escape?”

Bolden was surprised to hear this from his Mother. He wondered why she asked this,

“Her name is Jackie, Mom! Why do you ask?”

His Mother was firm in her tone of voice answering his question,

“I will include her in my prayers. The next time you see her give her a big hug and kiss from me. Tell her I said everything will be all right and that I hope I will get to meet her one day.”

Bolden's Mom wasn't finished with what she had to say, as she continued forward with her calming voice, she said,

“Your Dad was telling me that you wrote to Dick Morahn. John B. you listen to what he has to tell you and follow his advice closely. I am sure he will lead you in the right direction. When you get home I will make your favorite dinner, fried chicken with mashed potatoes and gravy. Make sure you are eating right to keep your strength up. And remember to do your prayers! I Love You John B.!”

Bolden's Mother was always good at making him feel special and loved. She had a way about her that made everyone feel special and loved within her presence. She was a true angel of love and kindness. Anyone and everyone who came into contact with her, enjoyed being around her, and she always made sure that those around her had plenty to eat to keep up their nourishment. Bolden didn't want to hang up the phone. He wished to keep talking with her as he didn't know when the next time he would be able to hear her voice again, but he knew he had to go upon this journey on his own and face what was to come. His eyes started to water as he held back his tears, then said,

“I Love You Too, Mom! I will call you when I can and let you know what is happening. And Yes, I will say my prayers. And Yes, I will let Jackie know what you said and of course there will not be a problem with giving her a big hug and a kiss.”

His Mother's voice came across the phone quickly,

“You be good John B.! If I find out different, I'll tan your hide and burn your fried chicken!”

The tears that were about to come from Bolden's eyes, stopped as the both of them began laughing with each other on the phone. The both of them had to have the air of happiness in the atmosphere to keep the positiveness flowing in the right direction. When their laughter slowed down, Bolden still chuckling said,

“I will be good Mom. You already know that. I'm always good! Love you and talk with you again soon.”

His Mother responded back,

“I know you will be Son! Love You!”

With those last words from his Mother's voice repeating in Bolden's thoughts, he heard the click from the other end, signifying the end of their conversation. Bolden walked back up the stairs and then returned to his room. His next move was to wait for a response from Dick Morahn to decide on what he was to do.

Tuesday, September 9th, 1986. Mail call, was at the end of the day, with the platoon formation. Bolden heard his name being called out. He marched up to his platoon sergeant, who handed him a single letter. He saw the return address on it being from Lt. Colonel Richard "Dick" Morahn, United States Army, Retired. Bolden went back to his place in formation and was anxiously awaiting the release from the platoon formation. As soon as the order of, "Dismissed", was given, he ran up to his room and opened the letter, where he began reading his family friend's response.

To: Specialist 4th Class John A. Bolden
United States Army, Infantryman

Dear John,

Upon reading your letter, I am amazed to learn about what you have done in West Berlin as a soldier. You asked me to write to you as a soldier to another soldier, an officer to an enlisted man, and this is what I am going to do. You may not like what I have to say to you. I have talked with your Father and Mother about this and have told them my thoughts concerning you. I thought they should know, what I think may happen to you and they should be prepared for it. The one thing that you did wrong was to disobey a direct order. Though this order was not given to you verbally, it is in the Uniform Code Of Military Justice. These are written standing orders to be obeyed at all times. You have violated the U.C.M.J., by bringing over unauthorized personnel into West Berlin. I can tell you this, you will be punished and it is up to your Battalion Commander on what to give you. He will be following his orders, that will be coming from the

General of the Brigade. It is quite possible that you may be dishonorably discharged. If they offer you an Article 15, then I suggest you take it and move on. What you have to understand is, “That You Disobeyed A Direct Order!” This can not be tolerated by anyone, officer or enlisted man. In order for any mission to be accomplished successfully, all orders must be obeyed and carried out to insure mission accomplishment. The safety and security of West Berlin is your mission! West Berlin stands as a symbol of our strength, integrity, and commitment to a free society! This must be upheld to show the world how dedicated we are toward this great way of life! What you have done may seem honorable or noble to you, granted, that such a heroic act is constituted within it's nature, but that is not your mission! With your act of heroics, you have placed the whole Berlin Brigade at risk as well as the city of West Berlin! I have known you since you were a very young man and have always seen goodness in you. What you did was out of kindness and generosity from your heart. I know that your honor and integrity are still intact. I am hoping that your superior officers will see that in you and your punishment will be according to your behavior on how you act through this whole thing. Do not go public with this! If you do go public with this then they will make an example out of you! I know you will make the correct decision on what to do and what has to be done. I wish you the best of luck with everything and will see you when you arrive back home.

Best Regards,
Richard Morahn

The letter was short, bittersweet, and straight to the point as Bolden expected it would be. From reading it he knew what he had to do. All that was left to do was wait on his superior officers to make their final decision on what to do with the three soldiers. Bolden exited his room, took a right down the hallway, stopped in front of Broadways door and knocked. He had promised Mike that as soon as he received his letter that he would let him read it. Broadway opened his door and saw Bolden standing in front of him handing him the letter. Mike didn't invite him into his room. He took the envelope from Bolden pulled out the letter then read it. It only took about a minute. Broadway folded the letter back up and placed it into the envelope handing it back to Bolden. He looked at him and said,

"I guess we know what we have to do now, don't we?"

Bolden nodded his head in agreement, then said,

"Yes we do! Have you heard anything from Ray? We have to get a hold of him and see what he is going to do."

Broadway quickly answered,

"No! Haven't heard anything from him. I have called his house a couple of times and left messages but haven't heard back from him."

Bolden nodded his head in affirmation to what Mike had told him, then said,

“Okay Mike. Have a good night. I will talk with you later.”

Broadway waved his right hand at Bolden then closed his door. Bolden walked back to his room. He sat on his bunk and thought about Ray. With the uncertainty that was in the air about him, Bolden's thoughts were on trying to get a hold of him and to let Ray know what was going on, so he could make a good solid decision as well. For right now, patience was the key for understanding. In due time, the pieces of the puzzle would soon develop to be placed in to the proper positions, hoping for a nice even fit.

Wednesday, September 10th, 1986, Bolden was working on his mortar gun tube at the motor pool. Working diligently and with total interest upon his task, he is interrupted by his platoon sergeant, when he heard the voice of SFC Horton yell out,

“Bolden, You and Broadway get your asses up to your rooms and change into your best pressed and cleaned BDU uniforms right now! The General wants to meet the both of you in an hour! Scrub up, take a shower, or do whatever it is you have to fucking do and you better look good in thirty minutes standing in front of the CQ Desk when I get there!!! Is that understood?!!! Make sure your boots are fucking shined too!!! I told you before I don't have time for this fucking bullshit!!!”

Bolden looked up and saw Broadway standing next to his platoon sergeant. He immediately went into the position of parade rest and shouted back,

"YES SERGEANT!"

Bolden looked at Copsovic, the gunner of his squad, shrugged his shoulders at him, then left his position on the mortar track to stand next to Broadway. They had their orders then proceeded up to their rooms by themselves. Halfway through the motor pool Bolden looked at Broadway and said,

"You know, I hope I get to see Horton in the civilian world so I can kick him in the ass and put some sense into his head."

Broadway with his sarcasm, gave a hmmph to Bolden then said,

"Yeah??? You and who's army?"

Bolden with a smug smile on his face looked at Broadway and said,

"YOU!!!"

Broadway rolled his eyes into the air shrugging off Bolden's comment. They continued on to their rooms to get ready. They were prompt at the CQ Desk with their best pressed, clean, BDU uniforms, and shined boots. SFC Horton showed up with First Sergeant Dean, CSC 6th/502nd Infantry Battalion's First Sergeant. He stood about six feet four inches tall, muscular, with a big frame to his body. He had black hair with a trimmed mustache. The combat patch he carried on the right shoulder of his BDUs indicated he was a Vietnam Combat Veteran. First Sergeant Dean took the lead with his calm heavy voice that carried a slight southern drawl to it,

“ All right you two, we are going to meet with the General in less than thirty minutes. He wants to meet all three of you and is going to give you guys some good advice. Actually it is not going to be advice. It's going to be an order and you better take it!!! You keep your mouths shut. Listen to what he has to tell you!!! And don't dare say a word back to him!!! Is this understood?!!!”

Bolden and Broadway immediately went to the position of Parade Rest and yelled back,

“YES FIRST SERGEANT!!!”

First Sergeant Dean, without showing any emotion expressed back,

“Good, now that we have that out of the way, let's get going. We are going to meet the General at the museum. He will be coming in with his Huey. We will know when he is here. Let's move it out!!!”

The four of them headed down the steps, into the parking lot, across the street, then entered the museum, where the American Flag was laid to rest at night. When they entered the museum Bolden looked around and saw that there were many officers standing in the room they had just entered. They walked through the open hallway toward the end that opened up into a bigger room. Bolden and Broadway spotted Williams standing there with his NCO from supply. Both of them wanted to talk with Williams right away but knew they had to be silent for the moment. Time ticked by slowly as they waited for the Generals appearance. Officers and NCOs talked among themselves as the three "Freedom Fighters stood in silence awaiting their silent orders. The time approached as the blades from the General's Huey Helicopter could be heard. The echoes of, thud, thud, thud, were knocking on the roof of the museum, from the aerial blades, grasping the air, from the sky, to present a soft landing upon the helipad on the ground. The knocks became silent as did the room in the museum. The door creeks open and the sound of a strong voice is heard in the air, where even silence is forbidden,

"ATTENTION!!!"

One unison click is heard from everyone standing in the room. The General presented himself and walked straight over to where the three "Freedom Fighters" were standing. He paced excitedly, back and forth between the three of them. He was thinking of the words he had to express to them and knew that what he had to tell them had to be expressed and received clearly within their thoughts. When he was finished thinking, he stopped. He looked at the three of them with pride, then with disgust, then with sadness, then came the stern voice of completion,

"You three men have been keeping me up late at night, wondering what I should do with you. Can't say that I like it much! The three of you have done something, that us as American Soldiers should never had done, but do, all the time!!! This unanswered question is what keeps me up at night, not you men!"

Without moving a muscle, the General's eyes became fixed upon Specialist Bolden. His stare penetrated Bolden as Bolden stared back at him, with respect, while many others stared into the open air. Bolden wasn't nervous. He was attentive, as to what the General was about to say, as it would determine their fate.

"I don't wonder about what you men did because I know why you did it! This is what is important! I am telling you right now!!! If you would have taken money from her or if you would have had sex with her, I would have your asses in Mannheim right now!!! BUT I KNOW WHY YOU DID IT!!!! YOUR COLONEL IS GOING TO OFFER YOU AN ARTICLE 15 AND YOU BETTER TAKE IT!!!"

Without saying another word, the General and his staff marched out of the room and closed the door behind them. The order was given to, "AT EASE". Most of the men in the room began to relax, all except for the three "Freedom Fighters". Sergeant First Class Horton gave his orders to Bolden and Broadway,

"Well you two got that, now get your asses back down to the motor pool and do your jobs."

First Sergeant Dean stepped in with his orders,

"Sergeant First Class Horton, have these two men come to my office immediately. I have to talk with them."

SFC Horton complied with the First Sergeant's order. Looking at Bolden and Broadway he said,

"You two heard what he said. Follow the First Sergeant up to his office and listen to what he has to say to you."

Bolden and Broadway did as they were ordered to do. When they reached the First Sergeants office, he instructed them to have a seat, then commenced to telling them what they were there for, with his southern heavy voice he said,

"All right, you guys, this is what is going to happen. I have been instructed to guide you through your proceedings. I need to know what you plan to do. The General has just given you a very kind offer, that I suggest you take, but the decision is up to you. You may go in front of a court martial and hope for the best, by pleading your case. You will be appointed an attorney through JAG, the "Judge Adjutant General". I suggest you talk with your assigned attorney first, before making your decision. As of this moment, what do you plan on doing?"

Bolden and Broadway were silent for a moment, then Bolden broke the silence as he stated,

“Top, Mike and I are thinking about taking the Article 15 and moving on. We haven't been able to talk with Sergeant Williams to see what he would like to do, so I can't speak for him.”

First Sergeant Dean stepped in with his comments to enlighten the two men sitting in his office,

“I have already talked with Sergeant Williams and he has decided to go in front of a court martial stating his innocence, as he did not know anything, of what happened that night. Let me ask you guys this. Did Sergeant Williams know that you were bringing that woman over to West Berlin?”

With that question being presented to Bolden and Broadway, it had left the air wide open to admit their guilt, in the activities that they were being accused of. They were silent, wondering whether to answer the First Sergeant's question or not. If they answered the question truthfully, then the First Sergeant would be involved, but on the other hand the First Sergeant was already involved, seeing that he had been ordered to guide and instruct Bolden and Broadway on what to do, based upon their decisions. Bolden and Broadway went with their gut instincts and decided to trust First Sergeant Dean as they looked at each other, eye to eye, without saying a word, they nodded their heads slowly, in agreement, confirming, to First Sergeant Dean, that Sergeant

Williams was involved and knew about the escape of Jackie into West Berlin. First Sergeant Dean slammed his fist down upon his desk. It produced a thundering echo in his office that got the attention of Bolden and Broadway as they heard First Sergeant Dean's heavy southern voice,

"Well son-of-a-bitch! They should be giving you men medals instead of an Article 15! You men are heroes in my book. As for Sergeant Williams, he should be staying by your side. If you plan something together, you should always stand by each other, no matter what!" He is talking about going public with this and this is something that you men do not want to do. They will make an example out of you should you proceed forward with that!!!

John and Mike knew that Ray was staying with the story, they had all agreed upon with the plan, prior to Jackie's escape. They all had agreed, upon maintaining their innocence, for this very, just in case, scenario. Mike and John had to talk to Ray to let him know what was going on with them and with what Jackie had agreed to, by being her own liberator. Sergeant Williams was holding on strong to their agreement not knowing of the new developments that had taken place. Bolden intervened, being polite and respectful, he said,

"First Sergeant, as I stated earlier, we have not been able to talk with Sergeant Williams to let him know what we have decided upon. We have to get together with him soon so all of us can decide on what to do."

First Sergeant Dean was adamant with his demand,

“Then you two better get with him soon and talk this over among yourselves. This is a very serious matter and you men do not want to take this lightly. If they have to, they will crucify all three of you on this! Your strength, right now, is being “United” together! I suggest that you three, “GET IT TOGETHER!”

Bolden, being understanding and considerate to what the First Sergeant had expressed to them, said,

“Yes First Sergeant, we know how serious this matter is being taken. We know the deal “Top”, “WE'RE EXPENDABLE....”

First Sergeant Dean stopped Bolden from completing his sentence by forcefully interrupting him with his heavy voice, which was now, raised another octave,

“AND WHAT MAKES YOU THINK YOU ARE SO FRICKING SPECIAL, SPECIALIST BOLDEN?!!! WHY HELL, EVEN AT MY RANK AND MANY YEARS OF SERVICE, I'M EXPENDABLE! AS A MATTER OF FACT, EVERY SOLDIER IS EXPENDABLE TOWARD THE FREEDOM THAT WE DEFEND! AND I'LL TELL YOU ANOTHER THING ABOUT BEING EXPENDABLE, THIS INCIDENT IS SO SERIOUS THAT EVERYONE IN THE CHAIN OF COMMAND IS BEING REPLACED. AS SOON AS THIS MATTER IS RESOLVED, I AM BEING REASSIGNED TO ANOTHER COMPANY IN WEST GERMANY!”

Bolden and Broadway sat in their chairs with stunned looks upon their faces. They were dumbfounded as to why this would happen. Broadway, who had been silent through the whole meeting, voiced his opinion, as he was curious, and so was Bolden, as to why this was happening. Broadway asked with curiosity and concern,

"Why are they doing that "TOP"? You, just got here! You didn't have anything to do with this! Out of all these years of service, from what I have heard, your wish was to serve in the "Berlin Brigade". Now that you are here, they are going to ship you out to another company, after what we have done? That doesn't seem fair at all First Sergeant! You didn't have anything to do with this!!!"

First Sergeant Dean gave the explanation to Broadway's question,

"Fair doesn't have anything to do with anything Specialist Broadway. The reason why the present chain of command has to be replaced with a new chain of command, is in case the Soviets push this issue of how three American Soldiers helped an East German citizen escape their allied GDR country. You have to know the Soviet Union is an ally to East Germany because the East Germans serve their best interest right now. We have to prove to the Soviets that this was not a planned mission from the United States Army, besides that, all of this is sensitive information. Do you men get it now? As for me, I'm proud of what you men did! It is one of the reasons why we are soldiers. I don't mind being reassigned to another post because of this. To me, this is an honorable and noble reason. My mission right now is to make sure you men are going to be okay, that you are treated fairly, and to instruct you on what to do in order for this to happen. Once this is done then my mission will be complete here in Berlin and it will be time to move onto other things. With that said, let all of us get it together so we can move on in life. Understood?"

The bigger picture was beginning to unfold before Bolden and Broadway. They were beginning to see the sacrifice of others that were not directly involved with their actions. They had full trust and confidence in First Sergeant Dean, as well as respect for him. He was the stronger leader that they had to have to help them through their situation. First Sergeant Dean carried the lighted torch that would light up the pathway to safety, security, and well being for these three men. There was no other man for the job as First Sergeant Dean was a well qualified leader for humanities sake. Bolden and Broadway acknowledged the First Sergeant in unison,

"Understood, First Sergeant!"

First Sergeant Dean continued on with his instructions,

"Our superior officers will notify us of when they have made their decisions. In between time, there will be other departments calling on you men to ask you questions. Answer their questions truthfully but do not admit to any guilt of your participation of this incident. I will let you know when your appointment will come up with the Judge Adjutant General. That's it! You two better get back down to the motor pool and show your presence to your platoon sergeant. I will see you men soon, and for God's sake, keep your mouths shut about this!"

Bolden and Broadway stood up, shook the First Sergeant's hand, and expressed their gratitude to him for his help. They returned down to the motor pool and made their presence known to their platoon sergeant. For the remainder of the day they continued on with their normal duties. Both of them had heavy thoughts on how they were going to be able to talk to Sergeant Williams and they hoped that it would be soon. They had to come together and make an agreement between themselves. It was all they had left. Being united would be their shield that would defend them and keep them safe, physically, mentally, and spiritually!

43
J.A.G.

Sunday. September 14th, 1986. It was late in the afternoon when Bolden heard a knock on his door. He was wondering who it could be as he didn't recognize the knock to be that of his friend Mike. He opened the door and saw Ray and Mike standing together. Bolden with a smile, feeling much relieved to see Ray, welcomed the two of them in to his room and offered them a seat. Each of them sat down and began to discuss the situation they were in, so they could come to a formidable agreement between them. Bolden started first,

"Ray it is good to see you. There is a lot we have been wanting to tell you with new developments that have come up on our end. Has Mike clued you in on what we have decided to do yet?"

Mike came in to the conversation quickly,

"No, I haven't told him anything yet. He just got here and I thought it would be best if all of us talked about this together."

Ray came in with his comments,

"I think all of us should stick to our plan that we made before. We did good with what we have done and they know that. We haven't done anything wrong. If we go public with this and let people know of what we have done then they will have a difficult time punishing us. We can get away with this and proceed on with bringing others from the East over here to the West, like we planned on doing! Besides that, my wife just got promoted where she works and she is making really good money. They can't just up and send us off somewhere else without proper notification. We have to stick to our guns here men!"

Bolden and Broadway looked at each other with a bit of concern. They knew Ray was staying with the plan but he didn't know the new developments. Bolden began to enlighten Ray upon their situation,

"Ray, look. Mike and I know what all of us agreed upon in case this scenario happened, but, things have happened that are out of our control right now. The last time we talked with Jackie was at the Ku'dorf a couple weeks ago. She agreed to being her own liberator, saying that she hid herself under the back seat of the van while we were away up in the disco, but that doesn't matter right now. What happened that same night was that Mike and I, and Kevin Festerman had a run in, with GREPO. These East Germans are looking for us Ray and they were here in West Berlin. Jackie warned me about this happening before it even happened. She said Tanye told her that the Stasi already know who you guys are but they don't know anything about me. With that incident happening Ray, I don't believe we are going to have another chance of bringing anymore East Germans into West Berlin. If we ever did get a chance to go back to East Berlin then they will be watching us closely. Mike has already come to terms with this and he knows now that we are not going to be able to do this anymore."

Mike came in to the conversation, confirming to Ray, what John was telling him,

"It's all true Ray. We had a rough time with those two men that night. I already know that we aren't going to be able to bring Jacqueline and her son over here. We are going to have to settle this quietly and hope for the best. Top told us you were thinking about taking this public and he said it would be best if we didn't, as they would make examples out of us, if we decide to bring it out. It is best if we keep this a secret. John and I have decided to take the Article 15. We know you have more to lose than we do but we are hoping you will do the same. If we accept the Article 15, it will keep us out of Mannheim. Once the proceedings are done, then they can't go back on us for anything about this incident. It would be double jeopardy on their part and that is what the General is really trying to say to us. It is weird but I think they are trying to protect us, in a funny sort of way. When this is all done, we can go about our lives and get it all back."

Ray listened to what each of them had to say, then started shaking his head in disagreement with them,

"No, I'm not going to accept the Article 15. They offered me a letter of reprimand, which I am not going to accept either. We did nothing wrong, Mike...., John. We have done what we believe to be right. We have done our duty, above and beyond the call. This is what we are here for. I can not accept what they are offering us, and you two men shouldn't either!"

Mike and John were able to see Ray's point in the whole situation, but their instincts were telling them to accept the light form of punishment, which was the Article 15. It would be their shield, defending them, from any other aggressive movements toward them. They knew their superior officers were trying to protect them the best way they knew how. It was up to them to accept their protection, if these three men refused their protection, then their superior officers would have no other choice but to prove, to any other service men, that if they should have the same ideas, then be prepared for what would happen to them. The example would definitely have to be shown. Bolden knew he was the lowest ranking man between the three of them. He also knew, that if an example was to be made, then he would, most likely be the one that they would choose. Bolden began pleading with Ray. His voice was calm, hoping that Sergeant Williams was able to see his point,

"Ray! I am asking you, if you will take this light form of punishment, for me, and possibly Mike, here! I have read the statements that You, Mike, and Jackie have given to C.I.D. The interrogating officer told me that all three of you gave me up and that I was the only one that created the plan, and helped Jackie to escape. I do not believe these statements, at all!!! What I do believe, is that they will chose me to make an example of, as all the evidence that they have, points to me. Being the lower ranking man, among us, I know they will pick me, to place all the blame on. If we go public with this Ray, and I am not looking for any publicity, or medals, for what we have done, on this, but I know, and I believe even Mike knows, what I am going to have to go through, in order for things to be settled, in a political sort of way. They will chew me up and spit me out Ray! I can go through this, I am prepared for it, but I chose not to, because I think it is in the best interest for all of us to take the light form of punishment! At this time, we must live to fight another day!
Please Ray! Take the letter of reprimand and move on with this. They will not take any rank from you, money, or extra duty. You will come through this, pretty much, unscathed. We have to stay together on this. Being united among the three of us is the only strength we have left in this situation. We have to look out after each other!"

Broadway piped in with his thoughts,

"Ray, I'm going to stay by John's side. They will have the two of us to place the blame upon. I'm not going to let him go through this by himself. Your an NCO and they are going to keep us separated through the whole process. We are going to have to come to an agreement here today. Who knows when we will see you again. We have to go see JAG in a few days and talk with our attorney and see what he has to say. Both John and I have already chosen to go through the Article 15 proceedings but we would like to here what the attorney has to say. Ray, that letter of reprimand is nothing compared to what we might get from the Article 15. All of this is a slap on the wrist for what we have done, for what we have accomplished here. Not only are we a part of history, being here, all of us created an event within the history of the Berlin Wall, and that will never be taken from us! Take the letter of reprimand that they are offering you. John and I will give them, the meaty portion, they are looking for, to satisfy them. All of us can walk away from this unharmed in every way! What will be your decision here Ray!?"

Sergeant Williams had listened intently to Bolden and Broadway. By the look on his face, they could tell he did not like what he was hearing, but in another aspect, his eyes held concern for Mike and John. Ray knew the sacrifice he had to give to help his friends. His head moved downward as his eyes stared at the floor, thinking of what to do. It only took a few seconds to make his decision. He looked at the both of them and said,

"I don't like what I am hearing from you men, but I know, what you are saying here. If you have to have a decision right now, then this is it. I will take the letter of reprimand, as you men have already decided to take the Article 15, but let's keep our options open for the time being. We shouldn't let them know what we have decided here today, in case something new develops. We have some time to play with for right now. As long as they don't know what we plan on doing and with the possibility that we still might make it public, we still may be able to get out of all of this, without anyone one of us taking a hit. Are we all in agreement with this?"

Mike and John knew what Ray was saying to them, and that was, to keep the playing field in play, or in other words, keep your options open. They all knew it was a closed matter, but, like the Cold War, which was present, it was a gray area of matter, that showed uncertainty, upon everything in life. Though this gray area is considered null and void, it held within it, a certain power, that held time in place, that provided the moments, to make an accurate decision, that would be based upon the positive forward movement, for the greater good of all. This was democracy at it's finest! The freedom to move forward into the future, based upon faith, of knowing, the unknown. This is what all soldiers, all warriors, are called upon to defend within a democratic society. These three men, these three soldiers, in all actuality, were living their dream and showing proof of what they truly believe in. With Ray's statement to Mike and John, it opened up a vision for all of them, to protect and defend their belief of Freedom for everyone. Bolden and Broadway were in agreement with Sergeant Williams. As they ended their conversation among them, they all stood up and shook each others hands. Their confidence was high as their strength was still intact by being united together. All that was left to do was to have patience and wait for the appointment to be set to talk with their attorney at JAG. That day was soon to come.

Thursday, September 18th, 1986. Bolden and Broadway are called out of platoon formation and ordered to wait in their platoon sergeants office for further instructions. They did as they were ordered to do. SFC Horton upon entering his office, which was located downstairs and into the Mortar Platoons Area of Operation. Broadway gives the order to "At Ease". Bolden and Broadway went into the position of "Parade Rest". Sergeant First Class Horton gave the order to "At Ease", then proceeded giving his instructions to them,

"All right you two, the time has come for you to see your attorney at JAG. He is located at Brigade Headquarters on Clayalle. Do you know where that is at?"

Broadway answered the platoon sergeant,

"I know where it is Sergeant but I don't know where the JAG office is located at in the building."

SFC Horton continued on with his instructions,

"Okay, then make sure you take Bolden with you and show him where to go. When you get there ask someone where the JAG office is located at. I am sure someone there will be able to tell you where it is. You are to be there at 1000 hours, so I suggest you put on your best uniforms and boots. Make sure you are looking sharp when you get there. You might just run into the General again, while you are there. If you do, make damn sure you don't say anything to him. I don't know how long you will be there but it shouldn't take all day. I expect to see the both of you down in the motor pool before the end of the day. You better get up to your rooms, get ready, and then head out. I hope you men have decided to take the Article 15 and to keep this quiet. This is out of my hands and there is nothing that I can do for either one of you. So get going!?

Broadway and Bolden did as they were ordered. They changed into their best BDUs again and put on their highly shined boots. They were both quiet on the bus ride to Brigade HQ. Taking in the scenery of the hustle and bustle activity of the American Sector in West Berlin. Mike broke the silence between them saying,

“Hey, you know what we should do? We should go see Jackie this weekend and her new place. I've got her address. We will have to try and find it. Who knows how much longer we have left here in the city. I would like to know how she is doing. Besides that, we are going to the Grunewald for field maneuvers soon for a couple of weeks. It will do us good to get out and about instead of being cooped up in the barracks.”

Thinking that it was a good idea, John nodded his head in agreement with Mike and a plan to visit Jackie was silently made between the two of them. Their bus arrived in front of Brigade Headquarters and the two of them stepped off the bus and walked toward the entrance way of HQ. There were many officers in the outside area as John and Mike were continually saluting them as they walked by them. Looking at the board on the wall to see where the JAG office was located at, they found the room number, but did not know where the room was located at. They saw a Captain walking toward them and asked him for the location to JAG. He pointed them in the right direction where they proceeded down the wide hall, took a left into a smaller hallway. Three quarters of the way down that hallway, they found the office. They both stopped and looked back. There were two men standing at the beginning of the main hallway that Bolden and Broadway had just come from. Broadway, looking at John, said,

"You know who that guy, standing on the right is, don't you?"

Bolden winced his eyes a bit to focus them. He saw the sillouhettes of the two men but he couldn't make them out. John looked at Mike with a bit of confusion then answered his question,

"No, can't say that I do Mike. Can't really make them out from here. Why? Are they important?"

Broadway being sarcastic in his tone of voice, said

"Come on Johnny! Are you serious? That's the General! You know, the guy we met at the museum, and chewed our asses out."

Bolden dismissed Broadway's sarcasm, then said,

"Really? He looks much shorter than what I remember him. Must be the distance we are at right now. He seemed to be a pretty tall man when he was yelling at us!"

Mike gave a smile and a little chuckle, then said back,

"That's because you were scared at the time Johnny!"

Bolden chuckled back at Mike, then with a casual voice said,

"Whatever, Michael! Let's get in here and get this over with. I'm very curious as to what this guy is going to say to us."

They walked into the JAG office and announced their presence to the secretary. She offered them a seat, which they took, then waited to be directed to their attorney's office.

After a few minute wait they were told to enter into their attorney's office. The door was already opened as they walked up to the entry way. With a slight knock on the door from Broadway, they heard the voice of their attorney saying,

"Come in and take a seat. This is going to be short and sweet."

Bolden and Broadway walked in together then stood at the position of "Attention" giving him a salute as they discovered his rank was that of "Major". Broadway began with the usual presentation but was rudely interrupted by the Major,

"You don't have to go through that formality. Have a seat and let's get this over with!"

They took their seats as they were ordered to do and silently waited for the Major, who was to prepare their defense, in case they chose to go for the court martial. Bolden looked at the Major, who wasn't looking at him directly. The Major sat in his reclining chair, that was turned to the left side of Bolden and Broadway. Being silent the Major was rocking back and forth in his chair with his left leg crossed over his right knee, flipping the pages of a report, that were in a folder, he was holding in his right hand. He was overweight for being a soldier, which was kind of odd to see, as Bolden was used to seeing infantry officers being in great muscular shape. He wore wire rimmed glasses which he would remove from his eyes, from time to time, as he studied the documents that were before him. The Class B uniform he was wearing looked a bit wrinkly and unkempt. After a few minutes, he placed the folder back down on his desk, turned his chair forward, put his elbows on the top of his desk, put his hands together, and interlaced his fingers together, forming it into one fist, then said,

"Well, I hope you two men have decided to take the Article 15, if you don't, and I am going to speak plainly to you, then you guys are pretty well screwed. So tell me what you men want to do with this."

Bolden began first,

"Sir, what other options do we have right now? What is the best course of action for us?"

The Major was quick with his response. Being very rude, he says,

"You men don't have any other options available to you. If you decide to go through a court martial with this, I can tell you right now, the both of you, will be doing two years in Mannheim, with hard labor, and at the end of that time, you will be dishonorably discharged..., and I am going to help them do that to you! I guarantee you that!!!"

Bolden and Broadway were surprised and had stunned looks upon their faces when they looked at each other. They were not sure how to respond back to the Major, who was supposed to be helping them, but were now finding out, that this was not to be the case. Broadway began with his question,

"What about Sergeant Williams? He is talking about taking this public and we are agreeing with him if they want to push it this far. What other choice will we have but to do this?"

The Major, sitting back in his chair, placing his hands behind his head. With a slight laughter and smile on his face, he said,

“Sergeant Williams is going to walk. He didn't know anything about what you two men did. I just got done talking with him before you men showed up. He has agreed to turning evidence against you two. I'm going to save his rank and everything else. He will be able to stay in Berlin and continue out his service with an Honorable Discharge, maybe even retire from the Army, later on, if he decides to do this, while the both of you are screwed. I am going to make sure this happens and it won't matter if you decide to take it public or not, they will sweep this under the rug and nobody, no one, will ever know this incident ever happened. As a matter of fact, either way you go with this, all of this is going to be placed into the “Restricted Files”, the only one that has access to any of this will be the President of the United States! Take the Article 15 and be appreciative that our superior officers are protecting you. There is nothing I can do, nor do I want to, for you men! You men placed this whole Brigade and City of West Berlin at risk with what you have done and I have no qualms with what they want to do with you men!”

Bolden was next with his questions,

“Sir, if you are representing Sergeant Williams and if he is going that route, then isn't that a conflict of interest on your part? Shouldn't we get us another attorney?

The Major, without hesitating, answered Bolden's questions,

"No, not really a conflict of interest. Good luck on getting assigned to another attorney. No one wants this case because it is a losing case. I just happened to get stuck with it and I will tell you the truth. I am not happy about this at all!!! I have to look out after the best interest of this case and that is what I am going to do!!! Take the Article 15!!! Sergeant Williams will get a letter of reprimand. Like I said, this incident is going to be placed in the "Restricted Files"! All three of you will be separated and assigned to other companies. It might be in West Germany or it could be anywhere the Army needs you at. Your security clearances will be taken away from you. You will not be able to return to West Berlin, as long as you are in the military. You will not be able to serve in another border patrol unit. As for your Article 15 punishment, that will be up to your Colonel, as to what he decides to do with you. After that, you will be able to continue on with your military service, receive an Honorable Discharge, or retire from military service, when it is time, and receive a pension. I have to know what you men want to do with this before you leave here!!!"

To Bolden and Broadway, it was pretty clear to them, from what the Major just told them, on what they had to do. Their decision had already been made before walking into the Major's office. The story that the Major told them about Sergeant Williams, was totally unbelievable, as their strength was from the meeting they had on that prior Sunday in Bolden's room. Bolden and Broadway knew the Major was, as they say, “Blowing smoke up their ass”, to scare them in to taking the Article 15, which didn't work with the two of them, but the Major didn't know that. Knowledge Replaces Fear, as the saying goes, with the unity of Ray, Mike, and John being together undivided, they moved forward with their decision, as Bolden and Broadway advised the Major of their decision, to take the Article 15. Bolden had one more question for the Major,

“Sir, what can we expect from this? Will it be the maximum?

The Major with a huff in his voice said,

“If I were you two men, I wouldn't be too worried about that right now. Just be grateful to your Colonel for whatever he gives you. You two are dismissed! Now get out of my office!”

Broadway and Bolden stood up from their chairs and went in to the position of Attention and then to give the proper salute to the Major. The Major abruptly stopped them by saying,

“GET OUT OF MY OFFICE!”

Bolden and Broadway did as they were ordered to do without saying a word. They exited Brigade Headquarters saluting as many officers that walked by them then stopped at the bus waiting area, eager to leave the area of the Berlin Brigade HQ. Silent while waiting, they boarded their bus to take them back to McNair Barracks. Once they were seated, Bolden was the first to say something,

"Man, what an asshole, eh Mike?"

Mike was chuckling as he responded back,

"Yeah, with an attorney like that, who needs enemies?"

They both started laughing, because they both knew what they were going to do before they even got there. It was an experience that was unforgettable and would remain with them their whole lives!"

44
THE PUNISHMENT

Sunday, September 26th, 1986. Bolden met Broadway at the CQ Desk at 1000 hours. They were dressed in casual civilian clothing. The plan for the day was to see if they could find Jackie at her new apartment, located in the French Sector of West Berlin. They made small talk with Specialist Schmidt, the CQ Runner, for a few moments then decided it was time to head out. They boarded a couple buses on the way there. Upon their arrival in the French Sector, Bolden said to Broadway,

"I hope you know what you are doing here because I sure don't."

Broadway was hopeful with his voice, when he responded back,

“We will walk around until we find the street. It's not going to be that difficult. Follow me and you will be alright.”

“What choice do I have?”

Was Bolden's thought. They walked down a few streets looking for their destination. Thirty minutes later they found their street, then found the apartment complex building that Jackie had written down on the piece of paper for Mike. They walked up a couple flights of stairs and found the apartment number. As Broadway was about to knock on the door, Bolden being cautious said,

“Are you sure this is the right place? Hope we don't bother somebody on a Sunday that we don't know Mike.”

Broadway being sarcastic, responded back,

“Johnny, this is the right address that's on the piece of paper, right here! You want to see for yourself?”

Bolden shook his head, shrugged his shoulders, then with a wave of his right hand, said,

“All right! Go ahead and knock!”

Mike did his usual signature knock of continuous rapping. There was no answer at the door. He continued on. They both were anxious and excited, hopeful that Jackie would be standing there in front of them. There was still no answer. They heard a door open up behind them as a middle aged woman stepped out of her apartment and looked at them with curiosity. Mike was inquisitive with his question to her,

"Do you know the lady that lives here?"

It was apparent from her reaction to Mike's question that she didn't understand what he was saying to her. She was uncomfortable being around them as she quickly closed her door then walked down the hall toward the stairs. Mike knocked upon the door a couple more times. There was still no answer. They were still unsure if they had found the right place of Jackie's new home in West Berlin. Not sure of what to do next, Broadway asked Bolden,

"Well, what do you think? Should we head back to the barracks and call it a day?"

Bolden shrugged his shoulders, then said,

"Let's walk around the area and see if we can find Jackie. She might be out shopping or walking around. We might bump into her somewhere around here. We can take a look around the neighborhood maybe get us some lunch if your hungry."

Broadway with a smile on his face said,

"Good idea Johnny! I knew I brought you with me for some reason."

Bolden responded back with a smile on his face,

“Yeah, Yeah. Whatever Mike. You know you would be lost without me.”

Both of them began laughing and with a joyful attitude toward each other headed down the hallway, to the stairs, where they had once came from, arrived at the ground floor, then exited through the door. They walked a couple of blocks where they were standing at an intersection. Waiting for the walk symbol to appear on the signal light, to cross the intersection, Bolden looked up and to the left. He saw some type of artistry, that had illuminated to him, on the top side of a long cement building in the business district of town. He took a couple of pictures of it, with his kodak disc camera. Mike with a disturb, confused look on his face asked him,

“What are you doing taking a picture of that thing? It's not the greatest piece of art I've ever seen.”

John with a hopeful smile upon his face said,

“I'm thinking, that if we ever get to see Jackie again. I can show her the picture to show her that we came to see her before we left West Berlin. If that was her new home then this is close to it. That thing is big enough to remember. It will serve it's purpose someday Mike. You'll see. It might be a few years before we see her again, but we will see her again, I'm sure of this. You said just a little while ago, you brought me with you for some reason.”

Mike being pessimistic but with a humorous attitude, said,

"Yeah, well that's not one of them."

Bolden shook his head and took Mike's attitude as being one with a light demeanor to it. John with his right hand, placed it over his stomach and said,

"I'm getting hungry. Let's find us one of the busiest places around here and grab a bite to eat. If we don't see Jackie by that time then we can head back to the barracks."

Mike being in agreement, lead the way. They found a small imbiss stand where a crowd of people were gathered around enjoying their lunch. They saw that many people were passing by as well and decided that, with as much foot traffic going by in that area, it will be a good place to have their lunch. They placed their orders in for curry wurst and pomme frits with a coca cola. They found a small table that they were able to sit at, with a great view of the foot traffic, then proceeded to eat their lunch. After eating their delicious meal, they waited another hour then decided to head back to the barracks. Their hope for being able to see Jackie had diminished. They knew their time in West Berlin was coming to an end soon. Who knew when or if they would be able to see Jackie ever again. Being silent upon their ride back to McNair Barracks, their thoughts were upon their prayers, with hope and faith held high, that someday they will reunite with her and that their best wishes will always be with her upon a good life, a great life, that held with it, the promise of freedom, forever binding upon her granted wish.

Monday, September 29th, 1986. It was close to the end of the business day when Sergeant First Class Horton presented himself down at the motor pool. He found Bolden and Broadway then began giving them his instructions,

"All right, you two men! It's time! Get up to your rooms and... well, you know the procedure. You better be looking good as you stand before the man!!! The both of you are excused from regular platoon formation. I will meet you in "TOPS" office at 1715 hours. He will instruct you on what you are to do. I'm going to tell you right now, what he is going to say to the both of you. When you are receiving your Article 15, you will not say anything to the Colonel. If you have a request before the proceedings, then tell First Sergeant Dean, what it will be. He will then relay it to the Colonel and it will be up to him to grant, whatever it is, that you will be asking. Sergeant Williams will already be at Battalion Head Quarters before you two men will arrive there. The three of you will not speak among yourselves and will be separated as the proceedings begin. Do you understand what I am saying to you?"

Broadway and Bolden went in to the position of "Parade Rest" responded back, together,

"YES SERGEANT!!!"

Sergeant First Class Horton dismissed the two men so they could go about their duties, as they were instructed to do. They were silent to each other, hoping that their punishment, from the Colonel, would be light, so they would be able to continue on with the obligation that they had provided the United States Army, when they said their oath, upon their voluntary enlistment. Bolden and Broadway stood at the CQ Desk dressed in their best B.D.U. Uniforms and highly shined boots awaiting their punishment, at 1700 hours. By 1715 Hours, First Sergeant Dean made his entry way, through the double set of glass doors, in to the Company area. Specialist Schmidt sounded out the First Sergeants arrival by yelling the order of,

"AT EASE!!!"

Everyone, present, went into the position of "Parade Rest". First Sergeant Dean, being in a hurry, did not call out the usual protocol order of, "Carry On!" With his right hand, he motioned Broadway and Bolden in to his office, where both of them stood at the position of "Parade Rest" in front of his desk. First Sergeant Dean began with his instruction to the two men,

"All right, you two! This is it!!! You follow my orders exactly as I give them to you, and both of you will be fine! Are we in agreement with this!!!?"

"YES FIRST SERGEANT!!!",

was the reply from Bolden and Broadway. First Sergeant Dean continued on with his orders, they were as their platoon sergeant had stated to them earlier,

"When we get down to Battalion Head Quarters, I will ask the three of you, if there are any special requests, from either one of you, that you, would like to request from the Colonel. It is this time, and only this time, that if, you have something to say, you say it, otherwise, through the whole proceedings, you will keep silent! What I am saying to you is this, the least, any of us know about this, is for the better for everyone involved. Do you understand what I am saying to you!!!"

Specialist Bolden and Specialist Broadway, sounded off in unison,

"YES FIRST SERGEANT!!!"

First Sergeant Dean continued on,

"Good, then let's get down there and get this over with. Sergeant Williams is already there awaiting us. Neither of you will speak to one another. I will tell you this right now, Sergeant Williams will be receiving a letter of reprimand, where the two of you, will be receiving your Article 15. This is the arrangement that has been made. Are the two of you in agreement with this!!!?"

Specialist Bolden and Specialist Broadway sounded off in unison together again,

"YES FIRST SERGEANT!!!"

With the agreement being confirmed, First Sergeant Dean motioned with his right arm, to head out, toward Battalion Head Quarters. The three of them walked out of the First Sergeants office. When their presence was made, Specialist Russell Schmidt stood at the position of "Attention" then saluted Specialist Broadway and Specialist Bolden. Everyone that was standing in the near area, repeated the same step. Bolden and Broadway looked around and saw these men standing proud, with honor, and gratitude in their hearts. The only regret Specialist Broadway and Specialist Bolden had, was that they could not return the respect to those that were giving it to them, at that moment. Their hearts sank within their chests, wishing, hoping, that these men, who were giving them honors, knew that they were appreciated! Specialist Broadway and Specialist Bolden held much gratitude, to all of them! It was a memory that will last within their thoughts, forever!!! As they walked down the hallway, other soldiers, that they passed, did the same thing. They walked passed Specialist Broadway's room, then past Specialist Bolden's room, through the opened set of double glass doors, then descended down the steps to the next floor. They entered into Battalion Headquarters where they saw Sergeant Williams waiting for them. Standing tall, they nodded to each other, giving each other, the confirmation, of their Unity. Undivided, their strength together, was fully intact, as they awaited the decision, that their superior officers, had made, for their fate. Sergeant First Class Horton, the mortar platoon sergeant, made his presence known as he walked in behind them. First Sergeant Dean began asking the question he stated in his office before entering into Battalion HQ. He started with Sergeant Williams,

“Sergeant Williams, do you have any special requests to the Colonel before going in to his office?”

Sergeant Williams stood tall and was direct with his answer,

“No, I do not have any special requests, “TOP”.”

First Sergeant Dean continued on to Specialist Broadway,

“Specialist Broadway, do you have any special requests to the Colonel before going in to his office?”

Specialist Broadway was direct with his answer,

“No, First Sergeant, I do not have any special requests.”

First Sergeant Dean, turned to Specialist Bolden,

“Specialist Bolden, do you have any special requests to the Colonel before entering his office?”

Specialist Bolden, standing tall, said,

“Yes, First Sergeant, I do have a special request to the Colonel. Hopefully he will be able to grant it. First Sergeant, all of us work very hard at our jobs. I feel that we excel, greatly, in what we do. If at all possible, I ask that the Colonel will not give us any extra duty. He can take our rank and our money, for we can always get them back, as for extra duty, we do that every day First Sergeant, above and beyond!"

Every one stood in amazement at Bolden, from what, he had just expressed. They could not believe what he had said as a request. It may have seemed small to them but to Bolden it was a big request. First Sergeant Dean looked upon him with a smile on his face, then said,

"I don't think the Colonel will be able to grant your request, but I will ask him." Good Luck to the three of you!"

First Sergeant Dean continued on,

"I have to separate the three of you now, so we can start the proceedings. Your platoon sergeant will be with you in the Colonel's office. Sergeant Williams, stand next to Sergeant First Class Horton, you will be going in very soon. Specialist Broadway, go over to the other end of the room, and stand in that corner. You don't have to turn your back and put your nose in it, if you don't want to."

The laughter ensued among the group of people that were standing in the area. It was a type of whispered laughter as the proceedings were to be of a serious nature, but there had to be some type of humor involved to release the tension that was apparent in the room. Specialist Broadway did as he was ordered to do. He arrived at the corner, did an about face, went in to the position of "Attention", then in to the position of "Parade Rest", where he stood silently, still holding back the laughter generated from “TOP'S”, humorous comment. First Sergeant Dean continued on,

“Specialist Broadway you will be going in, right after Sergeant Williams, once he exits the Colonel's office. Specialist Bolden, go wait in the Battalion X.O.'s office. I don't know if he is occupying his office or not. Knock on his door, see if he is in there, if he is, then ask him permission to wait in his office.”

Bolden proceeded with the First Sergeant's order. He knocked on the X.O.'s door and heard a strong voice coming through it,

“Come In!”

Bolden opened the door and saw the Major sitting behind his desk. Specialist Bolden marched to the front of his desk, stood at the position of “Attention”, presented the Major with a salute, then said,

“Sir, Specialist Bolden asking permission to wait in your office until I am called upon to see the Colonel, Sir!”

The Major, following proper protocol, returned the salute back to Specialist Bolden, then said,

“Have a seat Specialist Bolden.”

Specialist Bolden, dropped his salute, did an about face, walked over to the chair that was directly opposite of the

Major's desk, did another about face, then sat down in the chair. Specialist Bolden looked at the name plate that was displayed upon the Major's desk. It read, Major Victor Bero. First Sergeant Dean entered Major Bero's office, to explain to him what was happening,

"Sir, I had to split these men up. They are here to receive..."

Major Bero interrupted First Sergeant Dean. With respect, he said,

"I know what he is here for First Sergeant. He will be here when the Colonel is ready for him."

First Sergeant Dean responded back,

"Thank You, Sir!"

First Sergeant Dean exited the room closing the door behind him. The X.O.'s office was silent between Major Bero and Specialist Bolden, as they looked upon each other. One thing was for sure, Specialist Bolden was impressed with the Major, by the way he presented himself. Major Bero was a strong, muscular man. His eyes were strong, like steel, as he looked at Specialist Bolden. The Major's B.D.U. Uniform was immaculate. His demeanor was one of strength, and straight forwardness. His aura, that surrounded him, held a strong sense of purpose. Specialist Bolden could tell this man was a true infantry officer, a valuable leader to his soldiers. The silence was broken as Major Bero's strong voice and choice of words came through the air, like an arrow being released from a bow, strong, with a true aim, intent on hitting it's target,

“What In The World, Were You Thinking, Specialist Bolden?”

The arrow of intent had hit it's target as Specialist Bolden sat up in the chair he was sitting in, then said,

“I do not know what you are talking about Sir!”

Specialist Bolden knew exactly what the Major was asking him but he was ordered to keep silent about the incident and the order was being adhered to with serious intent. Specialist Bolden did not know if the Major was testing him upon this. It would be to his benefit, not to discuss it with anyone. For some reason, he trusted the Major, and a quick thought came through Specialist Bolden's mind, that Major Bero wished to know the whole story about what happened, but this was not to be discussed. The Major squinted his eyes and with strong intention said,

“Do You Realize What You Have Done, Specialist Bolden?”

Again, Specialist Bolden, answered the Major's question with,

“Sir, I Do Not Know What You Are Talking About, Sir!”

"Do You Realize That President Ronald Reagan, The President Of The United States, Knows Of What You Have Done Here?"

With Confusion and wonderment in his eyes, Specialist Bolden looked at the Major and asked,

"Why would, the President of the United States, be interested in these proceedings, that are happening here today, Sir!?"

Major Bero looked at Specialist Bolden with confusion and wonderment in his eyes, then realized that Specialist Bolden's question was real and authentic, because Specialist Bolden, was being truthful, in his inquisitive question. The Major, with his eyes of steel, answered Specialist Bolden's question,

"It's because the Soviet Union are our Allies!!! The President has to know everything, that has occurred here, in case, the Soviet Union wants to prosecute you in their court system. You see, Specialist Bolden, Not only did you violate our law, you violated the laws of our allies! The President, has to be prepared with a statement, in case, they ask the United States, that you men, be handed over to them, to be tried in their courts, for violating their laws!"

Major Bero's voice grew louder, making sure that Specialist Bolden, understood what he was saying to him,

"AND SURE ENOUGH WE WILL HAVE TO DO THAT!!! DO YOU REALIZE, NOW, SPECIALIST BOLDEN, WHAT YOU HAVE DONE?!!!"

Specialist Bolden was amazed, confused, dumbfounded, but totally alert, to what Major Bero had expressed to him, at that exact moment. He came to know, that, all of his training, for the past few years, was to be against an enemy, that was a friend. Specialist Bolden knew this all along, but..... it was not apparent to him, until that exact moment, what the true definition of "The Cold War" was all about!!! Major Bero had did something to Specialist Bolden, that no one had ever done before. The Major's knowledge, had lit a candle within Specialist Bolden and placed fear in his heart. Knowing, now, of the the truth, Specialist Bolden had the response of "Flight", from the concept of, "Fight or Flight", response that was presented upon the psyche of an individual. Specialist Bolden's thoughts were frantic, fleeting, from moment to moment, on what to do. Within seconds he calculated his risks, which were very high. He knew of no one that could get him home to his family, where he would feel safe, within his Mother's loving arms. He was a soldier, an American soldier, at that. There was no mistaking his identity, with his short hair cut, and speaking only one language fluently within a different country. There was no way out of this situation. Specialist Bolden knew, for sure, that his superior officers were protecting him, the best way they knew how. With the "Flight" response being out of the question, Specialist Bolden knew there was only one thing to do, AND THAT WAS "TO FIGHT, TO THE

END, IF NECESSARY!!! His response was quick and to the point with the Major,

"NO SIR!!! YOU WILL HAVE TO KILL ME!!! I DO NOT INTEND TO SPEND THE REST OF MY LIFE IN A GULAG!!!"

The Major's jaw dropped. He was not expecting the answer that Specialist Bolden had given to him. Specialist Bolden did not mean any disrespect toward him. Specialist Bolden was afraid of the realization, that was brought on to him, at the moment. There was nothing else that Specialist Bolden could do. Major Bero did something for Specialist Bolden. He had opened Bolden's eyes, with the realization of truth, and this truth brought with it, fear! No one else, not even the General, the Colonel, the Soviet Union, nor the East Germans, could do that, to Specialist Bolden, who was soon to be demoted. Major Bero had shown Specialist Bolden, the bigger picture, that brought with it, a new definition to him, about what "The Cold War" was all about. It was a big ocean filled with this milky, white, black, gray substance. Like the color of C4 explosive, that could ignite into an unstoppable wall of fire, with just one little spark. One event, no matter how small, it may seem to some, could be blown way out of proportion, should anyone decide to do so. "The Cold War" was to be silent among friends, but with hidden enemies, on both sides, that had a great potential for destruction. Specialist Bolden went from feeling special for what he had done for his beliefs, to being a pawn to serve only those that would see an opening for their advancement, should they decide to use such an incident. Specialist Bolden was now left open for such an event, should anyone desire to do so. He knew it, at that moment, and had no plan of action, to counter against it. Specialist Bolden could only rely on those that had superior knowledge of what Specialist Bolden knew to be true. He knew exactly what they were doing, protecting, not only him, but, Specialist Broadway and Sergeant Williams, as well. There was no way Specialist Bolden could show his appreciation to his Superior Officers, for protecting, either one of them, from their ignorance. As much as he wished to do so, to show his gratitude to these men, he could not. From that moment on, he had to remain silent, keeping the gray milky area, of not knowing, within it's existence, for protection! Major Victor Bero, the Battalion X.O., was Specialist Bolden's, Guardian Angel! He held within him, the Sword of Archangel Michael, that was present, in the Berlin Brigade Patch, that protected, truth and justice! Their eyes of steel were entranced with each other until it was disturbed by a knock upon the Major's office door. The Major's voice being strong, said,

"Come in."

As the door opened, both of them knew that, it was First Sergeant Dean, that was about to ask, for the justice, that Specialist Bolden was to receive, for disturbing the silence, the peace of unknowing, that "The Cold War" provided". First Sergeant Dean announced,

"Specialist Bolden! It's Time!"

Specialist Bolden stood up from the chair he was sitting in, marched up to the center of the Major's desk, stood at the position of, "Attention", saluting Major Bero, he said,

"Thank You, Sir!!!"

Specialist Bolden was hoping that Major Bero had realized what he had done for him. He hoped that someday that Major Bero would realize that what Specialist Bolden had done, came from what he believed to be true and right, within his heart. It was not an act of youthful folly, because of his young age, but an act of intention, feeling, believing, that all human life has the right to freedom, to be whoever, whatever, they wish to be. Specialist Bolden hoped that one day, this man, who held the sword of Archangel Michael, would know of the true story that had happened, and that, what he had given to Specialist Bolden, was the truth that he had to have, the understanding, that with goodness from your heart, toward truth and justice, that you are protected, guarded by a higher source, to move forward, toward a better life of goodness and right livelihood! Major Victor Bero presented his salute back to him. Specialist Bolden dropped his salute, did a left face, and marched out of the X.O.'s office with First Sergeant Dean closing the door behind him. First Sergeant Dean looked at Bolden and said,

"Are you ready for this?"

Specialist Bolden took a deep breath in, then let it out, to clear his anxiety, and said,

“Yes, First Sergeant, I am ready.”

Specialist Bolden went in to the position of “Attention”. First Sergeant Dean opened the Colonel's office door. Specialist Bolden marched straight to the center of the Colonel's desk, where he stood at the position of “Attention” and presented the Colonel with a salute. The Colonel returned the salute back, then started the proceedings,

“Specialist Bolden, you are charged with aiding and transporting unauthorized personnel into the American Sector of West Berlin. With your signature here today, upon this Article 15, you are agreeing to the punishment set forth by your superior officers, from this unlawful act, and you will agree to abide by this punishment. The punishment is set forth as follows,

“You will be demoted from the rank of Specialist 4th Class to the rank of Private First Class, you are ordered to give up two months pay...,

The Colonel paused for a moment, then looked at Specialist Bolden, and continued on,

“Your First Sergeant has told me of your special request of not giving you any extra duty. I can not grant this request, however, I can give you the minimum amount of extra duty, which is seven days. The extra duty will commence right after the end of these proceedings. Your security clearance will be stripped from you. You will be reassigned to another unit and you will not be able to return to West Berlin as long as you are in the military. These proceedings will be entered into the "Restricted Files", and no one, but the President of the United States will be able to see them. With your signature, Specialist Bolden, we will end these proceedings and bring forth the punishment that has been set forth, for you, here today!"

Lt. Colonel Hutchinson turned the paperwork around, that was the Article 15, then handed Specialist Bolden an ink pen to sign his name upon it. Specialist Bolden came out of the position of "Attention", moved forward, accepted the Colonel's ink pen, then signed his name upon the Article 15. After signing his signature, Specialist Bolden moved back to his original position, regained the position of "Attention" and without a word, presented a salute to the Colonel. Lt. Colonel Hutchinson gave Specialist Bolden a salute back, then said,

"Private First Class Bolden, you are now ordered to move forward and perform the punishment that has been set forth by declaration of this signed Article 15. You are dismissed!!!"

Private First Class Bolden dropped his salute, did an about face, and with straightforwardness, he marched to the exit way of the door. First Sergeant Dean was accompanying him. Bolden's march was true and defined until he was almost out of the Colonel's office where Private First Class Bolden's march had a jerky movement, due to hearing a "THUD" upon the Colonel's desk, caused by Lt. Colonel Hutchinson's fist,as he exclaimed,

“This is a sad day for the United States Army gentlemen. We've just lost three of the finest soldiers we will ever know!!!”

Private First Class Bolden regained his march out of the Colonel's office, with the door being closed behind him, by First Sergeant Dean. He didn't look back. He wasn't supposed to. First Sergeant Dean and Private First Class Bolden marched into the hallway of the staircase, where “Top”, gave him his instructions,

“You will meet Private First Class Broadway down in the parking lot where you will meet an E-5, who is also on extra duty. He will be your assigned NCO for your extra duty detail. When your orders come in for you to be reassigned I will be there to aid, You and Broadway, to make sure you will be departed from West Berlin safely. Do you have any questions for me at this time?”

Private First Class Bolden went in to the position of “Parade Rest”, then answered the First Sergeant,

“No, First Sergeant!”

First Sergeant Dean motioned with his right hand for Bolden to head out for his extra duty detail, which he did with promptness. There were no other words exchanged between them. Walking down the stairs, Bolden felt the sadness that surrounded him, but the strength that he held in his heart could be felt as well. Like tempered glass, forged in strength, through a hot fire, to withstand a direct hit, from any aggressive projectile, Bolden's pride was shattered into thousands of pieces, but his foundation, his belief, was still intact. Should it have been tapped so very lightly upon it's side, then his very foundation would have been shattered into millions of pieces, never to be recovered, for what Bolden, Williams, and Broadway, stood for. Bolden fully understood the value of freedom, the overbearing cost, that so many others, and their families, had given, to maintain this inalienable right. Though this cost was not fully exacted upon Bolden and his comrades, they surely knew what it meant for many others that had come before them, that had given them free and safe passage, in and out of West Berlin, to provide for the one soul, that desired her freedom so much. Their reward was not of anything monetary, nor egotistical. It was in knowing that one life, one spirit, will strive to the best of her ability, to be free, to pursue everything and anything, to live a fulfilled life of freedom! Their cost would be proven to be justified by her actions of living life to it's fullest, by way of right livelihood!

45
REASSIGNMENT

Wednesday, October 1st, 1986. Bolden and Broadway reported for their extra duty at the end of the day. The E-5 that was in charge of their extra duty detail was no where to be seen. They stood around in the parking lot for a little bit waiting for him to show up. Bolden picked up a broom and started sweeping the parking lot, of which, they had done for the past couple of days. Broadway sounded off with,

“Johnny, what are you doing man?”

Bolden shrugged his shoulders and said,

“I'm sweeping the parking lot like we have been doing. He's not going to show up. I figure we do this for an hour and head up to our rooms, or maybe to the chow hall to get something to eat.”

Broadway looked at Bolden and with a smirk on his face said,

“You're right! He isn't going to show up, which means we don't have anyone looking at us, besides if he does show up, he is here for a bit, then takes off. Put the broom away, if he doesn't show up in a few more minutes then we will head out. This is our last day of extra duty anyways. We are going to the field tomorrow, so this is it. I am positive we will get to skate on the next four days, without extra duty.”

Bolden put the broom back where he got it from. They waited another fifteen minutes. Deciding that the E-5 wasn't going to show, they headed for the mess hall, grabbed a bite to eat, then went up to their rooms to pack their gear, to get ready for the field. Bolden's thoughts were upon his old room mate Jack, and of how, his Article 15, for a stolen candy bar, of where he had received, the maximum punishment of the Article 15. Demoted to an E-1, three months pay, and 45 days of extra duty. It did not compare to Mike and John's Article 15, for these two men, the punishment they had received, was a slap upon their wrist. Bolden was thinking of how grateful he was to everyone involved. Of Jack's sacrifice, for a stolen fifteen cent candy bar, the change of command, that was about to take place soon after, the Yugoslavian Gentlemen that supplied Jackie with a safe night of rest, of Kevin Festerman, willing to protect Jackie, Bolden, and Broadway, from the night at the Ku'Dorf, Specialist Ivey, with the advice he had given to Bolden, with that special night on the town with him, in West Berlin, and of their Superior Officers, who were protecting them. So many people involved for one incident and the realization of it being so overwhelming, that no one else would see! Private First Class Bolden packed his gear and was ready for the next day to go into the field for training, not knowing when his orders for reassignment to another Company would present itself. He had been with "The Berlin Brigade" for only a little after nine months and was soon to be shipped out, to who knew where. In all actuality, he received his wish for, fighting against his orders, to be assigned to the Berlin Brigade, as he knew he was being transferred away from such a great assignment, but he also received his wish, in allowing his country to know of his gratitude, for giving him the knowledge and belief of his true self. With all of this weighing upon his conscience, he became tired, after a full day of work, a full stomach, and with filled emotions, he laid down upon his bunk and fell fast asleep.

Thursday, October 2nd,1986. CSC 6/502nd Infantry Battalion formed together to start their field duty. It was off to the Grunewald to do some heavy training. The only thought Bolden and Broadway had on their mind's was,

"When will they be shipped out of the Berlin Brigade!"

The company moved into the motor pool assembling their vehicles, then moved into a tactical formation, moving to the Grunewald. They arrived at their designated location and began to prepare for their mock battle. As the sun set in the west, the mock battle had begun. Moving quickly, the mortar platoon was advancing forward, to set up position, for their forward assault, against a fake opposing enemy. The Battalion was moving quickly, indicating, that they were on the offensive. The mortar platoon, moving from position to position, did not have enough time to set up their equipment, as they kept advancing forward. The mortar platoon encountered many assaults from the opposing enemy as they advanced forward. PFC Bolden had placed his M16A1 rifle into the AUTO position, in other words, continuous fire. He spared no ammo as he quickly exchanged ammunition magazines, firing upon the enemy. He knew that at the end of the battle, he would have a heck of a time, cleaning his rifle, as fired blank ammunition, left heavy gun powder residue, through the barrel of the weapon, when being fired through it. The Company won their mock battle for the evening then set up in a tactical position for the advancement on the next day. Once all the equipment was in position, PFC Bolden began to plan his movements, so that he would be prepared, to help the Company move forward, toward their goal. His weapon was filled with gun powder residue. He prepared to clean his weapon, then heard the voice of First Sergeant Dean approaching the track of his assigned squad,

"Where is PFC Bolden?"

Private First Class Bolden whispered out,

"Right here, First Sergeant!"

With PFC Bolden's words being heard, he discovered that four red lights, from flashlights, that held light discipline, were upon him. He looked to the left of the First Sergeant and he saw PFC Broadway, who was still wearing his Specialist 4th Class insignia, upon his BDU cap and upon his lapels. First Sergeant Dean expressed his orders,

"PFC Bolden, grab your gear and come with us! You are being reassigned to Frankfort West Germany, from their, you will receive your orders for your new assignment. Take everything but your weapon!"

PFC Bolden knew that, even though, Him and Michael had been demoted to Private First Class, that Mike was in denial and actually getting away with displaying his same rank insignia. Being that everything they were going through would be in the "Restricted Files" the only one that would know of anything would be the President and should he show up, well...., it was all good. Bolden was trained to keep his weapon cleaned at all times. It bothered him to leave his weapon uncleaned and exclaimed to First Sergeant Dean,

“But Top, I should clean my weapon first and besides that we are never to leave our weapon behind anywhere!”

First Sergeant Dean was adamant as he barked out his order,

“Some one will be assigned to clean your weapon!!! Now grab your gear and get in my jeep. Do It And Do It Now!!!”

PFC Bolden did not mean any disrespect toward First Sergeant Dean. He was doing what any infantry soldier would do and felt uneasy leaving his dirty, uncleaned weapon behind for someone else to clean. All of a sudden he seen a hand come toward him as the words of Specialist 4th Class Tracy Long, sang with pride, through the still air of the evening,

“I'll take care of this Johnny! It will be an honor to clean your weapon and turn it in to the armory, when we get back!!! Don't you worry about a thing!!! I got you covered!!!

This was a man, a soldier, that only a few months back, at the time, that Specialist Bolden, had complained about and demeaned, of how and why, he always had to clean, this man's weapon when he was assigned to weapons cleaning detail, and now, this soldier, was offering to take the reigns of such a great service for another infantry soldier, and with honor! It was at this time that PFC Bolden was beginning to see the clarity of how all things were becoming connected with each other. PFC Bolden looked at Specialist Tracy Long then said,

" I appreciate it Trace!!! Don't know if I will ever see you again, but please know that it was an honor to serve with you!!!"

They shook hands together and nodded toward each other. Bolden grabbed his duffle bag from the compartment that it laid in then departed the track vehicle he was assigned to leaving his squad. All of them shook his hand as he departed for his new journey. Bolden and Broadway followed First Sergeant Dean to his jeep, threw their equipment in the backseat, then sat down upon it. When First Sergeant Dean took his position on the passenger side, he motioned to his driver to move out. The jeep moved quickly through the night path that was barely illuminated from the headlights, hitting each bump, as it seemed, to their passengers. Thirty minutes later they arrived in the parking lot of CSC 6/502nd Infantry Brigade. The First Sergeant gave his orders to Broadway and Bolden,

"All right you two, get your field equipment cleaned and pack your personal things. The two of you will be on the duty train by 1800 hours taking you to Frankfort, West Germany. From their you will be assigned your new duty stations. I will meet the both of you at the CQ Desk at 0600 hours. Make sure all of your equipment is cleaned as you will be turning it in to the proper departments. Is this understood?"

Bolden and Broadway replied together,

“Yes First Sergeant!”

They were motioned with First Sergeant Dean's movement from his right arm to move out and carry on with the orders that they had just been given. Broadway and Bolden were silent with each other as they went up to their rooms to carry on with their orders. Upon entering his room, Private First Class Bolden emptied his duffle bag and began cleaning his equipment. As the hours passed, he knew there would not be enough time to clean his equipment, Clean his room, then pack up his personal belongings, to be ready to board the duty train, by the time it was to depart. He was in a hurry to comply with the orders that he had been given, hoping that he will be able to accomplish his mission. It was 0200 hours when PFC Bolden heard the continuous knock upon his door, indicating that it was his friend, Mike Broadway. PFC Bolden opened his door, then asked,

“Hey Mike, you got your things cleaned already?”

Broadway, with a smirk and a muffled laugh, asked,

“Are you joking with me? Are you seriously cleaning your equipment Johnny?”

Bolden looked at Broadway with a bit of confusion, then asked,

"What do you mean? Aren't you cleaning your equipment to turn it in later on today? We are leaving here at 1800 hours!!!"

Mike began shaking his head with disbelief, then said,

"Johnny, clean or dirty, no matter where we go to, they are going to have to take our equipment as is!!! You are wasting time! I suggest we get some rest and move on!"

He was correct in his statement as Bolden knew that time was of the essence and in less than four hours they had to meet the First Sergeant at the CQ Desk. Bolden looking at Mike said,

"Well I guess you are right Mike. It's time to get packed, get some rest, then head on down the road. I will see you in a few hours."

They shook hands and went about their duties. It only took a few minutes for Bolden to get packed up. With exhaustion, he fell upon his bunk to get a couple hours of rest before his last night in West Berlin.

0545 Hours Bolden is awakened by a knock upon his door. Opening the door he discovers Specialist Schmidt standing in front of him.

"John, First Sergeant Dean won't be here to meet you at 0600 hours. The new platoon sergeant from the scouts is here asking for your presence at the CQ Desk. He is the acting First Sergeant until we can get a new one. First Sergeant Dean is at home packing his things up to leave as well. The new change of command is starting with him."

Bolden still half a sleep nodded his head and said,

"I will be there in a few minutes Russell."

With only a few minutes left, PFC Bolden grabbed his gear and wearily walked toward the CQ Desk. As he was walking past Broadway's room he heard the clicking of the lock being presented into the open position. He stopped and saw Mike with his gear. Both of them joining each other they arrived at the CQ Desk promptly at 0600 hours. The acting First Sergeant was no where to be seen. They waited another hour and saw a silhouette walking toward them. Then they heard his orders,

"All right, grab your gear and follow me!"

They did as they were ordered to do. The first place they went to was to turn in their field equipment where they waited for two hours before anyone opened the doors. It was ran by civilians. In other words, they had banker hours, that had to be followed by the general population and the military. Bolden and Broadway heard the acting First Sergeant talking to the civilian in charge, then talking turned into argument. Loudly, the words of the civilian could be heard,

"YOU MEN DON'T HAVE AN APPOINTMENT, THERFORE I MUST REFUSE TO TAKE THEIR EQUIPMENT!"

The acting First Sergeant was adamant with his orders, barking back at the civilian,

“NO, WE DO NOT HAVE AN APPOINTMENT! WE HAVE AN ORDER STRAIGHT FROM THE GENERAL TO GET THESE MEN ON THE DUTY TRAIN TONIGHT! IT IS BEST FOR YOU IF YOU TAKE THESE MEN'S EQUIPMENT, RIGHT NOW!!!”

The argument kept on with the civilian as Bolden and Broadway were laying out their equipment on the table in front of them following the Acting First Sergeants orders.

“I WILL TAKE THIS MAN'S EQUIPMENT, AS HE POINTED TOWARD PFC BOLDEN, BUT I WILL NOT TAKE THAT MAN'S EQUIPMENT, AS HE POINTED TOWARD PFC BROADWAY. THAT MAN'S EQUIPMENT IS FILTHY AND DIRTY!!!”

It was clear, Mike didn't want to leave West Berlin. It was the best that he could do to be in defiance of leaving without his fiance. The Acting First Sergeant was adamant again with his orders,

“YOU WILL TAKE BOTH OF THEIR EQUIPMENT AND GIVE THEM CLEAN CLEARANCE. CALL BRIGADE HEADQUARTERS AND SEE WHAT THEY TELL YOU!!!”

The civilian barked back at the Acting First Sergeant,

“ I WILL DO EXACTLY THAT!!!”

The three of them waited for the next three hours. When the civilian returned he was silent. With a haughtiness and a look of disgust, he gathered all the equipment that was presented to him, then stamped the official paperwork as being cleared. The Acting First Sergeant, Bolden and Broadway walked out of the area. They were relieved from carrying the heavy equipment. As they went from station to station to be cleared, there was minimal resistance from anyone else, except for when they went to recover their dental records. In charge there was a full bird Colonel and with that much clout his word was given authority. It was getting close, a couple of hours before the duty train was to exit West Berlin and time was of the essence to fulfill the Acting First Sergeants orders from the General of the Berlin Brigade. He placed the order in asking for Bolden and Broadways Panorexes. These are what they call full scale, 360 degree, X-Rays, of their teeth. A small matter, it may seem. It is here that the Acting First Sergeant met the fiercest resistance. The secretary denied the order, stating that they needed a twenty four hour advance notice to collect the information in order to release the X-Rays. The Acting First Sergeant kept forward with his orders with the secretary until the full bird Colonel presented himself. With a loud voice, that everyone could here, he barked out his order,

"WHY ARE YOU GIVING MY SECRETARY SUCH A ROUGH TIME HERE SERGEANT!!! SHE HAS CLEARLY EXPRESSED THE RULES ABOUT GIVING OUT THE PAPERWORK YOU HAVE

ORDERED FROM HER!!! I SUGGEST YOU LEAVE THIS OFFICE NOW, GENTLEMEN!!!"

The three men came to the position of "Attention" then the Acting First Sergeant saluted the Colonel. The whole room was in silence as the respect of the salute was given back. The acting First Sergeant was still in the position of "Attention" when he said,

"SIR, WITH ALL DUE RESPECT, MY ORDERS ARE COMING FROM THE BRIGADE GENERAL, ORDERING ME TO GET THESE MEN ON THE DUTY TRAIN TONIGHT, SIR!!! I MUST HAVE ALL THE CLEARANCE TO ALLOW THEM TO LEAVE HERE!!!"

The full bird Colonel continued with his order,

"I DON'T CARE WHERE THE ORDERS ARE COMING FROM THIS IS MY OFFICE AND I WILL UPHOLD MY ORDERS AND MY STAFF IN DOING OUR DUTY HERE SERGEANT!!! IS THAT UNDERSTOOD?!!!"

The Acting First Sergeant was still adamant with his orders,

"SIR, REQUESTING PRIVATE CONSULTATION WITH YOU IN YOUR OFFICE SIR!!!"

The full bird Colonel, sensing the seriousness of the sergeant's request, granted him permission. A few minutes later the Colonel and the Acting First Sergeant made their presence known with the Colonel's loud voice being heard. Bolden and Williams snapped quickly to the position of "Attention". The Colonel barked out his order to his secretary,

"YOU GET THESE MEN'S FILES NOW AND GET THEM OUT OF THIS OFFICE IMMEDIATELY!!! THEY DO NOT BELONG HERE AND THEY DEFINITELY DO NOT BELONG TO BE IN OUR ARMY!!! GET THEM OUT OF HERE NOW!!!!"

The anger of the Colonel's voice was heard directly to all of those that were in his immediate area. Bolden and Broadway's heart sank within their chest listening to the words that the Colonel had just stated. They were in wonderment and confusion as to why the Colonel stated what he had said. It did not matter, as the secretary, nervously fumbled through her filed paperwork and found the Panorexs that she was looking for, then handed them to the acting First Sergeant. Once the paperwork was in hand the three of them immediately left the office. Marching down the pavement Bolden looked at the acting First Sergeant and saw he had a smile on his face. Bolden was confused and so was Broadway as to what happened back at the dental office. PFC Bolden had to know. He looked at the acting First Sergeant and asked,

"What just happened back there Sergeant? Why did the Colonel come out of his office acting like we were the worst things he ever saw in his life?"

The acting First Sergeant came forward with his answer. With a smile on his face, he said,

"You men need to know that I am following my orders. My orders are to get the both of you out of West Berlin safely tonight and that is what I am doing. I told the Colonel that the two of you were caught smuggling illegal arms to terrorists and you have to leave West Berlin tonight. That is why he reacted the way he did!"

Bolden and Broadway had a disgusted look upon their face as to what the acting First Sergeant had said to them. Bolden confused asked,

"Why didn't you tell him the truth Sergeant? That would have been much better than what you have told us!"

The acting First Sergeant was strict in his answer,

"IT'S BECAUSE I HAVE BEEN ORDERED TO KEEP THIS SECRET AND THAT IS EXACTLY WHAT I AM GOING TO DO!!! THE LEAST AMOUNT OF PEOPLE THAT KNOW ABOUT THIS, THE BETTER!!! WE RECEIVED WHAT WE CAME FOR AND THAT IS ALL THERE IS TO IT!!! WE ARE ALMOST DONE WITH EVERYTHING AND IN A COUPLE HOURS YOUR ASSES ARE ON THAT DUTY TRAIN TO FRANKFORT!!! YOU BEST GET SOME CHOW AND PREPARE FOR YOUR NEW ASSIGNMENTS!!! YOU GOT THAT????!!! DO YOU HEAR WHAT I AM SAYING TO YOU???!!!"

Bolden and Broadway immediately responded,

"YES, FIRST SERGEANT!!!"

The acting First Sergeant dismissed them to the chow hall and ordered them to be at the CQ desk by 1700 Hours. Bolden and Broadway did as they were ordered to do. When they received their meals at the chow hall they sat down at their table, Bolden looked at Broadway and said,

"Well I got two double cheeseburgers and fries, my favorite, I think it's like a last meal Mike."

Michael looked at Bolden with a bit of disgust and his usual sarcastic comment said,

"Good for you, I got beef strogganoff with a side salad. I hate this shit!!!"

Bolden looked at his friend with a smile and said,

"Tell you what Mike, I'll give you one of my double cheeseburgers and half of my fries if you give me half of your beef stroganoff and salad, cause that's like my second favorite. What do you say?"

Mike with a smile on his face said,

"I'll take it!!!"

They exchanged their agreement where both of them were pleased. It was like they were looking out after each other. Pleasing each other in their youthful ways. It was the pride they had among them. Both coming from poor families but the brotherhood they provided each other was the strength they had to have to carry forward. It was a common bond of sharing and sacrifice toward one another that brought strength to their unity. Only time could tell if that unity would still be bonded together. They finished their meal then walked up to the CQ desk to meet the acting First Sergeant. Promptly at 1700 Hours the acting First Sergeant was there to greet them. With personal effects in hand they followed the Acting First Sergeant to his jeep where they were escorted to the duty train station. The duty train promptly arrived at 1800 Hours. The acting First Sergeant stood at the position of "Attention" and saluted PFC Bolden and PFC Broadway, then said,

"It is an honor and a privilege to know you men!!!"

PFC Bolden and PFC Broadway stood at the position of "Attention" then saluted the acting First Sergeant back. No other words were exchanged between them as Bolden and Broadway boarded the Duty Train headed to Frankfort West Germany. With so much resistance that they had faced through out the day it would seem to those that the great City of West Berlin was reluctant to releasing these fine soldiers as she wished for them to stay with her and defend one of the most honorable posts ever given to a soldier, but it was time to let go of those that were needed elsewhere to serve another cause of that which is good for the greater good of all. As the doors closed upon the duty train to note it's departure. Bolden and Broadway waved good-bye to the acting First

Sergeant and to the city of West Berlin wondering if they would ever see each other again throughout time. Bolden and Broadway took to their assigned bunks. They talked among them for a few hours then exhaustion took them over, as they did not get enough rest from the night before, where they fell asleep upon their bunks and awaited their arrival into Frankfort West Germany where they would be assigned their next duty station. The sun was rising in the east as the announcement was heard that they were arriving at Marienborn West Germany, which was the indication that they arrived safely into West Germany. With the hours of sleep that were provided while they were sleeping, Bolden and Broadway opened the curtains of the duty train to see a new day of freedom. There were only a few more hours left until their arrival into Frankfort West Germany. There mouth dry from their awakened sleep, they quenched for thirst. Broadway saw that the door was opened to the Duty Train's lavatory and seen the flask that was sitting in it's dispenser waiting for the next person to enter and drink it's content. Bolden knew instantly what Broadway was thinking, then said,

“I wouldn't drink that if I were you. I've been there and from my experience, you won't like the results. I told you about that experience before when I went to see my best friend's brother in Carlstadt.”

Broadway looked at Bolden with a bit of disgust, then nodded his head, as he knew what Bolden was telling him. The next couple of hours came quickly as they departed the duty train in Frankfort and met their liason. Immediately upon their arrival they were assigned a bunk in the barricades that housed many soldiers that were awaiting their assignments to new duty stations. Bolden and Broadway stayed in Frankfort West Germany for a week until their new duty assignments were given. Within that time they frolicked in their youth discovering much of what the city of Frankfort West Germany had to offer to them. When the time came their orders were given to them. PFC Broadway was to report to Lichtenfeld, West Germany. PFC Bolden was to report a little bit further south to Bamberg West Germany. With their orders in hand they boarded the same train that was to take them upon their new journey. They traveled together, for what seemed a few short hours, then PFC Broadway had to depart the train to report to his new assignment. PFC Broadway and PFC Bolden shook hands, then hugged one another, upon their departure. Before departing the train Mike looked at John then said,

"Well Johnny, if you are ever in Rector Arkansas look me up will you? It has been an honor and a privilege to serve with you. You are my Brother, Sir!!!"

The tears were being held back from each soldier as the emotions were flowing heavy between them. Bolden with strength and confidence released his embrace from Michael then looked him straight in the eyes and said,

"Mike, I have a strong feeling I will be seeing you shortly before that. You keep your faith, your belief, your strength, and your courage up! What we have done together, what we have gone through together is something tremendous, beyond whatever we expected from ourselves. It is an honor and a privilege to serve with you as well, Sir!!! You are my brother, my strength, and my courage, that carries me forth, to continue on, that I am not alone in my belief of freedom! God be with you and may his blessings be upon you always in all ways Michael! I will see you soon!!!"

With their departing words between them, they both stood at the position of "Attention" then saluted each other simultaneously. Michael then departed the train as John looked upon him with honor and dignity. The train blew it's whistle then moved southward to carry PFC Bolden to his new duty assignment. PFC Bolden arrived in Bamberg West Germany then met his liason who was waiting for his presence. They provided a ride to his new duty assignment where he discovered he had a choice of which company he wished to serve at as the Specialist that asked him the question was being inquisitive,

"Where will you like to be PFC Bolden, we have Echo Troop 2/2nd ACR, Fox troop 2/2nd ACR, and... PFC Bolden stopped the Specialists questioning as he interrupted,

"Specialist, which platoon needs the most men available for their support? That is where I am needed the most. When you can answer that question then that is where I choose to go!"

The Specialist looked at him with a bit of confusion, then said,

"That would be Fox Troop 2/2nd of the Armored Cavalry Regiment. They are up at the Hof Border right now but will be back in a couple of weeks. I will assign you a room in their barracks. You will have to wait till they return from the border to report to your Platoon Sergeant. I don't recommend that you go there as their platoon sergeant is an E-6 but they could really use you there. I recommend that you go to Echo Troop, they are really a very squared away Platoon and their Platoon Sergeant is excellent!!! With that said PFC Bolden, where will you like to be assigned?"

PFC Bolden was adamant with his request stating,

"Specialist, if Fox Troop needs a soldier then I will go there. I have no question in my mind where to go!"

The Specialist shook his head, then said,

Okay PFC Bolden, I warned you. The best condolence that I can give you is, that their best leader is a Specialist 4th Class by the name of Tony Bisbee. You will get to know him. He is actually a very good leader!"

PFC Bolden piped up with excitement,

"Are you kidding me???!!!" He was in my Basic Training Company, Echo 7 1 in Ft. Benning, Georgia! I don't know him personally but I watched him during training. Busy Bee will be just fine!!! He might remember me, he might not!!! That is where I am supposed to be!!!"

The orders were cut and printed on paper. The only thing PFC Bolden had to do was wait for his new Platoons arrival home from the Hof Border, which seemed odd to PFC Bolden, as his Article 15 stated that he was not to be assigned to another Border Patrol Unit but in his mind, excellent experience should suffice excellent service, whenever presented. It was a perfect match within PFC Bolden's mind, well.... at least that was his thoughts. From what the Specialist had told him, PFC Bolden calculated he had a couple weeks to get squared away before meeting his new Platoon. He hoped for the best and was anxious to see what he had to offer toward his new assignment. The Specialist was not done with PFC Bolden for the time being. He looked at PFC Bolden then said,

“Our Company First Sergeant wishes to see you now. He is First Sergeant Harris and has been with us for a few months now. If you are ready, I will let him know you are available.”

PFC Bolden looked at the Specialist, then said,

“I knew a “Top Harris” when I was stationed with HHC 1/8th Cavalry Regiment about a year back, or so, not sure if he is the same one. I'm ready when you are Specialist.”

The Specialist got up from his chair, as he was finished with all his paperwork, then walked over to the First Sergeant's door and knocked upon it. The First Sergeant's voice could be heard through the closed door,

"Come in!"

The Specialist informed him that PFC Bolden was in the office and ready to report to duty. The First Sergeant was forward with the end of his day's duties, saying,

"Show him in!"

PFC Bolden got up from his chair, marched to the center of the First Sergeant's desk, then came into the position of "Parade Rest", saying,

"PFC Bolden reporting for duty First Sergeant!!!"

Upon one look at First Sergeant Harris, PFC Bolden recognized him as being the First Sergeant from HHC 1/8th Cavalry Regiment where they had been stationed at in Ft. Hood, Texas. Not only was he PFC Bolden's First Sergeant at Ft. Hood but he was also the First Sergeant at Ft. Benning, Georgia, where Private Bolden was placed on medical hold for two weeks. In order for the Army to consider him valuable to serve in the United States Army, because his left elbow was crooked due to an incident of falling of a pony when he was five years old. He had shattered the bone from his elbow up to his shoulder as he braced his fall with his left hand. The surgeons did the best they could do to save the use of his left arm, which they did, but left a mark upon him that was very noticeable. First Sergeant Harris was the man that ordered Private Bolden to do push ups, in front of him, to see if he was fit for duty, and to be able to complete the infantry basic training, at Ft. Benning, Georgia. Private Bolden completed the task, then afterwards, as a joke to the First Sergeant, when ever a medical officer would walk by, he would laughingly say,

“Hey Sir, look at this son-of-a bitch do push ups, with his fucked up elbow. Watch him and see if he is able to perform his duties. Private get in the leaning rest position and start doing push ups until I tell you to recover!”

Private Bolden did as he was ordered to do. He did this a couple more times, until his true medical officer arrived and approved him to be fit for training as an infantry soldier. Humiliating as it was, Private Bolden did not forget the First Sergeant's face. To be placed under this First Sergeant's command again was punishment enough for him. The first thing Top Harris said to him was,

“PFC Bolden you are in civilian clothes. What gives you the right to report to duty without your uniform?”

PFC Bolden still at the position of “Parade Rest” responded back,

“First Sergeant, my orders are clear!!! My orders are to report to duty in civilian clothes due to terrorists activities!!! I am following my orders First Sergeant!!!”

The rest of PFC Bolden's reporting to duty at his new duty station went the same way as he reported to his Captain and to his NCO's. PFC Bolden decided that day that he would no longer pursue his dream of being a soldier for the rest of his life. He thought for sure, that during his service in the military, that he would never be trusted again. His heart sank within his chest that day but decided that he would continue on, providing the best service that he could, to fulfill his obligation, upon his oath, to his country, and to the United States Army. He was assigned his quarters, a room to himself, where he felt alone, once again, awaiting for the arrival of his new platoon. A week had gone by when he heard the continuous rapping upon the door of his new room. He chuckled within himself as he was reminded of his friend's door knocking signature of Michael Broadway. As he opened the door, standing in front of him, was the man himself, in civilian clothing, and accompanying him, was Ray Williams. Bolden stood in astonishment wondering what was going on. He was happy to see his friends again. Broadway was the first to speak,

"Well, are you coming with us Johnny, or are you staying here?"

Bolden gave both of them a hug, then said,

It is great to see the both of you!!! Where are we going?"

Ray was next with his comment, answering Bolden's question,

"Wherever we want to go. First off, we are going to Munich and go to the original Oktoberfest!!! Are you coming with us?"

Bolden didn't hesitate on his answer,

“You bet I'm going with you guys!!! I've got another week before my new platoon shows up. Let's go!!!”

He grabbed a few personal things, closed his door, then locked it. Bolden was happy, very happy, to be in good company once again. They arrived at the parking lot where Ray had parked the White VW “Freedom Van.” All of them jumped in taking their usual spots. They began their conversations, each of them learning about each others new duty assignments. Ray had been reassigned to a company in Erlangen, West Germany, a little south of Nurnberg, West Germany. He had found Mike stationed in Lichtenfeld West Germany, picked him up there, where Mike told him where Bolden was stationed in Bamberg West Germany. It was then that they had decided to travel a bit further south to pick him up and enjoy the last few days together that they had. They drove to Munich, West Germany, spending a couple days at the Oktoberfest, sleeping in the White VW “Freedom Van”. They then decided to visit some of the castles that West Germany had to offer. The best one was the “Rothberg Castle, it was there that the three of them carved their initials into the old wood gates that offered security to the old sentries of the time, as they walked their post, to keep them from falling to the ground. From their they traveled up to Frankfort, once again, frolicking in their youth. As the time went by quickly, it was time to head back to their new posts. Broadway was first. They pulled into the parking lot, in Lichtenfeld, where Mike was stationed. John gave his friend one last hug as they did not know when they would see each other again. Ray and John departed Mike's company. They traveled south upon the autobahn arriving in Bamberg West Germany, where Ray and John shook hands. It was the last time that they would see each other. Those few days gave to each other a Unity of Strength among the friendship that they held with one another. It was time to separate from one another and continue on with other things in life. The future of each one of them was yet to unfold. John, Mike, Ray, and Jackie had a life to live that was beyond their unification in West and East Berlin Germany. The only question that could be asked at their time of departures was.......?

It was actually a question that everyone asks of themselves because, as the second hand of the clock tower, at McNair Barracks, clicks away, it unfolds the future, as time waits for no one, nor should it, for it is, the keeper of history, the value of the present, and the creator of the future. The clock tower located on 4th of July Platz, at McNair Barracks, will always, stand in the memory of an infantry soldier, as it is a pillar of strength, that upholds his honor, dedication, and courage for the time he spent defending the city of West Berlin, as a member of The Berlin Brigade!!!

46352185R00298

Made in the USA
Middletown, DE
29 July 2017